DOING ARCHAEOLOGY

DOING ARCHAEOLOGY
A Hands-On Laboratory Manual

PATRICIA C. RICE
West Virginia University

Mayfield Publishing Company
Mountain View, California
London • Toronto

Library of Congress Cataloging-in-Publication Data
Rice, Patricia C.
    Doing archaeology : a hands-on laboratory manual / Patricia C. Rice.
    p.   cm.
Includes bibliographical references and index.
    ISBN-13: 978-1-55934-845-4
    ISBN-10: 1-55934-845-3

    1. Archaeology–Laboratory manuals.   I. Title
CC75.7.R53   1997
930.1'07'2–dc21   97–27878
                                                                            CIP

Manufactured in the United States of America
10   9   8   7   6   5   4

Mayfield Publishing Company
1280 Villa Street
Mountain View, California 94041

Sponsoring editor, Janet M. Beatty; production editor, Melissa Kreischer; manuscript editor, Michelle Fillippini; design manager, Susan Breitbard; text and cover designer, Anne Flanagan; cover photo by Patricia Rice; art manager, Robin Mouat; illustrators, Joan Carol and John & Judy Waller; manufacturing manager, Randy Hurst. The text was set in 10.5/12.5 Baskerville and printed on acid-free 50# Butte des Morts by Banta Book Group.

Credits

Fig. 3.2 From Rubbish! The Archaeology of Garbage by William Rathje and Cullen Murphy. Copyright ©1992 by William Rathje and Cullen Murphy. Reprinted by permission of HarperCollins Publishers, Inc. **Fig. 6.1** From Pottery Function: A Use-Alteration Perspective, James M. Skibo, ed. Copyright ©1992 Plenum Press. Used with permission of the publisher and the editor. **Fig. 7.2** From Laboratory Exercises for Introduction to Archaeology by G. Rapp, Jr., S. Mulholland, J. Gifford, S. Aschenbrenner, 1984, University of Minnesota. With permission of the authors.

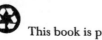 This book is printed on recycled paper.

# PREFACE

Most introductory archaeology courses are lecture courses that do not give students an opportunity to be active learners, working directly with archaeological objects and/or problems. This laboratory manual is designed to give students an active experience and introduce them to the scientific study of archaeology through direct work with archaeological materials.

Just as geologists cannot bring a mountain to the classroom, archaeologists cannot bring a ziggurat to the laboratory. But what we can do is actively introduce students to key methods used in gathering and analyzing archaeological data. Students will not only understand core archaeological concepts better through active lab participation, but they will also be better prepared to do fieldwork at an actual, nonrenewable site should the opportunity arise.

The laboratory exercises that follow contain both a reading component and a "doing" component. First, students will read about the subject of the exercise to fully understand its use in archaeological analysis and prepare for the exercise they will be doing in the lab. In many cases, the reading and subsequent exercise represent what has become an archaeological subdiscipline; pollen analysis and paleosediment analysis are good examples. Ten pages or so of written materials are not meant to summarize the work of experts, nor do the exercises replicate what these experts do. The readings do, however, introduce the concepts and nature of the subdiscipline, and the exercises give the flavor, if not the complications, of the work done by specialists.

Each of the thirteen hands-on exercises begins with clearly laid out objectives and directions for completing the exercise. In addition, each exercise contains a list of key terms and suggestions for further reading. Each exercise has been planned to fit the following profile as much as possible (though some subjects will take more time than others): 30 minutes for the reading on the subject of the exercise; 45 minutes to do the exercise, and 30 minutes to write up the findings. At the end of the workbook is a glossary of common archaeological terms as well as an index.

An accompanying Instructor's Guide provides all the information an instructor needs to set up a laboratory environment for the exercises in this lab manual. Included are a list of equipment needed and where to get it (or how to make or borrow it), an estimate on the cost in both time and money for each exercise, hints on running the exercises, a key matching the lab exercises to appropriate pages in major introductory archaeology texts, and three additional exercises for further experience in fieldwork.

We wish you luck in your archaeological adventure!

ACKNOWLEDGMENTS

Many thanks to various people who helped the project by loans, donations, services, and/or advice, including: Nick Ashton and Karen Perkins (British Museum); Warwick Bray, Ken Thomas, and Tony Barham (Institute of Archaeology, University College, London); Sebastian Payne (English Heritage); and Jean-Philippe Rigaus (University of Bordeaux).

And from West Virginia University I would like to thank Roland Guthrie, Leah Williams, and Dennis Quinlan (Biology Department); Frank Ammons and Bob Driscoll (Divison of Forestry); Charles Sicina (Physics); George Rice (Political Science); Richard Smosna (Geology and Geography); Trish Sahady (Sociology and Anthropology); and the lab managers.

I wish to thank the reviewers who made excellent suggestions, corrected mistakes, and caused me to learn a lot of "new stuff," including: Aubrey Cannon, McMaster University; Christopher R. DeCorse, Syracuse University; Gary M. Feinman, University of Wisconsin; Sheila Pozorski, University of Texas–Pan American; James M. Skibo, Illinois State University; Kevin E. Smith, Middle Tennessee State University; William C. Smith, Central Washington University; and Paul D. Welch, Queens College. I particularly thank James Skibo for providing new Kalinga insights.

I'd like to thank the staff at Mayfield for seeing this unusual project through to its end, beginning with Jan Beatty, sponsoring editor, to Robin Mouat, art editor, to Melissa Kreischer, production editor. Jan took a chance with this "odd" book, and I appreciate her willingness to go out on the limb with me.

And, finally, thanks and much appreciation for the financial support in setting up the labs go to the WVU Faculty Development Fund and Curriculum Grants from Eberly College of Arts and Sciences.

BRIEF CONTENTS

CONTENTS

1

Mapping

The map is as fundamental to archaeology as it is to geography. Without maps, archaeologists would have no idea where to excavate or how to incorporate excavated materials into a picture wider than a single season at a single excavation. Maps are one of our basic organizing tools: Maps must be made before excavation is even planned; they must be made on a daily and hourly basis while excavating a site; and maps are looked at constantly after the excavation is over. Archaeologists can be said to "think maps" before, during, and after the actual work of an archaeological excavation. And, because some of the people whose culture we are trying to reconstruct via the artifacts they left behind also made maps, prehistorians must be able to interpret prehistoric maps as well as use them in their roles as archaeologists-excavators.

Maps and mapping are not exclusively twentieth-century Western ideas. Many people at many times and places have found it necessary to represent visual phenomena in symbolic and graphic form. The Sumerians some 3500 years ago used cuneiform for writing but also made maps of rivers, city walls, canals, and temples. The Egyptians used hieroglyphics for writing but also made and used maps for tax-collecting purposes. As is well known all over Europe, the Romans took their mapping ideas with them when they conquered, establishing cities and roads based on these maps. Some feel that the famous Pech de l'Aze bone, a 300,000-year-old bone from central France, has an engraved "notation" on it that may well be a map of some sort.

People without writing are also known to draw maps, which show both natural and cultural features, usually in iconographic form. And there is at least indirect evidence for mapping in places such as Meso-American cities that have urban layouts so complex, yet so regular, that most experts feel some sort of mapping must have been used, even if those maps do not exist now. The famous and huge city-state of Teotihuacán in central Mexico, with its population of 100,000 people some 1300 years ago, is laid out with very regular streets into quadrants that are subdivided into neighborhoods. It is not likely that this feat could have been carried out without the use of maps of some sort, as the layout of the city spread over a much longer time period than one person's mental template of the city's future. In the 1970s, René Millon, an American archaeologist, spent several years surveying Teotihuacán, ending up with a map of its thousands of buildings. Assuming the people of Teotihuacán had some type of maps, it would be interesting to be able to match the ancient map with the modern Millon map of the same city.

There are many kinds of maps in cartography; maps can be taken by high-tech sensors or by people with paper and pencil. There are types of maps for

1

different professions and although they all have certain principles in common, they are all special tools for special jobs. The following details the types of maps for archaeologists. In simplified form, it describes how archaeologists use maps and why they are so vital to our work.

MAPS BEFORE EXCAVATION

Before a trowel is put to the ground, the archaeologist has already made a series of maps, each one taking from an hour to a day to complete, depending on the size of the area to be mapped and the detail needed. Pre-excavation maps are, above all, **convenience** maps and are made solely for the purpose of getting funds or doing proper excavation. Although archaeological maps must be made carefully and accurately, including convenience maps, they are not legally binding and will not be used by the U.S. Geological Survey (USGS) as maps to be emulated. They are made solely for the purposes of communicating information concerning archaeological excavation, analysis, and archiving. Often, archaeologists use their field data to generate computer maps that can accurately depict either contours or grids with or without cultural materials mapped in.

Intuitive Maps

Another kind of map is called an **intuitive** map. Like a convenience map, it is usually drawn before excavation. Because a map is a physical representation of some existing phenomena, the first step in doing archaeological mapping is asking, What do you want to map? The answer is fairly straightforward: Archaeological sites and their context. How archaeologists locate sites to excavate is a completely different topic and will not be discussed here; we will merely assume that archaeologists have found sites, one way or another. Once found, maps begin.

We begin a description of archaeological maps and their use on a personal note. I remember walking the Beune River in southwest France in 1990 from its meeting with the Vézère River at Les Eyzies to its source, about 10 kilometers to the east. The area was wooded, undeveloped, and a sylvan glade. On a smaller scale than its larger cousins, the Vézère and the Dordogne Rivers in the same area of France, the Beune cut through the limestone during the Jurassic some 200 million years ago, leaving rock shelters in various degrees of formation. Once undercut, rock shelters are suitable for human habitation, but in time, small-to-large boulders fall and collapse into a pile of large rocks. Having seen dozens of rock shelter sites and having been involved in the excavation of several of them, it was natural for me on that exploratory walk to note potential rock shelters, scuffle up surface finds of blades that were probably 30,000 to 10,000 years old, and imagine doing a real excavation in what until that time was a totally unexcavated area. At one particularly interesting spot, I made my companions sit down for a rest while I drew a sketch map of the area. This map was done on the spot and from my perspective (from the spot I was standing at); I mapped the river, rock cliffs, vegetation, the one fence (and the two cows on the other side), and the surface flint pieces, as if I were going to actually excavate that site one day. The map also included information on where the sun was at that particular time (I did not know where true north was), where the decayed chateau we started off from was located, and where we had left the car in case we needed the information later to get ourselves back to civilization. This was an "intuitive" sketch type of map (technically called a **Compass** map), but it demonstrates how intuitive it is for archaeologists to draw maps, even on vacation, and how vital such maps are to archaeologists—even before they think of applying for grants to excavate.

Preliminary Survey Maps

Once a decision has been made to do an excavation at a particular place and even before funds have been secured or the archaeologist decides to excavate on his or her own time and money, a "real," as opposed to an intuitive, Compass map must be made. This map need not be beautiful, nor done professionally, but it must adequately communicate what the archaeologist hopes to do in the excavation. It first maps in the person from whose perspective it is taken. Using line of sight (sometimes called "eyeballing"), the archaeologist systematically sketches in the horizon items (hills, mountains, rivers, buildings), including important vegetation; then items closer to him- or herself such as telephone lines or other boundaries, roads, and buildings are drawn in; and finally the archaeologist outlines the provisional place of the excavation. Figure 1.1 shows this kind of map. It would be submitted as part of the package to any funding agency in this rudimentary form, as an archaeologist would want to avoid spending days measuring or locating only to be turned down for funding. This map differs from a Compass map only in its systematic nature. Both are done from the perspective of the mapmaker, but all major and minor features are mapped in the **Preliminary Survey** map, whereas only those features thought at the time to be of importance show up on a Compass map.

Jumping ahead six months, let us assume the funds to proceed with the excavation have been secured and the excavation is planned to begin in another month or so. Before that trowel hits the dirt, the archaeologist would either hire a professional surveyor to do several kinds of pre-excavation site maps or, if properly trained, do them him- or herself. Depending on the size of the site, such maps might take a week to complete. (By contrast, the famous Teotihuacán maps took the archaeologists two years to draw, using both aerial photographs that produced an overall grid system and a lot of foot slogging to investigate every square meter in that grid.)

Figure 1.1 Hypothetical Preliminary Survey Map

Site Surface Survey Maps

At a minimum, the archaeologist would do a **Site Surface Survey** (SSS) map before the crew arrived. If the site is located in the United States, the archaeologist would first get official USGS maps that already contain a good deal of the information that archaeologists want: contours, locations of major physical features such as rivers, vegetation, mountains (and their heights), and cultural features such as roads and buildings. In most other countries, the same types of maps are easily secured from the proper civil authority. Cooperation is usually secured by promising to provide the civil authority with a copy of the redrawn maps, as the detail of the archaeological maps often supersedes what is on the basic survey map. This kind of map would communicate the relationship or context of the site to its surrounding. The exact latitude and longitude of the site need to be noted. Sites also need official designations and these are put on all maps as well. In the United States, official designations begin with a two-digit reference number for each state. Counties within states are given alphabet letters, and then the site is given a number in the order it is registered with the state archaeological agency. A site designated as 36WP297, for example, would be recognized as Meadowcroft Rockshelter in Pennsylvania.

Important features such as distance to water, placement of salt licks, shoals, likely migration routes of herbivores, and cul-de-sac valleys that would reflect good hunting strategies would be clearly marked. **Topographic** maps show relief by using contour lines and elevation measurements. The archaeologist can produce an SSS map using both contours (3-D) and features (2-D) showing the size, shape, and distribution of all important features relative to the site to be excavated. If the archaeologist subsequently decides to walk the landscape in four directions to try to find out how much food might be available in some environmentally related geographic area, this context map will be helpful. Traditionally, relief features are drawn in brown (mountains, contours); hydrological features are drawn in blue (shorelines and lakes, rivers); cultural items are drawn in black (houses, roads); and vegetation is drawn in green (trees, swamp scum).

The SSS map must include the following: information on contour line intervals (50 feet, 100 feet); the scale of the map (1 inch = 1 mile); the directions with true north indicated by an arrow; a legend in the lower-right corner for symbols standing for relief, natural items, and cultural items; and the date of the map.

In addition to an SSS map, the archaeologist would zoom in on the area scheduled to be excavated and, using the boundaries of the site, would do a more detailed topographic map of the surface of the site only, particularly noting every surface find. (But this map is getting ahead of the necessity to carefully mark the boundaries of the site to be excavated.)

Marking Boundaries

Depending on time, money, help, and the size of the potential site, the archaeologist must decide the boundaries of the excavation. If the site is very small, it can be excavated by one person in one season. If the site is very large, the archaeologist may decide it is feasible to only sample the area. But how does the archaeologist decide what "the area" is? In some cases, it is obvious: a city with a wall around it may determine the area; a single mound and ditch surrounding it may be the deciding factor. But more often than not, a site does not define itself by such obvious boundaries. Surface finds may or may not be good indicators: sometimes there are surface but no subsurface finds whereas sometimes highly stratified and concentrated assemblages of artifacts are subsurface with no surface indications at all. Archaeologists who are fairly confident a site exists may sink test pits equidistantly throughout the area to sample the amount of artifacts in each. Doing this often helps make the decision where to put the excavation boundaries. When an area is too large to excavate in its entirety, given the amount of time and money, or when it is better scientifically to *not* excavate an area entirely, leaving some excavation for the future when there are better techniques or better questions to be answered, **probabilistic sampling** is used. Employing statistical sampling, archaeologists use small samples of data to represent more general phenomena. Then the larger area must be mapped, showing the sample possibilities with the randomly sampled units identified. It's then possible to go back later to the same area and resample unexcavated units.

Again, before that first trowel is placed, the archaeologist has to decide what will be excavated when–time, money, and the amount of help available are important variables. Even when sampling units are used, decisions must be made as to which units will be excavated during which season. The archaeologist may have five years in which to do a planned excavation and be able to excavate from the top down on the entire site one level a year; more likely, he or she might stake out an area that can be excavated from top to bottom in a single season. By doing the excavation in the latter fashion, what is learned in the off-season can often be applied successfully to the next season's entire area. Regardless of specifics, plans for excavation by season will go on the area or site map, if only in dotted lines. Dotted lines can be inked in or changed as needed.

MAPPING DURING EXCAVATION

In theory, excavators should map everything excavated, from the largest to the smallest bit of ecofact or artifact material, but in practice, what is mapped depends on what the archaeologist believes is important. In some excavations, only building walls may be noted, with bits of pottery or flint regarded as a nuisance and merely sketched in (without measurements) and tossed in a communal pot. In other excavations, the tiniest of flint chips are measured and mapped as accurately as possible. Obviously in the first example, the archaeologist in question is probably in a hurry and only interested in reconstructing the major buildings in a town or city; in the second example, the archaeologist may be interested in reconstructing the hand ax technology of Acheulean foragers and as such, every bit of flint removed from a core during the hand ax manufacturing sequence is important.

What all archaeologists have in common relative to on-site mapping is their adherence to the general rule that all important materials must be accurately mapped, as once the artifact is removed, the mapping (and measurements that allowed the mapping) is all that is left to show the three-dimensional location of the object and its association with other artifacts. What is deemed important is of course subjective. Many a map has shown activity areas, for example, that could not be identified during excavations; often patterns show up only on maps.

To do precise measurement, some sort of system must be set up and adhered to during the entire excavation. First, a **datum point** is chosen. The datum point is the fixed reference point for the entire excavation, so it must be chosen carefully. Choosing a datum point that halfway through the excavation is found to be in an unsatisfactory spot can be disastrous; putting the datum point in the middle of the area to be excavated, for example, means you will want to excavate it later on. The best bet is to carefully decide where to put the fixed reference point on the basis of the boundaries and natural features of a site. In a rock shelter, excavators often paint a cross with a circle around it high up at the farthest point inside the shelter. If the site is in an open area, the datum point is usually placed so that a 90° angle can be set at two boundaries of the site. If the datum point is in the extreme southwestern corner, for example, then all subsequent measurements can be done in only two directions: north and east. Once the datum point is established, all other fixed points can be made, horizontal as well as vertical. Depths will all be made from that datum point position; horizontal grids will also be set up from this point. Once the datum point is set, all depth measurements of artifacts can be made, usually with a stadia rod and a recording device such as a transit, theodolite, dumpy level, or laser. Each has good and bad features, but each measures depths.

Lines are usually set from the datum point, taking care that they are done precisely to 90° angles. The metric system is preferred but sometimes American archaeologists still use yards, feet, and inches because U.S. Customary Unit equipment is easier to obtain in this country. From the datum point, the archaeologist sets out stakes and lines and measures off the appropriate number of full squares. **Grids** should be made permanent: a metal rod apparatus can be set up over the top of the site with strings and lead weights at each corner, falling down to just above surface level, or permanent stakes and strings can be put around the perimeter with internal lines strung between meters; these stakes and strings can be moved as the excavation proceeds. Measurements of artifacts are then made from the strings or from metal measuring rods as set from the ceiling grid.

Once the grid system is set up, numbers or letters are given to each gridded square. Traditionally, letters go in one direction and numbers in the other, so each square has a binomial designation, such as H-4 or N-3. Each grid square will have its own map, and there will likely be more than one map for each square before the excavation is completed, as maps get cluttered with information and need to be changed. When maps should be changed varies by site: sometimes layers are identified artificially and arbitrarily by "spits," consistent depths of soil about two centimeters (or about three-fourths of an inch) thick; sometimes more objective features, such as layers of cobbles, are used.

After the grid system is labeled, every artifact can be measured and put on that square's map. Maps for squares are usually made on graph paper with 10 × 10 square intervals and often subdivided within the 10 square divisions. Frames (heavy inked lines) can be drawn around the mapped areas, the four squares "next door" labeled, and the map itself labeled. The date and the excavator's name finish the labeling. The important items that are excavated are then measured and mapped before they are removed from the soil surface.

Although all grid-square mapping systems are somewhat different (depending on the kind of site and degree of accuracy needed), systemization requires certain rules:

- Pencil is always used on maps in case they have to be changed. They are usually inked in (or a fixative applied to prevent smudging) later;
- Scale of the map to reality is always given;
- A legend is drawn in a block in the lower right-hand corner. Symbols for artifacts, features, and natural items must be explained.

Some archaeologists change maps only when they get cluttered, but some draw maps of the surface daily; these will show everything visible at that precise moment. The next day's map will show everything that has been removed and give some indication of daily excavation.

USE OF MAPS AFTER EXCAVATION

As every archaeologist reminds his or her students, once a site is excavated, it is gone forever. If it is done wrong, it can't be repaired. Although this is a true statement, luckily, once excavation is completed, we still have the records of the excavation itself. We have photographs, card or notebook notations, narratives, and most importantly, we have maps. And if the maps are drawn correctly, they are a permanent record of the excavation itself and what was found. Some excavators put 3-D measurements of each find immediately into a computer program (sometimes even on-site) so they can look at vertical or horizontal relationships in micro or macro terms at any time. Others prefer to rely on the human eye and humanly drawn maps. Photocopies of each map for any given level can be cut and taped together to give a bird's-eye view of the ground surface. If the artifacts have not been disturbed by postdepositional effects (a rare situation) and are basically in situ, what went on in a site—its activity patterns—should be discernible. Some sites do show such patterns, as if people had simply gotten up one morning and walked away. Without accurate maps, residual activity debris would not be displayed.

CONCLUSIONS

It is vital for archaeologists to have accurate records (maps) of archaeology sites before, during, and after excavation in order to plan, get funding, run a proper excavation, and to use as a permanent record of the archaeological event. Most professional archaeologists have picked up the skills of surveying and mapping while apprenticing at real sites and learned the additional technical details by taking supervised courses in map interpretation, map drawing, and using survey equipment. Any serious student wanting to be a professional archaeologist is well advised to take courses in map interpretation and drawing, as well as a basic course in surveying.

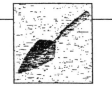

THE EXERCISE

Mapmaking and interpreting skills are required for any successful excavation. In this exercise, you will play the role of an archaeologist who has just decided to excavate a particular physical spot. The spot (hereafter called "the site") has enough surface finds on it to make you believe there is a real site underneath. Your state archaeological unit has in the past been willing to give seed money to professional archaeologists to further investigate the likelihood that what looks promising will indeed be a successful venture. Although the site is not large relative to places such as Teotihuacán in Mexico, it is too big to be excavated on weekends by you alone, so you do want funds to pay for your salary, equipment, and the minimal needs of five student volunteers for what you estimate will be a three-year project (summer months only). To get a grant for even seed money to run test pits, you need to make a map. The Preliminary Survey map will be attached to your grant application. Assuming you will receive the grant, do the test pits, and receive further funding to do the excavation, you will have to do a Site Surface Survey map as well. In this exercise, you will learn how to make the kinds of maps that are important to any archaeological work.

OBJECTIVES

In this exercise, you will

- learn how to draw a Preliminary Survey map of a site.
- learn how to draw a Site Surface Survey map.
- learn how to draw the surface finds on a one meter square map.

DOING THE EXERCISE

1. This exercise is set up for a three-person team to do at one time to save wear and tear on the site, to encourage cooperation as on real sites, and to lessen the time it takes to draw maps so that you can draw three of them. Each of you should produce three separate maps, but you may cooperate to set up stakes and take measurements.

Get instructions from your lab manager about where to go to map. Permission to map the site has been secured, but there are rules that must be followed. You will move or remove nothing from the area. You are to map only what is there. If people ask what you are doing, tell them it is for your archaeology course and that should satisfy most. If not, give the person your instructor's name and telephone number and tell the person to phone for details. If some official, such as a police officer, tells you to stop and leave, do so until the matter has been resolved.

Take the equipment in the box labeled "Survey/Mapping Equipment" with you. You will need the following equipment: measurers in metric units (at least three meters long), scissors, string, compass, hammer, stakes, clipboards, paper, graph paper, small card with large red asterisk marked on it to use as a datum point, pencils, and sticky tape. When you get to the site, you will make three maps.

2. First, do a Preliminary Survey map. Use your compass and find true north. With the compass pointed true north, walk to the spot that gives you the best view of the area's expanse with true north facing out in front of you. Use a half sheet of plain paper and pencil for this map. Mark yourself at the bottom of your map (you can draw yourself later). Draw what you see of the area using Figure 1.1 as a model. Draw natural features (hills, rivers, vegetation), and cultural features (buildings, roads—label them if you know their names). With a dotted line, mark where you think the site should be, based on surface finds.

Later, back in the lab, you can ink in the features, draw your legend, and paste your map on Figure 1.2.

3. Next, do a Site Surface Survey map. The three of you on your survey team should agree where the site is, based on surface finds or the "lay of the land." Decide the vague scope of the site and, based on that, where you will put your datum point. Use a bit of tape and put up your datum point card (be sure to take it down when you leave). Use your measurer and bring the reference point to the ground. Hammer in a stake at that point. One person should hold the measurer and the stake and one should walk off the appropriate number of full meters. Put in a stake at the end point. Tie a piece of string on the first stake and run it to the end, adding stakes at each meter. Do the same for the other end of the datum point so you have a 95° angle grid. Using the measurer, find the last stake of the square or rectangle and pound it in, adding string. Your

boundaries are now set. Run strings between each meter so you have a site that is delineated by strings. Draw the Site Surface Survey map on graph paper, drawing a frame as necessary, depending on the shape of your site. Again, you can finish up your map back in the lab. Paste your map on Figure 1.3.

4. Pick any one square in your gridded system and eyeball the surface finds, drawing them on an additional piece of graph paper and labeling them as best you can. Back in the lab, you can finish up the map and paste it on Figure 1.4.

Before you leave the site, take down the datum point card, remove the stakes, knot the cut strings and rewind them on the string ball, and bring all equipment back to the lab.

Finish up your maps and paste them in your manual.

☐ **Check with your lab manager on all three maps for full credit.**

KEY WORDS

convenience map

intuitive map

Compass map

Preliminary Survey map

Site Surface Survey map

topographic map

probabilistic sampling

datum point

grids

FOR FURTHER READING

Barker, Philip. *Techniques of Archaeological Excavation,* 3rd ed. London: Batson, 1993.

Hester, Thomas R., Harry J. Shafer, and Kenneth L. Feder, eds. *Field Methods in Archaeology,* 7th ed. Mountain View, Calif.: Mayfield, 1997.

Jaukowsky, Martha. *A Complete Manual of Field Archaeology.* Englewood Cliffs, N.J.: Prentice Hall, 1980.

Millon, René. "Teotihuacán: Completion of the Map of the Giant Ancient City in the Valley of Mexico." *Science* 170 (1970):1077–82.

Napton, L. Kyle, and Elizabeth Anne Greathouse. "Archaeological Mapping, Site Grids, and Surveying." In *Field Methods in Archaeology,* 7th ed., edited by Thomas R. Hester, Harry J. Shafer, and Kenneth L. Feder, 177–234. Mountain View, Calif.: Mayfield, 1997.

Figure 1.2 Preliminary Survey Map of Site

Figure 1.3 Site Surface Survey Map

Figure 1.4 One Square Meter

Ethnoarchaeology: The "Lunch Site"

With its usual three-inch headlines, the latest supermarket tabloid reports "Archaeologist Discovers Purple Headhunters in New Guinea." You say to yourself, There they go again, confusing archaeologists with cultural anthropologists, who—if anyone—would have discovered those "purple head-hunters." Archaeologists, as we all know, study the cultural remains of dead people; they study ancient tools and hearthstones, pottery and postholes, but the people who made the objects are often thought of as background noise. People had to make the artifacts that archaeologists focus on, but the people themselves are long gone, were never seen by archaeologists, and were never interviewed. By contrast, cultural anthropologists focus on living people in the flesh, people who can be observed, interviewed, and joked with on occasion. Under these circumstances, the "purple headhunter" discovery by an archaeologist must be another of those journalistic errors, as these "purple headhunters" are still alive. Or is it an error?

Think of the following real-life happenings in the recent past: (1) An archaeologist lives with a group of Ju/'Hoansi, once called Bushmen, in the south African Kalahari Desert for two years, focusing on the materials the group dropped and tossed aside during the time they spent in camp; (2) an archaeologist counts the number of fish and shellfish every person in a group of aboriginals in coastal Australia ate for a year; and (3) an archaeologist and his family live with a group of aboriginals in central Australia for several years, with the goal of studying their entire culture. These are all fairly recent examples of **ethnoarchaeology**, showing some of the places and topics of interest to the archaeologist-turned-cultural anthropologist.

Sometimes called "living archaeology," ethnoarchaeology uses the present as a bridge to the past and is based on analogies with modern people, but not direct analogies. Just because the Mbuti Pygmies of Congo in central Africa are hunter-gatherers and practice preferential sibling or first-cousin marriage exchange does not mean that whenever an archaeologist uncovers evidence that a group of prehistoric people were hunter-gatherers, they too practiced this form of preferential marriage. But knowledge about a present-day population does allow us to hypothesize about some unknown aspect of culture in the past. In another example, if a contemporary Australian aboriginal group of foragers claims to draw cave pictures of the animals they want to kill and eat—a type of hunting magic—then if we find cave pictures of animals that date to prehistoric times, we might hypothesize that prehistoric foragers used pictures of animals in a kind of hunting magic activity as well. At this point, the archaeologist must use evidence from the prehistoric group under study, and not from the group that provided the stimulus for the hypothesis, to test the idea. This use of knowledge about modern foragers makes analogies indirect, but scientifically proper.

Ethnoarchaeologists often focus on modern societies themselves, and actually live with people for extended periods of time, studying their behavior and artifacts. It is from these observations that they generate hypotheses about past human activities and material items. Perhaps the role and goals of cultural anthropologists, sometimes called ethnographers, and ethnoarchaeologists can become clearer by looking at a real-life happening in the 1960s. At that time, a number of anthropology faculty and graduate students from Harvard University were spending anywhere from months to years working in the Kalahari Desert with a group of foragers known to them as !Kung Bushmen. The term *Bushman* is pejorative and has been dropped from all modern references and even the term *!Kung* is no longer used because it is what other people living in the Kalahari called the group, not what they call themselves. Their term for themselves is *Ju/'Hoansi*, and we will refer to them by that name, though the earlier literature called them Bushmen or !Kung or San.

Among other graduate students, Richard Lee (now at the University of Toronto) and John Yellen (now anthropology director of the National Science Foundation) spent years in the Kalahari with various Ju/'Hoansi bands of foragers. But because of their training and interests, their roles and goals differed. Richard Lee is a cultural anthropologist; as such, he was interested in the culture of the contemporary Ju/'Hoansi. Although he specialized in trying to understand their strategies for food gathering and staying alive under difficult conditions, he also collected data through observation and interviews on their entire way of life: economics, social organization, political organization, and religion and magic, to cite the major, if arbitrary, categories cultural anthropologists usually consider.

By contrast, John Yellen is an archaeologist; he was interested in what modern Ju/'Hoansi culture could tell him about past cultures. As he could not assume that what he observed them doing today was true in the past, he could—and did—use what he observed them doing to hypothesize that their ancestors did the same thing in the past. If he had followed this into a second phase, he would have tested his hypotheses—generated by modern Ju/'Hoansi—by excavating sites known to have been lived in by their ancestors. This is ethnoarchaeology, and the role and goals of ethnoarchaeologists differ from those of cultural anthropologists by virtue of time. Cultural anthropologists and ethnoarchaeologists may use some of the same methods and study the same people, but whereas cultural anthropologists are interested in describing and explaining the culture of existing groups of people, ethnoarchaeologists are interested in describing and explaining the culture of groups that no longer exist.

Ethnoarchaeology has a strong materialist bias, and most ethnoarchaeologists, by training and expectations, cast their eyes more on what people *make* in their society than what the people do or believe in. This is for good reason, as beliefs, rules, and behaviors per se do not fossilize to become part of the archaeological record. Only when behavior, beliefs, or rules lead to material objects do cognitive or behavioral elements of culture have a chance to become part of the record of the past. This is not a hard and fast rule, however, as will be seen, because ethnoarchaeologists have sometimes been able to hypothesize about social phenomena, such as activity patterns and demographic features.

What were those archaeologists mentioned earlier really doing when they were living with modern foragers? Where is the archaeology in their ethnography? John Yellen (1977) lived with the Ju/'Hoansi in southern Africa for two years; his archaeology can be found in the predictions he subsequently made about prehistoric hunter-gatherers, based on what he learned by living with the modern Ju/'Hoansi. Betty Meehan (1982), living with the Anbarra in northern Australia, counted the fish and seafood eaten by an entire group of gatherers for a full year, observing how many people consumed how much food for how long. Archaeologists interested in Mesolithic population size in Denmark could use Meehan's quantitative findings to hypothesize what the population sizes of large *kitchen midden* sites in Scandinavia were 8000 years ago. (A kitchen midden is a conglomerate of seashells and fish skeletons compacted into thick deposits.) Finally, Richard Gould (1977) excavated a prehistoric site in Australia called Puntutjarpa and then lived with the contemporary descendants of the people, called the Ngatatjara, who left their debris at that site, comparing the way of life of the contemporary group with their prehistoric ancestors some 6800 years ago, and finding considerable continuity in their material culture.

Although it was common for archaeologists in the past to use ethnographic data to generate or test their ideas, it was rare for an archaeologist before the mid-1960s to work directly with informants who were alive. The swing away from pure description or the reconstruction of ancient life ways to a broader base from which to attempt to discover the processes involved in forming the archaeological record continues to be at the forefront of archaeological theory and practice today. This is a large part of what goes on under the umbrella of middle-range theory (see Glossary), and ethnoarchaeology plays an important role in this new thrust. But are there any forager groups left for archaeologists to live with? Are there any more hypotheses to generate about prehistoric life ways? One or two groups from each area of the world's foragers have been sampled, but this is only the tip of the ethnographic iceberg. What one ethnoarchaeologist may observe in a contemporary foraging society may not trigger an association with any material objects that he or she has seen in an excavation; a different ethnoarchaeologist may make the same observation and be able to associate social organization and a particular hearthstone pattern, triggering a memory of similar patterns found in a recent excavation.

CONSTRAINTS OF ETHNOARCHAEOLOGY

There are a number of good reasons why archaeologists do not use knowledge of contemporary societies as direct explanations of prehistoric findings. As John Yellen (1977) suggests, the lifestyle of living foragers may be very different from that of any prehistoric group. Living foragers are often the result of "civilized" people pushing them into the most remote, usually inhospitable, regions of the world: the Arctic and the desert. Although the Mbuti Pygmies of Africa live in what appears to be a hunter-gatherer paradise, they share with many of the world's other foragers the fact that they have lived there for a relatively short time; the material culture of each contemporary foraging group is specialized rather than generalized, and this suggests recent migration and adaptation.

A second constraint concerns the curious lack of variability among most modern forager cultures; do we assume a similar lack of variability in prehistoric cultures? Most of us envision a kind of model of prehistoric foragers, with all groups being a variation on a very general theme. Even professional archaeologists until recently fell into the trap of presenting a picture of all prehistoric foragers as being variants of Cro-Magnon. Modern foragers do display many similar characteristics that characterize them as foragers: small amount of material culture, portable shelter, and low population density, among other traits. They also display many similarities in political and social organization, but they differ considerably in supernatural beliefs and practices. Surely 500,000 years ago or even 10,000 years ago, there was considerably more variation than is witnessed in modern foraging societies. When we use contemporary foraging societies as ethnoparallels, we therefore restrict the variety that probably existed in the past to the narrower range of the present.

Third, there are numerically so few foraging societies left in the world that attempting to make statistically valid statements about them is unjustified. Because most foragers are located in only a few refuge areas, the sample is biased toward only three or four spots on the earth: Australia, southern and central Africa, the Arctic area. The *Ethnographic Atlas* (Murdock 1967) describes selected culture traits for 179 foraging groups (many of which no longer exist), but much of the data were often collected by nonscientists many years ago. Reliable ethnographic literature exists on only a dozen foraging groups, and statistically, this is meaningless.

Finally, there is the problem of assessing cultural capabilities in the past. Today, all people belong to one biological species and have the same capacity for culture, although obviously cultural groups vary in the manner in which they display those capabilities. Two and a half million years ago when archaeologists note the first stone objects that were patterned enough to call artifacts (tools), our human ancestors were quite different from modern humans, and the artifacts may have come from the hands of several different genera and perhaps as many as six species. The capabilities for culture at this time are unknown and using knowledge about modern *Homo sapiens* to assess some archaeological aspects of pre-*Homo sapiens* invites trouble. Although archaeologists know to avoid this trap, opinions differ as to when our ancestors became anatomically modern. Some experts feel our species in its anatomically modern form goes back 200,000 years—at least in Africa—whereas others will not use that designation until considerably more recently. A further problem lies in the potential difference between anatomically and behaviorally modern humans. Where such distinctions are made, experts believe anatomically modern humans may be modern in bone structure but are not behaviorally modern, meaning they had different cultural capabilities from modern *Homo sapiens*. Although caution suggests we use ethnoparallels only with groups regarded as definitely modern in cultural capabilities, in order to satisfy all experts, the accepted time frame for ethnoarchaeological analogies is in the neighborhood of only the last 40,000 years.

Although it is perhaps overly pessimistic to question whether any modern foraging group is representative of—much less replicates—any past behavior, set of rules, or material remains, and although we must recognize that the time frame for ethnoarchaeological use is relatively short, ethnoparallels at the very least do suggest the range of behavior into which prehistoric cultures *probably* fell at least during the last 40,000 years. Ideally, and used with caution, ethnoarchaeological findings allow archaeologists to go beyond the limits of the archaeological record in interpreting the past.

USES OF ETHNOARCHAEOLOGY

In the past, archaeologists have been somewhat quicker to use ethnoparallels between contemporary and prehistoric material remains than with nonmaterial remains. One is on more solid ground hypothesizing the function of a spearthrower from knowledge of Native Americans than hypothesizing about some aspect of social organization, if only because the known and unknown spear-throwers are visibly comparable; by contrast, predicting that a prehistoric group had sibling exchange based on the fact that some foraging groups have it today is using a very weak analogy. Material and nonmaterial remains will be discussed separately.

Studies of Material Remains

Richard Gould (1977) had little trouble (and little criticism) when he compared the stone tools excavated from a 6000-year-old prehistoric site in western Australia to the tools made and used by the contemporary descendants of the prehistoric group. Not only was he comparing objects made by two anatomically and behaviorally modern populations that had an ancestral/descendant relationship, he was comparing the edge damage of observable material items. Because he was comparing stone tools in both cases, his observations at least appear to be more valid than if he had been comparing social systems.

But studies about another aspect of prehistoric material culture—the integrity of toolkits and the activity areas we assume they represent—have recently been questioned, based on findings from ethnoarchaeology studies. Until recently, archaeologists have assumed that when certain tools were found together in more or less direct association on archaeological occupation floors that the tools were used at the same time and formed a single toolkit, suitable for a single activity. Underlying this idea was the assumption that most daily activities today are performed by job-specific and special-purpose groups that are spatially segregated from each other during work. If this were true in the past as well, then archaeology sites should show clustering of tools associated with special activities in areas that are separated from each other across the occupation floor of the site. Such activities might include food processing, sleeping, cooking, butchering, tool manufacturing, hide preparation, to name just a few.

This long-held assumption of an association between activities and areas was based on collective common sense and archaeological analyses of material remains by well-respected archaeologists. We all know that certain behaviors happen in dining rooms that do not happen in garages. Kent Flannery (1986) in the 1960s and 1970s led an interdisciplinary team into Oaxaca, Mexico, focusing on the origins of farming in the New World. In the course of excavation, the team noted that debris was not randomly scattered on the living floors of the cave of Guila Naquitz, and a number of hypotheses about the activities that likely went on there were generated. Although Flannery predicted that activity areas would have overlapped and blurred borders, he and members of his team carefully noted every discard and used a statistical program that used clustering and densities of food residue and flint discards to identify potential activities. Based on the statistical analysis, they concluded that there were areas where the two genders worked separately at a number of food-processing tasks; that both genders made their own flint tools; and that gender division of labor intensified over time. The project is a classic example of archaeological analysis of **activity areas,** but unfortunately there is no way to verify the conclusions via ethnoarchaeological means because there are no modern Mexicans living the same kind of life as their ancestors did thousands of years ago.

On the one hand, many archaeologists firmly believe activity areas are discernable at sites. A recent analysis of Abri Dufaure in the foothills of the Pyrenees suggests that Upper Paleolithic people some 12,000 years ago were deliberately dumping debris away from meat-roasting and tool-manufacturing areas. This suggests three activity areas: cooking, tool manufacturing, and dumping. Refits of tools are the evidence for the tool manufacturing area. At three other

French sites about the same age, but over 700 kilometers to the northeast in the Paris basin (Pincevent, Etiolles, and Marsangy), concentrations of bone splinters adjacent to hearths suggest an area devoted to breaking bones to get to the marrow for food. Additionally, the following activities are mentioned by the excavators: processing meat for storage, carcass dismemberment, the first stages of butchering, and sleeping.

On the other hand, recent work by John Yellen and others has shown that among some modern foragers, debris gets jumbled up so much that what tool belongs to what activity cannot be determined. In addition, observation of these modern foragers suggests that most activities take place in more than one place and are not activity specialized. Ethnoarchaeologists working with the Hadza in East Africa (a sometime-foraging group) found too much overlap of activities to be able to discern single-purpose activity areas. They specifically stated that they could not discern any gender-associated areas, which places into question the assumption that prehistoric camps will necessarily show activity areas via toolkits.

Lewis Binford does not agree with Yellen that *no* modern foragers have job-specific activity areas. In his work in Alaska, Binford (1978) observed the Nunamiut Eskimo and concluded that they displayed both sides of the activity/place argument: in some cases they did job-specific activities and left debris in discernibly different areas; in other cases they performed several activities in one place and as a result, discards were jumbled. In this study of the Nunamiut, he observed the activities and subsequent material debris that resulted from the group of hunters congregating at hunting stands to watch for caribou (reindeer) and discussing strategies for hunting them. Because of the cold, the men had built a hearth, and four or so men huddled around it, with an opening to the area of observation. As the men watched, they snacked by breaking open caribou long bones to get to the marrow, dropping bits of broken bone around the hearth. Binford called this area, appropriately, the "drop zone." When they ate entire meals, however, the hunters deposited large items such as whole bones, pop cans, or sardine cans in quite a different manner by tossing the larger items away from the immediate hearth area where they had congregated. Binford called this the "toss zone." When asked why they tossed some items and dropped others, the hunters simply said, "Who wants to sit down on a large bone?" If this hunting stand had been immediately covered by soil with no disturbance by animals or wind, the two distinct zones could have remained intact for an archaeologist to excavate hundreds of years later. The drop zone, with its small, lightweight bone chips would have been spatially distinct from the toss zone with its larger, heavier bones and cans. Because the drop/toss zone resulted from the same activity—eating food—the activity was not spatially distinct in the sense of all food residue being in one place. Here, Binford's findings seem to agree with Yellen's. However, in an attempt to reduce boredom, the Nunamiut also made masks, carved horn, and repaired caribou socks while they waited for the caribou. These activities did leave distinct debris in spatially segregated areas.

Archaeologists might predict similar behaviors to those described for the Ju/'Hoansi or the Nunamiut if they found similar distribution patterns on archaeology occupation floors (see Glossary for "occupation floor"). Binford, using an overlay made by Andre Leroi-Gourhan for one of his habitation/hearths at Pincevent, a 12,000-year-old late Magdalenian site in central France, found it "fit" the Nunamiut site in terms of debris patterns. Not all toss/drop zones would be identical in all modern sites or in all prehistoric sites, however, as the size and shape of the activity pattern can be affected by unknown variables. In the case of the Nunamiut, the zones are in a 360° circle; a hearth against a rock shelter wall would result in a 180° semicircle. Because some foragers prefer ring-shaped habitations with hearths in a circular pattern, and others prefer linear habitations, with hearths in a row, variability is to be expected in prehistoric patterns as well. In one ethnographic observation of habitation patterns, the physical characteristic of shade versus constant sun was the major criterion for placement of huts and hearths. If toss and drop zones were present on a habitation floor, however, they would be easily differentiated on the basis of type of item and weight/size of the debris.

David Hurst Thomas recently used these ethnoarchaeological findings to generate a hypothesis concerning the debris pattern found in a site he excavated in the 1970s. At Gatecliff Shelter in Nevada, Thomas (1989) found that the only statistically valid difference between the discard in two large areas was one of weight/size. He hypothesized that prehistoric Native Americans dropped small bits of food and flint and tossed the larger pieces against a wall, because dropping and tossing explained his observation better than assuming different activity areas.

Thomas also used this ethnoarchaeological hypothesis to relook at some maps from the Coxcatlan site in Mexico, originally excavated by Richard Mac-Neish in the 1960s. MacNeish, the head of the interdisciplinary team that excavated this site, using an idea that was accepted then, interpreted some layers as displaying different activity areas, including food preparation, skin preparation, hunting, tool manufacturing, burials, woodworking, ceremonial activities, and weaving in six segregated areas. Thomas has relooked at these maps and suggests that the distribution appears to be the result of the inhabitants differentially discarding debris by size. Although Thomas's interpretation is in no way proved, it does suggest using caution in immediately assuming that discard patterns are always the result of activities.

Ceramic studies might initially be thought to yield evidence of activity because pottery is so closely connected to cooking. However, people do not normally leave their pots where they break (in the kitchen, one assumes) but instead usually take them to the dump or sweep them over a hill to get rid of them. Only when some catastrophic event occurs and people drop what they are doing to escape are we apt to find ceramically related activity areas (and catastrophic events such as floods, fires, or volcanic eruptions are very rare events). Indeed, the pieces of a single pot may be found with a distribution of 200 meters, suggesting the pot was not broken or left where it was last used.

In summary, archaeologists once assumed that toolkits and activity areas would be discernible in the archaeological record. Ethnoarchaeological studies of modern foragers suggest that it is likely that for some activities, no observable discard would form but for other activities, they would. In particular, hearths may show special-purpose activities because they were commonly the focus for domestic projects.

In contrast, patterns of discard may not represent specific activity areas (where all members of a group did a particular activity in one spot) but may at least minimally represent a domestic unit (where only members of a social unit such as a nuclear family were active and left debris and where each unit is spatially separated from other such units by empty space). Foragers in base camps that incorporate nuclear families, for example, leave debris in dimensions that are roughly circular to their shelter and hearth, separate from other piles of debris. At Verberie, a 12,000-year-old Upper Paleolithic site near Paris, experimental archaeologists—on the basis of comparing the bones in several spatially separate piles of similar debris—have concluded that the inhabitants shared meat. Very recently, John Yellen, working in Congo, found two clusters of artifacts and fish bones that conform to the debris pattern made by modern forager nuclear families (such as the Ju/'Hoansi he studied in south Africa 20 years ago), in which production tasks (making tools or processing food) are done by nuclear family units. The importance of this work is that the site Yellen describes here is 14C dated as being over 40,000 years old, thus pushing back the time when archaeologists can look for activity areas or areas represented by social units.

Studies of Nonmaterial Culture

Much of what people do, think, and believe can never become part of the archaeological record because it does not result in artifacts. Are ethnoarchaeologists thereby limited in what they can observe to bridge into the past for archaeological explanations? Several archaeologists would say no. John Yellen made predictions about the size of prehistoric populations, the number of social units in a camp, and the duration of a camp's use by observing the patterning of the camp debris. Binford applied Yellen's predictions to Nunamiut debris patterns and found that two of the three predictions did not hold. Apparently, Yellen's predictions only work under certain circumstances.

A project connecting material culture with social organization and possible activity areas was attempted by William Longacre at Carter Ranch in Arizona. Longacre hypothesized that because women are the potters in Zuñi and Hopi society today, they were likely to have made the pottery in prehistoric times as well; he also postulated matrilocal residence based on the same ethnoparallels, with women staying at home near their female relatives after marriage, bringing their husbands into their families. He assumed that if his hypotheses were true, the evidence would show up on their ceramics, with more similarities in style showing up within matrilocal clusters (nearby apartments) than between such clusters. He also postulated that women were apt to make their pots together if they were closely related, with gender-related activity areas the result. Males, by contrast, should have their own activity areas for weaving, rituals, and gambling. To verify the male activity of weaving beyond ethnoparallels, Longacre pointed to loom equipment found in graves with male bodies and two loom holes in a kiva where, today at least, males are involved in ritual activity. Some of Longacre's predictions have not been supported, but the work demonstrates that ethnoarchaeology is not restricted to hypotheses about material remains alone.

Activity-area analysis has also been used to attempt to identify individual as opposed to group behaviors, as exemplified by the Ju/'Hoansi and the Nunamiut. This kind of analysis is not likely to be successful unless the archaeology site in question is in situ; otherwise, it is not possible to separate behavioral events by time. The late Upper Paleolithic site of Meer, some 9000 years old on the Belgian coast, provides a good example of attempting to identify individual behavior based on the refitting of the site's flint debris back into cores. The excavators have concluded that in one area separate from the main camp, two flint knappers made a fire and sat down to knap flint. One was right-handed and the other was left-handed; one was a better knapper than the other; they worked on different materials. Although the excavators also concluded that the two knappers were male, no evidence was given to substantiate this idea and the gender of the individuals remains open. The excavators were able to come to conclusions about individual behaviors because of the unusual segregation of activity areas.

A great deal more needs to be done using ethnoarchaeological principles, particularly in the area of nonmaterial culture, in which archaeologists have so little solid evidence.

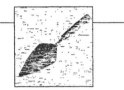

THE EXERCISE

It seems clear that ethnoarchaeology studies can trigger ideas in the heads of creative archaeologists, ideas that can translate into hypotheses about life in ancient times that can then be tested by excavating archaeology sites. Just such an idea occurred to John Yellen when he observed the activity patterns of the Ju/'Hoansi he was living with, resulting in his conclusion that if the camps he was observing were archaeology sites, archaeologists would not be able to discern where specific activities had taken place. Yet Lewis Binford's work with the Nunamiut suggests that at least some forager activities are observable in the present and would likely be discernible under archaeological deposition conditions. If we conclude that some modern forager groups do and some groups do not have specialized toolkits and use special activity areas, then archaeologists can, cautiously, proceed to at least being on the lookout for such toolkits and single-purpose activity areas. Perhaps the drop and toss zones that are observed in modern forager societies (Nunamiut and Ju/'Hoansi) and reconstructed from debris patterns in the past (Gatecliff Shelter and Coxcatlan) are well suited for investigation, with activity-related patterns emerging from them.

In Exercise 4 in this book, you will be assessing the function of flint tools. In the reading for that exercise, Semenov—the "father" of microwear studies—was criticized because he did both parts of his experiments himself: He made the experimental tools and used them for various activities, causing microwear to occur on the tools; he then matched prehistoric tools to them, concluding the artifacts were made in a certain way because they matched his experimental tools. It took a blind test by two investigators, one making tools and one "blindly" attempting to discover what the tools had been used for, to verify microwear studies. Without such verification, microwear analysts could justly be accused of knowing too much and letting that knowledge unconsciously bias their assessment of function.

But it is precisely that beforehand knowledge that gives the ethnoarchaeologist the bridge from the present to the past. It is knowing that a group of foragers does or does not have special activities relegated to specific areas of a camp that has allowed ethnoarchaeologists to hypothesize that prehistoric people may have had activity areas as well. And as long as cultural anthropologists use modern cultures to only generate hypotheses, the beforehand knowledge is scientifically valid.

In the following exercise, you will see how this kind of knowledge serves archaeology. In the first part of the data analysis, you will be in the dark relative to any individual's behavior and will have to make a prediction about such behavior based only on the debris you mapped after a specific activity, just as an archaeologist would if he or she excavated the specific activity 1000 years from now. In the second part of the analysis, you will have use of the observational record only an ethnoarchaeologist would have, and your reconstruction of individual behaviors will be valid because you were there to record them! The exercise uses the drop/toss zone model of debris, previously explained in connection with Binford's Nunamiut study.

In this exercise, you will be doing a very simplistic bit of ethnoarchaeology. There is not time or money to send you to Australia or south Africa, and you'd need to take at least 10 cultural anthropology courses and learn the language of the people you were going to be living with even if you did go. Therefore, the ethnology part of the exercise will be role playing; you will be "going native" for 30 minutes. This is a group exercise, with two of your labmates functioning as "lunch partners." It can't be done alone; a total of 3–4 people is ideal. The group part will take only 30 minutes.

OBJECTIVES

In this exercise, you will

- role-play, with others, a small microband of foragers who are away from base camp at mealtime. You will eat then discard your refuse, but remember where you discarded *your* debris.
- make a map of the discarded refuse; analyze the map for information on individual behaviors of the people who left the debris.
- look at the size of the debris in various areas and decide if the patterning matches the drop/toss zone model.
- map in the three of you. Identify *your* debris. Reanalyze the map for individual behaviors.
- contrast what an archaeologist can reconstruct with confidence from knowing only the pattern of debris at a site with what the ethnoarchaeologist knows because he or she was there.

DOING THE EXERCISE

1a. Decide with your two labmates when you want to do the exercise. The word *lunch* is not necessarily to be taken literally. Depending on what time your lab meets, you can do this exercise during your regular lab, or you can plan to meet at a more convenient time for 30 minutes at the site some time during the next three days. The term *lunch* will be used in the exercise, even if you have supper or a large snack. Be sure the lab is open when you come, as you will need to use lab equipment. Also decide ahead of time who is bringing what for lunch (you may bring your own lunch, or you may share). You must follow one rule: The food you bring must leave debris. Do not bring a sandwich, eat it, and leave. If the lunch leaves no debris, there is no point to this exercise, as it is the debris that you will be analyzing. To be safe, *each of you must deposit at least 10 items of lunch debris during your meal.*

b. Take the lunch tarp outside on the grass if you want to brave the elements, or do the exercise inside.

c. Put the simulated log "campfire" in the middle of the tarp (remember that in foraging societies, this is often the focus of activities), bring out your lunch items, sit down on the tarp–arranging yourself so you won't get "burned" by the fire, yet can get its "warmth"–unwrap your lunch items and get started. Eat your lunch, dropping and tossing lunch debris (at least 10 items) as you please, but try to keep it on the tarp. While you are eating and dropping or tossing, try to remember where you deposited *your* debris. (Do not have food fights!)

d. After lunch, get up as carefully as you can without disturbing the debris on the tarp. If you have food on your lap, let it drop naturally on the tarp.

2a. Put the "lunch grid" over the tarp area. Get a site map (graph paper) that shows 10 × 10 centimeter spaces and draw a map of the "lunch site," eyeballing each piece of debris to the closest centimeter. Draw the size of each bit of trash as accurately as possible for later analysis. (Normally, mapping would need to be far more accurate, as in Exercise 1, but what you need to see on this map can be done without technical measuring.) If the lunch grid is smaller than the debris area (and tarp), put it over the area that has the most debris. Adjust your map by drawing the grid area inside the given graph paper and eyeball the placement of debris that falls outside the grid frame. Tape your map on Figure 2.1.

b. For this part of the analysis, forget that you were part of the activity; here you are an archaeologist excavating a 1000-year-old site. Look at the debris patterning on your map. On the basis of the observed patterning, hypothesize how many people made this debris and who did what. Justify your conclusions based on the pattern and write a paragraph in the space provided for (1) following Figure 2.1.

c. Analyze the patterning you observe. Does it match Binford's drop/toss model, with small food dropped and found in one area and large items tossed and found in another? Decide yes or no, and why, and write a statement in the space provided for (2) following Figure 2.1.

3. Now you are an ethnoarchaeologist with previous knowledge firmly in the forefront of your mind about who sat where and who did what at the "lunch site." Map in the three lunchers and assign them numbers (make yourself number 1). Mark each piece of trash that *you* tossed with 1; identify the trash of the others with numbers as best you can. Now, reanalyze the map, using your knowledge of what was going on at that event; write a paragraph of analysis in the space provided for (3) following Figure 2.1, concerning individual behavior at this site: How many people were involved; who did what?

4. Properly dispose of your lunch debris; return the tarp, grid, and "campfire" to your lab manager.

5. The contrast between (2) and (3) should be obvious, but write a paragraph for (4) following Figure 2.1, identifying what an ethnoarchaeologist knows that a "regular" archaeologist cannot know and how this kind of information can help archaeologists with their work.

☐　**Check your Figure 2.1 answers with your lab manager for full credit.**

KEY WORDS

ethnoarchaeology
activity areas

FOR FURTHER READING

Binford, Lewis. "Dimensional Analysis of Behavior and Site Structure: Learning from an Eskimo Hunting Stand." *American Antiquity* 43, no. 3 (1978):330–61.

Binford, Lewis. *Nunamiut Ethnoarchaeology.* New York: Academic Press, 1978.

Flannery, Kent, ed. *Guila Naquitz: Archaic Foraging and Early Agriculture in Oaxaca.* Orlando: Academic Press, 1986.

Gould, Richard A. "Puntutjarpa Rockshelter and the Australian Desert Culture." *Anthropological Papers of the American Museum of Natural History* 54, no. 1 (1977).

Hietala, H. J., ed. *Intrasite Spatial Analysis in Archaeology.* New York: Cambridge University Press, 1984.

Hill, James. *Broken K Pueblo.* Tucson: University of Arizona Press, 1970.

Kent, Susan. *Analyzing Activity Areas.* Albuquerque: University of New Mexico Press, 1984.

Kroll, Ellen, and T. Douglas Price, eds. *The Interpretation of Archaeological Spatial Patterning.* New York: Plenum Press, 1991.

Longacre, William A. "Archaeology as Anthropology: A Case Study." Anthropological paper no. 17, University of Arizona Press, Tucson, 1970.

Meehan, Betty. *Shell Bed to Shell Midden.* Canberra: Australian Institute of Aboriginal Studies, 1982.

Murdock, George P. *Ethnographic Atlas.* Pittsburgh: University of Pittsburgh Press, 1967.

Thomas, David Hurst. *Archaeology,* 2nd ed. New York: Holt, Rinehart & Winston, 1989.

Yellen, John. *Archaeological Approaches to the Present: Models for Reconstructing the Past.* New York: Academic Press, 1977.

Figure 2.1 Lunch Site Map

1. Looking only at the above Lunch Site map, how many people do you believe made the debris, who did what, and why? _____
   _____
   _____
   _____
   _____

2. Does the pattern of your map match the drop/toss model and why or why not?
   _____
   _____
   _____
   _____

3. After mapping in the people involved and checking off your litter and what you can recall the others tossed (mark on map), reassess the map. How many people were involved in the "Lunch Site" activity?_____ Who did what? _____
   _____
   _____
   _____
   _____

4. What can an ethnoarchaeologist know that an archaeologist cannot know, and of what importance is it?_____
   _____
   _____

3

Rubbish, Trash, and Garbage

There are many clichés describing what "we are"—"we are what we eat," "we are what we were"—so one more seems appropriate to introduce this exercise: "We are what we throw away." As in all clichés, there is a measure of truth to the saying. "We are what we eat" suggests nutrition is the key to our body's well-being; "we are what we were" pays homage to history in assessing present conditions; and "we are what we throw away" points to human discards as clues to our past, 10,000 years ago or yesterday.

In most archaeology classes, the instructor brings up the following point several times during the first week, so most students hear it at least once: Archaeology can be defined as the science of trash. One instructor tries to explain that definition by asking the class members to mentally follow a Neandertal hunter going through a normal Neandertal day, hunting, repairing a flint spearhead, butchering a small animal, picking berries, bouncing his children on his knee; at the same time, students are asked to mentally watch what that Neandertal drops, saves, or discards. This discard is, the instructor claims, his trash, and if multiplied by the same amount for 10 days and if added to the trash of the other 22 members of his band, there would be the equivalent of a trash barrel full of broken spears, moldy fur garments, cherry pits, and horse bones. This might be followed by a "you can be followed around too" statement, whereby you are watched dropping gum wrappers, pizza crusts, and beer cans. Multiply by hundreds of other college students' discards, and the result is trash barrels of garbage. The point is that there is a garbage-to-culture equivalency here: just as what today's people leave as trash represents their **culture,** so too what yesterday's people left behind represents their culture.

The first time a neophyte archaeologist excavates a site, he or she is overwhelmed with a sense of identification with the person or persons who left behind the first dozen or so excavated artifacts—that person's trash. The excavator can't help but stare at the artifacts and wonder who discarded them, what he or she was doing at the moment of discard, and often ends up building an entire mental scenario of who, what, where, and why. After a while, the novelty wears off, but for that first hour or so of invading the personal space and history of someone never seen who lived hundreds or thousands of years ago, the present and the past are tightly linked by what else? Garbage.

Rubbish, trash, garbage—it has a nicer archaeological name—**material culture.** The term encompasses all of the objects that humans make or alter. Material culture is only part of the wider term *culture* because it includes only items that are made, altered, or objectified, meaning made into objects. Human culture—our way of life—that consists of the learned portions of human behavior, cognition, and emotion that is shared with other humans in social groups, is composed of things made (material culture) and things that are not directly made (nonmaterial culture), such as rules or beliefs. A rule that allows women to have more than one husband at a time will never leave material remains; a belief in spirit ancestors will not leave any objects. Rules and beliefs can of course become objectified as material items when people make things that represent their rules or beliefs. Believing a recently deceased person goes to heaven is a belief and by itself nonmaterial, but if people act on this belief relative to the rules in their culture and build coffins and tombstones, dig holes in the ground, or place favorite possessions next to bodies, material objects will result. But unless cognitive and emotional components of culture are objectified, they cannot become part of the record of the past. For this reason, we often talk of ethnographic cultures and archaeological cultures.

Ethnocultures are not inherently different from **archaeocultures:** they both result from people who learn or learned much of their behavior, learn and conform more or less to the rules of their society, form attitudes and values that are similar to the people they live with, and even react to events in similar ways. But in ethnocultures, scientists who specialize in studying modern human culture—**ethnologists** or **cultural anthropologists**—have the entire spectrum of human behavior, cognition, and emotion to study and try to make sense of, whereas the scientists who specialize in studying ancient human cultures—archaeologists—are limited to what has survived biodegradation in the ground, material culture. As the archaeologist sees it, however, because material culture is the *result* of the interplay of human behavior, cognition, and emotion, it can be said to *represent* the culture, even if it is not the entire culture. The prime job of the prehistorian, as compared to the prime job of the archaeologist, is to interpret material culture and make inferences based on material data about culture in the past. Prehistorians and archaeologists are, of course, usually the same people, merely changing hats and foci at times. Archaeologists excavate for the remains of material culture and prehistorians interpret the remains in the context of current knowledge.

The preceding discussion is a traditional synopsis of the differing roles of some anthropologists. Traditionally, anthropologists study humans: their biology and their culture. Technically, cultural anthropologists study culture in the past or in the present, in contrast to **physical anthropologists,** who study human biology in the past or in the present. Regardless of technical accuracy, however, the term *cultural anthropology* is usually restricted to the study of modern cultures and is synonymous with ethnology. Ethnologists are the anthropologists who study modern cultures—usually other than their own—and archaeologists are the anthropologists who study past culture. But is this a realistic and unalterable dichotomy of studying culture? No. A number of anthropologists who were trained as archaeologists have lived with modern hunter-gatherers, studying their modern way of life in order to gain insights into what past cultures might have been like. In the same vein, in 1972, an archaeologist at the University of Arizona in Tucson (who was once a Mayan specialist) began a study of modern material culture that grew into what is now called "The Garbage Project" (TGP), or with tongue squarely in cheek and a nod to the French who have been so important in furthering knowledge of the past, "Le Projet du Garbage." (Garbage is not a French word, no matter how we try to pronounce it in "ze French manner.")

TRASH AS A DATABASE

Before discussing The Garbage Project, a few words are in order on behalf of garbage as an archaeological database. First, trash is an ubiquitous sign of humanity. Although other animals can be said to leave rubbish behind (chimpanzees leave banana peels and cracked nuts; birds and beavers leave nests), trashiness is next to humanness if we look at the correlation between human biological evolution for the last three million years and the amount of discard left behind; even factoring in the huge increase in population numbers over time, it is still true that the more we evolved, the more stuff we made and discarded.

Second, garbage links the present to the past. **Middle-range theory** tells us that the present is the key to the past, and in the last 30 years, a number of archaeologists have found it useful to live with modern hunter-gatherers to observe their use of material culture. The study of garbage is a kind of experimental- and ethnoarchaeology.

Third, garbage often tells the truth when other data do not. (The reliability of interview data will be discussed subsequently.) As one example of "truth telling," consider the well-known fact that there were French forts up and down the South Carolina coast during the sixteenth century. The inhabitants of Beaufort, South Carolina, lobbied Congress many years ago to put up a monument to the French fort Charlesfort on nearby Prairie Island; they also gave their streets, shopping centers, and developments French names in honor of this French fort. But as a result of excavating and analyzing the fort's garbage, modern archaeologists discovered that it was the Spanish fort of San Marcos, and not a French fort, as the French did not use either Spanish olive jars nor Seville pottery.

Although there are good things to say about trash as data, there are ethics involved in collecting and analyzing it. The "Peeping Tom" version of garbage collection and use is quite unethical as it intends to make use of what specific people have thrown away that they would not want other people to know about. Many tabloid reporters have made their fortunes rutting through celebrities' garbage cans to find story materials. In contrast, TGP insists on anonymity of householders.

THE GARBAGE PROJECT

The Garbage Project had a modest beginning, but over the 20 years since its inception, it has involved the study of rubbish from at least five cities, gone international, used over a thousand volunteers, and spawned a specialized literature.

In 1971, two students in William Rathje's archaeological methods class at the University of Arizona analyzed the trash from four households as part of a term assignment relating artifacts and behavior. What started as a game for undergraduates became a serious study of modern material culture. Rathje, the archaeologist who saw the potential impact of studying modern trash on a large scale, has taken a lot of ribbing over the years about being a "garbologist," yet the long-term study has resulted in the identification of methodological principles of importance to social scientists and in the gathering of information about waste in America in hopes of curing one of America's ills. Although Rathje was not the first to advocate the study of material culture by studying trash, he went way beyond a study of a trash can or a dump. He points to the pioneering work of A. V. Kidder, a well-respected Harvard archaeologist who, in the 1920s, excavated the Andover, Massachusetts, town dump.

The original Garbage Project study involved the city of Tucson, where there was plenty of data to study, and plenty of student volunteers to sort, note, and analyze the data. Rathje believes that archaeologists make assumptions about how material culture is related to behavior; to him,—it makes no difference if the material culture is old or new, someone else's or ours—archaeological insights can occur anywhere. He also believes that applying the methods of archaeology to a modern society might provide insights into that society itself. And so the project began.

Data Collection

To gather the data (rubbish), Rathje enlisted the help of the Tucson Sanitation Department. Once placed at the curb, trash became the property of the city of Tucson, so the cooperation of the sanitation department was vital. Although technically TGP did not have to inform residents that their rubbish would be analyzed, Rathje made sure there were no ethical problems: all garbage was analyzed anonymously with no specific association of trash and household, unless written permission was given. In the original survey, Tucson was divided into census tracts and the refuse randomly collected from two households in each tract. No individual households were followed over time, and all data were aggregated.

Initially, there was some concern over whether kitchen-sink garbage disposals (or pets) would void the results of trash analysis. It was easy enough to eliminate households with pets, as they could be identified by dog or cat products in the trash. To check on garbage disposals, a five-week comparison of trash in a subsample of 32 households without disposals to those that had disposals gave the project directors a "garbage disposal correction factor" (GDCF). They found that up to 50% of a household's refuse went down the disposal and that certain food was more likely to be disposed of in a disposal (orange rinds, for example) than others (candy). This means that certain wastes (food and scraps of food) do not show up in the totals, but most findings were not affected by the GDCF.

For this initial survey, after the trash was taken to the sanitation department maintenance yard, student volunteers sorted the trash into categories. To protect against accidents or disease, volunteers donned lab coats and gloves and were immunized. The sorting process underwent several modifications over the years, and is now made up of 150 categories of trash (see Figure 3.2 for a variation of this classification). For each sorting session, volunteers used data collection sheets made specifically for the project (see Figure 3.3 for a data collection sheet). For each item in the sample, volunteers noted the collection date, code and name of item, census tract, original weight or volume, cost, material composition of container, and weight of the discarded food (if pertinent).

Later, in a project with somewhat different goals, a number of householders were asked to participate in a more closely monitored study. In this project, garbage was matched to the household that produced it as well as to interview data that were taken earlier. All results were still treated anonymously because all data were aggregated and no individuals could be identified. At first, the investigators predicted that people would change their behavior after they knew their garbage was no longer anonymous; it was believed that some might take empty liquor bottles to work to toss in the bin in the washroom, for example. But, based on before-and-after data, this **reactivity phenomenon**—where knowledge that behavior is being monitored is the cause of behavior change—did not show up.

Some procedural changes occurred over the years, particularly in regard to the condition of garbage before sorting. It is bad enough to sort through two-day-old milk containers or mashed potato remains at the bottom of a plastic bag, but much worse to sort garbage that has piled up for a couple of weeks—particularly old tuna cans in the hot Tucson sun. Based on knowledge gained from doing a garbage project in a northern city that had cold winters, TGP purchased a huge freezer and froze the backed-up Tucson garbage (one suspects there might have been a fall mutiny when student volunteers returned to campus if the garbage had continued in its ripe condition).

Initial Findings: Waste

A number of findings emerged from the original survey and special projects. The large amount of wasted food reported by Rathje became the basis of subsequent special studies. One interesting finding refutes the so-called common knowledge that conspicuous consumption is correlated with upper-income groups. TGP found instead that the middle class rather than the rich or poor wasted the most (one guess is that the poor can't afford to waste and the rich became rich in the first place by making it a habit not to waste). Middle-class Anglo-American families were found to eat certain kinds of meat (ham, lamb, pork, chicken) more often than African American, Native American, or Asian American families. Rathje reported that the lowest-income households consume the largest quantities of vitamins and liquor, yet use the highest-cost educational toys for their children.

In what Rathje called the "first principle of edible food loss," the project found that when people eat their old standby food, they waste less; panic buying and trying out something new that doesn't turn out well so it ends up in the trash appears to be the cause of excess waste. Rathje and his colleagues predicted that waste in Mexican American households would be less than in Anglo-American households because Mexican American meals are based on fewer ingredients, with most meals being variations of the same ingredients. What isn't used in the tacos today can be used in the burritos tomorrow. By contrast, Anglo-American households use many different ingredients that don't translate from one meal to the next; much that is not used is trashed. This prediction was supported by the garbage data. Rathje and his colleagues also predicted that regular white bread would show less waste than specialty bread; they found 5–10% of white bread was wasted, versus 40–50% of specialty bread.

Initial Findings: Interview Reliability

What people say they do versus what they really do (and how to tell the difference) continues to be a problem for social scientists. Self-interviews (questionnaires), preferred by many social scientists because they are inexpensive and can be given to very large samples, have been attacked as establishing "ideal" rather than "real" culture, or what people claim they do or want others to believe they do versus what they really do. Findings based on self-interviews can only be as good as the data they are based on. Sometimes people claim they do or don't do things because the behavior is particularly sensitive: the amount of alcohol or tobacco consumed, the amount of drugs—legal or illegal—taken, the amount of meat consumed, are all sensitive issues to some members of modern society and people can thus purposely mislead. Sometimes, however, it is often a matter of just not remembering how much chicken the family ate last week. The matching of interview data against garbage data supported scientists' predictions: People do underestimate their consumption of alcohol, cigarettes, and meat. Garbage tells the truth. Matchings showed an overestimation of "good" food, such as cottage cheese, liver, tuna, skim milk, and high fiber cereals by 50%, and an underestimation of "bad" food, such as sugar, potato chips, candy, bacon, and ice cream by 50%.

LATER PROJECTS

Based on the success of the initial surveys, additional surveys were done in other areas and additional hypotheses were generated.

Milwaukee and Santa Cruz

TGP spread out geographically in the late 1970s to Milwaukee to see if the Tucson results could be extrapolated to other cities having different ethnic groups or climate. And because it was easy to identify Santa Cruz (100 kilometers south of San Francisco) as an upper-income city, it was added to the database. Two findings from the upper-income data are as follows: Rich people buy generic food for themselves while at the same time they buy gourmet food for their pets, and the higher the income, the longer the stem cut off of asparagus.

Mexico City

The Mexico City project brought several new dimensions to the study: It was the first major international offshoot involving a homogeneous, Third World culture. Some of the findings reinforced what was already known about Mexican economics. For example, although Mexicans actually produced higher amounts of trash than their American counterparts, most of that difference can be accounted for through different ways of producing and packaging food. Mexicans buy a chicken and toss the bones and skin; Americans buy boneless and skinless chicken tenders and toss the package they came in. Mexicans buy mangoes, bananas, and oranges and toss the peels; Americans buy a jar of peeled and sliced fruit and toss the jar (which was probably filled in Mexico). Mexico City **food debris** is 40% of total debris, as opposed to 20% in the United States. In both countries, about 10% of food is wasted and in both, upper-income groups produce more trash than lower-income groups. Although Mexicans have a "sweeter tooth" than Americans, they have a better overall diet.

Some final comments from the Mexico City study concern upper-income households. Wealthy families with servants and cooks might be predicted to serve "homemade" meals using only fresh ingredients; instead, these households rank very high in serving prepared and processed foods, the same as Americans. And try to explain the finding that upper-income Mexicans use six times as much toilet paper as upper-income Americans.

Applied Archaeology

In 1984, TGP applied its methods to problem solving, or applied anthropology/archaeology, when people interested in solid-waste management or recycling began to use TGP results. One project involved the contamination of groundwater, and another investigated tooth care among Anglo- and Mexican Americans.

MODERN MATERIAL CULTURE AND THE PAST

Rathje's work for the past 25-plus years has demonstrated one major point: Garbage says a lot about our own culture. But because Rathje and his colleagues are archaeologists, how does the study of modern material culture serve archaeology?

Alfred Kroeber, an influential anthropologist in the first half of this century, advocated the position that artifacts reflect the cognitive patterns (rules) of particular societies, and he used women's fashions (length of hemlines, for example) and their change through time to show the changes in attitudes and values they mirrored. Although Kroeber never claimed that historical events "caused" hemlines to change, he did conclude that hemlines were stable during normal times but that during times of stress, such as the Napoleonic Wars or the First World War, the established dress style was overthrown and hemlines were free to go up or down drastically. Other anthropologists have agreed with this principle that the study of artifacts (material culture) is an acceptable way to *begin* to study the entire culture of a past group. If Rathje and his colleagues had found all of their hypotheses supported, this principle could be used as a basis for all prehistoric reconstruction. But TGP's findings were (excuse the pun) a mixed bag. Their findings did not refute known facts so much as give us an incomplete picture of the culture under investigation.

What if we were for some reason forced to reconstruct American culture and only had modern material culture (rubbish)? Could we do it? Would our findings be accurate? Could we make accurate statements about social, political, or economic organization? Could we make accurate statements about the religious beliefs of the culture under study? For one reason alone, the answer is yes. And the reason is writing. In America, newspapers and news magazines make up 40% of the trash, so we would be able to reconstruct the total culture of this society. But take away writing and much evidence of nonmaterial culture is removed as well.

If we have no written words, can we perform **cultural reconstruction** based only on material remains? Many people say no. In the past, a few anthropologists and journalists have written that if future archaeologists used the contents of American basements, for example, they might reconstruct late-twentieth-century Americans as being box worshipers who used sacred garments (Halloween costumes) and sacrificial gowns (wedding dresses); if our bathrooms were excavated, future archaeologists might conclude we had tooth fetishes or kept spirits away from sacred water fonts by symbolically placing strips of thin paper over them. But of course these attempts to be humorous in reconstructing American culture ignore the fact that archaeologists have strict rules about sampling. If an archaeologist sampled Disneyworld (and found giant mice), the archaeologist would also sample a typical Florida house and grocery. If the basement and bathroom of a house were sampled, so too would a kitchen and living room. Archaeologists following their own advice would come to quite different conclusions about American culture than journalists have.

Although knowledge of one category of culture cannot give us accurate information about any other category, at least it is a beginning (in lieu of direct knowledge about some categories of culture), and the study of material culture is that beginning. When confronted with the job of reconstructing the entire culture of the Maya on the basis of one small "house" of paintings (Bonampak), art-history graduate student Marcia Menihan made a series of predictions about the culture. Because she was half incorrect (if one assumes knowledge gleaned from all sources about the Maya is accurate), the exercise might be used to condemn attempting to reconstruct a culture on the basis of very limited material remains.

But an important point is that she was also half correct in her predictions. If all we had of Mayan material culture were the Bonampak murals, at least we would be able to generate a series of hypotheses about their culture. If we were then able to find where the Maya discarded their household trash (their material culture), we could excavate and find out what they ate, what clothes they wore, and other bits of knowledge concerning their culture. If we could find and translate their writing (about 85% is now translated), we might know more about their religion and social organization. And in fact, it was the analysis of the Bonampak murals in the 1950s that gave archaeologists insights into the warlike nature of the Maya. The panels also provided hypotheses about social stratification and social organization. Prehistory rests on hypotheses that can be tested with evidence from the time and place under study: without hypotheses, we would not have science. If all we have is material culture, as with the Bonampak murals, at the very least we can generate hypotheses concerning all aspects of culture.

Art has been shown to be useful in gleaning knowledge about cultures even earlier than the Maya. Art in the form of cave paintings and figurines of females is well known for the Upper Paleolithic in western Europe, dating from 30,000 to 10,000 years ago. Based on analysis of these art objects (material culture), scientists have hypothesized and found that males and females likely had division-of-labor rules similar to modern hunter-gatherers; that social patterns concerning same-gender and same-age groupings go back that far; and that there is a direct relationship between what people painted and what they ate. Again, it is archaeologically sound to make predictions based on material culture alone, but support for the hypotheses must come from independent evidence.

Modern material culture serves archaeology in ways other than reconstructing culture. For example, archaeologists have been attempting for years to find a way to estimate population numbers of specific groups, with little success. An assumption made by TGP analysts is that the larger the household, the more garbage it will produce; this seems reasonable. Knowing how many people lived in a certain household (when permission was given to identify ownership of rubbish), TGP specialists could calculate how much plastic and total trash by weight was generated per person. Their formula is $0.02815 \times$ pounds of plastic in five weeks = number of people. This formula could be used to predict the number of people in a household whose number is unknown, or to predict the number of people in a community from knowing the amount of total trash and plastic they discarded. TGP specialists can also predict the number of infants in a population on the basis of $0.01506 \times$ number of diapers in five weeks = number of infants. They found no way to predict the number of males versus number of females, or any age breakdowns. Perhaps the principle behind these findings can be applied to prehistoric populations as well, as plastic and diapers obviously won't work for prehistoric sites.

Another service to archaeological theory regards activity areas and their identification in prehistoric sites. That people in some hunter-gatherer societies do different things in different areas seems established by Binford's work with the Nunamiut, yet Thomas suggested that in some cases, it is weight/size of artifacts and not necessarily usage that caused what looks like activity areas (see Exercise 2); this warrants caution in interpreting the clustering of objects as activity areas. An informative study done in the early 1980s in a college campus setting looked at trash as a predictor of activity areas. Probably to conform to standards of nutrition and to impress parents, downstairs kitchen trash suggested low-calorie, low-fat "good" food; upstairs trash suggested college "pig-outs," with an emphasis on pizza crusts and potato chip bags. In this case, the modern study confirmed different activity areas on the basis of different remains (trash). In the future, the application of these findings to archaeological occupation floors is not unlikely.

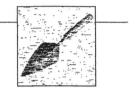

THE EXERCISES

Although it would be very instructive in many ways for you to do a miniversion of Rathje's garbage project, there are as many reasons for you not to do it. On the plus side, you would have learned how to convince people to do things they probably don't want to do, how to snatch trash bags away from garbage men, how *not* to smell like last month's garbage, and what to do with the "slops" at the bottom of garbage bags. You will be pleased to know that you will not be learning these things. If you were to do the project, you'd have to get permission from every garbage maker to use their garbage; you'd have to be immunized against any and all diseases (and because there is no immunization against AIDS, there would always be that small chance that someone infected with the virus would leave a sharp needle in the trash); and you'd have to pick up and get rid of whatever trash you analyzed. You can, however, do two garbage-related exercises that will not cause you to lose sleep: one will involve you in garbage-data analysis, and the other will ask you to reconstruct culture based on material remains—one exercise for each of the two major sections of your reading.

OBJECTIVES

In these two exercises, you will

- gain experience in sorting material culture.
- gain experience in filling out archaeological data sheets.
- compare the trash from three subgroups in your own culture and analyze the differences and similarities.
- creatively, but with restraint, reconstruct the culture of a group of people who left material culture in an archaeology site.

The first exercise is designed for two people, so get your lab partner and begin. If he or she is absent on the day you are scheduled to do the exercise, you can do it alone—a bit slower than if you had a partner. If there are two of you, alternate separating and then noting characteristics of garbage items on the Garbage Recording Form (see Figure 3.3).

DOING THE EXERCISES

1.   You and your partner will get one large sack of "prepared trash." Prepared trash differs from plain garbage only in the sense that "slops," recyclable items, and items that would identify the owner have been preremoved. The people who donated this trash (and yes, we have written permission to use it) were asked not to put any liquids in the bag, to dry off anything that had been

wet, and to not put anything "yukky" in the bag. So there should be no old mashed potatoes or grease or fish heads in your bag. Donators were also asked to continue to recycle newspapers, cans, and glass rather than put them in their trash. All donators continued to use their garbage disposals, but none used a trash compactor. Except for eliminating the "slop effect" and continuing to recycle, the donators were asked to put all of their discards in the bag for a week and not be selective. As far as we know, the instructions were followed.

2a. Sort the garbage in the bag first by categories and then by individual items. First, sort by the following major categories of discard items. Find a spot where you can sort the trash into piles. Use the following categories:

food (empty packages, cans, plastic wrappers with food names)

nonfood but consumable items (liquor, cigarettes)

hygiene, health, and nutrition (vitamin bottles, Kleenex)

beauty and grooming (shampoo bottles, makeup containers)

household cleaning (mops, sponges, soap bottles)

pet items (food cans, flea powder cans, cat litter bags)

yard and lawn care (weed killers, tools, leaves)

children's items (clothing, toys)

adult clothing (anything worn)

other

b. Weigh each category in grams (use preceding groupings) and place on Figure 3.1 (Trash Comparison Table) as "Sample A." Assume that this is the trash (material culture) from one household for one week (a standard value becomes $T = 1H \times 1W$) in your culture; further assume it is a representative sample of this particular community and represents other households similar to it. For comparison purposes, turn your gross weights into percentages: Total the sample in grams and calculate a percentage of the total for each category; write it as a percentage (%) on Sample A on the table (Figure 3.1).

3. Using the Garbage Project Item Code List (Figure 3.2) that is a modification of Rathje's list (minus the "slops"), fill out the Garbage Project Recording Form (Figure 3.3) (if you did a complete recording for the entire bag of trash, it will take longer than your lab time). Fill in as the form suggests: List code names of the first 20 items in your bag; then fill out the entire line for the first 10 items. For the weight section, put down the before-discard weight of the item (liquid or solid) in ounces (information is on the package; in the United States, weight is always in ounces and pounds), then weigh the packaging of the item in grams and put the weight of the pack on the form (the rest of the world weighs things in grams). This will give you an idea of what would be done if all data were to be used, but leaves time for other parts of the exercise for which you now have the necessary data. Before finalizing Figure 3.3, use the translation of ounces to grams card to change your ounces to grams. For liquids, use the old adage of "a pint's a pound," or one pint = 16 ounces (it isn't always true, of course).

(Note: The weight of the item and the weight of the packaging are not identical, obviously. Either the original weight of each item can be used, *or* an assumption can be made that because there is a loose relative relationship between all packaging and all consumed items, the weight of the packaging represents the weight of the original item. *In this exercise, the weight of each item in grams, or what it weighed before consumption, will be used.*)

Figure 3.1 Trash Comparison Table

The following percentages (for comparison purposes) represent two other samples (Sample B and Sample C) from other households. These samples represent many similar households, so A, B, and C are comparable kinds of samples. The trash from each of these three samples comes from each of the following: lower-income, middle-income, and upper-income households. Based on comparisons of percentages, predict or hypothesize which sample comes from each type of household. On what basis did you make your judgment? Write your answers where indicated below.

	Sample A		Sample B		Sample C	
	Grams	%	Grams	%	Grams	%
Food items	____	____		12		13
Non-food consumables	____	____		8		8
Hygiene, health, nutrition	____	____		10		14
Beauty, grooming	____	____		10		18
Household cleaning	____	____		20		23
Pet items	____	____		4		0
Children items	____	____		6		4
Yard and lawn care	____	____		8		0
Adult clothing	____	____		20		19
Other	____	____		2		1
Total	____					

Which sample represents upper-income households (A, B, or C)? _____

    Middle-income households? _____

    Lower-income households? _____

On what basis did you make this judgment? _____

_____

_____

_____

_____

_____

Figure 3.2 Garbage Project Item Code List

Beef 001	Sugar 044	Cigarettes 085
Chicken 002	Artificial sweetener 045	Cigars 086
Turkey 003	Candy 046	Pipe items 087
Bacon 004	Salt 047	Laundry cleaner 088
Other meat 005	Spices, flavorings 048	Household cleaners 089
Fish (any kind, type) 006	Baking additives 049	Cleaning tools 090
Shrimp, lobster 007	Puddings 050	House maintenance 091
TV dinners with meat 008	Gelatin (JellO) 051	Cooking/serving aids 092
Luncheon meat 009	Instant breakfast 052	Tissue containers 093
Cheese (incl. cottage) 010	Dips (for chips) 053	Toilet paper containers . . .094
Milk 011	Nondairy cream, whip 054	Plastic wrap containers . . .095
Ice cream (incl. yogurt) . . .012	Health foods 055	
Butter 013	Coffee (regular) 056	Bags, plastic 096
Margarine 014	Coffee (decaffeinated) 057	Bags, paper 097
Other dairy 015	Coffee (exotic) 058	Aluminum foil containers . .098
Eggs (any kind) 016	Tea (any kind) 059	Waxed paper containers . . .099
Beans (not green) 017	Chocolate drinks 060	
Nuts 018	Fruit juice (real) 061	Mechanical appliances . . .100
Peanut butter 019	Fruit juice (Kool-Aid) 062	Electrical appliances 101
Oil (liquid, Crisco) 020	Soda (tonic, bubbly) 063	Auto supplies 102
Flour 021	Soda (diet) 064	Furniture 103
Cornmeal 022	Premix cocktail 065	Clothing (child) 104
Rice 023	Liquor (hard) 066	Clothing (adult) 105
Other grains 024	Wine (any kind) 067	Clothing care supplies 106
Noodles/pasta 025	Beer 068	Dry cleaning, laundry 107
Bread (light) 026	Baby food 069	Pet maintenance 108
Bread (dark) 027	Pet food 070	Gate receipts (tickets) 109
Tortillas (etc.) 028	Take-out meals 071	Hobby items 110
Cereal (dry) 029	Soup (any kind) 072	Photo supplies 111
Cereal (to be cooked) 030	Gravy, sauces 073	Decorations 112
Crackers 033	Other food items 074	Yard/plant maintenance . .113
Chips, pretzels 034	Vitamins 075	Stationery supplies 114
Vegetables (fresh) 035	Prescription drugs 076	Jewelry 115
Vegetables (canned) 036	Painkillers 077	
Vegetables (frozen) 037	"Remedies" 078	Children's games or toys . .116
Fruits (fresh) 038	Drug paraphernalia 079	Children's books 117
Fruits (canned) 039	Contraceptives 080	Adult books 118
Fruits (frozen) 040	Baby supplies (diapers) . . .081	Adult games 119
Relish/pickles/olives 041	First-aid supplies 082	Miscellaneous items 120
Honey, jelly, syrup 042	Personal sanitation 083	
Pastries/cookies/cake 043	Cosmetics 084	

Source: Adapted from "Garbage Project Item Code List" (Rathje and Murphy 1992).

Figure 3.3 Garbage Project Recording Form

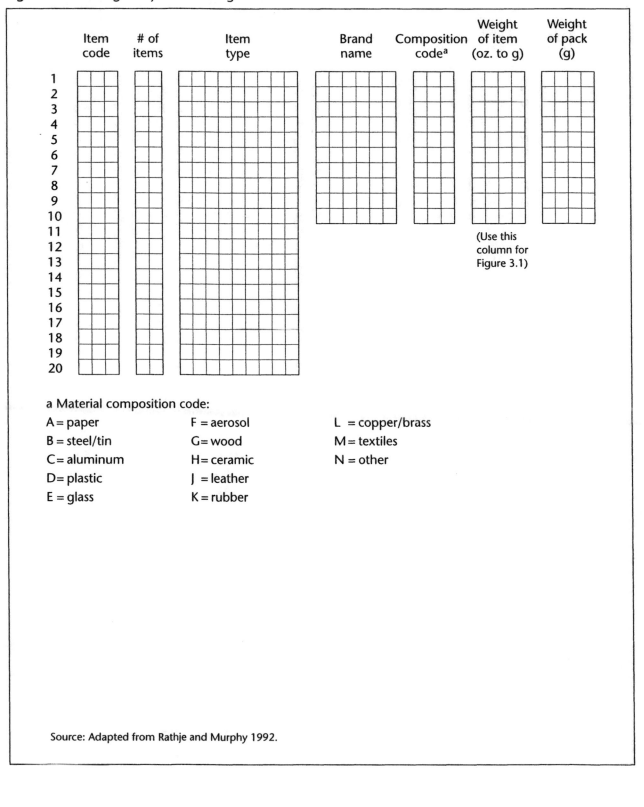

a Material composition code:

A = paper   F = aerosol   L = copper/brass
B = steel/tin   G = wood   M = textiles
C = aluminum   H = ceramic   N = other
D = plastic   J = leather
E = glass   K = rubber

Source: Adapted from Rathje and Murphy 1992.

☐ **Check with your lab manager when completing this part of the exercise for full credit.**

4. Use the information on the Garbage Project Recording Form (Figure 3.3) relative to your sample. Instead of analyzing the trash based on previous knowledge of the culture as you did in points (1) and (2) (your own culture in this case), assume you are an archaeologist in the year 2096. You've either come down from your home on a space platform or up from your home under the ocean (Ocean City?) to sample an Earth culture of 100 years ago, before the Great Pollution made spending more than a couple of days at a time on Earth unhealthy. A computer randomly picked the spot of the sample; you and your trusty assistant came to Earth, dug up your sample from under only a few inches of soil (your sample is only 100 years old, which is a drop in the archaeological bucket), and went right back home with it. You've already sorted the material culture produced by this group into gross categories (Sample A) as well as done a checklist of each item (filled out a recording form). Now is the time you must reconstruct the culture of the people who left this material culture. Remember that it is archaeologically acceptable for you to generate hypotheses (make predictions) about all of culture based only on material remains because hypotheses in this case are only good guesses.

Use the following standard categories of culture to complete Figure 3.4:

technology (basic economy—how did they get food and what food; what things did they make);

economics (production, distribution, and consumption of goods and services);

social organization (pair bondings or marriage, family, kin groups, associations or clubs, rules, group structure, relationships);

political organization (who wields the power, levels of organization, dealing with deviance, making decisions);

magic and religion (behaviors, practitioners, belief systems);

art (products and belief systems);

and worldview and philosophy of life.

Now reconstruct the culture based on the material remains. It might be helpful to relook at the "raw" objects in the original trash bag; sometimes there are clues that don't show up on a list. For example, you might have 10 chocolate-bar wrappers on your list. You might thus conclude that the culture had the technology to process cocoa into long bars, wrap them in foil, and put a printed outer wrapper on them. Or, by looking at where the chocolate bar was made, you might predict chocolate-bar making was a "cottage industry" (if you were sampling in Hershey, Pennsylvania, and if all the chocolate bars came from Hershey's Chocolate Company); or you might predict that people in this culture took trips to foreign lands (if the chocolate bars came from France, Belgium, and Switzerland). In the case of the latter, you might predict there is an international trade in chocolate bars. You probably would not have thought of these possibilities just by looking at "10 chocolate wrappers" listed on your Garbage Project Recording Form.

Try to be reasonable in your reconstruction. Avoid "cute" interpretations (that people ate babies because there is a picture of one on Gerber baby food jars, for example). Analyzing material culture is a serious archaeological endeavor, and archaeologists do it all of the time. If a collection of arrows and bows can predict hunting (in lieu of written confirmation), then a collection of broken pens and pencils can predict the culture had writing. In doing reconstruction, you may assume that you are able to read or translate what was written on your trash items. You will probably not be able to write much on every item in each cultural category, but try to write at least a sentence or so on each of the seven major groups. You will probably spend most of your time on the technological items, as technology is close to material culture.

KEY WORDS

culture

material culture

ethnoculture and archaeoculture

ethnologist

cultural anthropologist

physical anthropologist

middle-range theory

reactivity phenomenon

cultural reconstruction

FOR FURTHER READING

Gould, Richard A., and Michael B. Schiffer, eds. *Modern Material Culture: The Archaeology of Us*. New York: Academic Press, 1981.

Rathje, William L. "Modern Material Culture Studies." *Advances in Archaeological Method and Theory* 2. (1979):1–38.

Rathje, William L., and Cullen Murphy. *Rubbish, the Archaeology of Garbage*. New York: Harper Collins, 1992.

Rathje, William L., and Cheryl Ritenbaugh, eds. "Household Refuse Analysis: Theory, Method, and Applications in Social Science." *American Behavioral Scientist* 28, no. 1 (1984):5–60.

Staski, Edward, and Livingstone D. Suts, eds. *"The Ethnoarchaeology of Refuse Disposal."* Research paper no. 42, Department of Anthropology, Arizona State University, Phoenix, 1991.

Figure 3.4 Reconstruction of Culture X

Technology:
    How they got a living: _____

    Foods they ate: _____

    Things they made: _____

    Conclusions about technological level: _____

    _____

    _____

    _____

Economics:
    How they produced food and "things": _____

    How they distributed them: _____

      Internal (markets?): _____

      External (trade?): _____

    How they consumed them: _____

    _____

    _____

Social organization:
    Their marriage rules: _____

    Their families: _____

    Their kin groups: _____

    Their associations: _____

Political organization:
    Who ruled: _____

    How they dealt with deviance: _____

    How they made decisions: _____

Magic and religion:
    Their belief system: _____

    Their practitioners: _____

Art:
    Art products: _____

    Art beliefs: _____

Worldview and philosophy of life: _____

    _____

    _____

    _____

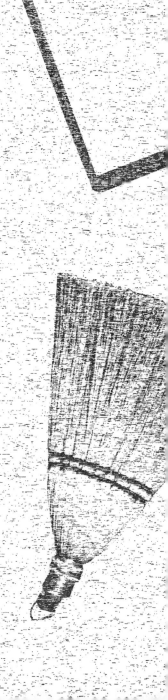

Experimental Archaeology: Lithic Use-Wear Analysis

EXPLAINING THE PAST: A HISTORY

Back in the early days of archaeology, before the 1900s, most archaeological debris was explained by *direct* reference to the present. If a material item—say an arrowhead discovered in a streambed in central Ohio—looked as if it was a hunting tool, then it was regarded as being one, with no questions asked. This direct explanation of the past by using the present was, of course, a mistake. Just because a piece of antler with a long, straight shaft and a knobby hook on one end, found in France and dated as 11,000 years old, looks like the kind of tool some Native Americans used and called an *atlatl* (spear-thrower) doesn't mean that the French prehistoric object was a spear-thrower too. Form does not always dictate function. As a French cartoon suggests, the object may have been designed and used as a back-scratcher or used in an intricate gaming activity, the hook having the function of moving pieces across some kind of board.

The New Archaeology's shake-up in the early 1960s resulted in a healthy, but changed, regard for explaining the past and the use of the present to provide clues to the past. Contemporary archaeologists will never argue that the form and function of something found in King Tut's tomb can now be identified because it looks just like some material object in today's modern society. But they will also not dismiss that such a possibility exists just because there are no known links between the two cultures. Instead, the present can be seen to "serve the past," but under new, rigorous, scientific controls; the operative term here is *science*. *To serve* is a term showing the *indirect* use of the present/past linkages.

The Scientific Method

Science is best understood as a frame of mind rather than as a bubbling retort or a scanning electron microscope; it is the method rather than the material that defines science. Most questions can be made scientific if they are phrased as hypotheses to be tested; if the tests are appropriate to the questions; and if the results are used to support or reject the hypotheses.

In regard to the present serving the past, let's go back to that French object of some 11,000 years ago, and, based on knowledge of what Native Americans did with similar objects, hypothesize that the French objects were designed and used as spear-throwers. To test this hypothesis, we might study some of the French objects and make and use exact replicas of the objects in the same way we know Native Americans used spear-throwers and see how well the objects work in performing spear-throwing tasks. We might do a microscopic analysis of the knobby hook on all three sets of objects (the French objects, the Native

American spear-throwers, and the replicas after they were used), noting similarities and differences of the marks made in the hook area from propelling shafted spears. Finally, we might use the replicas in other activities to see if the replicas worked better at doing something other than throwing spears. The list of tests is limited only by the number of ideas the archaeologist can come up with that are appropriate. Our conclusion would depend on the results of the tests, but they would support or reject the original hypothesis. This is the **scientific method** in action, testing the present based on the past. Note that we never claim to prove anything, concluding only that our tests support or reject the original statement about the function of the French objects.

The preceding is also an example of archaeological analogy; if we know the function of some object in the present because we can observe it being used, and we excavate something from the past that is identical in form to the known object, we can hypothesize about the function of the old object by knowing the function of the present, identical object. The spear-thrower from France is an example of this kind of analogy because the form is very similar in both the past and present objects, and the function of the present-day spear-thrower is known. We hypothesized about the function of the past objects by referring to that known function, using hypothetical experiments to test the hypothesis. In experimental archaeology, the archaeologist uses knowledge of the present to hypothesize about the past, runs appropriate tests (experiments), and comes to conclusions based on the findings of the experiments. As the previous materials suggest, there is a strong link among explanation, the scientific method, analogy, and experimental archaeology.

Experimental Archaeology

Archaeologists have been experimenting for decades, but only recently has this become a serious subdiscipline in its own right. Interestingly, there was hardly a mention of **experimental archaeology** in archaeology textbooks written prior to 1980, only technological descriptions of bulbs of percussion and descriptions of replicating ancient tools. Since 1980, however, it seems almost obligatory for authors to include a section on experimental archaeology. In earlier years, experimenters were rather casual about their work and did not use the scientific rigor used today. Experiments were primarily aimed at answering questions about how prehistoric tools were made or how long it might have taken to build a pyramid. (In one often-cited case, a Dr. Ball in Ireland blew a prehistoric horn so hard that he burst a blood vessel and subsequently died!)

One of the earliest goals of experimental archaeologists was to rediscover "lost" technological principles and skills, and many classic experiments were aimed at rediscovering these principles. The flint knapping work of François Bordes (France) and Don Crabtree (United States) showed experimenters how to properly assess their tool manufacturing experiments. Don Crabtree, for example, spent 40 years trying to rediscover the techniques of making Clovis and Folsom fluted projectile points before he was finally able to successfully replicate them. But he did so by using a technique known to exist not on the high plains of the United States where the fluted blades were found, but in Central America. And until material objects associated with the fluting technique (chest punches) are found with the projectile points, the "rediscovery" will remain only a hypothesis.

Today, in addition to following the scientific method, experimental archaeologists follow these rules: (1) The materials used in any experiment must have been available to the people whose artifacts are under question. In attempting to explain how Easter Island statues were transported to their present locations looking out to sea, only materials known to have existed on Easter Island at the time of the carving and transporting of the statues can be used. Thus, wood and rope from local vegetation are appropriate as experimental materials, not steel or plastic. (2) The methods or technology used in the experiments must have been known by the people under investigation. If the concepts of the lever and/or the winch were not known to Easter Islanders, then an experimenter cannot assume that these kinds of tools were used. Any attempt to explain the technology of the transporting of the statues must keep this in mind. (3) The experiments must be replicable by other archaeologists in case there is individual bias inherent in the experiment. An extremely strong male might be very successful at doing a task that an average female is not able to do. If that activity is gender-tied, the male bias may interfere with proper conclusions, particularly if it is not known which gender performed the activity. (4) The results of the experiment must be published so they can become general knowledge and so that others can replicate them for possible individual bias. The best experiment in the world is of little importance if only one person knows about it.

Two basic kinds of experiments are conducted by archaeologists: replication experiments and processual experiments. In replication experiments, archaeologists attempt to replicate artifacts or features (such as postholes) in order to rediscover "lost" technology or to infer functions of artifacts. In processual experiments, archaeologists attempt to understand the processes that were involved in the formation of the archaeological record. For example, archaeologists may clock the time needed for roving animals to totally obliterate the carcass of a dead animal, or may dump a known number of artifacts in the middle of a river (as prehistoric people may have done) and subsequently note the accumulation pattern downstream. The results of the latter experiment can be used to conclude whether accumulations of tools are the result of human habitation or river deposition.

Replication experiments have dominated experimental archaeology from the beginning of the subdiscipline: tool replication, in all of its complexity, and attempts to discover tool function, have been the focus of experimentation for decades (some feel this brings out the Boy or Girl Scout in many of us)

THE IMPORTANCE OF FUNCTIONAL ANALYSIS

The first thing an archaeologist is asked when he or she uncovers a "new" kind of artifact is, What was it used for? Instead of admiring the skill that went into its manufacture, or speculating on who made it, we ask, What was its function? Archaeologists want to know the function of artifacts too. Part of Exercise 6 focuses on the function of ceramics; in this exercise, the focus is on lithic (flint) tool function.

Knowing the function of an artifact (a stone tool, for example) and, by extension, all artifacts, would be of enormous help in reconstructing the behavior of our prehistoric ancestors. We could, through such reconstruction, envision people butchering dead animals, scraping hides, making projectile points, cutting and whittling branches to make pointed digging sticks for tubers or for hafting projectile points, or cutting soft plants to use as bedding or ground cover. If we could discover activity areas within archaeology sites by knowing the function of the artifacts that were excavated there, it would help reconstruct daily-life activities: hide work is done on the periphery of a site, butchering was done next to the fire, stabbing holes in hides for button attachment was done anywhere, and so on.

Functional analysis could also help in establishing cultural groups or cultural areas by time and space. For example, if we have an artifact from each of two areas that are equivalent in time, are very similar in form, and through functional analysis appear to have been used for the same purpose, we might use this information to assign the same cultural identity to the objects; we might assign a different cultural identity if the functional analysis suggests the objects served different purposes.

The job of inferring the function of tools from artifacts themselves may seem at first glance to be a fairly easy job. Or is it? As the old joke goes, an arrowhead is an arrowhead unless it is a backscratcher. How do we know if an artifact that looks like a projectile point was used as such? How do we know that something we call a "knife" was used to cut?

There are four ways to tackle the issue of flint-tool analysis: by analogy, by the context in which tools are found, by experiment, and by **use-wear.** Analogies with people who still make and use stone tools give clues and are excellent hypotheses generators, as the atlatl analogy showed in the introduction to this exercise, but as are all analogies, it is low-level evidence of function. The context of finding tools in associations, such as stuck in a bison rib, leaves little left to infer, but these are very rare events. Experimental archaeology is similar to using analogy, but the analogy is with modern archaeologists using tools in certain ways. Experiments are still only hypotheses generators, as they only tell us how tools *could* have been used. It is the last approach to lithic function that holds the most promise, as use-wear studies focus on actual use, not just potential use.

As some archaeologists surmised many years ago, artifacts themselves can often provide tantalizing clues to their function. Some clues can be thought of as direct, and some as indirect. If an archaeologist scans the entire surface of a tool, he or she may be lucky and locate a bit of substance, such as vegetal fiber or amino acid that adhered to the tool after use; this would be a direct clue. For the past five years or so, archaeologists have reported results of tests run on flint tools that presumably contained blood residue on their edges. Reports of human, bison, horse, and rabbit blood have made the headlines. Experiments with tools that were purposely bloodied, then buried for as little as two years, suggest that blood components break down very quickly, with the result that at present there is little to inspire confidence in identifying the species of blood on tool edges. Only rarely do organic substances survive. The classic exception to this generalization is silica gloss. It has long been known that cutting grassy plant substances will leave a shine on flint after a moderate amount of use. Experts differ on what they believe causes gloss, but experiments show that cutting plants with a fresh flint edge does cause the edge to become shiny.

Other clues to function are more indirect. Archaeologists began to notice that as tools made of flint or other finely grained minerals are used, edges become damaged; as artifacts are used, they become worn. In time, this insight developed into a highly specialized archaeological subfield: use-wear studies, **microwear analysis**, or traceology. Specialists may use different names, but they all agree on the principle: *Used tools contain clues to their former use;* we should be able to reconstruct the function of tools by using the clues. We assume that prehistoric people used flint tools to chop, scrape, slice, whittle, bore, cut, or saw various materials in their immediate environment that were vital to their lives: meat, plants, bone, hides, antler. We also assume that these materials and the motions used to perform certain jobs on them caused the flint to wear differentially: cutting wood should leave different wear patterns than scraping hides. In other words, we expect to find different "signatures" to be left on tools, which when properly interpreted, will provide vital information about the function of artifacts.

The signatures or patterns of wear damage on flint tools are evidence about some past human behavior concerning use of that tool. But, given *only* the tools, how do we know what specific damage resulted from specific action on specific materials? For example, how do we know with any degree of confidence that the shiny gloss on the edge of a flint piece was caused by cutting plants rather than from scraping a deer hide? How do we know that the scratches on a piece of flint are the result of dislodged grit that became embedded in the antler as the antler was being cut, thereby scratching the flint, and not the result of dirt scratching the artifact while it was being put in a sheath?

In order to bridge the present to the past, microwear experts have performed hundreds of experiments using as many variables of activity, motion, and material that they can think of to see exactly what happens under each circumstance. The resultant reference collection can be used to match the known to the unknown. If, for example, a microwear expert has designated four possible motions of the human hand on flint, eight activities likely to have been carried out by prehistoric people, and six different materials likely to have been used during this time, then there is a total of 192 combinations of these variables. The resultant 192 labeled experimental tools should show different, but known, signatures that can be used for comparison with prehistoric artifacts of unknown function. A microwear expert would not have to compare all 192 tools to each artifact under study, as there are certain clues that would be used to immediately shorten the list of possible matches. For example, an artifact of unknown function with a straight edge would not be compared to an artifact that has an end that looks as if it had been used as a "perforator," as it would be obvious that the use damage would not match.

A HISTORY OF USE-WEAR STUDIES

Interest in microwear and what it could potentially offer students of function goes back to the mid-1800s. But S. A. Semenov, a Russian archaeologist working from 1930 to 1960, is considered the "father of microwear" because he identified the basic principles that contemporary experts use in doing microwear analysis: (1) where the tool is damaged (**edge damage**); (2) the motion used in wielding the tool (**striations**); and (3) the polish that forms on the tool through contact with soft or hard materials (**polish**).

Working in Leningrad with his team, but isolated from Western archaeologists, Semenov made experimental tools and matched their damage patterns to Upper Paleolithic tools from Russian sites. His major work was published in the Soviet Union in 1957 and translated into English in 1964 as *Prehistoric Technology*. The translation produced a flurry of activity among Western archaeologists, but attempts to replicate his experiments met with considerable frustration when experimenters could not replicate his findings, particularly regarding striations. The problem appeared to be in the use of a microscope power that was too weak to detect wear.

Semenov regarded what he called "traceology" to be based on a composite of trends rather than on a single diagnostic trait to define an artifact's function, although he favored striations as the key to identifying function. He outlined three steps in the process: (1) visually examine each tool for edge damage, scratches, cracks, rounding, and polish, and hypothesize the tool's function; (2) make exact replicas of the tool (wherever possible) and experiment as in the stated hypothesis; if a hypothesis is made that the prehistoric tool was a "knife" used to cut meat, then the replica must cut meat; and (3) compare the use-wear on the two tools. If the replica is close to the original in use-wear, then the hypothesis is supported and provisionally accepted. If the replica is not close to the original, then the hypothesis is rejected and the steps repeated until satisfactory results are achieved.

Ruth Tringham, one of Semenov's Western-trained students in 1974, focused on edge damage traces when she returned from Leningrad, as she found striations were not as universal as Semenov implied. She hypothesized that when the edge of a flint tool was in contact with a particular worked material, it would develop signature edge damage in the form of scar size and shape that would be recognizable and would match the edge damage of prehistoric tools. As edge damage can be assessed at 10–40× magnification, her approach has the advantages of being quick, inexpensive, and easy to use in the field.

But not all specialists agree that either striations or edge damage or both are sufficient to identify function. Lawrence Keeley, for example, believed that polish formed by the action of tools on contacted material holds the key to tool function. Keeley (1980), in contrast to Tringham, used high-power magnification (200× and above), making his approach relatively time consuming and costly. But, he argued, polish identification is the only way to have confidence in signature criteria.

What are we to make of these various claims? Some experts claim there is little information lost by using only low-power analysis, whereas others argue that polish and striations are only visible under high-power magnification. Opponents of the low-power approach claim low power can only identify whether the material is hard or soft, not specific materials. Opponents of the high-power approach criticize use of polish as the diagnostic criterion because it is subjective and results in overlapping categories of polish, thereby causing ambiguity in statements about function. Perhaps the commonsense argument is this: If the maximum of information is needed, there is a lot of time, there is access to an expensive, nonmovable microscope, and the results are interpreted with caution, then high-power assessment of polish and low-power assessment of edges and striations are appropriate. If, however, it is not necessary to differentiate material as being other than soft or hard, and/or there is little time or money, or it is important to do only a preliminary analysis in the field, then the low-power approach is appropriate. Either way, the relative results are the same: Experts are more successful at inferring where and with what motion wear is patterned than they are at inferring the material worked.

The Keeley-Newcomer Blind Test

One strong criticism of early use-wear studies stated that because experimenters made their own tools, they knew what had been done to them; under these circumstances, matching the experimental tools to prehistoric tools and making statements about function were not valid. What was needed was a **blind test,** where the person analyzing the experimental tools and making statements about function did not know what had been done to them. In a classic blind test, Mark Newcomer, a flint-knapping expert at University College London, made 15 tools and used them in a variety of ways, each use likely to have been appropriate in the past. After thoroughly cleaning the tools, he gave them to Lawrence Keeley, then a graduate student at Oxford, who viewed them under his high-power microscope and reported back on the area used, the motion of the activity, and the specific worked material; in other words, he assessed each tool's function. Although he did not know what Newcomer had done, Keeley was 87% correct in his conclusions about what area was used, 75% correct on the motion, and 62.5% correct on the worked material. Keeley, in spite of the high-power microscope, had more trouble identifying the material on which the tool was used (using polish as the indicator) than either of the other areas of study. An overall rating of 75% correct gives archaeologists some confidence that statements about artifact function based on use-wear analysis are correct ones. Although 75% correct is considerably better than speculative guesses would be, it is only a middle C on a report card.

Despite some shortcomings, use-wear analysis has provided archaeologists with the most specific information on the function of tools that is available today. It has given support to some speculative hypotheses about some classes of tools and has rejected others. Semenov, for example, concluded that "end scrapers" were used to clean hides, contrary to earlier views that they were either all-purpose tools or "engravers" for wood or bone. Several use-wear specialists, working with a relatively small collection of artifacts from the Belgian seacoast, recently concluded that there were two flint knappers involved in the making of the tools, that they were both left-handed, and that one was a better knapper than the other. This study, though preliminary, gives us a rare look at the behavior of individuals in prehistory. In South Africa, several workers confirmed the importance of woodworking 15,000 years ago, as their experimental woodworking tools were the best match for the artifacts found there. In addition, use-wear is useful in identifying kinds of sites: home bases, kill sites, hunting sites. It also helps archaeologists draw boundaries around specific groups of people based on their lithic technology, some of which shows up in use-wear.

PRINCIPLES OF MICROWEAR ANALYSIS

Regardless of whether high- or low-power analysis is preferred, and regardless of whether edge damage, striations, or polish is favored as the best single indicator of function, workers in microwear analysis over the past 50 years have sometimes grudgingly agreed on what activity causes what damage using what material.

Edge Damage

Edge damage is the major clue used to determine what part of an artifact was used. Technically, there are four possible conditions of a flint flake's edge: undamaged, damaged due to nonhuman events, retouched by humans, or damaged by human use. These conditions and their variations are best viewed under a 10–20× microscope; some can be seen with the naked eye.

Because edges of flint are susceptible to damage for reasons other than use, the investigator must first rule out damage due to nonuse when a piece has been: nicked as it was detached from a core or as it struck the ground, trampled by a big-footed human or animal as it lay on the ground, nicked as it hit hard objects in the soil or as it rolled down a hill, hit by an archaeologist's trowel during excavation, rubbed against and nicked by other artifacts in an artifact bag on the way to the lab, or dropped by an overeager lab assistant. With this many possible causes, it is vital that the analyst first discount nonuse damage. Fortunately, nonuse damage can be recognized by its random distribution along the entire perimeter of the tool, lack of standardized size or shape of scars, and lack of areal concentration. By contrast, use damage is concentrated in the area of use and the scar damage is patterned (see Figure 4.1).

Analysts must also be able to differentiate between intentional (human) retouch along some of the perimeter and use-wear scars. Again, these differentiations can be identified with experience, as intentional retouch (either to shape or dull an edge) leaves large, regularly shaped and sized scars along an entire edge and may encroach far onto the tool. Use-wear damage is less regular in shape, size, and distribution, and never encroaches beyond the edge of the tool.

Edge Damage and Raw Materials

Regardless of what raw material a tool is used on, the first scars always have the same scalar shape (named for their resemblance to fish scales). If the material used is soft (skin, flesh), continued use even for a long time will continue to produce only scalar scars that are relatively small in size. If the material used is hard (antler, bone), subsequent scars can be large and irregular. If the artifact is used for even a moderate amount of time, new scars will obliterate the original scalar scars. The finding of certain scars identifies the relative hardness of the material, but not the specific material.

Edge Damage and Motion of Tool

By definition, longitudinal motion is parallel to the edge of the tool. Neither cutting (one-way) or sawing (two-way) motion results in any specific scar shape or size, and scar distribution is correlated with the area of use in cutting or sawing; sawing produces more and often larger scars. Transverse motion is perpendicular to the edge of the tool; scraping, engraving, shaving, and planing all result in scars only on the surface edge opposite that which has contact with the worked material, producing many scars the length of the use area. Rotary motion is circular in a clock- or counterclockwise direction or both; boring produces initial scalar scars, but crushing removes them during use.

Edge damage analysis makes it possible to distinguish which edge was used, whether the edges were used longitudinally, transversely, or in a rotary fashion, and whether the tool was used on soft or hard materials. However, because scars vary in size, shape, and distribution, and because only hard and soft materials can be differentiated, it seems reasonable to conclude that edge damage analysis by itself does not allow for confident statements about the function of tools.

Figure 4.1 Flint Damage

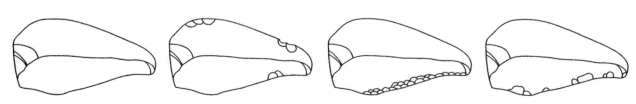

| Undamaged | Nonuse damage | Patterned retouch | Use damage |

Striations

Striations are scratches on flint caused by friction of particles against the flint, with the direction of the scratches indicating the motion of the tool. Once dislodged, grit, soil, or flint microchips can become embedded in the material being used and act as tiny diamond chips, scratching the hard flint as the tool is in use. Because foreign particles do not become embedded in all tools, striations are rather fortuitous and not as universal as Semenov believed. One experimenter found there were no striations visible in over 30% of his experiments. However, when visible, usually through the use of 200× magnification, striations are excellent indicators of a tool's motion.

Experiments suggest that transverse motion always produces striations that are perpendicular or diagonal to the working edge of the tool, whereas longitudinal motion always produces striations that are parallel or diagonal to the edge. Striations may form during rotary motion, but are obliterated rather quickly by crushing action during tool use. Although diagonal striations are ambiguous, perpendicular and parallel striations are absolutely signature in form.

Although striations are of enormous help in determining the motion of some tools, because they are not universal and cannot help differentiate among materials used means they are of limited value in functional analysis.

Polish

Polish (gloss) is the most controversial area of microwear investigation, ranging from claims that individual polish (plant, hide, bone, antler, wood) can be identified with confidence, to statements that there is no evidence that any polish can be unambiguously identified. The difference in assessment lies in the inherent subjectivity of assessing polish and the inability to put into words what is seen so that others can see and agree with it or not. Recent attempts to objectify different polish residues by computer analysis still give ambiguous findings. Although proponents of polish analysis claim they are able to distinguish among the many types of polish, overlap of characteristics produces ambiguity in some cases and; as a result, it is rare for any two people to assess polish in the same way.

After evaluating edge damage, striations, and polish, it seems safe to conclude that none by itself is sufficient to provide the necessary information to make statements concerning the function of any tool. Taken all together and used with care, the three principles appear to give enough information to assess function with some confidence.

LIMITATIONS

As any archaeologist doing microwear is quick to tell, the major limitation of the process is its time-consuming feature. Only a small percent of any collection will show microwear, yet one has to go through the entire collection to find that out. In addition, the presence of any wear depends on postdepositional effects; in some assemblages, all of the tools are covered in postdepositional polish, so separating use-polish for that incurred later is not possible.

Lithic use-wear studies are limited to specific kinds of raw material and certain time periods; for instance, quartzite tools do not show either striations or polish, thus limiting analysis to edge damage and what can be inferred from it. It is likely that the earlier the tools in the archaeological record, the harder it will be to establish **use-wear signatures**, and two attempts at establishing the function of the world's earliest tools in Africa during the Lower Paleolithic support this generalization. Finally, recent experiments of flint on root crops (manioc, taro, yams) have shown that root crops do not leave characteristic use-wear traces. Given these limitations, some experts have suggested that use-wear analysis be limited to asking and answering very specific questions about tool function, and not done on every site to every tool as some kind of normal activity.

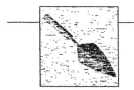

THE EXERCISE

In this exercise, you will play the role of an experimental archaeologist in the early stage of your career, who has an interest in establishing the functions of flint tools. But because you are just beginning your training and starting from scratch, your project mentor (Dr. Knowitall) tells you that you need to become familiar with already used tools first, then make a tool yourself and compare it to his reference collection of used tools (he knows what he did to them), and then you can try to identify the function of "real" tools. As your interest is in the European Upper Paleolithic (35,000 to 10,000 years ago), you will concentrate on that time period and the kinds of tools used then. Your mentor says he will do two nice things for you: You will look only at the tools in his reference collection that were made by motion in one direction (not combinations), and he will not throw in any surprises in terms of materials the tools were used on, but will use only wood, wet antler, dry hide, bone, meat, or plants. After you complete the exercise, you should have confidence (or not) in the role use-wear can play in assessing the function of prehistoric tools.

OBJECTIVES

In this exercise, you will

- become familiar with a small reference collection of tools that show different use-wear signatures.
- change an unworked flint flake into a tool by using it.
- compare the now-worked flint flake with the tools in the reference collection; decide which one it is most similar to, and write your findings of the comparison.
- identify the function of one "mystery tool," writing and justifying the results.

DOING THE EXERCISE

1. Look at each of the tools in one of the reference collections; in these cases, we know their functions because they were made by a modern flint knapper. Note that each tool is labeled with its function. Scan around the entire edge of each tool with the naked eye. Does the shape suggest any function or lead you to decide what areas to concentrate on for microscopic analysis? For example, if you have a tool that looks like a "perforator," you should concentrate on the tip area. If the tool looks like a "knife," you should concentrate on the edge

parallel to the backed (retouched) edge. Using 10- or 20× under the dissecting microscope, look at the edge perimeter for damage. Do the scars match those expected, as in Figure 4.1 and Table 4.1? Are there striations and do they match those expected? Can you detect any polish? (It is not likely that you will see polish under low power; the exception would be sickle gloss from cutting grass.) Look at each tool in the collection under the microscope to become acquainted with the signature damage resulting from different motions and materials, comparing them with the expectations.

2a. Select an unused flake or blade. Note it is in an individual baggie to protect its edges from nonuse damage. However, because the flint piece was detached from a core, hit the floor, and was gathered up along with other pieces before it was put in its own baggie, it is likely to already have nonuse damage on its edges. The flints in this box were flakes or blades made into potential tools by secondary retouch to shape them. Note that each is in a larger bag, suggesting activity: backed blade or burin. The working edge is identified. They are all unused. Write the type of tool selected in the space provided on Figure 4.2. You are encouraged to select a backed blade because it will show more damage in less time than any other type of tool.

b. So that you have a record of your undamaged or nonuse damaged piece, physically place the flint on the space provided at the top of Figure 4.2 and carefully draw around it with a pencil, being careful not to actually touch the edges of the flint with the pencil. This by itself could cause edge damage.

c. Place the flint under the microscope and scan the perimeter of the edge. Note all damage and copy the shape and size of scar damage on your outline drawing. This establishes the preuse condition of the flint.

Table 4.1   Traits Expected Through Use-Wear

Type	Description
Edge damage	Concentrated in area of use; not regular in shape or size; never encroaches beyond edge
Motion	
Cutting or sawing	Edge damage: in area of use and usually on both sides of tool
	Striations: always parallel or diagonal to working edge
Scraping, engraving, shaving, planing	Edge damage: only on surface opposite contact with material
	Striations: perpendicular or diagonal to working edge
Boring	Edge damage: removed by crushing
	Striations: removed by crushing
Raw materials	
Soft	Edge damage: only scalar scars
Hard	Edge damage: step or hinge scars
Polish	Variable, but sometimes visible to the naked eye

d. Decide what material you want to use your flint piece on: bone, wood, antler, leather. Then decide the motion of work: cut, saw, scrape, bore, whittle. You are encouraged to cut antler or bone to maximize results in a short time. Write down the activity (motion) and the worked material chosen in the spaces provided on Figure 4.2. Then do your activity for 1000 strokes (10–15 minutes) to simulate an average use event.

e. Look at the tool under the microscope again, scanning all edges used in addition to areas where there may be striations or polish. Note that after use, the flint piece is now referred to as a tool.

f. Redraw your tool by placing it on the space provided near the top of Figure 4.2, indicating edge damage, striations, and/or gloss. Compare the before and after drawings and conclude whether or not you have edge damage, striations, or gloss. Where, how much, and what do these conditions suggest for identifying function? Write your answers in the spaces provided on Figure 4.2.

Return your used tool to its baggie and give it to your lab manager. Do not return it to the box, as it is now used.

3. How does your tool compare with the tools in the reference collection, particularly the one made with the same motion on the same material (or as close as possible)? Why? Don't forget to factor in the nonuse damage noted on your first drawing. Write a statement about this comparison in the spaces provided on Figure 4.2.

4. Get a "mystery tool" from the box so labeled (the equivalent of your first "real tool" to analyze). Using the insights gained from doing (1), (2), and (3), assess the function of the tool by looking at the edge damage, striations, and polish under the microscope and by comparing the tool to the tools in the reference collection. Identify the tool by its number on the label in the space provided on Figure 4.2, assess its function, and justify your conclusions by stating the characteristics of use-wear you noted.

☐ **Check with your lab manager for full credit.**

Figure 4.2 Use-Wear Drawings

Drawing of flint piece selected for analysis

Type of tool selected: _____

What activity did you choose? _____

The motion was _____

The material was _____

Drawing of used tool

Comparison of preuse and postuse: edge damage, striations, gloss? Where? How much? _____

_____

_____

What do these conditions suggest for its function? _____

_____

How does your experimental tool compare with the appropriate tool in the reference collection? _____

_____

_____

Why? _____

_____

Identification of "mystery tool": number _____

assessed function _____

Justification for identification: _____

_____

_____

KEY WORDS

scientific method

experimental archaeology

functional analysis

use-wear analysis

microwear analysis

edge damage

striations

polish

blind tests

use-wear signature

FOR FURTHER READING

Keeley, Lawrence. *Experimental Determination of Stone Tool Use.* Chicago: University of Chicago Press, 1980.

Keeley, Lawrence, and Mark Newcomer. "Microwear Analysis of Experimental Flint Tools: A Test Case." *Journal of Archaeological Science* 4 (1977):29–62.

O Dell, George, and F. O Dell-Vereecken. "Verifying the Reliability of Lithic Use-Wear Assessments by 'Blind' Tests: The Low-Power Approach." *Journal of Field Archaeology* 7 (1980):87–120.

Schick, Kathy, and Nicholas Toth. *Making Silent Stones Speak: Human Evolution and the Dawn of Technology.* New York: Simon and Schuster, 1993.

Semenov, S. A. *Prehistoric Technology.* New York: Barnes and Noble, 1964.

Tringham, Ruth, et al. "Experimentation in the Formation of Edge Damage: A New Approach." *Journal of Field Archaeology* 1 (1974):171–96.

Vaughan, Patrick. *Use-Wear Analysis of Flaked Stone Tools.* Tucson: University of Arizona Press, 1985.

Whitaker, John C. *Flintknapping: Making and Understanding Stone Tools.* Austin: University of Texas Press, 1994.

Ceramics: Pots, Sherds, and Types

WHY STUDY POTS?

Archaeologists have strong emotions when it comes to pots: they either love them or they hate them, and there seems to be no in between. Those who specialize in the Paleolithic, Mesolithic, or Paleo-Indian periods seem to think **ceramics** are just a lot of containers, but those whose special interest is the Neolithic, Neo-Indian, or thereafter get that certain gleam in their eyes when they spot a piece of a pot while excavating or when they begin to sort a pile of 10,000 potsherds on their worktable. Even preceramic experts must admit that **pottery** analysis can potentially tell archaeologists a great deal about the pottery makers. The following exemplifies what ceramics can tell us about culture.

Ceramic analysis can place geographic boundaries around past cultures: Ceramic analysis can tell us that 4000 years ago culture X lived in this geographic area, whereas their neighbors who had different pottery lived over there. Pottery can also tell us about culture change in single populations, whether that change was slow or fast, internally or externally caused. In Britain, for example, archaeologists can point to a continuity of the Bucket-Urn tradition, with only its slow and occasional change from the third to the first millennium B.C., a period of over 3000 years. British archaeologists then point to new ceramic traditions in archaeological deposits that were introduced from the Continent by trade, invasion, or both. These Beaker, La Tene, and Gallo-Belgic pots show rapid change that was externally generated. Currently, ceramic studies provide the best method to determine the time and space dimensions of specific groups of people during the last 10,000 years, the time of ceramics.

Ceramics can date living floors, burials, or even entire sites (although this function's importance has lessened). Indeed, a single humble sherd can date an entire site by being cross-dated to a very similar sherd in a site that is well dated by some acceptable means. Before radio-carbon (14C) dating techniques, ceramic analysis was one of only two ways to actually date sites and layers, the other being through stratigraphy. Although 14C dating has since 1960 taken up the leadership role in dating archaeological materials, there are times when there are no bits of charcoal or bones to use to 14C date the layer or site, and times when the stratigraphy is so jumbled up or so complex that ceramic analysis is the only way to put the entire assemblage in proper chronological order.

Pottery also informs us about the culture of entire populations, not just the elite. Metalworking, for example, which came after pottery in both the Old and the New World (with one exception), was always an expensive process, whether the metal was gold or more humble iron or copper, and metals were never part of the personal world of the ordinary citizen. Metalworking has always been done by specialists of some kind who have specific statuses in their respective group, sometimes high and sometimes low ranked, but always "special," and because this expensive process is the product of specialization, the worked metals are widely traded over large areas. In contrast, pottery is, in most cases, a local product made by local women (or men in some cases) to be used by the potter and her or his family in doing domestic chores: food processing—cooking, transporting, storing—and eating and serving. Pottery is for the common folk, so its analysis tells us about entire groups, not just about specialist or elite metal users, workers, or traders. We presume this was as true in the past as it is in the present.

A study of pottery is the study of a group's technology in many respects. We ask questions such as, Did the group have the potter's wheel? Did men replace women as potters when the wheel was invented? Did they have open fire or oven firing? Did they have coarse terra-cotta pots that are low fired, or porcelain and earthenware pots that are high fired? Did they appear to understand the role of tempers (nonclay fillers) in firing pots? Did they adjust their recipes for making pots because they understood the cause and effect of use and use-wear? The "they" in these questions refers to numerous people, not just the first people to use pottery, as many details reflect changes in technical knowledge not available to early makers of pottery. The answers to these and many more questions will go a long way toward building knowledge of a group's entire technology.

Pottery can often indicate economic and social organization, intra- and interculturally. Although most pottery is for domestic consumption and remains local, occasionally pottery is so special it is traded long distances. Pots can often be identified as to their manufacturing place through microscopic analysis of the raw clay. Using this information in conjunction with maps of ceramic styles, archaeologists interested in trade, trade routes, or the nature of trading networks can often track the trail of trade by the track of the pottery.

We can often try to infer aspects of a group's division of labor (both gender and specialization) or its social structure through pottery. For example, William Longacre's and James Hill's projects at Carter Ranch Pueblo and Broken K Pueblo in Arizona, respectively, began with excavation of the pueblos, followed by an analysis both of ceramic designs and the function of rooms in the pueblos. Then hypotheses were generated about the social and economic organization of the prehistoric pueblo dwellers and validation made by matching their conclusions with modern pottery and social and economic systems of pueblo-dwelling Native Americans. The two archaeologists concluded that 1300 to 1100 years ago, women were the potters (an economic division of labor rule); the group practiced matrilocality (or at least had a rule that the couple lived with or near the bride's family after marriage); and that it was likely that these prehistoric southwesterners also had **matrilineages** and **matriclans** (social groups linked by common descent).

James Deetz used change in ceramics to postulate change in the social organization of a Native American group on the high plains. He hypothesized that in this matrilocal society, women were the potters, and that the group changed its social organization rules in the eighteenth century, probably as a result of stress caused by Anglo incursions on its borders. As a result, women no longer passed on their ceramic styles directly to their daughters (with whom they now no longer lived); rather, potters learned their work by watching anyone in their residence group. Change in ceramics was no longer patterned in matrilineal lines, but was random. When archaeologists see drastic and random change in ceramics that until that time had been locally patterned and slow to change, they may hypothesize that this resulted from a correlated domestic shift in social organization and look for further information to test that hypothesis. All this from pots!

In the cultural areas of religion and worldview, there is a wealth of information tied up in pottery, although the messages are harder to read than messages about technology. People often portray what is important to them on pottery, be it gods or symbols of their supernaturals. And an aspect of worldview can be demonstrated when modern potters purposely refrain from using the design elements of their neighbors, a kind of "us" versus "them."

With all of this information about past cultures to be gleaned from pottery, even the most avid pot haters have to admit that there is a good bit of worth to ceramic analysis. They may not want to do it themselves and may still sneer at a table of sherds to be sorted, but they do acknowledge that pottery probably tells archaeologists more about the collective questions archaeologists want answered than any other single class of artifacts.

A BRIEF HISTORY OF POTTERY

Pottery is almost ubiquitously found in archaeological excavations beginning about 10,000 years ago (with one exception) in the Old World and perhaps by 7500 years ago in the New World; the latter date for Amazonian pottery is somewhat controversial. By 5000 years ago in many parts of the Old World, pottery was commonplace. The principles of pottery making, which is actually making something out of nothing–a pot from dirt–were independently discovered in a number of places and pottery making is often, but not always, associated with farmers. But it is sedentary life rather than economics that is identified with pottery, as the first uses of what we normally think of as pottery (dishes or pots) came before farming in Japan. Here, the famous Jomon pottery is found in sites dated to 12,700 years ago, but evidence of true domestication of rice and barley is not found until 3000 years ago. In Japan, it was Mesolithic fishing-based people who were making and using the rough pottery, not farmers. It appears that foragers and herders must move too often to make pottery useful; they are better off using nonbreakable vessels made from leather, for example.

Interestingly, the first use of pottery seems to have been for nondish or pot objects. As the archaeological record now stands, fired clay "Venuses," small statuettes of the female form that date to about 30,000 years ago at a site called Dolni Věstonice in the former Czechoslovakian republic, demonstrate the first use of pottery. The people who ground up bone and added it to clay, molded the figures, and then baked them were not farmers, but mobile hunter-gatherers. This early use of pottery suggests that at least some people knew the principles of changing raw clay into pottery by means of firing long before practical use of this knowledge was turned into making dishes and pots.

Later, but still before the pottery-as-dishes or pots period, descendants of those Czech foragers used clay inside caves. They may have used clay in other contexts in unfired or low-fired conditions as well, but unfired or very low-fired clay dissolves in contact with water and is not preserved in the archaeological record. Inside caves, in what is now France and Spain, big-game hunters not only painted and engraved cave walls with primarily animal images, they also used clay to make finger tracings and, in a cave in the Pyrenees, sculpted two large and rather magnificent bison that are so well preserved that even after thousands of years, the fingerprints of the assumed sculptor(s) are still visible.

There appears to be no single origin of pottery; rather, when people settled down domestically, some of them used the principles they already knew and mimicked the shape of their previous containers that were made of leather, reeds, or wood to make their first pots. Translating raw materials such as leather, gourds, wood, soapstone, or baskets into pottery results in what is called *skeuomorphs,* and early pottery sometimes looks like cement-coated baskets or gourds rather than pottery. Pottery could have also begun by being used as liners for other raw material objects, perhaps because of the relative impermeable quality of clay. In an area in the Middle East where one independent discovery of pots-as-dishes occurred and dating to a time before true pottery was in vogue, people were using clay to line storage pits and perhaps experimenting with their knowledge of pottery principles, resulting in true ceramics by 10,000 years ago. Soon adobe bricks, toys, house models, loom weights, spindle whorls, as well as pottery for cooking, serving, and transporting, were made of fired clay. Open bonfires were followed by ovens (kilns); low firing was succeeded by high firing; pottery wheels and glazes were invented. Other areas of both the Old and New World had their own ceramic history, complete with inventions and discoveries, new uses, and increased importance.

MODERN TRENDS IN STUDYING CERAMICS

Ceramic studies, similar to all academic disciplines, underwent changes in aims and goals during the past 100 years, depending on changes in attitudes, new technological breakthroughs, or sometimes just the whim of an influential individual. The study of ceramics is almost as old as archaeology itself. At one time, archaeological pots were regarded as mere curiosities, sometimes considered to be "magic rocks" that either grew in the ground or were mined by gnomes in caves. This ignorance is not surprising, given the total lack of context for anything archaeological at the time. Over time, academics became interested in classical areas around the Mediterranean and in particular became interested in Etruscan, Greek, and Roman ceramics. Only in the late 1800s were archaeologists very interested in the ordinary ceramics of their local areas.

Modern pottery experts would probably agree that there are four main areas of ceramic analysis. The four main trends are as follows: (1) the reconstruction of pots from **sherds;** (2) **classification** or **typology** of pots and decoration, if any; (3) technological and compositional studies; and (4) functional analyses. As a note of historical interest, before 14C dating, ceramic studies were at the forefront of building chronology in archaeology and would have led the list of goals and aims. Times change.

Pot Reconstruction

It is rare to find entire pots in an excavation. Pottery is tough but of course it can be dropped and broken or cracked through thermal stress. After being slightly chipped or cracked, pottery can go from being used in cooking to roasting coffee beans or broken further to fine bits and used as temper in additional pottery manufacturing. In general, when pots break, they are either swept into the corner of a room, tossed outside the hut, or taken to whatever amounts to the village dump. People do not normally live on top of their broken pottery because it is simply uncomfortable to do so. Thousands or hundreds of years later, the pueblo, the yard, or the dump may be excavated and there are the pottery sherds from the original pots. Although it is sometimes akin to looking for that proverbial needle in the haystack to refit sherds to pots, it often can be done successfully. There are times when sherds are sufficient units of analysis, but more often, whole pots are preferable and, in some cases, necessary for analysis.

Refitting pots is based on logic, patience, luck, and a few clues as to how to proceed. When a ceramic inventory is large or jumbled up (as perhaps from a dump that was periodically destroyed by dogs and reshoveled back together), it is possible that not a single refit can be made. But in a moderate to small site, or one that has both good stratigraphy and in situ remains, the stratigraphic unit and the horizontal square meter unit can be used to divide the collection into meaningful units for refit searches. Under these conditions, it is often possible to refit partial or entire pots from the pieces spread out on a table. Clues and logic tell us to look for specific parts of the pot first: rim, base, handles, and decoration, in that order. Rims can be easily identified by their rounded edges, and bases can be recognized by either their flat or tapering areas (the base of a rounded pot that is suspended over a fire will of course not be flat, but it may be less rounded than its sides). Sides are the most difficult to refit, even if there is a total of only one pot and it has decoration on it. In these cases, the refitter, through trial and error, fits the pot as if it were a jigsaw puzzle, matching designs as well as matching the shape of the missing pieces. With undecorated pots, rims and bases (and handles if any) are refitted first, with sides taking longer to hit or miss with. And with any pot that has been tumbled in the soil for a few hundred or thousand years, edges become less angular and more rounded, leaving varying amounts of space between pieces.

In real-life situations, not a single whole pot may be excavated from a room or dump, and excessive tumbling may make it exceedingly difficult to put pot sides together. Nonetheless, for certain analyses, whole pots are either vital or important, so refitting is done when possible. Additionally, what museum wouldn't prefer displaying whole (or mostly whole) pots rather than a pile of sherds? Museum pots are seldom originally whole, but have been refitted with varying amounts of filler. Sometimes a pot can be reconstructed with only half of its pieces refitted because, with few exceptions, pots are bilateral in shape, and round. Almost the only place archaeologists find whole pots is in burials, where the intent was to take provisions to the "other world" or to take as gifts to the gods. Otherwise, ordinary people used pottery until it broke before tossing it out. When archaeologists get hold of that pottery, it is more often than not in fragmentary form.

Classification or Typology of Pottery

One of the most time-consuming jobs a ceramic archaeologist does is sorting ceramics, so the first question that needs to be answered is, Must pottery sherds or whole vessels be classified? (The terms *classify* and *type* are used interchangeably here, although some archaeologists use them in somewhat different ways. Both concepts refer to sorting a collection of pottery using one of many alternative ways.)

Classification is done primarily to make order out of what would otherwise be utter chaos. Can you imagine doing anything with a collection of 300,000 sherds of pottery, assuming they were even all of the same age, unless the assemblage was broken up into some sort of meaningful units? Without classification, every sherd or pot would be unique and we would be no further along in reconstructing culture. To be human is to classify; otherwise, we would spend our entire lives handling very small bits of information. We can't think, much less talk, without classifying objects. If every time we saw a robin we had to say, "Here is a medium-sized bird with gray top feathers and a red breast that eats worms and grubs," there would be no time to enjoy bird watching. In addition to the need for sheer manageability, there are two good and practical reasons why classification of ceramics is done.

First, ceramics can be used to date entire living floors or sites by seriation (see Exercise 7). Seriation is a kind of ceramic dating technique that differs from using ceramics to cross-date; in cross-dating, no classification is needed, just the observance of ceramic similarities between the two sites being cross-dated. In seriation, whole pots or sherds must be classified before the seriation process can begin. Second, classifications are the main tool used by archaeologists to define cultural or time boundaries. Culture X becomes "Pecos Brownware people" or "British Beaker folk" via ceramic classification, and the prehistory of the "Pecos Brownware people" can be tracked via their proxy—their pottery.

All archaeologists would agree that classification is an absolutely essential first step in pottery analysis, even if functional or compositional analyses are the end goal. What they don't agree on is how to do it. A great deal of time and effort have gone into justifying particular typology schemes. Perhaps it is not as volatile an issue as it once was, particularly among New World archaeologists, but there is still a good deal of acrimony over just how to do proper ceramic typing. Maybe the issue has died down somewhat in the past decade because archaeologists became tired of squabbling over something that cannot be systematized into a single taxonomy.

Do we want to classify the ceramic assemblage in question by size, shape (morphology), or function (use)? At present, there is no single agreed-upon answer to this question, and perhaps there never will be. As most archaeologists will tell us, "we classify by intuition" or "it depends on the collection." Because no two collections are alike, the chances that two archaeologists will use the same system are slim to none, unless they were trained using the same system. This lack of systematic typologies has led to a lack of comparability among collections.

It might be correctly said that trying to list, then categorize, all of the typologies used by ceramic archaeologists needs a typology of its own. Most can be placed into categories for easy discussion, but some defy classification. In no order of importance, they are as follows: *(a)* **intuitive typology;** *(b)* **type-variety typology;** *(c)* **quantitative typology;** *(d)* **physical properties typology;** *(e)* **treatment of decoration and surface typology;** and *(f)* **functional typology.** All of these "types of types" are considered convenient, designed, artificial, and arbitrary because they were invented for no other purpose than to help archaeologists organize their ceramic materials in some meaningful way, at least in the eyes of the archaeologist.

Intuitive Typology   Although intuitive typology is sometimes very successful, it is the least satisfactory typology to use beyond a very localized time and place because intuition does not travel beyond the cognition of a single investigator. To do this type of typology, the archaeologist puts the collection out on a large table in a big pile; picks up a pot or sherd and looks at its morphology—size, color, shape, raw material, weight, presence of handles or spout, probable volume (anything morphological); begins a pile; and gives the pile a name. He or she picks up another piece in the collection; it is either very close to the first piece in morphology or it is not; if it isn't, and if it differs enough to be recognized consistently and confidently, it is given another name and goes in a second pile. And so forth. The basis of this typology is the *perceived* similarities and differences within the collection, with the attributes being described after the classification. Presorting by stratigraphic level or geographic area can simplify what can be a very arduous process. If intuitive typology is used, it must be used consistently for the entire collection. One pot cannot be classified by its thickness and color and another by its shape and decoration; the guiding features must be applied consistently.

This is exactly what Nels Nelson was forced to do when he worked at San Cristobal Pueblo in New Mexico in 1914. He was the first to excavate in that area, and no ceramic typology existed. He had to create his own, and he did so intuitively. He took the 649 pieces and put them into five piles based on a gestalt composed of form, size, surface finish, and temper material. His intuition, along with a large dose of experience and logic, told him to group or type the pieces on the basis of his perception of a pattern of attributes, rather than using one variable at a time. This process of sorting into types is also called morphological typology and it is based on an overall morphology rather than on isolated attributes. It allows the archaeologist to use his or her judgment as to which attributes are the most important, rather than giving equal weight to each. Often intuitive typologies are the best way to classify single collections because this method may result in a classification that is close to how the potters would have classified their own work.

Type-Variety Typology   Intuitive typologies have problems when they are used beyond a single collection, as intuitions can't be compared. In response to this inherent problem and as a result of the hundreds of different typologies devised by individual archaeologists in the southwestern United States alone, the type-variety typology emerged in the 1960s. In this typology, a type is made up of a few important, diagnostic traits, such as the paste, decoration, or surface finish that pervade an area's ceramics, and not just a single collection. Each type in the collection is given a binary name (similar to using *Homo sapiens* in Linnaean taxonomy) that identifies both a geographic area and an important attribute: "Pecos Brown," "Gila Incised," "Colorado Burnished." The collection is then further divided on the basis of other variables, resulting in a dendritic system of more and more subcategories, each based on smaller and smaller units of similarity. As an example, a collection could first be divided by color into three subclasses: "redware," "blackware," and "grayware." Then each of these could be divided by the size of the full ceramic piece: large, medium, small; then, by function: bowl, dish, jar, pot; finally, by shape: straight-sided, convex, concave, convex/concave. After naming the type, it must be formally described so it can be used as consistently as possible by others as well as by the person who set it up. For this single system, if we stopped here, we would have a classification of some 144 types. The dendritic system can easily get out of hand and type pots down to the one type = one pot level.

Quantitative Typology   In quantitative typologies (there are more than one), an attempt is made to get away from the vagueness of qualitative typologies such as the intuitive and type-variety typologies and use numbers. Part of the problem with qualitative typologies has to do with the highly subjective decisions that must be made, such as how much difference there has to be between types, or how one knows where one type ends and another begins. Because all we have are sherds and not the people who made the pots, these decisions will always be somewhat subjective. Some typologists will always see fewer differences between attributes than others and therefore will classify fewer types in a collection. Comparing typologies made between typologists continues to be problematic.

One quantitative typology is a ratio-producing scheme that combines shape, volume, and likely function (what we might refer to as a "kind" of ceramic). For example, in this scheme, a bowl is a round hollow vessel, suitable for holding food; the height of a bowl must be one-third or more of its diameter but not greater than its diameter. A dish, by contrast, is shallower than a bowl and its height must be less than one-third but more than one-seventh of its diameter. To be classified as a jar, a piece must be taller than it is wide, with straight sides, whereas a vase is classified solely on its ornateness. Urns are classified on the basis of assumed function, which in this case is burial.

Another variation on the quantitative group of typologies looks at and tries to find patterned correlations between two or more dimensional measurements of pots. Although dozens of measurements can be taken on a single pot, the following are standard: maximum diameter, total height, height above the widest part. Once these measurements are taken, the archaeologist uses the quantitative results as the criteria for typing. For example, in a particular collection, the archaeologist may find that the vessel height and rim diameter are correlated. Whole or mostly whole pots must be used in this system, so whole pots or refitting is necessary.

Treatment of Decoration and Surface Typology   Another type of typology concentrates on the surface of vessels, assuming there is enough information in this area alone to type an entire collection. The underlying assumption of this typology is that factors such as the nature of the clay or the intended function of the pot can so influence the pot's end product that noncultural features are being classified; surface decoration and treatment, however, are purely cultural and some typologists believe that focusing only on cultural features will yield the best classifications. Although this may be true, and although pottery can be organized on the basis of decoration (painting, incising, stamping), or surface treatment (glazing, slipping, burnishing), many pots have no surface treatment or decoration at all. This makes the typology unusable on a global level.

Physical Properties Typology   In addition to a pot's color and shape, physical properties–hardness, texture, inclusions (sand, minerals, organic matter, old ground-up pots), luster, porosity (ability to hold liquid), or strength (resistance to breakage or abrasion)–can be used to sort pots. These properties are usually studied using petrographic microscopes that allow the expert to see light through thin sections (0.03 millimeters) of the pottery. Paint and glaze can be analyzed using chemical tests.

Functional Typology   If the ceramic archaeologist's main concern is to try to assess the function of pottery, he or she can do the typing by (assumed) function. But this typology is governed by an entirely different set of rules, assumptions, and problems, and will be the focus of Exercise 6.

Although all archaeologists would agree that it would be of considerable help to be able to systematically compare collections, at present there is no magic machine (mechanical or computer) that would allow them to put pots in one end and have a typology come out the other end, devoid of personal or collective bias. As a result, each classifier must decide on a classification scheme, explain why he or she is doing it that way, and do it. One way to check on a provisional classification is to observe a collection and do a typology (of choice). If the sample is huge, it can be done on a random sampling basis down to 200–300 sherds or pots. After it is done and the typology is recorded, it is put aside for a week, then redone. If the redone system is similar to the one put aside, perhaps that is the best typology that can be devised. If the two classifications do not match, readjustments would be necessary.

Once the decision is made, it needs no more validation than that it works. Many archaeologists who have been weaned on a certain scheme find a new collection does not "fit" the system they learned as students. To paraphrase Anna Shepard, the leading ceramics expert a generation ago, all archaeologists know how to classify their collections but are hard pressed to put into words what they know or how they know it. Is this situation unscientific? Yes, but seemingly inescapable. Modern ceramicists feel they are making progress toward systematization, but as soon as one expert puts forth a scheme that he or she thinks will work globally, it is either ignored or criticized. Typologies do not seem to travel well.

Regardless of what scheme is used to classify ceramics, one thing is certain—how experts classify is not necessarily how people who made the pots would have classified their own work, assuming they did. If we could discover how the potters or the members of their societies classified their own pottery (what cultural anthropologists call an *emic* classification), we would call them "cultural types," as the assumption is made that potters had a mental template—a set of cognitive rules—in their heads in order to make pottery that fits the norms of their culture. Some archaeologists working in modern societies where potters make pottery on a small scale and only for their own use claim they have looked at the total repertoire of ceramic types in that culture and made educated guesses as to folk taxonomy or cultural types; they say they can essentially classify them as the people themselves classify their ceramics. There is, however, no reason to believe that just because some modern ceramics experts can classify pottery similar to or identical to how real people do so today, that they can classify archaeological pots as their makers did in the past. We therefore regard all twentieth-century attempts at ceramic classification as being subjective and of the analytical kind, meaning it is set up solely for the purpose of analyzing prehistoric pots.

Technical and Compositional Studies

Some archaeologists study the composition of pottery (referred to as the "paste") in its own right, focusing on the physical qualities of the clay: its inclusions, firing techniques, and the technology of the pottery sequence itself. Such studies might focus on questions such as whether potters used hand or wheel techniques; whether they took big slabs of clay and made pinch pots or whether they used the coil method; how they kept the sides of the pots from slumping while making thin walls. Technological and compositional studies often take archaeologists into interdisciplinary and materials science arenas.

Functional Analysis

This area of modern ceramic studies will be the focus of Exercise 6 and merely needs to be noted here as one of the four trends.

CONCLUSIONS

Ceramic analysis has had a long history because, as has been somewhat wryly noted, What else are you going to do with all those sherds? But it is what ceramic analysis can tell us about the people who made the pots that is important, not the pots themselves. Although "pottery people" have been criticized in the past for studying pots as if they existed in their own right, modern ceramic experts fully apply their research to questions of chronology, cultural technology and function, and culture change. No other single class of artifact tells us so much about so many different facets of prehistoric people.

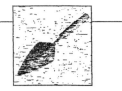

THE EXERCISE

In your reading, it was suggested that there are four modern trends in ceramic archaeology: reconstructing pots from sherds; classifying pots and sherds by typologies; studying the technology of making pottery and its composition; and the function of pottery. Technological and compositional studies normally involve highly complex equipment and even dangerous chemicals. The other three trends can be investigated further through hands-on exercises; in this exercise, you will learn how to reconstruct pots and do typologies (Exercise 6 will focus on ceramic functions).

OBJECTIVES

In this exercise, you will

- learn the basics of pottery reconstruction by putting together a pot from sherds.
- do several typologies using a single (small) collection of sherds.

DOING THE EXERCISE

1. Use one of the boxes for pottery reconstruction. Be sure to use only the sherds in your chosen box, and do not mix it up with the other boxes. If you think you have too few or too many sherds, get help before continuing the exercise. Lay the pieces out on the table (make sure you have enough room to lay them all out in a single layer) and sort by pot parts: put rim pieces in one pile, base pieces in another, side pieces in another, handles in another. Begin with the base pieces and fit them together, using pieces of masking tape to hold them together. Remember that because this pot may have been in the ground for several hundred years and been exposed to moderate amounts of tumbling action, its broken edges may have been somewhat dulled. Your jigsaw puzzle pieces may therefore not fit tightly against each other and there may be a bit of space around each. You must accommodate for this with your taping. Then take the side pieces and using the clues provided by the bowl's decoration and shape, build up the pot, taping as you go. Finally, add the rim pieces. There is no guarantee that every piece will be available for you to use. If you are not finished in

30 minutes, consider yourself finished. You may admire your reconstruction before you disassemble it. After you show your assembled pot to your lab manager, take it apart and put the disassembled pieces back in the box and return it to the shelf. (Toss the tape.)

2. Take a box marked "for typologies" and lay out the pieces on the table. This constitutes the collection to be typed. Also get a sorting page from the box, as it will help you keep your sorted pieces separate.

a. As if you were Nels Nelson in 1914 or an archaeologist who has recently stumbled upon a previously unknown area of prehistoric artifacts, do an intuitive typology, using pages 67–68 and the sorting page as your guides. You have sherds, not whole pots, but you can classify by sherds only. Write the names of the types at the lower edge of each separation of the sorting page as needed. After classifying the entire (small) collection, write the name of each type you decided on as well as a description of its attributes in the spaces provided on Figure 5.1. Assume this collection came from excavating the space between your building and one nearby, so use local names of buildings, streets, or campus icons as the first of the binomial names and use the major identifying attribute for the second name, as in Oglebay Plain or Scioto Burnished. On Figure 5.1 also indicate in the space provided whether the system worked or not. Were you able to type every piece in the collection? Erase or cross off the names on your sorting page.

b. Mix up the pieces in the collection. Do a type-variety typology using the information on page 68 and the sorting page as your guides. First, look at the collection and decide before you do any sorting what two to three diagnostic traits you wish to concentrate on; which ones seem to pervade the entire collection? Write your types in the spaces provided on Figure 5.1 along with the diagnostic traits and sort the collection by those types. Did this typology work? Were you able to type every piece? Were you overly influenced in your decision about types by doing your first typology? Write your answers in the spaces provided on Figure 5.1.

c. Mix up the pieces in the collection. Do a physical properties typology using page 69 and the sorting page as your guides. On Figure 5.1, write which types of physical properties you used in the spaces provided. Is there any important difference between this typology and the type-variety typology? Write your answers in the spaces provided.

Put the collection back into the "For Typologies" box and return it to the shelf.

d. On Figure 5.1, write a final statement on the three typologies that you did. Which worked best for this collection?

☐ **Check your typologies with your lab manager for full credit.**

Figure 5.1 Three Typologies

(*a*) *Intuitive typology:*

Types   Attributes

_____   _____

                                                _____

_____   _____

                                                _____

_____   _____

                                                _____

_____   _____

Did this system work? Did you type all pieces? Why or why not? _____
_____

(*b*) *Type-variety typology:*

Types   Diagnostic traits

_____   _____

                                                _____

_____   _____

                                                _____

                                                _____

_____   _____

                                                _____

_____   _____

Did this system work? Were you able to type all pieces? Why or why not? _____
_____

Were you overly influenced by doing (*a*) first? _____

(*c*) *Physical properties typology:*

Types   Attributes

_____   _____

                                                _____

_____   _____

                                                _____

_____   _____

                                                _____

_____   _____

                                                _____

Did this system work? What's the difference between this and the type-variety typology? _____
_____

(*d*) Of the three typologies, which seemed to work best for this collection? _____
_____

Why? _____
_____

KEY WORDS

ceramics

pottery

lineages (matri- or patri-)

clans (matri- or patri-)

sherds

classifications

typologies

intuitive typology

type-variety typology

quantitative typology

physical properties typology

treatment of decoration and surface typology

functional typology

FOR FURTHER READING

Anderson, Ann. *Interpreting Pottery*. London: B. T. Batson, 1984.

Barnett, William, and John Hoopes, eds. *The Emergence of Pottery*. Washington, D.C.: Smithsonian Institution Press, 1995.

Deetz, James. *The Dynamics of Stylistic Change in Arikara Ceramics*. Urbana, Ill.: Illinois Studies in Anthropology no. 4, 1965.

Gibson, Alex, and Ann Woods. *Prehistoric Pottery for the Archaeologist*. London: Pinter Publishers, 1990.

Hill, James. *Broken K Pueblo: Prehistoric Social Organization in the American Southwest*. Tucson: University of Arizona Press, 1970.

Kolb, Charles. "The Current Status of Ceramic Studies." In *Ceramic Ecology Revisited*, edited by Charles Kolb. BAR International Series, Oxford, 1988.

Longacre, William A. "Archaeology as Anthropology: A Case Study." Anthropological paper no. 17, University of Arizona Press, Tucson, 1970.

Nelson, Nels. "Pueblo Ruin of the Galisteo Basin, New Mexico." Anthropology papers, American Museum of Natural History 15, no. 1. New York, 1914.

Orton, Clive, Paul Tyers, and Alan Vince. *Pottery in Archaeology*. New York: Cambridge University Press, 1993.

Rice, Prudence. *Pottery Analysis*. Chicago: University of Chicago Press, 1987.

Rice, Prudence. "Recent Ceramic Analysis (1): Function, Style, and Origins." *Journal of Archaeological Research* 4, no. 2 (1996):133–63.

Shepard, Anna. *Ceramics for the Archaeologist*. Washington, D.C.: Carnegie Institution of Washington Publication no. 609, 1954.

Sinopoli, Carla. *Approaches to Archaeological Ceramics*. New York: Plenum Publishing, 1991.

6

Ceramics: Sherds and Functions

The identification of pottery's function is one of the goals of modern ceramics experts. In 1987, in her encyclopedic volume on archaeological ceramics, Prudence Rice did not include the study of pottery functions as one of the aims and goals she considered to be on the cutting edge of modern ceramic studies, but in her 1996 update on prehistoric ceramics, she claims functional analysis is at the forefront of modern ceramic studies. In less than a decade, an additional goal has been added. How can this be? Archaeological ceramicists have taken an interest in establishing the function of ceramics since the beginning of archaeology. However, until recently, archaeologists did not have confidence in the results of functional studies. It is now the hottest area of ceramic inquiry.

LOOKING FOR INFORMATION ON CERAMIC FUNCTIONS

Among all of the possible information pottery analysis is capable of providing answers to, what pottery was used for is one of the first-asked questions. It is easy to observe the use (function) of pots in modern societies; an anthropologist can see people making and using pottery and can ask questions about functions that may not be obvious: Is this pot used for cooking and that one for storing? Is the one with the long neck used to pour wine and the one with the short neck used only for making corn beer? But, in lieu of direct observation, archaeologists must use indirect methods of establishing ceramic functions: (1) **form and function** analysis; (2) written documents and art; (3) context in which the ceramics are found; (4) ethnological literature; (5) ethnoarchaeology; (6) observations on archaeological ceramics; and (7) ceramic experiments.

Form and Function Analysis

One of the first attempts to establish the function/use of ceramics merely assumed that form equals function, or at least that form covaries with function. Translated into ceramic terms, this assumes that whenever a particular pottery form occurred in the past, we could assume a particular function: A tall, narrow-necked vessel that we would call a "jar" was used for storage, or a low and wide vessel that we would call a "bowl" was used for eating. For much of the history of ceramic studies, the form-equals-function idea was assumed to be correct and not seriously questioned. More recently, it has become a hypothesis to be tested. Several recent studies have found that size and shape of vessels are strongly correlated with function in contemporary ceramic-producing societies, but statistical probabilities of modern pottery are no assurance that it was true in the past as well. Statistical probabilities are just that–probabilities.

Because whole pots are certainly better than fragments in establishing whether form is correlated with function, tests have been devised to turn fragments into estimates of entire vessels. If enough of a vessel is found (or can be refitted), there are several computer programs that are designed to take a series of measurement points to estimate shape and volume, both of which are useful in determining function. One program can estimate the volume of a vessel within 1% of accuracy by measuring 20 points on a vessel or on a large sherd or sherds. It is best to have a complete profile of the pot being analyzed, but large sherds will often suffice. Rims (orifices) are helpful as well, especially if rims and sides of single vessels can be refitted. A pot with a wide rim is likely to have a different function than one with a tall and narrow neck, where the rim would be relatively small. Pouring, for example, is much easier from a narrow-necked (and rimmed) jar than from a wide-rimmed bowl. For this reason, rims receive special treatment, more than any other part of a pot. Even pieces of rims can be used with a standard diameter measurement template to estimate the total rim size; add this to a sherd or two from the same vessel and estimates of size, shape, and function improve enormously.

Not all archaeologists are enthusiastic about functional studies because they (quite correctly) criticize the unflinching use of functional names in the discussions of kinds of pottery. It is very likely that particular archaeological pieces had several functions during their ceramic lifetimes, and we know from observing modern societies that differently shaped or sized pots often have the same function. As I look around my kitchen, bathroom, and office, I see at least six different functions of cups: In the kitchen, they hold pencils, small plants, and scissors; in the bathroom, they hold nail files, emery boards, and cuticle sticks; in my office, they hold vials of pollen; occasionally, they are used for drinking coffee. Some ceramics experts have suggested that it is probably wise (if more difficult) to refrain from using what sound like single functional names that imply single, known functions: cup, dish, bowl, jar. Instead, they suggest we use neutral units of identification, such as W, X, Y, and Z, or 1, 2, 3, 4. This practice, if adopted, would remove pottery one step further from people, culture, and behavior. However, because the aim of archaeology is to reconstruct the behavior, cognition, and emotions of prehistoric people and their culture, identifying an important part of people's lives using ciphers or letters goes against this established aim of archaeology. Perhaps the best compromise would be to continue using those seemingly functional words while realizing that any class of ceramic may have multiple uses in a given culture at a given time, and that when we use words such as *dish* or *bowl*, we are using analytical terminology and not necessarily using classifications that reflect prehistoric reality.

Written Documents and Art

Although historic people did not often write about their techniques for or uses of ceramics, they often indirectly provided information about function by writing about what was saved or used in pottery. It was important for people to write about the economics of how many bushels of corn were stored in pots, but to the archaeologist, the storing in pottery is what is important. The same is true of art and ceramic function. Artists did not often use pottery as the focus of painting, but pottery occasionally shows up in the background of paintings, and function can sometimes be inferred.

Context of Ceramics

If ceramics are found in archaeological contexts that clearly demonstrate their use as cooking vessels, for example, it does not take a leap of faith to assume at least a provisional function. Pottery sherds associated with a hearth or with bits of burned wood, for example, may be rare, but telling, nonetheless. Pottery urns found in tombs (often whole) give a fairly straightforward functional context, as does that rare coffin made of clay. But because pottery is usually sharp when freshly broken, it is often removed from the place of breakage and tossed in the village dump, where all context is irreversibly lost.

The Ethnological Literature

One search of the literature on modern or recently existing societies suggests pottery served 14 different functions in the present or recent past that can be subsumed under the three broad categories of storing (raw food), processing (cooking), and transferring (from a larger storage unit to domestic use, such as a pitcher). Another look through the literature came up with a total of 42 functions. Can we assume that pottery served the same 14 or 42 functions in the distant past? Use of **ethnoparallels** about ceramic functions is a start; at the very least it tells us the range of likely pottery functions in the past, and it does tell us what likely connections there were between form and function: tall vessels were probably used for liquid storage because this shape is best for pouring liquids; short and squat vessels were probably used for long-term dry storage; cooking pots were probably round, thin walled, coarse textured, porous, and tempered with materials that could withstand thermal stress. In regard to cooking, pots used for boiling (the most common way to cook) probably had wide openings with a smaller neck to restrict boil overs, whereas pottery for frying had flat bases. Pottery used for serving food probably had flat bases, and pots with concave bottoms were probably used for carrying water and foodstuffs (they fit the top of the head nicely). There are some odd or at least rare uses for pottery as well, such as ceramic baby bottles, honey collectors, coffins, or coverings for female pubic areas.

These predictions about prehistoric pottery functions serve well as hypothesis generators, but how do we know how the pots were really used? And how do we know that a pot had only one function in its lifetime of use? A pot might have been made especially for service as a storage vessel until it was chipped, then used as a flowerpot or a dog-food bowl until it was broken, then ground up and used in the next batch of pots as temper. Archaeologically, we only see that last function.

Observations on Archaeological Pottery

Recently, a number of archaeologists have argued that messages about ceramic function can be found on the archaeological ceramics themselves. Looking at ceramics and finding wear marks is one thing, but knowing that such marks were made by humans and not from rolling around in the ground, and knowing what the wear marks mean, is something else. Those archaeologists who claim that the ceramics themselves can tell us about their function during their use usually combine methods of (1) ethnoarchaeology (whereby a group is still making and using pottery for its own, noncommercial use); (2) observations on ceramics made by people using them and then comparing the use marks with archaeological ceramics; and (3) experimentation with ceramics, as needed. It is often difficult to separate the three methods.

The following observations, which indicate pottery use, can be made on pottery and, hopefully, on prehistoric pottery as well: (*a*) residue and soot marks on pots; (*b*) chemical changes in clay; and (*c*) use-wear as a result of abrasions and scratches. Each type of observation will be discussed.

Residue and Soot Marks   Occasionally, archaeological pottery will actually have residue or soot in or on it that gives obvious clues to function. Very recently, a yellowish residue in a pot originally found in Iran and stuck on a shelf in the University of Pennsylvania Museum for about 20 years was analyzed and is now claimed to be the earliest example of wine. The narrow-necked jar has been identified as to its function: It stored liquid and in this case wine. (This does not mean, however, that every similarly shaped jar in that collection, much less in the entire Middle East, was used to store wine).

Soot on the outside and burn rings on the inside of pots point to cooking, though by themselves they do not say what was cooked or for how long. One can observe sooting as a process in modern societies, but it is not known how long soot can last on archaeological ceramics. Soot and burn lines cannot be washed off, but that does not mean they survive very long in soil.

Chemical Tests   Chemical tests on the insides of pots can be run to see if the original contents were organic, or contained oil or resin. But many pots were likely used in cooking and unless there is a pot for every recipe or ingredient, such tests as are now available would not be able to single out individual ingredients. Such tests, however, can tell us if particular pottery pieces ever contained certain items (organic material, oil) or not, which would help sort out water vessels from oil or wine storage vessels, for example, or pots used to cook corn from those used to cook meat.

Use-Wear Studies   Though an archaeologist can always ask how old is this pot, where was it made, or by what means did it get to this spot, and usually find a way to answer the questions, the first and most important question is always, What was this pot used for? Pots can't speak for themselves, but recently a technique similar to that used to attempt to identify the function of lithic tools (see Exercise 4) has been successful in indicating the function of modern and prehistoric pottery. The technique is in its infancy and is usable only for a few types of pots at present, but it promises to be important in identifying ceramic function in the future. Many archaeologists are now looking at their own collections for insights into functional studies.

The new technique is called "pottery use-wear" or "pottery use-alteration," and it is based on the same principle as lithic use-wear analysis: As pots are being used, the use itself should change the pots in some way, either by adding to or subtracting from or modifying the original pieces. Different uses should yield different wear marks that are characteristic and identifiable pottery-use signatures; stirring, scraping, mixing, grinding, pounding, washing, putting lids on ceramic rims, and soot can leave long-lasting clues as to the pottery's use in the form of abrasion patches, pits, striations, and thermal spalls. Once archaeologists have a complete catalog of what happens to each kind of pottery through each functional use, they will at least theoretically be able to assess the function of individual ceramic pieces. If an entire small collection or a sample of a large one is analyzed in this functional way, an archaeologist could suggest the use frequency of certain kinds of pots in a particular culture.

At present, there are some problems with ceramic use-wear studies. If, for example, the surfaces of pots are badly eroded, it is very difficult to see use-wear marks. Pottery, unlike flint, does undergo modifications just by being in the soil. Tumbling by water can cause markings that theoretically appear similar to those caused by abrasion use. It is also difficult to assess a collection of sherds rather than whole pots because the location of use marks is important to the identification of the pot's function. Sherds would have to be refitted to be able to look at areas where use-wear traces show up, and this takes time. However, a quick look at rims, for example, or at bases—both areas of pots that are easily identified—would at least suggest whether a functional analysis is worth spending that extra time on. If there is no visible use-wear, the archaeologist does not need to refit the pots in the collection.

Nevertheless, all archaeologists will agree that reasonably long use of pottery in habitual ways should leave characteristic and identifiable marks. But saying use *should* result in use-wear marks is different from showing that they do; identifying specifically what caused what mark is an additional unknown. A number of early studies beginning in the late 1970s were instrumental in establishing a viable technique of ceramic use-wear. The first study analyzed scratches from eighteenth-century English lead-glazed earthenware, followed by analyses of the soot, oxidation, and surface pitting on Native American pottery in Georgia. And in 1985, Michael Deal (1988) began experimental work on prehistoric organic residues, finding that fatty acids can be identified in organic residues that are derived from prehistoric sherds.

All of these early studies have one disadvantage, and that is a lack of verification as to the relationship between which logically *should* produce use marks and what actually *does*. There is a great deal of speculation in these early reports. What was needed to establish ceramic use-wear as a viable and reliable step forward into functional analysis of ceramics was a study that would combine observation of modern pottery use to see what actually causes specific use-wear marks, experimentation on details of use-wear, and a collection of prehistoric pottery made by the ancestors of the people who are observed, in order to compare past and present use marks. The next section will describe just such a project.

Kalinga Ethnoarchaeology

The most energetic and thorough study of use-wear on ceramics for use in archaeological ceramic studies was done as part of William Longacre's long-term **ethnoarchaeology** study of the Kalinga of Northern Luzon in the Philippines. The Kalinga are a rice and vegetable farming people who live in small villages; they are relatively homogeneous in their culture (and different from their neighbors), and, of great importance to Longacre's study, they still make ceramics primarily for their own use. Unlike many modern people who still make pottery, the Kalinga are not influenced by the commercial market and do not make pots to please the public; their pottery is used only by themselves in their own domestic lives. This was, in Longacre's opinion, an ideal situation for a long-term project in ethnoarchaeology, a major part of which was a kind of ethnoceramic study. He and many of his graduate students, who have gone with him since the early 1970s, have used the Kalinga as an ethnographic storehouse for generating hypotheses about the past.

Longacre and his students are archaeologists, but similar to the ethnoarchaeologists in Exercise 2, they live with the Kalinga in an attempt to gain insights about modern material objects that will be usable for archaeologists studying material objects in the past. They hope to be able to use those insights as hypotheses about the past, using the same kind of material objects in an archaeological context to test the ethnologically driven hypotheses.

Until 20 years ago, it was common to sneer at ethnoparallels or at the use of ethnoarchaeology, but studying modern people and their cultures to gain insights about the past has become more rigorous and more scientific, and therefore more respected. Ethnoarchaeologists intentionally collect data on the people they are observing so the data can be used by archaeologists. For example, an ethnoarchaeologist might be interested in the breakage patterns and rates along with who broke what for what reason; or ceramic vessel usage along with demographic data on who used what pot for what reason; or use-wear data coupled with information about who the potters are and how they learned their trade.

James Skibo is the archaeologist who as a young graduate student went to Luzon in 1987 to study one specific aspect of Kalinga ceramics for his dissertation: use-wear traces. Other students of Longacre studied firing techniques, spatial boundaries of the Kalinga and their neighbors via their different ceramics, economic exchange of pottery (rare), and Kalinga basketry. Skibo used the term *pottery use-alteration* for his work, but the term *use-wear* will be used here because the shorter term has the advantage of mirroring the terminology in Exercise 4 on flint use-wear, and once the theory, method, and reference catalogs are developed for pottery use-wear, its proponents feel confident pottery use-wear will provide the same level of specific information as lithic use-wear studies. The term *pottery use-wear* can then be applied globally, keeping the term *pottery use-alteration* for the local Kalinga project.

Skibo tells us that the Kalinga make three kinds of pots (pots being one class of ceramic): water pots, rice pots, meat/vegetable pots. The latter two are used in cooking. The three kinds of pots cannot be distinguished by shape, as all essentially have the same shape. Figure 6.1 shows representative pots and their

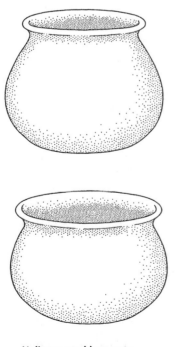

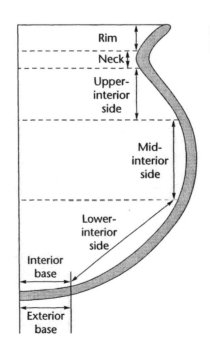

Figure 6.1 Kalinga Pots and Pottery Parts

Kalinga cooking pots   Vessel location terminology parts. Although individual potters may make water pots somewhat larger than rice pots or meat/vegetable pots, some potters make all pottery larger than other potters, so size would not be an effective measure of function in an archaeological context. All three kinds of pots are made from the same clay paste, and have the same temper in addition to having the same basic shape with rounded bases, so none of these attributes can be used to separate functions. Here is a case where form does not equal function, as the same form (and size) equals three different functions.

Many details about modern Kalinga pots and cooking have no archaeological importance, but those details that affect use-wear patterns need to be discussed. Kalinga pottery is made from clay that contains a sufficient amount of sand as temper material so that no additional temper is needed, which has a certain effect upon cooking. Pots are fired in open bonfires at quite low temperatures (only about 700° Fahrenheit) and only for about 20 minutes per firing. This too must affect cooking qualities. While still hot, the pots are removed from the fire and resin from local pine trees is smeared over the inside and the outside of the pots to enhance impermeability of liquids. The Kalinga do not boil their rice in pots over open fires beyond bringing the rice and water to a boil. When fully boiling, the covered rice pot is removed from the direct heat and set on a three-legged support apparatus next to but not over the fire. It is close enough so that the rice continues to absorb the water and becomes tender without burning. The pot, covered and not stirred, is turned every 20 minutes or so while the meat and vegetables are cooking in another pot directly over the fire, uncovered, and stirred to prevent burning.

Before he attempted use-wear analysis, Skibo tried to identify the function of Kalinga pots by other means. Phosphorus tests and carbon-to-nitrogen ratios were considered, but the literature on these tests suggests they would not be successful. He did, however, do an analysis of fatty acids (lipids) because, theoretically, they are absorbed and preserved in the pottery, they survive normal cooking temperatures as well as indeterminable periods of deposition in the soil, and they can often be identified at the species level. Skibo studied the fatty acids he found in modern sherds relative to what he knew the Kalinga did or did not do in cooking, sampling those pots that had contained only water versus those known to have been used to cook only vegetables and meat and those known to cook only rice. All pots used in cooking contained fatty acids; the water pots did not. Then, using chemical analysis on 10 pots taken from a recent excavation, Skibo attempted to separate rice-cooking pots from meat and vegetable pots. He was confident that all 10 pots had been used in cooking, as all showed some fatty acids; in this case, he did not know beforehand what had been cooked in the pots. The pots with low amounts of fatty acids were likely rice-cooking pots and the ones with a large amount were likely used to cook meat and vegetables, based on the principle that rice has less fatty acid than meat (and the vegetable/meat pots were always used for both ingredients). If a pot had been found with no fatty acids, he would have concluded it was a water pot.

So far, so good: Skibo could tell what was cooked in the pots and which ones were likely used to carry water. But there are two possible problems about inferring any further: First, fatty acids appear to have variable survival rates, depending on variable preservation conditions; second, knowing what was cooked is somewhat different from knowing how the pots were used. Sometimes fatty acids do become entombed in low-fired pottery and can be used to sort out specific food. There was no way of knowing if the people who made the excavated pots used them in exactly the same way as the modern Kalinga use their pots.

Skibo then proceeded to investigate surface attrition to answer the question, Can pots that change through use be accurately identified as to specific function or behavior? Skibo watched Kalinga women use their pots in cooking and later did experiments on Kalinga pots himself to test his assertions. He found five kinds of attrition (Table 6.1) on the outside and inside surfaces of pots: chips, abrasion spots, striations, pits, and thermal spalls (caused by overcooking with all moisture gone). Spalls are always circular and from 1 to 3 centimeters in diameter. The use-wear marks are summarized in Table 6.1, giving the area of use-wear, the type of use-wear (attrition), and the known cause(s). (See Figure 6.1 for names of pottery parts.)

All of these use-wear marks leave traces of behaviors (see "Cause" column) but some of them also allowed Skibo to differentiate between water pots and cooking pots, as water pots showed no use-wear marks at all. The use-wear marks on Table 6.1 with asterisks (*) differ for meat/vegetable and rice pots and need to be explained: Vegetable/meat pots will show more abrasion on their interior rims and necks than rice pots because they are stirred with metal tools; rice pots will show some abrasions, but directly on the neck where the tops are put off and on. Only rice pots will show thermal spalls on various parts of the pots because they are covered, not added to nor stirred once the cooking process has begun; occasionally, overcooking causes thermal spalls to occur. In contrast, vegetable/meat pots are half full of water at all times, being added to and stirred as they boil down, and they are not covered. Abrasion occurs on the lower interior and base only on meat/vegetable pots as a result of being stirred. In contrast, rice pots are lined with leaves before the rice and water is added (the Kalinga say the rice tastes better this way), and rice pots are not stirred. Finally, carbon rings can form on the interior of rice pots if the pots are not turned after sitting next to the fire every 20 minutes or so; after several such episodes, a patch becomes a ring. Carbon rings on the interiors of vegetable/meat pots are always lower because they occur essentially at the boiling water mark, which is kept well below the rim to allow for stirring during cooking.

Table 6.1   Attrition in Kalinga Pots

Area	Type of Attrition	Cause
1. Lower-exterior side	Striations parallel to rim	Washing pot on ground
2. Exterior base	Circular, 3–6 cm abrasion	Contact with ground; dragging
3. Midexterior side	Striations parallel to rim	Washing pot on ground
4. Upper-exterior side	Very fine scratches	Carrying with rattan carrier
5. Rim	Chips	Putting top on/off
	Linear striations around rim	Contact with ground in washing
	(Attritions (1)–(5) are all on outside of vessels.)	
6. Interior rim and neck	Abrasion*	Putting top on/off; stirring
	Thermal spalls*	Overcooking to burned stage
7. Upper-interior inside	Pits	Stirring with utensils
	Thermal spalls*	Overcooking
8. Midinterior side	Thermal spalls*	End of cooking cycle
9. Lower interior and base	Abrasion*	Stirring; scrubbing; washing
	(Attritions (6)–(9) are all on inside of vessels.)	
10. Exterior	Carbon patches/soot marks	Penetrating food charring
Interior	Carbon patches/soot marks*	Penetrating food charring

*Traits differ for rice and vegetable/meat pots.

This detailed account of Kalinga pots and cooking, use-wear marks and causes, is intended to do two things: First, to give you an idea of how pottery use-wear studies have begun on a single, well-studied modern society. We are cautioned about using principles of use-wear gained from only one major study on a global scale. Eventually, however, there will be a catalog of marks, movements, and causes that is just as detailed as what now exists for lithic use-wear studies. It took 40 years for lithic use-wear to get where it is today in theory and practice. By contrast, pottery use-wear studies have only been around for a few years. And second, this account should help you to do the exercise.

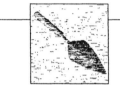

THE EXERCISE

For this exercise on ceramic functional analysis, you are to play the role of an archaeologist just assigned to William Longacre's group in the Philippines. The group has just located another archaeology site nearby its main camp. The archaeologists believe on the basis of surface finds that the people who left the debris behind at the new site are not only the ancestors of the modern Kalinga (their pottery is very similar and different from any of the Kalinga's neighbors' ceramics) but also earlier by several hundred years than the people who left the archaeological materials Skibo used in his early 1990 work. Skibo is not available for this work, so you have been assigned to perform the prehistoric use-wear analysis on the collection. You have read Skibo's dissertation and all of Longacre and his students' work from the past, you have spent several months watching Kalinga women cook and use pots, and you are confident that you can recognize cause and effect in their modern pottery. Finally, you realize that Skibo's catalog of attrition is usable only for the Kalinga until it has been verified.

OBJECTIVES

In this exercise, you will

- do a **functional typology**.
- use a rim diagram to give a preliminary functional identification to a sherd.
- investigate use-wear on pottery from an ethnoarchaeological perspective based on Kalinga pottery; look at a small reference collection of attrition use-wear marks; make an abrasion mark on a sherd with a metal utensil and match the mark with the abrasion mark in the reference collection; and attempt to identify the function (use) of several pieces of Kalinga pottery.

DOING THE EXERCISE

1.   Get abox prepared for typologies like you used for Exercise 5 on ceramic typology. If you have done that exercise, you will realize that this is an additional type of typology—this one is based on assumed function rather than on any morphological traits. If you have not yet done Exercise 5, this functional typology will be your first. It doesn't matter whether you have done a previous sorting by types; either way, remove the sherds from the box and put them on your sorting table. Using a sorting sheet, look at each sherd and try to decide its

function. You are using only sherds, not whole pots, so it may not be possible for you to type every piece in the collection. You cannot be very specific, as you can assume little beyond general function or kind of vessel. The best you can functionally sort will be

- cup (assumed function is for drinking liquids);
- dish (assumed function is for eating food);
- bowl (assumed function is for eating food);
- pot (assumed function is for cooking food, storing food, serving food);
- jar (assumed function is for storing food);
- urn (assumed function is for burying ashes of the dead);
- vase (assumed function is for decoration, perhaps to hold flowers).

Use the following measurements (do not actually measure, just eyeball them): the height of a bowl is one-third or more of its rim diameter; the height of a dish is one-third or less but more than one-seventh of its rim diameter; the height of a jar is one-half or more of its width. Use the line drawings in Figure 6.2 to help you determine the type of pot along with its assumed function. Pick up each piece, try to match it to a drawing, use the measurements, and decide what kind of pottery piece it is. Start a pile using the sorting sheet. The pile now has a name, such as "bowl," or "jar," or "dish." Pick up another piece and do the same. When you have typed the collection by assumed function and have a feel for the work, go back to your pile of unknowns and see if you can now type all pieces. On Figure 6.3, write the names of the functional types, the number of sherds you classified into each type, and the total number of sherds, converting to percentages, where indicated on the figure. Next to "Unknown," indicate how much of the collection you could not type.

2.   Get the "Kalinga Reference Collection." To isolate the use-wear marks, they are labeled in the reference collection to identify where the marks are on the pot and what the type of attrition (and soot marks) is. Look at the reference collection and note where and what each attrition use mark is. Use the material on page 83 and Table 6.1 for clues. In the spaces provided on Figure 6.4, write the kind of use-wear mark and the characteristics you see for that signature mark for each piece in the reference collection.

Figure 6.2   Kinds of Pottery

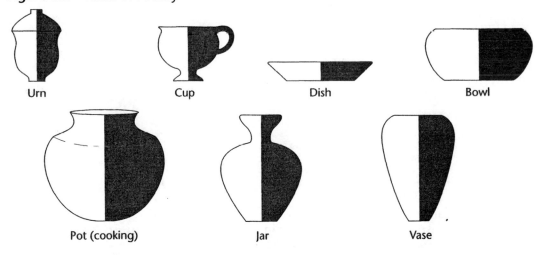

Urn   Cup   Dish   Bowl

Pot (cooking)   Jar   Vase

Figure 6.3 Functional Typology

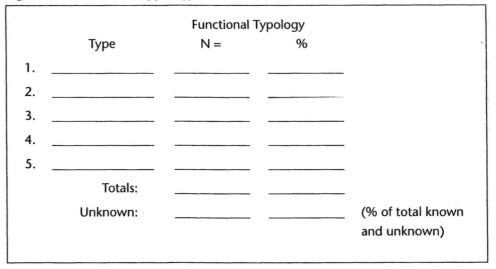

Figure 6.4 Kalinga Use-Wear Marks—Reference Collection

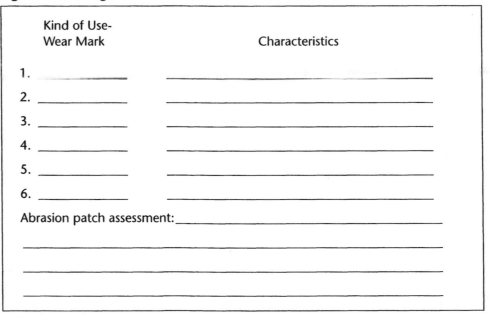

Figure 6.5 Template for Rim Measurment

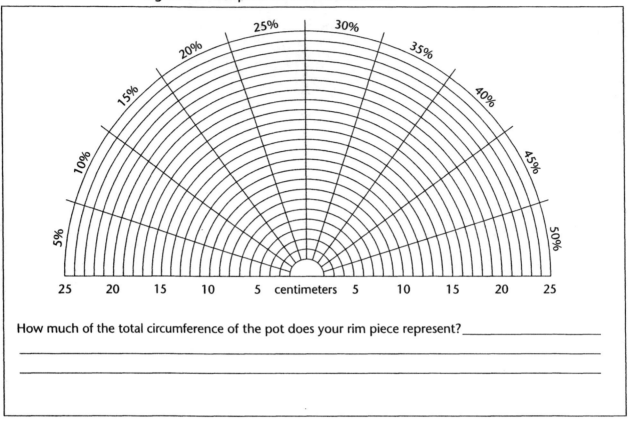

How much of the total circumference of the pot does your rim piece represent?_____

_____

_____

Figure 6.6 Archaeological Kalinga Sherds

	Sherd #	Area of Pot	Attributes	Assessed Function
1.	_____	_____	_____	_____
2.	_____	_____	_____	_____
3.	_____	_____	_____	_____

3.   Get a rim piece. Figure 6.5 is a template used to measure the rim (orifice) radius of a pottery sherd to establish the percentage of the total rim size. As rims provide a considerable amount of information on the size and shape of a pot, it is the first step toward assessing a pot's function. Do not use the template shown in figure 6.5 as it is only a model and not the correct size. Use the template provided by your lab manager that has the correct centimeter measurement. Put one edge of your sherd against the left edge of the template, fitting the sherd curve to the template curve and measure how much of the total piece you have. On Figure 6.5, indicate how much of the total circumference of the pot your rim piece represents.

4.   Get an unused sherd. Use a metal spoon as if it were a stirring utensil and rub it back and forth against an inside surface of the sherd for 5–10 minutes to simulate a year or so of stirring in one spot. Look at the abrasion patch and compare it with the abrasion patch in the reference collection. Does your patch match the one in the reference collection? Write your findings in the space provided on Figure 6.4. Do not put your sherd back in the box of unused sherds, as it has been used. Give your used sherd to your lab manager.

5.   Get the "Archaeological Kalinga Sherds" and choose three sherds to functionally identify. List by number on Figure 6.6 in the spaces provided. For each sherd, first decide where it likely belongs in the area of a Kalinga pot (rim, base, side); then scan the entire piece and see what attrition marks you can see. Using the knowledge gained by looking at the reference collection, assess the piece in terms of attributes of attrition. List the attributes you see in the spaces provided on Figure 6.6. Assess the function of the piece and write it in the spaces provided on Figure 6.6 based on those attrition attributes. Function should be stated as: water vessel, rice-cooking pot, or vegetable/meat-cooking pot.

☐   **Check with your lab manager when completing this exercise for full credit.**

KEY WORDS

form and function

ethnoparallels

use-wear

ethnoarchaeology

functional typology

FOR FURTHER READING

Deal, Michael, and P. Silk. "Absorption Residues and Vessel Function: A Case Study from the Maine-Maritimes Region." In *A Pot for All Reasons: Ceramic Ecology Revisited,* edited by C. C. Kolb and L. M. Lackey. Philadelphia: Laboratory of Anthropology, Temple University, 105–25, 1988.

Griffiths, Dorothy. "Use-Wear Marks on Historic Ceramics: A Preliminary Study." *Historical Archaeology* 2 (1978):68–81.

Hally, David. "Use Alteration of Pottery Vessel Surfaces: An Important Source of Evidence for the Identification of Vessel Function." *North American Archaeologist* 4, no. 1 (1983).

Heron, C., and R. P. Evershed. "The Analysis of Organic Residues and the Study of Pottery Use." In *Archaeological Method and Theory 5*, edited by M. B. Schiffer. Tucson: University of Arizona Press, 247–84, 1993.

Kramer, Carol, ed. *Ethnoarchaeology*. New York: Columbia University Press, 1979.

Longacre, William. "Kalinga Pottery: An Ethnoarchaeology Study." In *Pattern of the Past,* edited by I. Hodder and N. Hammond. Cambridge: Cambridge University Press, 1981.

Longacre, William, and James M. Skibo, eds. *Kalinga Ethnoarchaeology*. Washington, D.C.: Smithsonian Institution Press, 1994.

Rice, Prudence. *Pottery Analysis*. Chicago: University of Chicago Press, 1987.

Rice, Prudence. "Recent Ceramic Analysis (1): Function, Style, and Origins." *Journal of Archaeological Research* 4, no. 2 (1996):133–63.

Schiffer, Michael. "A Research Design for Ceramic Use-Wear Analysis at Grasshopper Pueblo." In *Pottery Technology*. Boulder, Colo.: Westview Press, 1989.

Schiffer, Michael, and James Skibo. "A Provisional Theory of Ceramic Abrasion." *American Anthropologist* 91 (1989):102–16.

Skibo, James. *Pottery Function: A Use-Alteration Perspective*. New York: Plenum Press, 1992.

7

Dating with Pots: Seriation

ARCHAEOLOGICAL DATING

If all archaeologists want to do is describe particular cultures in the past, the lifeways of those groups could be described without needing chronological context. But two of the other goals of archaeology—beyond reconstruction of past cultures—are to explain how and why cultures changed and to explain the archaeological record itself (what has happened to artifacts between the time they were deposited and the time they were excavated). Both goals rely on being able to put the explanatory data on a firm chronological footing. Indeed, the fourth goal, to date archaeological materials, is usually cited first because the others depend so highly on it: to date archaeological materials.

Time seems to penetrate Western thought, particularly when objects are known to be old to begin with. All archaeologists are asked from time to time to look at artifacts or collections from "Grandmother's attic," artifacts or collections that are usually unprovenienced, and after the usual question of Is it worth anything? (for which the answer is usually a resounding no), the next question invariably is, Well, then, how old is it? as if at least it has some intrinsic if not monetary value if an age can be established, the older the better. Anyone who has done museum work knows the first thing that is written on an accompanying card after the object's name is its assumed date. Nonarchaeologists as well as archaeologists need time frames in order to feel comfortable.

Archaeologists use a number of techniques in their attempt to properly date their artifacts. Some methods only give **relative** dates, which indicate which artifact in a collection is older than which others, and some methods—called **absolutes**—give dates that can be tied to the Western calendar and are given in "years ago," or as B.C./A.D. Some methods are well established, with archaeologists confident with their results, and some are still considered experimental. Some have fairly fine-grained resolution, and some are probable within rather large ranges of time. Some rely on logic and have only a few inherent assumptions, and some are based on unverifiable assumptions that may or may not be accurate. Some can be used to verify others.

Chronometric Dating

Specifically which **chronometric** dating technique dates what materials with what range of dates and accuracy is beyond the scope of this exercise; any basic archaeology text can be consulted for a discussion of 14C, thermoluminescence, electron spin resonance, potassium-argon, fission tracking, and obsidian hydration.

Relative Dating Methods

Until the mid-1950s, only relative dating methods were available to archaeologists, but since the 14C "revolution," which essentially began with the first issue of the journal **Radiocarbon** in 1959, chronometric techniques that tie artifacts to the Western calendar have taken over our thinking about dating. Regardless of whether chronometric methods are more or less accurate or based on more or less verifiable assumptions than are relative methods, it is somehow more comfortable putting an actual year to an object or an event than saying the year was either before or after another object or event. For this reason, archaeological thinking about dating and dates has undergone a revolution as assuredly as the invention of the chronometric techniques themselves. A good deal of archaeology was done before 1959, however, and relative dating, in its own quiet way, is still being used; it just doesn't get archaeological headlines.

All relative dating methods are based on the same principle of establishing order of deposition. Through the use of chemical tests, stratigraphy, or ceramic dating, artifacts can be ordered by the oldest, followed by the next oldest, and so on.

Chemical Tests

The three chemical tests (fluorine, uranium, nitrogen) are sometimes called the FUN tests; all are done on bone, teeth, and antler, and basically establish whether the bones in a deposit are of the same age or not. The FUN tests normally are used only when there is no proper stratigraphy or when the bones are obviously redeposited and mixed up in a deposit; often they are done to merely separate ancient from modern bone. The basis of the testing is that fluorine and uranium exist in groundwater and are absorbed by deposited bone; the longer the bone has been in water, the more fluorine or uranium it will absorb relative to the other bones (of any species, mixed or not) in the deposit. The principle behind nitrogen dating is that bone is composed of about 5% nitrogen and that the element deteriorates when it is deposited. FUN dating has one major limitation, and that is that it is dependent upon local conditions: There are variable amounts of fluorine and uranium in groundwater (in some areas it can be three times higher than in a different bed a few kilometers away), and nitrogen deteriorates differentially depending on the type of soil in which the bone is deposited. Both the addition of fluorine and uranium and the loss of nitrogen in bone are too variable from one geographic spot to the next to establish chronometric schemes.

There has been some notoriety attached to fluorine testing because it was used to assess the antiquity of the infamous Piltdown Man and other bone materials in the same deposit; fluorine testing found that the skull contained a good deal more fluorine than the mandible. It has subsequently been found that the skull is modestly old at 620 years (it was originally purported to be several hundred thousand years old), whereas the mandible was probably only a year or so old in 1913, when the first bones were "discovered." Less dramatically, but on a more positive note, when the third piece of the Swanscome skull (believed to be over 100,000 years old and found in eastern England) of a single individual was found in 1956 (the previous two pieces were found in 1935 and 1936), it was almost too coincidental to be true. The bones were subjected to fluorine analysis and found to contain considerable and comparable amounts of the element, thus demonstrating the three skull specimens were the same age.

Stratigraphy

Stratigraphic dating is based on the **law of stratigraphy**, which states that, unless disturbed, the oldest deposits in a site are at the lowest level (bottom) and the youngest are at the top. This law, in turn, is based on the **law of uniformitarianism** and the **law of gravity;** the law of uniformitarianism states that the forces that cause the earth's surface to change in the present are the same forces that caused change in the past. This means that the earth's surface is added to by mountain building and volcanoes, and subtracted from by erosion, now and in the past. The law of gravity claims that high materials will fall to low spots; thus, newly formed soil will fall down hills or be moved by rain or rivers onto the lowest spots to settle more or less permanently as horizontal beds of sediment. These beds will be covered by soil and sediment through succeeding similar events until a set of stratified layers has built up. Obviously, whatever cultural remains (artifacts) have been deposited in those undisturbed layers are then associated with the layers, and an ordering of the artifacts based on the order of the layers, with the oldest on the bottom to the youngest at the top, can then be worked out.

However, the important word here is *undisturbed,* as many factors can disturb horizontal layers to turn them into a geologist's nightmare: synclines and anticlines, river gouging, glacial movements, differential surface uplifting, and redeposition are just some of the potential disturbances to horizontal stratigraphy. In addition to natural disturbances, humans can alter stratigraphies as well by putting in postholes, burying their dead, or digging storage pits. Fortunately, geologists are very good at working out the proper sequences of layers, and the basis of stratigraphic dating has withstood time. A large proportion of archaeological artifacts has been dated by stratigraphic association, and it will continue to be the workhorse of archaeology. Even if 14C were economically feasible for every excavated artifact, probably 99% of archaeological artifacts cannot be dated by 14C, as the two most commonly found objects—flint and pottery—are not organic and cannot be dated by 14C. In addition, 14C only dates consistently to 40,000 years ago, leaving 2,460,000 years of cultural events where 14C cannot be used. Because of its expense, 14C is usually used only to establish the date of each layer in a site by dating two or three items, including charcoal from hearths, if present; the rest of the artifacts in that same site will be dated by their association within the now 14C dated layer in which they were found. Stratigraphic dating may not be as glamorous as its chronometric cousins, but *all* objects were dated by relative methods until 1960, and probably 99% are still dated by stratigraphic association.

Ceramic Dating

The use of pottery to date artifacts, living floors, and entire sites has a long history. Before chronometric methods were established, dating by ceramics was one of the few ways archaeologists could date their cultural debris. For the most part, **ceramic dating** is relative dating. The exceptions are the fairly new, still experimental methods of thermoluminescence (TL) and optical stimulated luminescence (OSL). Thermoluminescence was developed specifically to date pottery, and because it theoretically dates beyond the 40,000-year limit of 14C, it should date any pottery, as pottery's limit is 10,000 years ago. As of now, its margin of error is quite wide, around 10%. OSL differs from TL only in that it uses a laser to gauge the luminescence it gives off.

Ceramics as a relative dating technique comes in four forms: (1) ceramic/stratigraphic dating, (2) signature dating, (3) cross-dating, and (4) the various forms of **seriation dating.**

Stratigraphic Dating Before the turn of the century, dating by ceramics was one of the only dating techniques. Once the natural (as opposed to the cultural) stratigraphy had been set up for a site, ceramics that were in the layers were automatically dated, with the oldest at the bottom of a site to the youngest at the top. The order of pottery "types" could then be observed and noted in chronological order.

Signature Dating Although this "actual date" technique is very rare, occasionally a piece of pottery's actual date of manufacture is stamped or engraved on the pottery itself. Williamsburg cups were made (then buried and eventually excavated) in Virginia in 1600 to commemorate the restoration of Charles II to the throne of England. Any artifacts that are in good association with one of those dated cups is of course also dated, but it is a minimal date only, meaning the cup was *made* in 1600, not necessarily broken or thrown away in 1600. It could have been heirloomed, stored on a shelf for 50 years, and tossed away with artifacts that were made in 1650, but the cup and its associated objects could not predate 1600. In the Old World, pottery to commemorate coronations, births, or weddings was sometimes dated (or has likenesses of famous, historically datable people on it). One type of pottery with coin images in its decoration is found in Tunisia and is always associated with the local Roman period. This particular coin is known to have been issued between A.D. 238 and 244; the pottery cannot predate this range and likely the coin images were used when the coins were freshly minted, not decades later, and it's likely that the pots can be dated to around the same period. Finally, some Roman *amphorae* (jars or vases used to transport liquids such as wine and olive oil around the Roman world) have painted descriptions of their contents, the name of the shipper, and the date of the bottling on them. Finding a cache of amphorae at the bottom of the Mediterranean Sea dates the shipwreck as does finding them in a storehouse in France. This kind of direct signature dating is quite rare and has a limited geographic and temporal use.

Cross-Dating Ceramic stratification dating can be used to cross-date when the ceramics found in a new layer or site are very similar to another well-dated site. Another form of cross-dating dates the ceramics by use of nonceramic objects. This would occur, for example, if a cache of coins with dates printed on them were found inside a pot. This could be analogous to moderns stashing (dated) coins in piggy banks. The pot could not be later in date than the coins in it unless the coins were heirloomed, and the piggy bank is older than the oldest coins in it unless the coins were heirloomed. Heirloomed coins or not, the coins and pots are not likely to be too different in age and the coins thus cross-date the pot.

Seriation Dating *Seriation* is the name of a technique used to date different kinds of artifacts, but ceramic seriation has been the most frequently used variation since the "invention" of seriation in the late 1800s. Although there are several types of ceramic seriation, the two types that concern us are sequence seriation and frequency seriation; these seriation types are sometimes called similarity seriations. Both sequence and frequency seriations are based on the same principle: Things change over time. What this means is that styles of "things"–be they knobs on kitchen cabinets, lengths of skirts, or decorations on pots–have a beginning, a time of popularity, a decline, and a disappearance. As a simple example of this principle, one could seriate hemlines beginning in the late 1940s in the United States and use fashion photos in magazines as data to observe the change in hemline popularity through time. Using relative terms, hemlines can be thought of as being short (above the knee), medium (between the knee and midcalf), or long (below midcalf). Perhaps because people or the garment industry wanted to conserve cloth during the Second World War, skirts were fairly medium in length in the 1940s, with few being of either extreme. Then the "new look" came in, with its new fashion style of longer skirt lengths; it became popular and then it departed. In the late 1960s, short skirts (miniskirts) had the same style cycle. Since then, there have been less drastic changes in hemlines, but hem-length fashion trends continue to occur. Seriation of hemlines would show each individual style's change (short, medium, long) through time and each hemline would show its relative popularity to the other lengths at any given time as well. A hemline seriation might look like that in Figure 7.1. Figures are given in percentages by decade.

Figure 7.1 Hemline Seriation

Decade	Short	Medium	Long
1986–1996	30	30	40
1976–1986	40	50	10
1966–1976	60	35	5
1956–1966	30	35	35
1946–1956	15	25	60
1936–1946	10	80	10

(a) Variability of length

If 5-year periods between reports were used instead of 10-year reports, the seriation graph that follows would be smoother, but the principle would remain the same. Traditionally, seriation graphs depict trends that show observable patterns. Each of the three sets graphed below show a midline, with the frequency of each 10-year report showing on both sides of the line. One can compare across each time report or look at the change in each variable individually.

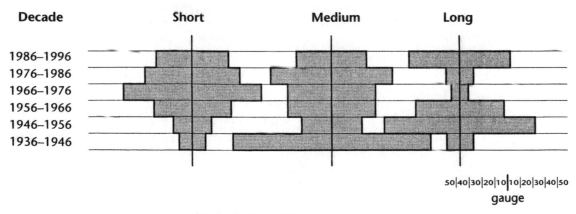

(b) Data from (a)

How seriation is involved in dating, using the hemline example, might go like this: You find an esoteric catalog of women's fashions but somehow the cover, which likely had the date of the catalog on it, has been ripped off, and for some reason this was the only date in the entire catalog. There is an unusual form of turban worn by some of the models in the catalog, a style of turban you've never seen before. As a fashion designer, you want to "revive" that turban and will undoubtedly be citing its previous history in your advertisements. But what was that elusive date? Knowing that the fashion industry keeps records of styles and that a seriation graph exists for hemlines at least, you decide to do a seriation of the hemlines in that esoteric catalog. After classifying each hemline relative to the three possible length variables, and finding a simple percentage for each, you come up with these figures: short 55%, medium 30%, long 15%. Using the graphs in Figure 7.1, what is the decade of your turban? If the hemline reports had been in increments less than 10 years, you might have been able to narrow the date down even further, but the principle remains the same: styles of things—in this case, hemlines—change through time as one style is invented, becomes popular, declines.

Many things can be seriated: lithic tools, for example, over a long period of time, are invented, become popular, and decline, to be replaced in popularity by another style while the first is declining. Parrot-beaked burins in France were unknown until Magdalenian II times, became popular during Magdalenian III, and all but disappeared by Magdalenian IV. Prehistoric French bone harpoons came in four types, each based on the number of barbs it has. All four types of harpoons were not invented at the same time, but rather changed through time as numerous small changes were made; one style did not replace earlier styles overnight, though as a class of weapon the harpoon changed through time from nubs to double barbs. Bone harpoons can be seriated from their beginning in Magdalenian IV for a period of several thousand years. An archaeologist finding a site with a number of parrot-beaked burins and harpoons could date that site by comparing the frequency of different kinds of burins and different styles of harpoons to the "master" seriation.

Recently, a seriation on various animal bones was done to try to date hominid (early human) remains in an undatable site in South Africa, where sites are notoriously difficult to date by conventional means. The investigator looked at the variability of 246 species of animal bones that were found in 17 south African sites, ordering the sites into oldest to youngest on the basis of the greatest similarities of specific animal bone frequencies. He assumed that the number of identified species in two sites that are close in age should be more similar than the identified species of sites further apart in age. This assumption is basic to seriation studies, whether the units being compared are ceramic pots or hemlines or species of animals. Once graphed, the undated site could be placed into a "best fit" spot in the graph. Because several of the sites could be dated by conventional means and the others given relative dates within that scheme, a provisional date was given to the hominid finds.

To test the statement that most anything can be seriated and to see just how it is done, I undertook a seriation project in the spring of 1996, on "English women's heel shapes." Realizing through observation that the shape of the heel on women's shoes is variable, I plunged into the project of observing and noting the shape of women's shoe heels (with the expectation of turning the notations of heel shapes into percentages when the project was concluded). Having worn shoes with different heel shapes in the past, I wrote down my observation of heel shapes without thinking about it very much: no heel, short and squat heel, high and squat heel, high wedgie heel, and high and narrow heel. Almost as if I were doing an intuitive typology of heel shapes (see Exercise 5 for this process), I later added attributes to each heel shape: for no heel, I wrote down "less than 1 inch high, no visible separation of heel and sole" and noted athletic shoes (with brand names such as Reebok, Nike), tennis shoes, some heelless sandals; for short and squat heel, I wrote down "had to be less than 1 inch high, had to be fairly straight-sided, and had to have a separation between the heel and the sole," noting moccasin-type shoes, oxford tie-up shoes, hiking shoes and boots, and some sandals. And so on. I made up new rules as I went along, as appropriate, though I did not change my classification of heel styles. When spring turned to summer and it was obvious that sandals were the shoe of choice because of the warm weather, I stopped my data gathering. When it was obvious that the women whose shoes I was seriating were not of European descent, I did not use them in the sample, though I am sure I inadvertently included many who were foreign. I also did not take data in parks or on university campuses, or functions that could have been biased by age, status, or activity. Nonetheless, it was only a convenience sample and it was taken for practice rather than for any scientific project. I sampled 1668 heel shapes; for posterity, the breakdown is as follows: type I (no heel), 19%; type II (short and squat heel), 29%; type III (high and squat heel), 21%; type IV (high wedgie heel), 8%; and type V (high and narrow heel), 22%.

What can I do with this 1996 seriation of heel shapes? Absolutely nothing. If I had had the foresight to know that I would be taking this sample in 1996, I would have begun the project in 1980, sampling every year or so. I can put the project aside and, in subsequent years, count heel shapes, coming to a conclusion about change in frequencies over time. On a personal note, although it is easier to do observations on feet than on eye color, for example, where people look back at the collector, I admit that I am tired of looking at feet and will not continue. I have learned, however, that one can seriate most anything, if one has the will and patience.

CERAMIC SERIATION

Using principles previously described, one finds that ceramics are a natural for seriation studies. People seldom have (or had) only one style of ceramics at a time, and even within whole categories of ceramics (bowls, for example), there are varieties that fit the popularity theme necessary for seriation. Within that category of bowls, any style of bowl may be in any stage of its seriation: rare because the style has just been invented; plentiful, at the peak of its popularity; or about to disappear because it is considered old-fashioned. A particular style of bowl may never become very popular relative to the other styles of bowls, but will always have a relative popularity with other bowls even if it is always low; it will have a beginning and an end as well, if one looks long enough for them.

There are two basic kinds of seriation: **sequence seriation** (sometimes called **contextual seriation**) and **frequency seriation.** Both types are based on the principle of similarities of material objects within and then between groupings of a general class of material objects and how these groups change through time. Recall the four-heel-shapes project: The class of object in this case is heel shape, but the variables are the individual shapes—flat, squat, wedgie, high, and so on. The presence of each shape has a history of being introduced, being popular, and declining, and the seriation is the tracking of the popularity of each shape. The names of the two types of seriation are of some help in differentiating them. In sequence (contextual) seriation, it is the presence (or absence) of a number of the variables that is used to seriate the entire class of objects. In frequency seriation, popularity (coming, in fashion, going out of style) is expressed in percentages of totals, which of course over time will increase and decrease. The hemline example and the heel-shape project are frequency seriations because the frequencies are expressed in numbers. The seriation of animal species in south African sites is a modern example of sequence seriation.

Sequence or Contextual Seriation

Sir Flinders Petrie literally invented what he called "sequence dating" in 1890. Petrie was the stereotypic British academic Egyptologist at what is now University College London (when he wasn't in Egypt). Petrie spent most of his professional life slogging away in the hot desert, digging, sorting, identifying pottery, but definitely not getting the headlines of Schliemann and his Troy. As a professional, rather than a pothunter, Petrie was as interested in the lowly sherd as he was in the whole pot. And he was the first to appreciate the use of pottery in dating prehistoric objects. What Petrie did—being concerned with the bead as much as the pyramid, the sherd as much as the urn—has become so commonplace in archaeology that it is hard to believe that his creativity almost 100 years ago was setting tradition.

In the 1890s, very little was known archaeologically about ancient Egypt, least of all the dates of Neolithic predynastic happenings. Once the Egyptians started using hieroglyphics and dates, king lists could be translated into the Western calendar, but the events of predynastic Egypt were a complete mystery in terms not only of calendar dates, but in terms of what happened in what order. Artifacts looted from tombs or sites, debris from what few "legal" excavations there were, tombs from the Valley of the Kings, and so forth—none had any chronology whatsoever.

Petrie spent four years (1899–1903) looking at royal cemeteries and tombs to gather data to accomplish his goal, which was to do a relative dating of all the prehistoric things into successive periods. If the tombs had had a stratigraphy, one on top of the other, there would have been at least some clues as to relative dates, but only a few tombs showed any superpositioning; the rare occurrences were used as a check on ordering. The contents of the tombs—the ceramics—provided the only real clue to ordering the tombs themselves. There were 27 cemeteries, 900 tombs, and 4000 graves in the tombs; there were ceramics as well as bodies, yet no way to date anything. But Petrie knew enough about Egyptian predynastic times to realize that although the tombs contained different pots, many of them were variations on themes and some seemed to occur together from one tomb to the next. In typing the huge collection of pots, knowing he would be using the sorted types as his way of chronologically ordering the materials in the tombs, he looked for unusual attributes, such as the shapes of handles on vases, from fully functioning wavy handles to globular handles to just wavy lines representing handles. He reasoned that, given the 917 different types of pots in what he referred to as the "corpus" or total assemblage, if one tomb contained, say, 15 different types of pots and another contained the same 15 types, they were likely to be the same age. He also reasoned that these 15 types did not emerge suddenly, but had a history of being invented, had some popularity for a while, and then disappeared. Putting this together in a chronologically challenged mind, he reasoned that if he found a tomb with 13 of those pots but 4 different ones as well, it was not exactly the same age as the other 2, but closer in time than a tomb with only 3 of those types. This scheme of matching types (not frequencies) of many different kinds of pots was the basis of his seriation scheme.

His system is complicated, but worth summarizing, as it was the birth of seriation dating. As Petrie excavated, he sorted pots by what we would now call an intuitive typology (see Exercise 5). Each type of pot was given a letter designation and all pots with this letter were very similar. In addition, when types could, on the basis of less similarity, be divided into subtypes, they were given numbers. A type might be designated as H and a subtype as H4. Every pot could be placed into this scheme. As he finished excavating each tomb and classifying the pottery in it, a tomb slip was made identifying the tomb and the pottery types found in it. All together, he ended up with 900 tomb slips, each representing the ceramic inventory of a single tomb. Using the principle previously described, he arranged all 900 tombs in chronological order. The details of ordering all 900 slips is not important to our discussion here. He of course did not know how old each tomb was even after seriating it, but he knew the tombs' relative order to each other, and that is the nature of relative chronology. Theoretically, a finished seriation has two end points, but it is not known which end is the beginning and which is the end in terms of earliest and latest. In Petrie's case, however, he knew enough about datable dynastic Egyptian pottery to be able to distinguish the early end from the late end. Because each tomb represented a one-time-only event, he assumed—and, it turns out, quite accurately—that by dating the ceramics and the tomb, he was dating an event. Everything in each tomb is dated as well: mummies, furniture, clothing. Almost 100 years later, archaeologists have concluded that Petrie was essentially correct in the ordering of the tombs.

The first use of sequence seriation in the New World was done by Alfred Kroeber in 1915 at a Zuñi pueblo in Arizona where he was working at that time. The ceramics he seriated were a surface collection, rather than from a sealed excavation layer, but he was able to do a sequence dating that was probably fairly short-lived. He collected over 2000 pieces of ceramics from 15 surface sites by enticing four of the children in the family he was staying with to pick up sherds for him. Others have done surface seriation with seeming success, but some archaeologists feel these collections might be biased by differential pothunting or trampling in modern times.

Frequency Seriation

Another kind of seriation is frequency seriation, first begun by W. S. Robinson and G. W. Brainerd in 1951, when they seriated Mayan ceramics by using the frequencies of different types of wares. Stratigraphy was a problem in this project and there was no method other than seriation to order the chronology of the ceramics.

Clear understanding of the principles of seriation have allowed archaeologists to do frequency seriation all over the world: Ecuador, Venezuela, Peru, Mexico, Guyana, and in the United States, Louisiana, the Ohio valley, and New Mexico, to name but a few locales. In addition, frequency seriation of flint artifacts and harpoon heads in the Arctic have been successful. The difference between Petrie's type of seriation and frequency seriation is that in frequency seriation, the actual frequencies are given and used in determining the beginning, the popularity, and the decline of the various types of items that are being seriated.

CONCLUSIONS

It may be old-fashioned to do seriation dating in an archaeological world that has so many high-tech dating techniques. But there are times when no other method is available. If done well, seriation dating is just as credible as stratigraphic dating because the weaknesses of each are independent of the other's. When done together, they have an additional advantage of validating each other. And in the presence of jumbled stratigraphy, seriation may be the only dating game in town.

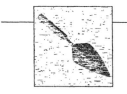

THE EXERCISES

The principles of seriation can be learned and understood intellectually by reading about Petrie's sequence seriation or about the more modern frequency seriation, but the best way to learn the principles is by actually *doing* seriation. Before beginning the exercises, remember that the value of seriation is to relatively date the material objects used in the seriation, in this case, ceramics. Seriation is not done to establish typologies (though the items to be seriated have to be sorted/typed).

OBJECTIVES

In these exercises, you will

- see how Petrie did his sequence seriation back when little was known about Egyptian archaeology and no dates had been established for any predynastic (prehieroglyphic) artifacts.
- order an already typed and counted group of ceramics by "best fit" seriation principles.
- do a seriation of ceramic sherds.

DOING THE EXERCISE

1. Paper Contextual Seriations:

a. Look at the drawings of drinking cups from Mycenae, Greece, in Figure 7.2. Note that they are all similar in basic design (each has a base, a stem, a body, a rim, and at least one handle), but you will also note there are differences in the details of these attributes. Instead of cutting up the pictures of the cups in the figure, take an enlarged copy of the "Mycenaean Cups" and move them around on the table, eventually placing them in proper order. While doing this, assume that there were changes in Mycenaean pottery during the 350 years of the late Bronze Age, but that the changes were gradual and not abrupt. Order the pots to maximize gradual change and to minimize abrupt change. In the spaces provided in Figure 7.2, write the order of the proper sequence; then write your justification for your ordering, particularly justifying the beginning and the end. What traits were most important?

Figure 7.2 Drinking Cups from Mycenae

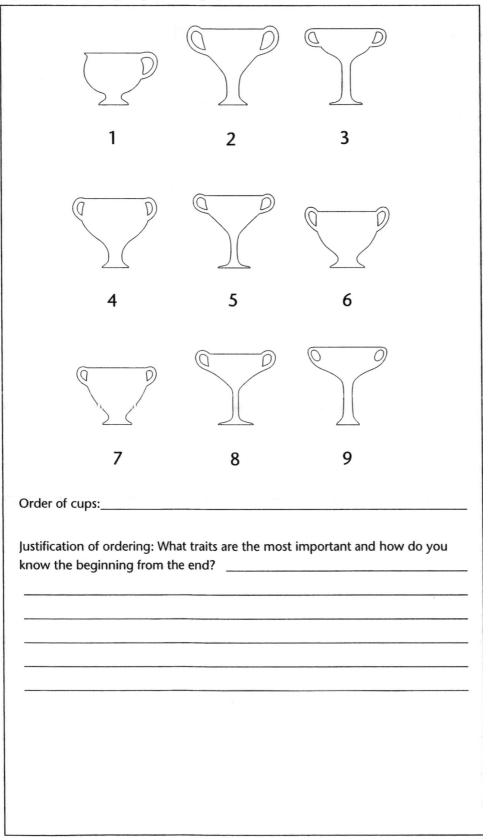

Order of cups:_____

Justification of ordering: What traits are the most important and how do you
know the beginning from the end? _____

_____

_____

_____

_____

_____

Figure 7.3 Petrie's Predynastic Egyptian Pottery Types

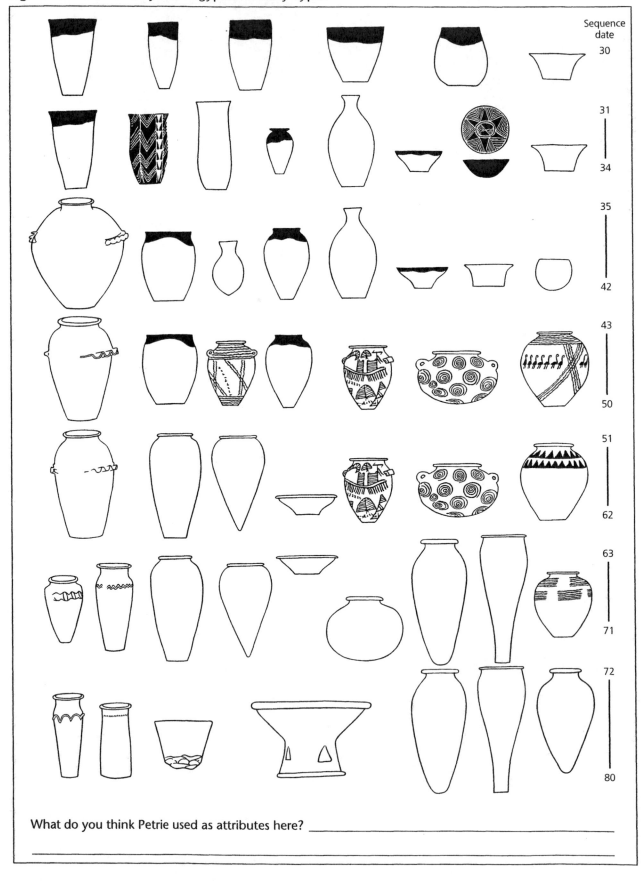

What do you think Petrie used as attributes here? _____

_____

b. Having used one principle—the principle of similarity/difference—now look at a much more complex group of pots: part of Petrie's predynastic Egyptian pottery types, as shown in Figure 7.3. There were always a great number of *types* of pots in each tomb that often appeared together (we would say today that they co-varied, but archaeologists did not speak statistics in 1903). (Remember that Petrie was not concerned with the *number* of pots in each type.) Petrie classified 917 types of predynastic pots, 765 of which he referred to as "common types." The 765 were grouped by him on the basis of similarity into 9 "forms," and he gave a name to each, such as "black-topped pottery" (163 types); "polished red" (135 types), "wavy-handled" (30 types), and so on. Figure 7.3 shows 52 of those types. "Black-topped" includes the first five pots (from the left) in the top row; "polished red" includes the third and fifth pots from the left in the second row; "wavy-handled" types can be seen as the first pots in rows 3 and 4. See if you can see other black-topped, polished red, and wavy handled pots in lower rows, as there are examples of each type in these rows. The beginning of the seriation is at the top, the first row showing one of each type of pot in a particular tomb; the second group of pots was seriated by Petrie as coming after the pots in the first row, and so on down the rows until you get to the last (bottom) row that represents the ceramics in the last dated tomb. The sequence dates given at the right on the figure are Petrie's subsequent ordering plans and need not concern us.

Look at Figure 7.3 and see if you can determine what attributes Petrie used to order the series of pots as he did. Remember that each row represents a tomb. Look at the top row that shows 5 black-topped pots and one polished red pot, and the second row that has black-topped pots, three polished red pots, and one cross-lined pot. Draw a line between the pots in the first two rows that more or less "match"; give the well-matched pots a heavier line than the moderately matched ones. Then look at the pots in rows 2 and 3 and, using the same principle, draw lines between those pots that match. Finish the seriation via lines between every two rows; some rows will have multiple lines; some will have only one. Some pots may have multiple lines from previous rows. If you look at the pots in the first and last row, you will note there are few similarities beyond all having a base and a body. Pots in row 1 have no rims and all pots in the last row have rims. Did you catch that? In the space provided on Figure 7.3, write what you think Petrie used as attributes of similarity and difference in making this seriation.

2. Paper Frequency Seriations:

a. Pots or sherds must first be typed to do frequency seriations. When doing seriation typing, it is important not to type too finely or the data will not seriate; however, if archaeologists sort the material objects into only two types, it will also be difficult to seriate the results. Most archaeologists sort into three to five types for seriation purposes. Figure 7.4 (*a*) gives an unseriated set of frequencies for three types of pots from eight different rooms in Pueblo Eberzo in New Mexico. We know that not all rooms in a pueblo were used at the same time—some rooms were abandoned or just not used for long periods of time; some rooms were also added on. We want to know when each room in that pueblo was used. The ceramics for this seriation were sorted into three types based on their similarities and differences. The sample was sufficiently large to warrant confidence that there is a representative sample of each of the eight units to seriate (each of the eight rooms is treated as a unit). The archaeologist counted the number of pots of each type, used a slip of paper with the midline drawn for each of the three types, drew in the frequency percentage of each type, and did a "best fit" seriation. Note the use of the gauge in showing the percentages of each type. Figure 7.4 (*a*) shows the unseriated frequencies and (*b*) shows the best fit of the eight slips of paper. Note the battleship shape for each type. What if a ninth room was suddenly excavated? Could you, the archaeologist in charge of this new excavation, "fit" the ceramic popularity of the three types you sorted and counted into the now-existing seriation and thereby date the ceramics in that new room? Use a slip of paper provided and decide where it best fits into the existing seriation. Using an arrow, draw where it fits on Figure 7.4 (*a*). Remember that although we were able to seriate and find the best-fit order, either 1 or 8 on (*b*) could be the oldest.

b. Do a paper seriation with the data in Figure 7.5 (*a*). You are an archaeologist working at a late Neolithic site in Turkey, where there is a lot of pottery. Because the local government forced you to use local untrained labor much of the time, during excavation of the site the excavators worked without supervision as the archaeologists were called away for long periods to justify the excavation's importance to the local politicos. As a result, at the end of the excavation you have a lot of pottery sherds and no provenience for most of them. The late Neolithic in Turkey is not well known and you need to date the layers in the site to tie the events to the early Neolithic, which is well known in Turkey through classic sites such as Çatal Hüyük and Çayönü. Seriation of the ceramics seems to be the only solution and you may be able to match the beginning of the seriation with the early Neolithic sites and the end of the seriation with early metalworking sites in the area. The archaeologist in charge typed the ceramics into four groups and then counted the sherds. The units to seriate (listed as layers G, P, N, F, Q) are the five piles where the untrained workers dumped the ceramics. You have some confidence that one pile equals one layer in the excavation. Note that the layers—the five piles—are given nonconsecutive labels because the order is not known. Also note that some types are much more common than others.

Use the partially completed chart on Figure 7.5 (*b*) and get five slips of paper. Then draw the center marks for each of the four types following the model on Figure 7.4 (*b*). Using the gauge on Figure 7.4 (*a*), draw the appropriate percentages for each type on each slip. Now arrange the slips in a best-fit graph, remembering the principle of the battleship shape. Tape them on Figure 7.5 (*b*) in the space provided.

3.   You are now ready to do a seriation from typing to ordering, and on real sherds. Use five "Utah Seriation" boxes. In this exercise, the sherds in the five boxes are from the surface of five sites in Utah (see Figure 7.6). They are geographically within a kilometer of each other and seem to be the top debris of five villages. The pottery as a total assemblage resembles Anasazi pottery in other parts of the southwest desert, where the cultural period dates from A.D. 1 to 1300. You want to know the relative chronology of these villages because you have the funds to excavate only one of them below the surface. Because the early Anasazi period and where the makers of Anasazi pottery came from are still questions not properly answered, you want to excavate the earliest of the five villages. But which one is it? A fairly inexpensive (and not overly time-consuming) way to find out is to seriate the surface finds you already have. To do this seriation:

Figure 7.4 Pueblo Pottery (Unseriated and Seriated). Figures are given in percentages.

Room	Type 1	Type 2	Type 3
1	32	30	38
2	26	40	34
3	20	50	30
4	15	60	25
5	30	50	20
6	35	50	15
7	40	45	15
8	60	30	10

(a) Pueblo pots (unseriated)

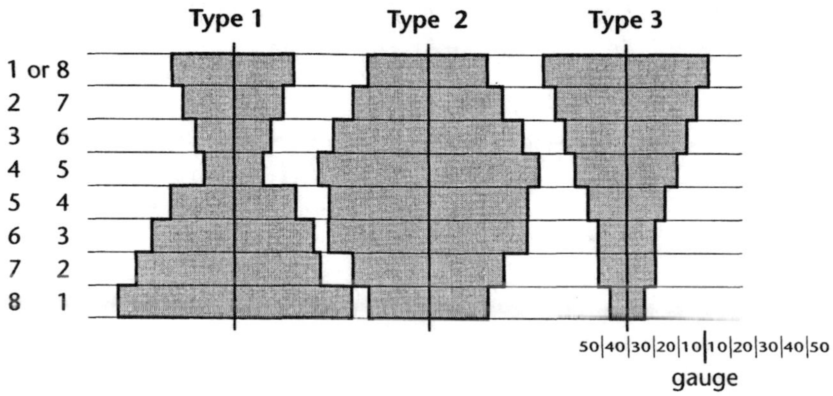

(b) Pueblo pots (seriated)

Figure 7.5 Turkish Ceramics (Unseriated and Seriated) Figures are given in percentages.

Layer	Type 1	Type 2	Type 3	Type 4
G	75	0	20	5
P	50	0	45	5
N	40	40	00	20
F	75	5	15	5
Q	75	20	0	5

(a) Turkish ceramics (unseriated)

Layer	Type 1	Type 2	Type 3	Type 4
5				
4				
3				
2				
1				

50|40|30|20|10|10|20|30|40|50
gauge

(b) Turkish ceramics (seriated)

Figure 7.6 Utah Seriation

Villages

5

4

3

2

1

50|40|30|20|10|10|20|30|40|50
gauge

a. Lay out the sherds in the first box you pick and decide how to sort them. Remember that you are doing a typology only for the purpose of the seriation of this collection in the five boxes (the assemblage); do not oversort into too many types, yet sort finely enough to make your seriation work. You should have three to five types. Use the principles of similarity/difference to make your typology decision and use attributes appropriate to sherds rather than to whole pots. You must use the same typology throughout this seriation. You cannot use size; rim shape would be unusable, as you may have no rim pieces; and assumed function would also be difficult to determine on the basis of only sherds. Use obvious sherd attributes such as color, overall decoration, and paste qualities (thick, thin). Once this unit (in the one box) is sorted, get five slips of paper, one for each village. On one side of the slip, label your unit with an appropriate name or number (it is arbitrary, just as it was arbitrary which box you chose to seriate first). Make the appropriate number of midlines down the slip. Regardless of how many types you are working with, be sure to keep your types in consistent sequence and space across the slips or you can't seriate. Count the number of sherds in each type and, using the frequency-width gauge in Figure 7.4 (*a*), mark in the frequency "band" for each of your types for this unit on the slip of paper. Return all sherds to that first box. Do not mix up sherds in separate boxes.

b. Lay out the sherds from a second box in the series. Do the same thing as in the preceding, using the typology that was established. Continue for the rest of the boxes. You now have five lettered slips, each giving the frequency of ceramic types from one surface collection of one village.

c. Seriate your slips relative to their frequencies, doing a best-fit, battleship-shaped seriation. Tape them in the appropriate spot on Figure 7.6, matching midlines and villages.

☐ **Check with your lab manager for full credit.**

KEY WORDS

relative

absolute

chronometric

law of stratigraphy

law of gravity

law of uniformitarianism

ceramic dating

seriation dating: sequence or contextual

frequency seriation

FOR FURTHER READING

Brainerd, G. W. "The Place of Chronological Ordering in Archaeological Analysis." *American Antiquity* 16 (1951):301–13.
Dethlefsen, Edwin, and James Deetz. "Death's Heads, Cherubs, and Willow Trees: Experimental Archaeology in Colonial Cemeteries." *American Antiquity* 31 (1966):502–10.

Kroeber, Alfred L. "Zuñi Potsherds." Anthropological papers of the American Museum of Natural History 18, no. 1 (1916):7–37.

Marquardt, William. "Advances in Archaeological Seriation." In *Archaeological Method and Theory* (1), edited by Michael Schiffer. New York: Academic Press, 1978.

Petrie, W. M. F. *The Cemeteries of Abadiyeh and Hu*. London: The Egyptian Exploration Fund, 1901.

Robinson, W. S. "A Method for Chronologically Ordering Archaeological Deposits." *American Antiquity* 16 (1951):293–301.

Environmental Reconstruction: Paleoflora

ENVIRONMENTAL RECONSTRUCTION

This is one of several exercises concerning how archaeologists attempt to reconstruct environments in the past. This interdisciplinary study is referred to as "**paleoenvironmental** reconstruction," and it involves the disciplines of biology, ecology, geology, paleontology, geography, and of course, archaeology. From the archaeologist's perspective, the aim of paleoenvironmental reconstruction is to be able to infer environmental contexts for cultural (archaeological) events. The importance of environmental reconstruction is discussed in more detail in Exercise 10. Paleofloral analysis—literally, the analysis of old plant remains and the focus of this exercise—is an important part of the larger field of environmental reconstruction.

INTRODUCTION TO POLLEN ANALYSIS

In 1992, an almost entire skeleton, complete with skin and the clothing of a 5200-year-old Neolithic man, was found on the Austrian/Italian border in the Alps, a probable victim of cold weather. Since his discovery, archaeologists have been instrumental in describing his cultural remains, from his tattoos to the tools he carried. In addition, paleoenvironmentalists have begun the long-range work of attempting to reconstruct the environmental context in which the "Ice Man" lived. Only when we know the larger environmental context can we properly assess the man's clothing, tools, and tattoos. Did he stuff grass in his boots for comfort in walking or to prevent frostbite? Was his clothing warm enough for the altitude he was walking in when he died, or was he a victim of a sudden storm? Do the remains in his intestines suggest a diet that was sufficient to sustain mountain life typical of a stock breeder, or was he a valley farmer who got caught in a freak storm up in the mountains as he was crossing to visit relatives? The "Ice Man" continues to be a cultural question in search of an environmental context.

Twenty years ago, based on the research of Arlette Leroi-Gourhan, Ralph Solecki astounded the world by telling us that Neandertals, at least in the Middle East, not only buried their dead, but buried them with what appears to be a very modern (and Western) touch: flowers placed on the graves. Based on the species of **pollen**—bachelor's buttons, hollyhocks, grape hyacinths, among a total of eight species—Leroi-Gourhan suggested that burials were in the spring when these flowers were in bloom (and the soil, even in a cave, was not frozen).

Because the pollen remains of the flowers were thickest around the head of the deceased male from Shanidar (Iraq), she also suggested that garlands of flowers were placed around his head. As the flowers did not grow inside the cave where the man was buried, it seems sensible to assume the flowers were part of an organized burial. How did Leroi-Gourhan determine what species the flowers were, as they would have totally biodegraded since then?

Why did people begin to farm when, from all that we can discover, foraging was a less time-consuming and more predictable way to get food? Hunter-gatherers today spend only a few hours a day collecting berries, nuts, and tubers and hunting large and small game, whereas farmers normally spend eight hours a day clearing land, planting crops, keeping wild animals (and people) away, and harvesting. If a climatically bad year dries up a group's favorite supply of nuts, foragers go to second-choice foods and seldom starve; by contrast, if a farmer loses the entire crop because of drought, it is likely that everyone within miles is affected the same way, and many people may starve. So the question is, Why would people farm? If we knew what they farmed, how long it took for the whole process of domestication to take place, and whether animals were involved in initial domestication or were an afterthought, then we might know more about that elusive question, particularly when it appears so sensible for them to have remained foragers. Did the environment change, as many experts believe, "forcing" people to take up farming in order for everyone to get enough to eat? Here is another cultural question in need of an environmental context.

When we hear the phrase "Ice Age art," what do we usually conjure up? Do we think of Europe as being in some sort of a deep freeze, with tundra covering a huge expanse of barren ground, with only a few scrubby trees and howling winds? Do we see artists going deep into caves to stay warm and taking up painting the cave walls out of boredom? You might be surprised to know that scientists have recently determined that the Ice Age was not so icy after all, and that between 20,000 and 15,000 years ago, Europe was in a deep freeze for only part of the time, having periods of relatively temperate climate, with pine and birch forests and lush summer meadows during other times. And because the insides of caves were very cold, damp, and housed cave bears, people were better off living outside (except for the month of January), perhaps at the lips of caves where they probably hung animal hides to keep out the draft, or under cliff overhangs, or even out in the open in hide tents. Experts believe the insides of caves were used for special events rather than as housing; here, people painted and engraved the animals they saw, hunted, and ate. Add this to the list of cultural questions with an environmental context.

What do the "Ice Man," Neandertal burials, the first animal and plant domestication, and Ice Age art have in common? Obviously, they all are part of environmental archaeology, as they all involve the reconstruction of paleoenvironment to facilitate the understanding of the cultural events the archaeologist finds of prime importance. In addition, they all specifically involve using pollen and its analysis to do the reconstruction of past environment. It is the pollen in the soil surrounding the "Ice Man" that will provide clues to the climate of the Neolithic Alps; it was the pollen around the Shanidar Neandertal that suggested what eight species of wild flowers were used as "funeral" flowers; it is weed pollen more often than pollen from domestic plants—which produce little pollen and are usually self-pollinating anyway—that informs us of initial domestication because weeds can find a place to sprout and grow only after humans have cleared the land for crop planting; and it was recent pollen analysis of ice-age France that changed the image of our prehistoric ancestors from one of stalking large game in the barren, frozen, treeless tundra, to that of hunting large herbivores, such as reindeer or horses, in open woodlands and meadows. Our focus in this exercise is pollen, its analysis, and its use in reconstructing paleoenvironment in order to put the cultural picture into an environmental frame.

What Is Pollen?

As any sufferer of hay fever can attest, pollen is microscopic and often airborne. What most do not know is that pollen is the male sexual reproductive element, born on structures called anthers that, when ripened in the spring or summer on a warm and dry day, can be dispersed by the wind and become part of the "pollen rain." If the pollen lands on the female sexual organ of the species (called the pistil), fertilization occurs, and seeds are produced. But fertilization is a fairly rare event; more often, pollen falls to the ground, where it becomes part of the soil and ultimately concentrated in stratified layers considerably below the original land surface on which it first landed. Pollen, as any organic material, would quickly biodegrade except that the outer shell of the pollen (the exine) is very resistant to biodegradation and survives for thousands of years. The shedding of pollen usually goes unnoticed by all but biologists or hay fever sufferers, usually occurring just before a tree's foliage develops in the early spring.

Pollen does not directly tell us specific information about paleoenvironment. Rather, scientists infer climatic change through data that suggest vegetational change through time; vegetation (trees, shrubs, plants) depends on climate (sunlight, rainfall, and temperature) for survival and is therefore a sensitive barometer of climatic change. Some types of vegetation react relatively quickly to climatic change, as was the case during the Ice Age, which we now know had several periods of intense cold each followed by a period of relatively warm climate. Because variation in rainfall or temperature can cause vegetation to change, scientists can look at evidence of change in "paleovegetation" to infer change in environment. By vegetation change, scientists are referring to either a change in dominance of one species of tree over another that might indicate a change to colder or wetter conditions, or to a change in the range of a species that might indicate similar kinds of change. If the climate becomes colder and a particular species of tree does better in a colder climate, the range of the species might be extended for hundreds of miles in a short period of time.

Both macro- and microbotanical fossils can be used to infer aspects of climate. Seeds, stems, and leaves are all macro plant parts, but unfortunately they fossilize only under very special conditions, such as extreme aridity, waterlogging, or carbonization (see Exercise 12 for more information on macro plant remains). Micro floral remains (pollen, spores, and phytoliths), however, can be longer lived. Because of a number of constraints (to be discussed shortly), pollen analysis can never give us a true and accurate picture of paleoenvironment. Instead, we have to be content with inferences about climatic change, which is the best approximation possible, given the nature of our data and the inherent constraints of the analysis. However, most experts agree that an analysis of pollen is probably the best single indicator of paleoenvironment for archaeological contexts. It is as simple (and as difficult) as this: *Pollen percentages that fluctuate through time indicate a corresponding fluctuation in environmental conditions.* Therefore, through pollen analysis, we can infer temperature, humidity (rainfall or moisture), and ground cover for specific time periods, as we are able to infer change in those environmental factors through time.

A Brief History of Pollen Analysis

Until 20 or so years ago, with some exceptions, archaeologists paid little attention to any nonartifact materials; they simply were not interested in anything except cultural materials. Animal bones, soils, and the pollen in soils were just tossed onto the back dirt and forgotten. Until the contextual importance of environment was realized, palynologists—experts in pollen identification and analysis—worked more as biologists than as archaeobotanists. Recently, this picture has changed, and now archaeologists depend on palynologists to help provide what they now realize is so vital to archaeology: reconstructing the environmental context of their cultural findings. Even if archaeologists don't actually do the pollen analysis themselves, they must understand the technique, the constraints, and the inferences made by those who do.

Modern **palynology** began in Sweden in 1916 with the pioneering work of Lennart von Post. Although his original work was on the forest trees in Sweden, pollen analysis was eventually extended to all pollen-liberating vegetation in Europe and, somewhat later—in the late 1920s—in North America. We now have, for example, a pollen core from eastern France (Grand Pile) that contains environmental information spanning the last 130,000 years. Recent work in Africa (Burundi) from 356 sites representing the past 40,000 years has recently been completed; it is the first continuous paleotemperature record ever reconstructed for the tropics, and it indicates that the climate was 30% wetter in this part of Africa 40,000 years ago than it is today.

Palynology was initially used by a few archaeologists in cross-dating before radiometric methods, such as 14C, were available. For example, a vertical column of soil in an excavation might show that domestication occurred in that area because of the presence of initial weed pollen in a certain part of the column; the domestication layer could then be dated using data from other sites where documentation dates are known by 14C.

But since 1950, palynology in archaeology has been mostly used to help reconstruct paleoenvironments. Multivariate analysis is currently providing a new methodological tool to attempt quantitative estimates of how cold or how wet it was at certain times and places that mirror modern climatological proxies. A great deal has yet to be learned about pollen analysis, but enough has been firmly established to make it the prime tool of environmental reconstruction.

The Technique of Pollen Analysis

The technique occurs in three locations: in the field, in the lab, and in the office. In all of these work places, knowledge, skill, and patience are required. In the field, uncontaminated samples of pollen must be collected from sediment, soil, or rock. In general, any pollen in pre-Quaternary deposits (before 1.8 million years ago) is generally in rock and has to be broken up to be released; post-Quaternary pollen generally resides in sediment and peat and is usually easier to extract.

When attempting environmental reconstruction (as opposed to reconstructing diet, for example), archaeologists have decided that it is better to do sampling a short distance away from sites rather than from inside archaeology sites, as humans can contaminate sites by bringing in pollen on their feet (shoes) or by bringing in pollinating tree limbs for some purpose. In addition, nomadic prehistoric habitation sites were often rock shelters or cave lips, and in both cases, windblown pollen, which is quirky, does not correctly represent the environment of the immediate area. So that environmental conditions are represented as they existed in the past, sites are sampled nearby the human sites that are being put into environmental context, but not so close as to be contaminated. Because it is difficult to assess which area best represents the environment accurately, many archaeologists sample a number of nearby sites and average the results.

Soil or sediment samples that contain pollen must be carefully collected; because the samples are small (a full matchbox is sufficient), the person doing the sampling must be sure not to smear the sampling trowel down the column of soil or the sample will reflect an incorrect pollen event. It is preferable to cut into the column, with the surface end then disposed of, leaving a clean and representative soil sample for the layer. Once the samples are collected, the first phase of laboratory work begins. The aim of this lab work is to separate the pollen from the soil, remove the extraneous matter, concentrate the pollen grains, make them as visible as possible, and mount them on a glass slide for counting. Some methods take up to seven months; others less than a day. The process begins by dissolving the soil sample in water. Through the alternation of acid baths and centrifugation, nonpollen materials are removed and the pollen condensed down to an eyedropper of concentrated pollen. One drop on a prepared slide, covered and sealed, is representative of the pollen spectrum in the sample; however, the palynologist will usually make as many slides as there are drops in the concentration in case a question of bias comes up.

There is no standardized direction for viewing pollen under a microscope; however, the viewer must be certain not to count the same pollen grain more than once as the slide is traversed. Master sheets, with expected pollen species noted, are used for counting. Figure 8.1 shows a typical "master pollen count sheet." Scientists also differ as to how many grains of pollen they believe must be counted before there is a statistically reliable number: The figure 200 seems to satisfy most, though rare pollen will have a lesser chance of being recognized if the analyst stops after 200 grains. The raw figures are then converted to percentages of the total sample. Identifying pollen under the microscope is often tiresome and not easy, but some of the more common pollen grains can be identified once the diagnostic morphological traits are learned. A master chart of pollen diagrams is always available for reference and consulted when rare species show up. One expert predicts that an automated SEM (Scanning Electron Microscope) technique will soon be able to identify pollen grains through shape and texture, eventually replacing the slow manual counts and identifications.

One sample of pollen will not tell an archaeologist very much because it represents but one cultural point in time, and it is the *change* in flora that allows us to infer climate. The counting of pollen grains from slides for the entire stratigraphy of a site results in a **stratigraphic pollen diagram;** each stratified layer from the earliest to the latest layer will be sampled. This is the main analytical tool for the reconstruction of environment through time because it records change. Therefore, an archaeologist will always start the diagram by using modern pollen frequencies and go back into the past. The pollen diagram may include only arboreal pollen (AP) that is wind driven and that represents trees only, or it may include both AP and NAP (nonarboreal pollen, such as shrubs and grasses). The use of both AP and NAP is helpful in separating tundra—where there are few if any trees—from taiga and temperate climates.

Figure 8.1 Master Pollen Count Sheet and Conversions (Typical)

Master Pollen Count Sheet

Oak (AP)	Pine (AP)	Birch (AP)	Grass (NAP)
ⵂⵂ ⵂⵂ ⵂⵂ ⵂⵂ ⵂⵂ ⵂⵂ ⵂⵂ ‖	ⵂⵂ ⵂⵂ ⵂⵂ ⵂⵂ ⵂⵂ ⵂⵂ ⵂⵂ ⵂⵂ ⵂⵂ ⵂⵂ ⵂⵂ ⵂⵂ ⵂⵂ ⵂⵂ ‖‖	ⵂⵂ ⵂⵂ ⵂⵂ ⵂⵂ ⵂⵂ ⵂⵂ ⵂⵂ ⵂⵂ ⵂⵂ ⵂⵂ ⵂⵂ ‖‖	ⵂⵂ ⵂⵂ ⵂⵂ ⵂⵂ ‖‖‖

Conversion Indices

Species	Total Grains	Conversion Value		Number of Grains	Conversion Grains	% of Total
Oak	31	.44	x	31	16.3	19%
Pine	69	.55	x	69	38	44%
Birch	58	.55	x	58	32	37%
Grass	24					
Total grains:	188			Total	86.3	

Figure 8.2 shows a hypothetical pollen diagram from a single, stratified site representing 10,000 years of time. The diagram shows the relative proportion of different species of arboreal pollen (AP) on the left, and the proportion of arboreal versus nonarboreal pollen (NAP) on the right. The species of arboreal trees (with common names) are indicated on the top of the diagram above their respective columns. The small "+" means that the species are present but in small amounts. Relative pollen proportions for individual layers (strata) of the eight-layered site were plotted, and points were vertically connected for each pollen species to show change in frequency through time. Note that as hazel (a "warm-loving" shrub/tree) increases in prevalence over time, pine and birch ("cold-loving" trees) decrease, and when hazel decreases, pine and birch increase.

Analysis of the diagram now begins, and so does the real work. As in other historical sciences, the principle of uniformitarianism is invoked: An assumption is made that the special requirements of certain plant species that exist today also existed in the past; to assume otherwise would be to deny use of any paleo-data. If magnolia trees today cannot survive in climates where the winter temperatures go below zero, then the same is assumed to have been true in the past. Therefore, pollen analysts must have a good working knowledge of the specific tolerances, growing requirements, and preferences of contemporary trees and shrubs, grass, and herbs. Some plants reflect very specific climatic conditions because they have very narrow requirements, such as ivy, for example; other plants are more tolerant and reflect more general environmental conditions, such as birch and pine trees.

Figure 8.2 Stratigraphic Pollen Diagram for Hypothetical Site

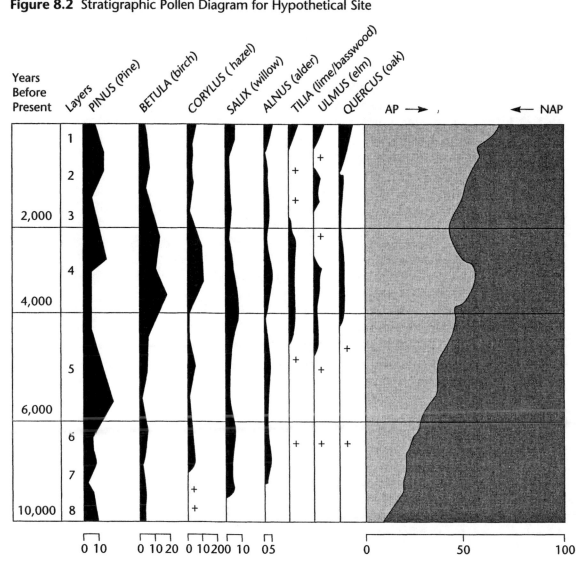

Constraints of Pollen Analysis

Palynology tells us about paleovegetation, but the data have to be interpreted in order for them to be used in environmental reconstruction. How accurate are pollen slides (samples) in terms of a true environmental picture of the past? In general—and with constraints—experts conclude that pollen analysis does reflect paleoenvironment. But the following constraints are worth discussing:

- With a regular translucent (slide) microscope, most pollen cannot be identified at the subspecies or species level because its morphologies do not differ enough; SEM can often identify what regular microscopes cannot because they allow us to "see" the surface pattern of pollen. Although most pollen can be identified at the genus level, a few (such as grass) can only be identified at the family taxonomic level. This can be unfortunate, as some species differ

within their genus in terms of preference and tolerance, and it would be helpful to be able to use this information. It is not necessary, however, to know the
species of pine in order to know if the climate was warm or cold at a particular time, as all species of pine have the same general requirements and tolerance and give the same general climatic information.

• Although worms can cause pollen to move downward in soils, it is believed
that worm action is generally confined to the upper 4–6 inches of the soil.
Soils compact due to pressures from new soils and gravity, with bottom levels
not being susceptible to the action of worms. Once compacted, the pollen
horizon does not appear to change, thus keeping the relative sequence intact.

• Pollen can "fly" thousands of kilometers, limiting the reconstruction of local
environment. There are wonderful accounts of windblown pollen being found
in Greenland, Antarctica, and in the middle of the Atlantic Ocean (in a vacuum cleaner bag), where there are no trees. Light and small pollen can travel
up to 55 meters from its parent tree and heavier and larger pollen only 2
meters; 100 kilometers is the maximum limit of most pollen, with 50 kilometers a more likely distance, and straight to the ground the most likely route.
The sheer quantity of locally produced pollen overwhelms the amount of fly-
ing pollen, making long-distance pollen travelers relatively insignificant. Doing
multiple samples and averaging them eliminates most of these problems.

• Because trees produce different amounts of pollen, there is not a 1 to 1 representation in the pollen record: one pollen grain does not equal one tree. This
is a correct statement in that the manner of dispersal and differentially produced pollen do affect the relative amounts of pollen in a sample; however,
palynologists are cognizant of this problem and convert raw pollen figures to
relatively representative figures. There is an inherent bias in pollen samples
due both to differential pollen production by species and different dispersal
mechanisms. Pollen that is insect-dispersed is underrepresented in the pollen
record relative to pollen that is wind-dispersed because insect-dispersed
pollen remains fixed on plants until the proper species of insect comes along
and behaves correctly. Wind-pollinated trees, by contrast, are overrepresented
in the pollen record because most of the pollen ends up on the ground under
the tree or shrub that shed it, where some of it will become embedded in the
soil. Relatively speaking, even if insect- and wind-pollinated trees produced
the same amount of pollen, more wind-dispersed pollen than insect-dispersed
pollen would end up in a sample.

It is also true that some plant species simply produce more pollen than others. In terms of known frequencies of various species of trees in a specific area,
pine, for example, is likely to be overrepresented; spruce is relatively properly
represented; maple is underrepresented; and larch is very rarely represented in
the pollen sample because it does not produce much pollen. An example of differential pollen production is the estimate that a single anther (male sexual
organ) of pine can produce 70,000 grains of pollen a year, whereas insect-polli-
nated trees produce 1000 or less grains per anther.

If pollen analysis is to be used to reconstruct regional environmental conditions, palynologists must compensate for these distortions in their analyses by
use of conversion indices (Table 8.1). Two indices used currently are based on
pollen in northern Europe. The indices are overly simplified and a palynologist
would include factors such as the age and health of the trees when compensat-
ing for distortions, but they are combined here and modified and will suit our

Table 8.1   Pollen Conversion Index

Birch, alder, and pine	Multiply by 0.55
Oak	Multiply by 0.44
Basswood (lime), willow, maple	Multiply by 2.00
Beech, ash, fir	Multiply by 1.00
Elm and spruce	Multiply by 1.75

Source: Adapted from *Textbook of Pollen Analysis,* 4th ed. (Faegri, Ekland, and Krzywinski); *Quaternary Paleoclimatology* (Bradley 1985).

purposes (Faegri, Ekland, and Krzywinski 1989; Bradley 1985). Note that these are all aboreal (tree) pollen grains. Grass, including weeds, is a nonarboreal pollen, but because it tolerates all varieties of temperate and tropical climates, it indicates a lack of extremes such as arctic and desert probably more than it indicates climatic preferences.

The Pollen "Er Curve"

Using present-day tree tolerances and preferences, and the relative frequencies (given in percentages) of pollen as are found in particular layers of soil, the variables of temperature, rainfall, and ground cover can be inferred and plotted as a vertical graph. Figure 8.3 gives an example. (See Exercise 10 for a fuller description of the "er curve," which is slang for a relative gradient.) The **pollen "er curve"** (warm*er*, cold*er*, wett*er*, [dri*er*]; more or less forest/grass) is only as accurate as the data it is based on and on the interpretation of the data, but because it is an "er curve" and not a definitive statement about "how cold," "how dry," or "how many trees," it is likely to correctly reflect the environment being reconstructed. Remember that it is but one indicator, and its verification depends on other indicators, data, and techniques.

Figure 8.3 Pollen "Er Curve" for Hypothetical Site

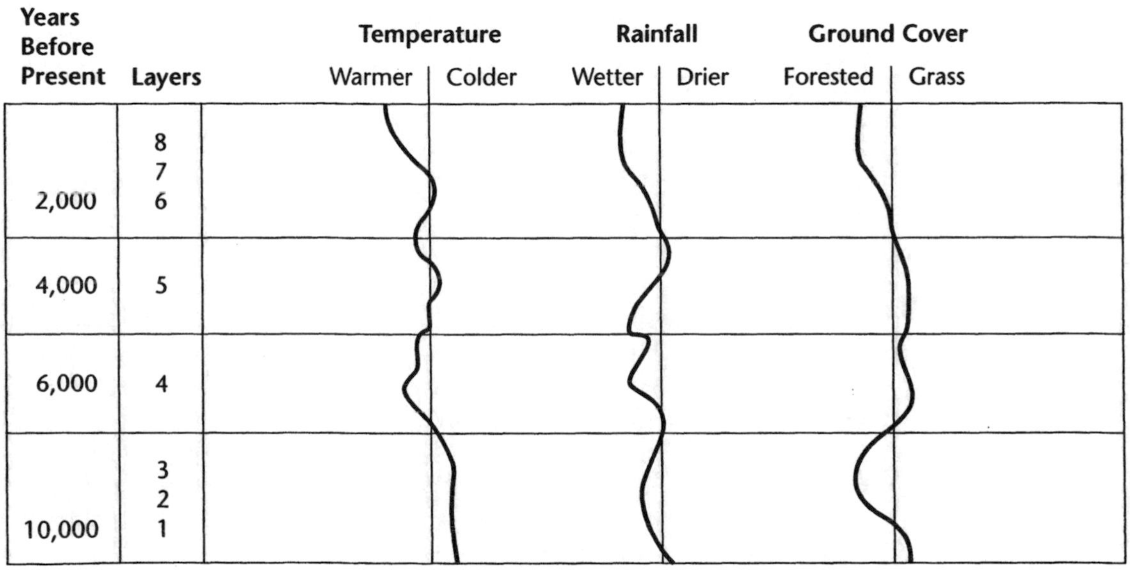

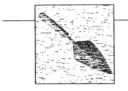

THE EXERCISE

(Note: If you have never used a slide microscope before, please get instructions from your lab manager so you know what you are looking at and don't smash the pollen slides.) In this exercise, you will play the role of a palynology-trained archaeologist concerned with reconstructing the environment of a 12,000 to 8000-year-old Native American–stratified site in upstate New York. At the beginning of the time period under analysis (12,000 years ago), the landscape would have looked quite different from today's landscape, as North America was still under the rigors of a major phase of the last Ice Age; there would be few if any trees. Later, birch and pine trees would colonize from the south, to be replaced by mixed forests of oak, beech, and alder. The stratified sequence would show these changes in pollen frequencies that in turn would be used to infer climatic changes. In your role, you will begin with the raw data and finish by inferring the environment 12,000 years ago in upstate New York. Then you will have an environmental context in which to reconstruct the life of the Native Americans who left their cultural debris behind.

OBJECTIVES

In this exercise, you will

- learn to identify certain species of pollen.
- identify and count pollen grains on an already prepared slide.
- do a paleospectrum by figuring percentages of pollen (you may not have time to observe and count 200 grains in 30 minutes, but you will learn how this step is done).
- fit this spectrum into the given "er curves": temperature, rainfall, ground cover for pollen zone III after reviewing the pollen conversion index (Table 8.1).
- interpret your findings relative to the finished pollen "er curves": put in words what was happening to the vegetation over time and, from this, infer the temperature and rainfall.

DOING THE EXERCISE

1. Before looking at pollen under the slide microscope, look at the "Pollen Key" (Figure 8.4). Size is variable within a species, so size is not an important diagnostic trait in identifying particular species, although all pine pollen is larger than all birch pollen. Color may or may not be helpful, depending on whether stain has been used to bring out features of the grains. Do not rely on it. Ask yourself these questions: Does the grain have a **porate** (pore) or a **colpate** (furrow) or neither? (Birch has pores; oak has furrows.) How many pores or furrows does it have? Are the pores or furrows equidistant around the equator? Is it an **aperturate**, with no pores or furrows?

Get a set of "pollen identification" slides and look at each under the microscope. Look for the traits previously listed: size; color (but see preceding); presence or absence of pores, furrows, apertures, and their placement on the pollen. The pollen slides used to learn identification of species contain only one species

Figure 8.4 Pollen Key

Under a low-power (20–40×) translucent microscope, pollen grains have definite morphologies (shapes). Use this key to identify the following pollen grains.

Pollen	**Description**
 *Betula* (birch)	A trizonoporate; it has three pores equidistant around its axis
 *Quercus* (oak)	A trizonoporate; it has three furrows equidistant around its axis
Pinus (pine)	An aperturate; it has no pores or furrows, but has two "sacs" or wings (Mickey Mouse ears) around the central area
Gramineae (grass)	A monoporate; it has but one pore

of pollen on each slide. So that you can refer to these traits when you are looking at a slide with mixed pollen on it, write the names of the pollen grains as you see them under the microscope, along with three to four key identifying traits next to them.

Name   Identifying Traits

_____   _____

_____   _____

_____   _____

_____   _____

2. Get one "counting pollen" slide, and put it under the microscope. Starting with the upper-left-hand corner of the slide, traverse horizontally across the slide using only one directional knob on the microscope, staying as systematically on the same hypothetical line as possible. As you spot pollen grains, stop and identify each by using your trait list, marking where indicated on the "master pollen count sheet" (Figure 8.5). After one traverse across the slide, return to the extreme left edge, move down one complete notch on the slide and continue. Do this for 30 minutes.

3. Count the pollen grains for each species and mark where indicated on Figure 8.5. Return all slides. (Count and mark your grass pollen grains on Figure 8.5, but ignore them in this part of the analysis, as grass will not help in identifying aboreal treed climates.) Write the total grains counted (including grass) in the space provided. Even if you don't have 200 grains, it is likely that your number will be adequate to infer environment.

4. Convert the raw total grains using the pollen conversions from Table 8.1. The important factor is the converted percent of the total arboreal grains for each species of pollen. Based on the **pollen indicators of environment** (Tables 8.2, 8.3, and 8.4), make a decision as to what your relative percentages are likely to mean in terms of temperature, rainfall, and ground cover, and briefly write your interpretation of the findings where indicated on Figure 8.5. Based on these findings, fill in "pollen zone III" on Figure 8.6. (See Exercise 10 for further details on "er curves.")

5. In the space provided in Figure 8.6, put into words what was happening to the vegetation that was inferred by your analysis. You need not do this for temperature, rainfall, and ground cover throughout all pollen zones, but as you will need to be able to interpret a pollen "er curve" on a lab exam, it would be good practice to write out, in relative terms, the general happenings in the period right before your data entry, the period of your data entry, and the period after your data entry, using appropriate "er" words.

6. If this is your third "er curve" and you've already done paleosediments and paleofauna, use these pollen data to finish your composite "er curve" and fill in Figure 10.5 in Exercise 10.

Pollen Indicators of Environment

Based on knowledge of modern preferences and tolerances, palynologists can place species of trees and nontreed plants into relative order of temperature, rainfall, and ground cover. Each variable will be discussed, followed by the relative order of major types of trees.

Temperature Although all plant species have a range of tolerances and preferences for temperature and rainfall, one variable is often more important than the other. For example, if a tree grows in an area that has good soil and proper rainfall for its needs, the tree can tolerate more extreme temperatures than if it is in an area that has poor soil and improper rainfall. It is therefore not possible to be definitive as to which species always indicates colder or warmer climate relative to another species, as each species has a range of temperature and

Figure 8.5 Master
Pollen Count Sheet

Master Pollen Count Sheet

Oak (AP)	Pine (AP)	Birch (AP)	Grass (NAP)

Conversion Indices

Species	Total Grains	Conversion Value	Number of Grains	Conversion Grains	% of Total
oak	_____	_____ x	_____	_____	_____
Pine	_____	_____ x	_____	_____	_____
Birch	_____	_____ x	_____	_____	_____
Grass	_____				

Total grains: _____   Total _____

Interpretation of findings of arboreal pollen:

_____

_____

_____

Figure 8.6 Pollen "Er Curve"

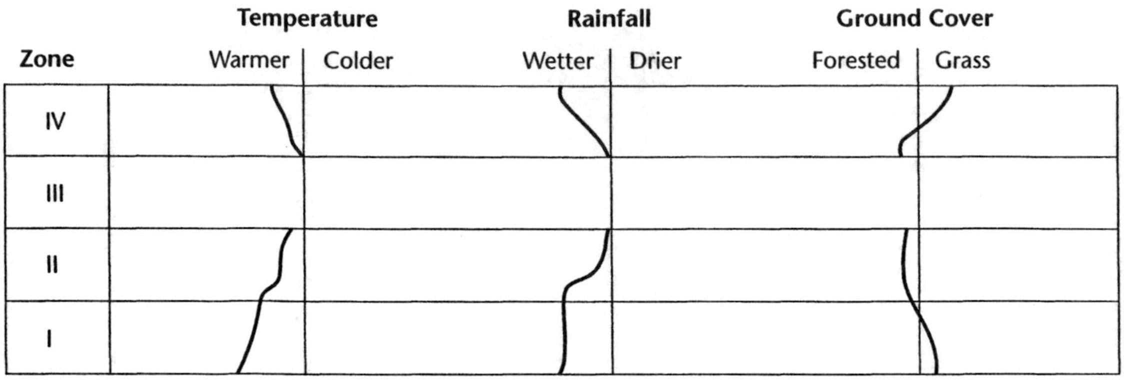

Zone	Temperature		Rainfall		Ground Cover	
	Warmer	Colder	Wetter	Drier	Forested	Grass
IV						
III						
II						
I						

What does the inference made by your pollen analysis suggest was happening to the environment

through time? _____

_____

_____

_____

Table 8.2   Range of Temperature for Tree Species

Species	Range of Temperature	Environment Type
No arboreal species (no trees)	Coldest	Tundra
Dwarf birch Dwarf willow Birch Pine (pines, spruce, juniper)		Forest tundra (birch-dominant)
Willow Aspen Alder		Taiga (conifer-dominant)
Poplar Sweet gum Beech	Moderate	
Oak Hazel Ash Elm Maple Hornbeam Chestnut Walnut		Deciduous woodlands
Hickory Holly	Warmest	

amount of rainfall in which it is most successful. The chart of tree species in Table 8.2 represents the general picture of the temperature variable. Although it is clear that birch pollen indicates colder temperature than does walnut pollen, it is not possible to make statements comparing elm and ash, for example.

Rainfall   All plant species have a range of rainfall (moisture) tolerances; this variable is affected by other variables as well. Although it can be said that willows prefer more moisture than do pines, it is not true that all willows will grow only in wet areas and all pines in dry areas. The chart of tree species in Table 8.3 represents the general picture of the rainfall variable.

Ground Cover   Absence or presence of particular pollen species and their frequencies relative to each other help scientists conclude what the ground surface probably looked like at any given time (Table 8.4). It does not, however, say whether an acre of land had one or one thousand pine trees on it.

KEY WORDS

paleoenvironment

paleopollen

pollen

palynology

stratigraphic pollen diagram

pollen "er curve"

porates

colpates

aperturates

pollen indicators of environment

Table 8.3   Range of Rainfall for Tree Species

Species	Range of Rainfall
Willow	Most
Alder	
Poplar	
Chestnut	
Elm	
Aspen	
Hazel	
Oak	Moderate
Birch	
Hickory	
Aspen	
Pine	
Ash	
Beech	Least

Table 8.4   Ground Cover Indicators and Conditions

Indicator	Condition
No tree pollen	Arctic tundra (no trees; presence of sedges)
Sedges and grasses only	Prairie (no trees; grasses)
Pine, birch, willow	Taiga (not forested; groups of predominantly birch trees) or conifer forest (pine predominant)
Oak, beech, ash, elm, maple	Mixed forest (deciduous trees predominant)
Basswood (lime)	Temperate forest

FOR FURTHER READING

Birks, H. J., and A. D. Gordon. *Numerical Methods in Quaternary Pollen Analysis.* Orlando, Fla.: Academic Press, 1985.

Bradley, R. S. *Quaternary Paleoclimatology.* Boston: Allen and Unwin, 1985.

Crowley, Thomas. *Paleoclimatology.* New York: Oxford University Press, 1991.

Faegri, K., P. Ekland, and K. Krzywinski, eds. *Textbook of Pollen Analysis,* 4th ed. New York: Wiley, 1989.

Goudie, Andrew. *Environmental Change.* New York: Oxford University Press, 1992.

Greig, James. *Archaeobotany.* Strasbourg, Fr.: European Science Foundation, 1989.

Lamb, H. H. *Climate: Present, Past, and Future.* London: Metheun, 1972.

Moore, P. D., and J. A. Webb. *An Illustrated Guide to Pollen Analysis.* New York: Wiley, 1991.

Solecki, Ralph. *Shanidar: The First Flower People.* New York: Knopf, 1971.

West, R. G. *Studying the Past by Pollen Analysis.* Oxford: Oxford University Press, 1971.

9

Environmental Reconstruction: Paleosediment and Paleosoil

ENVIRONMENTAL RECONSTRUCTION

This is one of several exercises concerned with an interdisciplinary field referred to as "paleoenvironmental reconstruction," whereby archaeologists attempt to reconstruct environment in the past. In order to infer environmental contexts for archaeological events, geologists and geographers study **soil** and **sediment;** paleontologists study small mammals; and paleobotanists study paleopollen. The importance of environmental reconstruction is characterized by this recent quote by Brian Fagan (1997, 52): "Some of the most sophisticated research in archaeology is being done in the open-system ecology format [and] such studies can be conducted only with detailed background knowledge of the specific environment in which the culture flourished, changed, and eventually died."

INTRODUCTION TO PALEOSEDIMENT AND PALEOSOIL

To many archaeologists, the most commonly found item in all archaeology sites is unimportant, a nuisance, and something to be gotten rid of as soon as possible. Yet this most commonly found item contains a wealth of information concerning the context of the cultural debris that is the focus of archaeological investigation. And what is this most commonly found item? Dirt. Technically, *dirt* is a colloquial term that should not be used in professional writing, although specialists and laypersons alike use the word in everyday conversation. In technical writing, scientists use the words *soil* and *sediment* to refer to that most commonly found item in archaeology sites. It is soil and sediment that contain a wealth of information about the environmental context of archaeology sites—temperature, moisture, ground cover. And soil and sediment contain a great deal of information about local site formation processes and the differential survivability of artifacts as well.

Of the three major tools used to reconstruct paleoenvironment—paleopollen, paleofauna, **paleosoil/paleosediment**—the last is the one tool that theoretically is the most usable and important because, of the three, it is the only true common denominator of all archaeology sites. Some sites have no bones and some have no pollen, but they all have soil or sediment. Although it is obvious that a 10,000-year-old Paleo-Indian site in Colorado will be underground and thus dominated by that most commonly found item, even classical sites in the Near East with their huge ziggurats, temples, and pyramids contain a considerable amount of soil and sediment.

Some sedimentologists feel that the specific history of sedimentary deposits is too complex to yield accurate information about paleoenvironmental conditions, whereas others claim sedimentology studies form the backbone of paleoenvironmental reconstruction, with pollen and faunal findings being secondary, providing only reinforcement or detail. Henri Laville, a French sedimentologist who worked with archaeologists for years, analyzed sediment with the goal of reconstructing paleoenvironment clearly in mind. He made statements about paleoenvironment in the form of hypotheses and was able to substantiate them with data. Working regionally in southwest France, Laville built up an environmental picture for this archaeologically well-known region that covered the past two million years. Most experts feel that, used with caution, the study of paleosediment and paleosoil can provide archaeologists with reliable information about past environment. As with paleopollen and paleofaunal analyses, sediment and soil analysis should be thought of as one set of hypotheses to be tested by using other kinds of data. If consistent, the findings verify each other; often, they complement each other, giving different data at different spatial and temporal scales. Because soil and sediment take longer to show the changes caused by new environmental conditions than either flora or fauna, soil and sediment change may lag behind the other two indicators. Although archaeologists in the past often ignored the important clues inherent in paleosediment and paleosoil (and some still do), most modern archaeologists either ask experts to be integral members of their interdisciplinary teams, or they themselves become expert enough to infer environmental conditions from the sediment or soil in their sites.

To answer questions about paleoenvironment, archaeologists need to know what the sediment and soil were originally composed of, where they came from, how they got there, what happened to them on their way to the archaeology site, and what happened to them after they got there. These are complex processual questions, but they are some of the same questions experts ask about soil and sediment in general, so that the basic difference is one of focus: Archaeologists want the answers to these questions as environmental context for their primary focus on cultural remains. If, for example, the study of a site's soil or sediment suggests cold and dry conditions, the archaeologist might infer that the people who lived at that time and place were exploiting a landscape that was meadow or steppe occasionally broken by stands of conifers. If later sediment or soil is shown to have been laid down or modified by milder and wetter conditions, the archaeologist might infer that the people at that time and place were exploiting a parkland of grasses and mixed deciduous trees. There is, of course, a large step between a soil or sediment sample and the conclusion that it was cold and dry or milder and wetter, and that step concerns the specialized work of the sedimentologist and soil scientist and is the focus of this exercise: How do specialists conclude that the sediment or soil of a layer at an archaeology site indicates a specific environmental condition at the time that people lived there? The answers to this basic question form the majority of the material in this exercise.

Soil, Sediment, Peat, Rock

Although it may all appear to be "dirt" to us, there is a difference between sediment and soil and between **rock** and sediment or rock and soil. And is **peat** soil or sediment? Sediment is the sand, gravel, and clay that is deposited or redeposited on the floor of an ocean, a lake, the channel of a stream, or within a swamp (to become peat). Soil, however, is the in-place product of the alteration of bedrock by chemical, physical, or biological agents. Bedrock (sometimes called "parent rock") can become either soil (by alteration in place) or sediment (by erosion, weathering, transportation, or redeposition). Soil and sediment compact progressively lower in sites, and, given time and geological stability, they will stratify horizontally into strata or layers. Usually, strata represent single geological events, though such events may be thousands of years in duration. Because such an event is homogeneous in cause, the strata will be of a more or less single color, texture, and composition, and can be differentiated from other layers based on those variables. A vertical cut, much as on a modern highway, shows these more or less horizontal strata as thin-to-thick bands of rock and soil or sediment, each looking different from its neighbor. When archaeologists date artifacts, they date them in strata, and if the layer can be dated (by relative or chronometric dating), then so too can the artifacts be at least roughly dated. Peat is usually considered a sediment, consisting primarily of organic materials, whereas soil is rock-derived. Peat is composed predominantly of plant remains (up to 80%) that were deposited in swampy areas where oxygen levels, which normally decompose dead plants, were low.

The "parent-child" relationship between bedrock and soil/sediment is a complex one that perhaps needs further elucidation, even if in an overly general and simplified fashion. Rock is formed in three different ways and constitutes three groups: igneous, sedimentary, and metamorphic. **Igneous rock** is formed when volcanic eruptions bring molten materials to the earth's surface, or when all rock material on top of the igneous material is eroded. **Sedimentary rock** forms when older rock is weathered and eroded into sediment, which is then transported by water or wind to be deposited elsewhere. **Metamorphic rock** is sedimentary rock altered by pressure or heat, generally deep within the earth. By far the most common rock found in archaeology sites is sedimentary rock. In summary, rock can become soil when it weathers and decomposes at the earth's surface. Sediment becomes rock when chemicals released by water and pressure cement it under compacted conditions. Earthquakes, glaciers, mountain building, river formation, gravity, and rain cause rock to come to the surface and expose it to weathering; the cycle continues. This very simplified summary should provide a brief look at the relationship between rock and sediment, sediment and soil, peat and soil, and back to sediment and rock.

In any discussion of sediment and sedimentary rock, it is quite proper to pay homage to the eighteenth-century geologist James Hutton, who proposed the principle of **uniformitarianism** that is so vital to all geological work and to the work of those who use geological applications, such as archaeologists. Uniformitarianism, based on several hundred years of research, proposes that whatever causes rock to become sediment, and causes sediment to become rock today (ongoing geological processes), had the same causes in the past. Here again, the present is the key to the past. Scientists, including archaeologists, also use the principle of uniformitarianism in equating past and present pollen and fauna principles.

Sediment, Soil, and Archaeology

To pose the question simplistically, How can a sedimentologist take a bag of sediment or soil (a sample) from a layer in an archaeology site and make inferences about the environment during the time that layer (and its cultural remains) were deposited? First, an assumption is made that if a layer of sediment or soil contains cultural debris such as flint flakes, tools, animal bones, or sherds that the soil or sedimentary matrix was usually deposited at the same time as the cultural material. It does not take a leap of faith to assume the clues provided by the sediment and soil will allow the archaeologist to infer the environmental context of the people who left the cultural material. Sometimes, however, cultural material becomes redeposited in sand or on floodplains, or even in glacial material, and the scientist must be aware of these possibilities.

Because sedimentology and soil science serve archaeology only when they answer questions about paleoenvironment, archaeologists are interested primarily in those aspects of paleosoil/paleosediment that attempt to reconstruct aspects of paleoenvironment: temperature, moisture, ground cover. They are less interested in knowing the exact composition of a soil than what the composition can tell them about the temperature at the time of formation. Temperature and rainfall can often be inferred by the color or texture of the sediment or soil. Ground cover is inferred by climate (temperature, rainfall), vegetation, and soil generally interrelating so as to form predictable patterns. Examples of these patterns include black soil, moderately heavy rainfall, and tall grasses; light-colored soil, cool and moist climate, and conifer forests; red soil, high temperatures and heavy rainfall, and rain forests; brown soil, moderate temperatures and rainfall, and short grasses or temperate deciduous forests. Each of these patterns includes soil (by color), amount of rainfall, and ground cover. The inference of temperature and rainfall first and ground cover second on the basis of the interlinkage of the three patterns is the opposite of paleofaunal analysis, in which ground cover is inferred first. As long as the pattern holds, it does not matter which element is inferred first.

PALEOSEDIMENT AND PALEOSOIL INDICATORS OF ENVIRONMENT

Certain characteristics of soil and sediment, based on a history of their formation, provide clues about paleoenvironment. Color, texture, and transportation will be discussed in order.

Color of Sediment and Soil

Color seems to be associated more with the climatic variables of temperature and rainfall at the time of sediment deposition or soil alteration than with the type of "parent rock" that was being deposited or weathered. In other words, when a rock is decomposing at the surface of the earth, the color it forms is more likely due to the existing climate at the time of decomposition than because it is igneous, sedimentary, or metamorphic in nature. The following are some examples of this association of color and climate: Soil formed under dry conditions tends to be brown, and soil formed under wet conditions tends to be reddish; soil formed under hot conditions tends to be red, and soil formed under cold conditions tends to be lightly colored, such as yellow. Note the word *tend*, as these are tendencies, not absolutes. Note also that in the examples just given that the first set refers to moisture and the second set to temperature. Complications occur when both moisture and rainfall are combined. Some ambiguities occur, but, in general, soil formed in warm and humid conditions tends to be red, and soil formed under moderate rainfall and temperature

Table 9.1   Tendencies of Sediment and Soil Color: Temperature and Moisture

	Dry	Moderate	Wet
Cold	Yellow gray	Black	Gray-green to black
Moderate	Gray Yellow	Brown/ Black	Gray-green or gray with red flecks
Hot	Red	Red	Red to black

tends to be dark brown/black. Table 9.1 provides general conclusions about color in soil or sediment and inferences that can be made about moisture and temperature.

Color is not always an indicator of past environment, however. Forest fire burning or human activity (use of hearths, for example) can be the reason why a sediment or soil is red in a particular layer rather than because it was formed during warm climate. This conundrum can be resolved by a laboratory test. Black color may be due to the presence of charcoal (as in natural or human-made fires), to high amounts of humus, or to the presence of manganese dioxide rather than to being deposited or altered under cold conditions. Both charcoal and manganese dioxide can be detected by microscopic examination (or with a hand lens), and humus can be detected by a laboratory test. Gray color may be due to the presence of ash from fire rather than from deposition or alteration under dry conditions, but phosphate tests can confirm the presence or absence of ash. Some special conditions also exist that cause soil and sediment to have a characteristic color. For example, color can indicate the condition of drainage when the sediment was deposited or the soil was formed; red or yellowish may indicate good drainage and gray blue may indicate water-saturated conditions. These special conditions can be eliminated as the primary cause of color if the expert knows the conditions under which the soil or sediment was formed.

To eliminate as much subjectivity in assessing color as possible, experts match soil and sediment color directly to color chips in the standardized Munsell color chart. By use of number alone, other experts can identify color by using their own Munsell charts.

Texture of Sediment and Soil

The texture of a sediment or soil provides clues to the original process of formation, which in turn can be used to infer the environment during the time of formation. Texture of sediment or soil refers to several characteristics of the grain: size of grain, size of frost spalls (if present), and/or shape of grain.

The size of sediment or soil grains can be measured and proportions of size quantified. Sedimentologists refer to this as the pebble-sand-silt-clay (largest to smallest) fractions, or PSA (**particle size analysis**). Pebbles are further divided on the basis of size, from boulders down to gravel. A sediment that is high in **sand** and devoid of **silt** and **clay** suggests it was deposited as a beach sediment. A bimodal sample of sand and silt that is devoid of clay suggests a bimodal process of deposition involving sand being deposited during wave/sea activity, and silt deposited during a quiet, estuary activity. Sediment high in clay but low in sand and silt indicates a depositional climate of still water, such as in a lake.

Table 9.2   Dry Texture Test (Feel Test)

Type	Characteristics
Sand	Grains will grate against each other in the hand; handful will fall apart when squeezed and released; grains are individualized and loose
Coarse sand	Individual grains are large enough to see with naked eye
Fine sand	Individual grains are barely visible with naked eye
Silt	Individual grains not visible to naked eye; sample feels smooth and soapy and perhaps slightly sticky and/or gritty; when wet will form sludge; will leave color on fingers
Clay	Individual grains not visible to naked eye; forms clumps or clods; when wet is very sticky and can be molded into pellets; will leave color on fingers

Loess, a silt-sized sediment, is associated with cold and dry conditions during its deposition; only in a cold and dry climate—in which there were few trees and little moisture to keep the sediment particles consolidated—could the particles of fine silt blow off steppe landscapes to be redeposited in low-lying areas. Thus a sample high in silt suggests cold and dry environmental conditions.

Under relatively cold conditions, large fragments of limestone can spall off cave walls and ceilings due to the constant pressures of water and/or ice on the rock, and can further be shattered by frost conditions following deposition on cave floors. Large fragments indicate colder conditions than do smaller fragments in the same place, but both indicate formation under cold conditions.

The shape of sediment and soil particles, often visible only under a microscope, can provide clues to formation environment—grains become angular under fairly strong energy forces, such as rivers, whereas grains become rounder under quieter forces, such as lakes. The surface of sediment grains also suggests the mode of their deposition; grains with dull surface texture are generally windblown (such as loess) and associated with cold and dry conditions, whereas grains with glossy surfaces are generally the result of water transport.

Archaeologists and soil experts often do on-the-spot "feel tests" while in the field to note the texture of a sediment or soil. Such tests can be done on wet or dry samples. The characteristics listed in Table 9.2 will identify the type and size of soil or sediment.

Sometimes texture can influence color; finer sediment and soil have more color than coarser sediment and soil, so silt and clay tend to be darker than sand.

Transportation of Sediment

Where a sediment is transported to often provides clues to the environment during its final deposition, depending on whether the mode was wind, river, or sea. Sediment can end up on beaches or on floodplains of rivers; as sand dunes; or in low-lying areas of accumulation.

In summary, sediment and soil studies often provide clear and direct indicators of the climatic condition that existed at the time the sediment and soil were deposited. Angular limestone fragments from caves are such indicators, directly and clearly indicating cold conditions. Some sediment studies offer less, or ambiguous, information. For example, a standby test used by sedimentologists tests whether a sample is mostly sand or clay or silt or a combination of the three (as determined by PSA). Although this analysis can quantitatively indicate the agent of transportation of the sediment (wind, river, sea), and the environment of the final deposition (beach, floodplain, low-lying valley), except in the case of loess, which indicates cold and dry conditions when deposited, the results of particle-size analysis do not at present give clear or unambiguous indications of the climate at the time of deposition. Even the classic glacial tills, so clearly indicated by their heterogeneous sediment (no heavy bias in favor of silt or clay or sand), are not very helpful, as humans never actually lived on glaciers for glacial tills to indicate human activity and cold climate. Instead, other clues, such as frost-fractured limestone, are used to indicate this condition.

IN THE FIELD AND LABORATORY

"A sedimentologist at work on a section not only looks at it, but also scrapes and pokes it with a knife, rubs its surface by hand, crumbles a handful of its matrix, chews some of it, and then spits on another handful and repeats the process" (Laville, Rigaud, Sackett 1980, 80). As this somewhat humorous statement by Henri Laville, the geologist of the three, suggests, there is as much art as science in field sedimentology; as much intuition as experience. For every sample, the expert must remove the possibly contaminated surface of the sediment or soil and carefully remove a vertical slice of each layer; this is referred to as a "sampling column." While scraping and poking, the expert uses his or her eyes, ears, and the feel of the sediment or soil. Dry and wet samples are given the "squeeze and sludge" tests as previously described: A small amount of each dry sample is squeezed in the hand to see if it will fall apart or form clumps; moisture is added to each handful to see if it forms sludge. The results of these simple field tests will give preliminary classification to each sample and tell the scientist if the sample is predominantly sand, silt, or clay. Classifying samples in the field often allows experts to question certain findings and seek answers while still in the field and able to answer them. In addition, experts can note the composition of the sample (presence of minerals, charcoal, humus) by using a hand lens, and match color against Munsell color chips.

In the laboratory, each sample is dried, and nonsediment and nonsoil material, such as flint chips and small bones, are removed. Laboratory technicians then run PSA tests, sedimentation tests that separate samples into sand, silt, and clay by suspending the grains in water; redo wet and dry color matchings; look at roundness/flatness of grains under the microscope (often with an SEM); check for pH (acidity or alkalinity) values; and check for ash and humus content. Once the results of the tests on each sample are completed, the expert interprets the overall findings and infers their environmental implications. Usually, the interpretations are stated for each sample, representing one layer of a site. Laville, for example, described one Upper Paleolithic stratum in France as being "a limestone eboulis dominated by blunted stones and frost spalls having a matrix of sandy silty clay that is slightly plastic and of firm consistency and that shows a fine crumbly, moderately developed structure; its color is brownish yellow" (1980). Some of the reported findings for this sample are of environmental importance, particularly the sediment's color, the shape of the grains, and the presence of frost spalls. Depending on the description of the previous layer in the stratigraphy that would be provided for comparison purposes, a scientist might conclude that it either became colder or that it remained cold in this part of France at this time, as yellow color, blunted stones, and frost spalling all suggest relatively cold conditions. The environmental inferences could then be placed on a relative amplitude scale (a sedimentary/soil "er curve") for that time and place. Note that Laville described the sediment in the stratum in great detail without making claims for the environmental conditions under which it was formed. Only when compared to previous or successive strata can climatic inferences be made.

SEDIMENTARY/SOIL "ER CURVES"

Because of the nature of the data, sedimentologists and soil scientists are on safe ground inferring paleoenvironment if they report their findings as gradients rather than as absolute values, and are careful to make statements that are hypotheses to be tested rather than statements as "facts." It takes a good deal of experience and intuition to infer paleoenvironment even in gradient form; anything more definitive than this is beyond today's scientific knowledge.

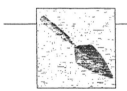

THE EXERCISE

Sediment and soil analysis provide different degrees of usefulness to archaeologists who will use the findings to infer paleoenvironment. At present, the best indicator of paleoclimate is the color of soil or sediment, which can indicate both temperature and rainfall amount. In addition, due to the usual associated pattern of soil or sediment color with ground cover, inference of vegetational cover can also be made. Certain conditions of texture are also guardedly used; loess is the classic case, but angularity and surface texture of the grains can also suffice.

In your role as an expert in paleosediment and soil, you have a very specific question to answer: Why did the people in Zimbabwe cease building at A.D. 1450? Zimbabwe, in south-central Africa, influenced surrounding areas for several hundred years and appeared to be an important trading center for the transporting of gold, iron, and textiles. Why did the people there stop building and apparently leave? One hypothesis is that south-central Africa became drier at this time, and if Zimbabwean herds of cattle overgrazed the now somewhat drier grasses, production might be down just enough to contribute to lower crop production as well. Before this hypothesis can be substantiated, archaeologists must be able to show that the area did become drier. The Zimbabwe excavator has asked for your help in inferring the climate of the area right before and right after the assumed exodus, and has brought you several samples for analysis. Once the environment of A.D. 1450 has been established, the archaeologist can interpret the cultural findings and hopefully conclude whether climatic change did or did not have an effect upon the abandonment of the site.

OBJECTIVES

In this exercise, you will

- assess the color of the soil or sediment of sand, clay, and silt samples.
- assess the three samples of sediment or soil by feel to gain practice before you get the Zimbabwe sample (analysis sample) for analysis.
- assess the PSA of the analysis sample provided; also assess the color.
- infer from your reading and the results of the three preceding objectives, the environmental condition under which the analysis sample from Zimbabwe was formed.
- fill in zone III in Figure 9.3 for the "er curve." Use your findings to answer the questions in Figure 9.3 about the Zimbabwean exodus.

With sophisticated laboratory equipment (and more time), experts can run many tests on samples. For example, they are able to do x-ray diffraction on clay; to do chemical analysis to determine the degree of chemical weathering; to determine mineral composition; to determine amounts of humus or phosphate; to do a pH value of sediment acidity. In addition, many labs are equipped to electronically shake the PSA sieves; sort and weigh the fractions; measure the degree of roundness or angularity of grains by machine; or even do PSA more accurately (sedimentologically rather than with sieves; this takes several days). However, these additional laboratory tests serve to complement and add detail to the tests that you will be doing in the exercise.

DOING THE EXERCISE

1. Use the color chart and match as closely as possible the three samples (one clay, one silt, one sand). Large laboratories would use a Munsell color chart, as used by geologists and sedimentologists; assessment of color would be made by number only and would be comparable to other color assessments. Unfortunately, Munsell charts are expensive. Our color chart is usable for our purposes. Write the color numbers and describe in words the color of each sample on the Sample Report (Figure 9.1). Gray with bluish tinge, or dark red, is sufficient here.

2. Use the "Dry Texture Test" chart in Table 9.2 of (qualitative and subjective) characteristics concerning the feel of sediment or soil. One could do this test in the field or in the laboratory. You will do only the dry test. Do the test on the three samples: Pick up a small handful from the bag and squeeze it. (Do this over a container.) Look at the characteristics in Table 9.2 and write what you felt during the squeeze test in the spaces provided in Figure 9.1 under "Feel Test." Put the handful back into the proper bag after use.

3a. Write the weight (in grams) of each empty sieve—marked on the sieve itself—where indicated in Figure 9.1. The sieves do not weigh the same, as the mesh of the wire changes size and weight. Take the Zimbabwe sample and empty it onto the top of the nest of sieves, checking to see that the sieves are nesting in proper order (the coarsest should be at the top, with the finest at the bottom; they should be in numerical order as well) and that both the bottom and top are covered. Gently shake the nest for about five minutes. Weigh the sample in each sieve; list the weight of each sample in grams in the space provided in Figure 9.1 under "weight of soil or sediment." Subtract the sieve weights for each. Then put the sieved sample back into the original bag. Figure a percentage for the weight of each of the types of soil or sediment relative to the total weight and write the percentages in the spaces provided in Figure 9.1. Report your findings on both the pie diagram in Figure 9.1 and on the triangular diagram in Figure 9.2. In Figure 9.2, the triangle shows a sample finding of 70% sand, 20% silt, and 10% clay, with the dot in the appropriate place within the triangle. Using the results of the Zimbabwe analysis sample and the percents of sand, silt, and clay, place an X on the triangular diagram in the appropriate place in Figure 9.2.

b. Get a 2-inch strip of double-sticky tape. Dip the upper sticky part of the tape into your analysis sample to get a coating on it, then attach it to Figure 9.1 in the space provided at the top right. Assess the color via the color chart and write its description and number in the spaces provided in Figure 9.1.

c. Do the feel test (as you previously did on the clay, silt, sand samples) on the analysis sample and write what you felt doing the squeeze test in the spaces provided in Figure 9.1 under "feel test–analysis sample."

4. Fill in zone III material on the first two "er curves" in the spaces provided in Figure 9.3. Then infer the ground cover and add it. Based on these findings, answer the inference question concerning environmental conditions in existence when your sample was formed in Zimbabwe; write your answer on (4) in Figure 9.1. (See your lab manager if you are not familiar with a pie diagram.) If this is the last of your three "er curves" (that is, if you have already done Exercise 8 and 10), complete the question on all three "er curves" in Table 10.5.

☐ **Check all results with your lab manager for full credit.**

KEY WORDS

soil
sediment
paleosoil/paleosediment
rock
peat
igneous rock
sedimentary rock
metamorphic rock
uniformitarianism
particle size analysis
sand
silt
clay
loess

Figure 9.1 Sample Report

1. **What color is it?** Match the four samples (sand, clay, silt, and the analysis sample given to you by your lab manager) with the chips in the color chart.

	Color ID #	Color Description	Attach your analysis sample double-sticky tape here:
Sand sample	_____	_____	
Clay sample	_____	_____	
Silt sample	_____	_____	
Analysis sample	_____	_____	

2. **Feel tests:** Squeeze a small handful of each sample and release. What characteristics does each show?

Sand sample _____   Silt sample _____

Clay sample _____   Analysis sample _____

3. **Particle size analysis:** Sieve the analysis sample.

Weight of Soil or Sediment (grams)	Sieve (grams)	% of Total
Gravel:	_____ – _____ = _____	_____
Fine gravel:	_____ – _____ = _____	_____
Sand:	_____ – _____ = _____	_____
Silt:	_____ – _____ = _____	_____
Clay:	_____ – _____ = _____	_____
Total weight:	_____ – _____ = _____	<u>100%</u> _____

Pie diagram

4. **Sample Conditions.** What were the likely environmental conditions under which this sample was found in Zimbabwe? _____

_____

Figure 9.2 Ternary or Triangular Diagram

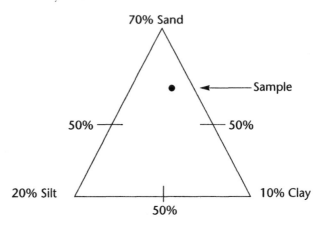

Figure 9.3 Sedimentary/Soil "Er Curve"

Zone	Temperature		Rainfall		Ground Cover	
	Warmer	Colder	Wetter	Drier	Forested	Grass
IV						
III						
II						
I						

Zone III refers to the time directly before the Zimbabwe exodus. What does the inference made by your soil sediment analysis suggest was happening right before the Zimbabwe exodus? Did the environment change after the exodus? _____

_____

_____

_____

_____

_____

_____

FOR FURTHER READING

Bell, M. G. and Michael Walker. *Late Quaternary Change*. New York: John Wiley and Sons, 1992.

Boggs, Sam, Jr. *Principles of Sedimentology and Stratigraphy*. Englewood Cliffs, N.J.: Prentice Hall, 1995.

Courty, Marie Agnes, Paul Goldberg, and Richard Macphail. *Soils and Micromorphology in Archaeology*. New York: Cambridge University Press, 1989.

Fagan, Brian M. *In the Beginning*, 9th ed. New York: Longman, 1997.

Hassan, Fekri. "Sediments in Archaeology: Methods and Implications for Paleoenvironmental and Cultural Analysis." *Journal of Field Archaeology* 5 (1978):197–213.

Keeley, Helen, and Richard Macphail. *A Soil Handbook for Archaeologists*. Bulletin 18. London: Institute of Archaeology, 1981.

Laville, Henri, Jean-Philippe Rigaud, and James Sackett. *Rock Shelters of the Perigord*. New York: Academic Press, 1980.

Selley, Richard. *Applied Sedimentology*. San Diego: Academic Press, 1988.

Shackley, Myra. *Archaeological Sediments*. London: Butterworth, 1975.

Stein, Julie K. "Deposits for Archaeologists." *Advances in Archaeological Method and Theory* 11 (1989):337–98.

Stein, Julie K. "Interpreting Sediments in Cultural Settings." In *Archaeological Sediments in Context*, edited by Julie K. Stein and William Ferrand. Orono, Maine: Center for the Study of Early Man, 1988.

10

Environmental Reconstruction: Paleofauna

ENVIRONMENTAL RECONSTRUCTION

This is one of three exercises concerning the very important field of paleoenvironmental reconstruction. In this interdisciplinary field, geologists and geographers attempt to reconstruct paleosoils and sediments; paleozoologists attempt to reconstruct the small mammal population; and paleobotanists attempt to reconstruct the flora of times past. From the archaeologist's perspective, the aim of paleoenvironmental reconstruction is to allow us to infer, with some hope of being correct, the environmental context for cultural (archaeological) events. Before we can consider **paleofauna** data for its role in the reconstruction, however, the stage first needs to be set for the importance of this work.

Only when we know the basic parameters of cold/warm, wet/dry, prairie/tundra/forest/grasslands can we begin to properly interpret cultural happenings. For example, what might logically be inferred if an archaeologist found evidence of small ivory beads near the wrist bones of a man who was buried 26,000 years ago, the beads positioned as if they had been around the bottom of a sleeve (though the sleeve has biodegraded) and down the rib cage of the man as if they had been sewn down the front of a shirt (although again, the shirt has biodegraded), as well as the archaeologist finding buttons near the rib cage, with bone needles and flint scrapers off to the side? If the archaeologist knew the climate was very cold at this time, the inference might be that tailored clothing was made for survival under frigid conditions; thus, the presence of sleeves. If the archaeologist knew it was quite warm at this time, the inference would be that tailored clothing was more likely due to style preference. The point is, unless we know what the climate was like, we cannot accurately interpret the cultural remains.

And when we want to explain why certain things happened in the past, often that explanation is environmentally tied; at the very least, environmentally focused explanations should be tested. Many explanations of plant and animal domestication, for example, have been tied to environmental change, such as the environment getting drier, or getting hotter, so that people had to change their basic economy from foraging to farming. But unless we are fairly certain that the environmental suppositions are accurate, our explanations for change are only hypotheses yet to be tested.

Archaeologists must become at least conversant with the various ways paleoenvironments are reconstructed. Techniques are often borrowed from other sciences; in most cases, specialists become part of the archaeological team, operating in the field as well as in the lab in order to collect data, observe the cultural context, and infer the paleoenvironment based on all information gathered. Some archaeologists, however, specialize in reconstructing environments, and are trained in both archaeology and some environmental specialty.

In Exercises 8, 9, and 10, the three most commonly used reconstruction techniques are explained, and you will be reconstructing the paleoenvironment of hypothetical sites. Each reconstruction is analyzed separately because each involves the specialized work of a single subdiscipline: palynology, **zooarchaeology**, and sedimentology. Each technique has its own strengths and weaknesses, and its own set of problems. The common thread among them is that they all result in **"er curves."**

"ER CURVES"

Environmentalists are generally unable to make absolute statements of fact about any aspect of paleoenvironment. The technical terms for an "er curve" are *relative amplitude* or *gradient*. It is not possible, given our present state of scientific knowledge, to say that on April 5, exactly 10,132 years ago in what is now central Wyoming, a band of Native Americans hunted at two o'clock in the afternoon; that it was sunny in the morning and rainy in the afternoon; that the day reached a high of 61°; and that there were three lodgepole pine trees and two Englemann spruce trees on the nearest hillside, and two willows and one quaking aspen along the nearest stream, with the rest of the landscape in grass and shrubs.

Based on the available environmental clues scientists use to reconstruct paleoenvironments, they could state—with some confidence of being correct—that 10,000 years ago in what is now central Wyoming, a band of buffalo hunters lived in an environment that was somewhat warmer than it had been in the previous millennium and that it was also somewhat wetter than in the past; and that although the area would be classified as a prairie, with grasses and shrubs predominant, there were some large trees such as pines, spruce, willows, and aspen in the area. Note the use of comparative and nonspecific terms: *colder, wetter, some*. In most cases, paleoenvironmental reconstruction clues give indicators of change rather than indicators of absolutes.

Figure 8.3 shows the first of several "er curves" in this text. The figure is an "er curve" for a hypothetical site that is stratified into eight layers or strata. By tradition, the oldest (first to be laid down) layer is at the bottom; it is labelled (1). The three "er curves" represent three climate-related phenomena: temperature, rainfall (moisture), and ground cover. Within each curve, there is a comparative range: for temperature, the range is warmer and colder; for rainfall, the range is wetter and drier; for ground cover, the range is forest and grass. Note that for ground cover, the range is not in comparative terms, but rather represents the results of temperature and moisture: warm and wet conditions usually produce forest (tree) ground cover, whereas cold and dry conditions usually produce tundra or prairie (grass) ground cover. The line down the middle of each curve represents a midpoint in the range, a kind of average from which colder/warmer is judged. An archaeologist plotting the temperature curve would plot an appropriate point for each layer based on the existing evidence for temperature at that time. The comparative gradients (points) for each layer would then be joined by a "wavy line" or curve as in Figure 8.3, showing gradual change through time. The same approach is used for the other two gradients. These are known as "er curves," and they can be "read" as in "It was quite dry 6000 years ago but became wetter by 5000 years ago."

Although there are a number of techniques used to infer paleoenvironment, some are of little interest to archaeologists because they represent times when humans did not occupy the area. For example, the presence of glaciers is easily inferred by the evidence of glacial tills as the predominant sediments at a site, but humans never lived on glaciers. It must be emphasized, however, that palynology (analysis of pollen), paleofauna (analysis of small mammal remains), and paleosedimentology (analysis of sediments and soils) each offer clues to but one piece of the environmental puzzle. Each stands alone as a technique, but each must be verified by similar findings from other data and techniques. At the end of the last part of this exercise, you will be able to see if the three techniques cross-verify each other or not. In real-life situations, generally, archaeologists have found that in cases where there are sufficient data for all three techniques they do indeed cross-verify. For example, in France, where all three techniques have been used for many years, the findings are surprisingly consistent for thousands of years.

Back in 1669, a physician named Nicholas Steno claimed that flora and **fauna** should be expected to occur together in the same environment, but scientists and the lay public alike were not yet ready to accept such a revolutionary finding. In addition to a number of French studies using all three environmental indicators, a substantial body of data exists for the Levantine Middle East (Israel, Lebanon, parts of Syria, and Jordan) for the past 11,000 years (since the end of the last glaciation), including data on culture change. The various paleoenvironmental data confirm the onset of dry conditions at the same time that tool frequencies suggest a transition from the early to the late Natufian: pollen diagrams show a replacement of Mediterranean flora by steppe (drier) flora; microfaunal studies show a change from woodland to more open habitats; and paleosediment data show a dramatic change to arid conditions, as evidenced by the 2–3 meters of drift sand that overlay early Natufian deposits. Middle Eastern clues cross-verify as well.

Closer to home, a group of environmental scientists recently working in Arizona reported "excellent correlation" between sediments and pollen. Because this was a multisite project involving nine different pollen columns each from a different bog, it gives archaeologists a regional climate pattern based on several environmental databases, not just information from a single site that at best is localized and at worst is biased.

Composite "Er Curves"

After you have finished Exercises 8, 9, and 10, you will be in a position to see if the three "er curves" cross-verify each other or not. Realizing that no two indicators will react to climatic change at the same rate, you will compare all three and come to a conclusion about whether or not they reasonably cross-verify.

INTRODUCTION TO PALEOFAUNAL ANALYSIS

Zooarchaeologists specialize in identifying and analyzing animal bones in and around archaeology sites for the information they contain about human activities. The term *archaeofauna* is often used to refer to the animal bones found in an archaeological context that form the database; in addition to providing information about human activities, such data, zooarchaeologists believe, are also important in the reconstruction of paleoenvironment. Theoretically, there are three methods that can be used to obtain archaeofaunal data: (1) the presence or absence of specific animals; (2) the relative abundance of various animals within the fossil assemblage; and (3) the body size of the individual members of the animal species found.

The mere presence or absence of a species in a sample the size of archaeo-faunal samples (usually small) can be extremely misleading, as absence or presence merely indicates whether a species is present or not, not how much is present. The finding of a very rare species might give entirely erroneous implications in a small sample. Therefore, this method is not often used. And although Bergmann's rule states that average body size will increase with cold climate, within the body size range of a species, the rule is not universal. Richard Klein and K. Cruz-Uribe (1984) actually found that among modern dune rats in South Africa, the correlation was between size and rainfall rather than between size and temperature; they found bigger rats in areas of higher rather than lower rainfall. They applied this trend for modern rats to the rat archaeofauna in South Africa and inferred that the area had higher rainfall between 11,000 and 9,000 years ago than during the previous 7,000 years, as the rats were considerably larger during the latter period. This is a classic example of using the present to predict the past.

The abundance or relative frequencies of various animals at the same time and place provides the most revealing archaeofaunal information about past climates. As Simon Davis (1987, 61) rather optimistically puts it, "Animal remains may indicate whether the environment was forested or open grassland, whether it was hot or cold [or] whether the seashore was nearby or not." Theoretically, archaeofaunal data give us inferences about temperature, rainfall, and ground cover, but, as shall be discovered later, it is ground cover that is inferred first, and, from that, further inferences about temperature and moisture are drawn. For example, if microfaunal remains indicate that the ground cover was tundra sedges, this in turn infers severely cold climate, with low rainfall. As in other environmental reconstruction techniques, uniformitarianism must be assumed: The tolerances and preferences for certain types of ground cover today were the same in the past. If we can infer the ground cover, we can infer the temperature and rainfall.

Owl pellets (discussed shortly) contribute more remains of small mammals (shrews, voles, mice, rats) to the small mammal sample than do any other contributor. A small mammal sample is of interest to general biologists, ecologists, and, as will be discovered, archaeologists as well. By counting the frequency of the prey species (shrews, voles, mice, rats) from a sample of owl pellets (mostly barn owls), biologists and ecologists believe they can obtain a fairly accurate picture of the relative frequency of the small mammal community made up of these elusive nocturnal animals. Though the frequency of prey species remains relatively stable over a short period of time in a given area, the prey species differ in their respective frequencies from one environmental region to another at a specific time, and also differ in their relative frequencies in a single geographic area through time, which is of importance to those interested in change-through-time studies. This is when the archaeologist takes notice. Although most small mammal species have a range of habitats in which they live, as all species of life, some species do better in certain, preferred habitats and numerically outnumber other species, whereas they do worse in other habitats that other species do well in. This variability causes different frequencies of often the same four or five small mammal species in two or more adjacent geographic areas or in two or more time periods. Today, and probably in the past as well, small mammals do vary by climate. In Britain, for example, field voles—the most common prey species—represent 50–65% of the diet of barn owls, but on the Continent, shrews are the most common prey species. This makes sense, as in colder, wetter

Figure 10.1 Common Prey Species in Europe

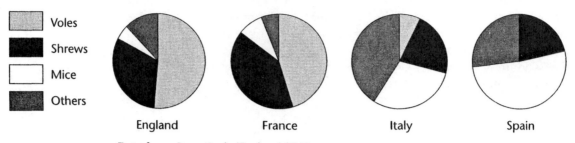

Voles

Shrews

Mice

Others

England   France   Italy   Spain

Data from *Barn Owls* (Taylor 1994).

Britain, long, moist grass is particularly attractive to field voles, whereas dry, short pastures on the Continent are attractive to shrews. In the driest parts of Europe, such as in Spain, mice are the most common prey species. See Figure 10.1 for comparable prey species in Europe.

Insects (especially beetles) and snails, as well as small mammals, are very sensitive indicators of climatic change and are much faster at indicating change than trees, for example. Though the relative frequency of different species of trees changes in response to climatic change, it does so slowly, whereas a change in climate can find a change in animal population literally overnight. Trees can't move even if climate changes; animals can and do.

Small versus Large Mammals as Environmental Indicators

Macrofauna are sometimes used to reconstruct paleoenvironment; extinct mammoths are one notable example of this methodology. Five of the major six species of large herbivores became extinct or migrated from western Europe at the end of the last Ice Age because they were cold-adapted animals and the temperature became considerably warmer. But whereas large mammals have a relatively wide range of climatic tolerance, small mammals are more sensitive to small change, thereby making small-mammal analysis ideal for environmental reconstruction. Often, only very large environmental changes such as ice ages or interglacial periods can be inferred from changes in macrofauna.

Small mammals, as opposed to large mammals, are an example of what ecologists call "r strategy": high rates of conception, large litters, short growth phases. These factors allow them to survive in relatively small, specialized econiches in comparison with large mammals' which have more generalized econiches. This in turn causes small mammals to reflect the immediate environment more reliably than large animals, due to several reasons. Large animals often move many kilometers in a single day searching for food, or hundreds of kilometers in a single migration; in contrast, small mammals tend to stay within a few kilometers of where they were born. Additionally, human hunters likely traveled great distances to hunt, kill, and bring back to the archaeology site the carcasses of large herbivores, many kilometers from where they were killed; if humans hunted small mammals, they likely did it locally, as part of the foraging, rather than the big game hunting pattern.

Another reason why small mammals are more likely to reflect local environments is because large mammals appear to reflect the "cultural choice" of human selective hunting as much as or more than they reflect the paleoenvironment; bones of large animals in archaeology sites reflect what hunters wanted for food, clothing, sinew, and other material items, rather than the actual frequency of the area's animals. Once hunters became efficient at killing (certainly as far back as 40,000 years ago), they could afford to be choosy about what animals they hunted; in certain areas where several species of animals dominated equally, archaeofaunal evidence of one species' bones can dominate at one site; at another site of the same age, the predominant animal was a different species; and at a third site, the third species was apparently chosen for specialization. "Cultural choice" will not likely mirror the actual animal population. If ethnoparallels accurately predict the behavior of past foragers, small mammals, such as voles and rats, were seldom hunted by humans, and "choice" would not likely be a factor in predicting the frequency of small mammal bones in archaeology sites. For all of these reasons, small mammal remains provide a more reliable picture of the local environment than do large mammal remains.

Students of evolution, paleoenvironmentalists, and archaeologists are, for the most part, concerned with the longitudinal long-term aspects of studying small mammals. Obviously, evolutionary studies of any species are studies of change through time, but paleoenvironmentalists are not very interested in biological changes, per se, but rather use the changes in relative frequencies of small mammals to infer changes in environment. Archaeologists are of course not interested in either the evolution of small mammals or changes in environment, but rather are interested in what these different frequencies can tell them about environmental change during human occupation.

Paleo-Owl Pellets

The prey (voles, shrews, mice/rats) found in owl pellets are used as a tool by biologists and wildlife ecologists interested in present-day environmental conditions; archaeologists (and evolutionary biologists) are interested in owl pellets that can be compared through time. Fossilized owl pellets are not nearly as common as paleosediment or paleopollen, and a larger number of them in any or all parts of the world for all time periods would be most welcome. But we can only use what data we have. Our total fossilized owl pellet sample is small because pellets fossilize only under fairly extreme conditions. Normally, they break down in a day or so due to rain or trampling animals and never become part of the fossil record. Only when owls roost in dry caves and disgorge their pellets there are pellets likely to become fossilized. The earliest known fossilized owl pellets are Neolithic in age, so their use at present is chronologically limited to the last 8000 years. What is an owl pellet? An owl pellet is the regurgitated remains of prey (bones and fur) after an owl's highly acidic gastric juices have broken down the soft parts of small mammals and allowed digestion to take place. After nightly hunting routines, owls regurgitate one or two pellets. The pellets average about $1\frac{1}{2}$ to 2 inches in length and 1 inch around and have practically no odor other than a vague "woodsy" smell. The consolidated owl pellet, when dry, has a shiny surface, and is almost black to dark brown in color.

Barn Owls and Prey

The barn owl swallows its prey whole after killing it with a quick bite to the neck, and therefore little damage is done to the prey's bones. In addition, the barn owl is the "ideal" owl to use for environmental reconstruction, at least in temperate climates, because it is a generalist, hunting and eating what is most available, in contrast to other owls that specialize in shrews *or* voles *or* rats/mice. Barn owls do have dietary preferences in that they do eat more voles, shrews, and mice/rats than birds, amphibians, fish, or reptiles, but within the triad of small mammals (voles, shrews, mice/rats), the prey and the resultant pellets are in proportion to their relative availability. Scientists who stick with the triad can use the analysis to reconstruct the paleoenvironment it represents. Because barn owls take what is most available, their pellets reveal the relative abundance of the small mammal community at one time and place. The barn owl normally stays within a 5 kilometer range on its nightly forays, as do the small mammals; thus the prey species reflect the local rather than the regional environment. This is an ideal state of affairs for paleoenvironmental reconstruction.

The Technique of Owl Pellet Analysis

As in the analysis of paleopollen and paleosediment, there are three segments to owl pellet analysis: analysis in the field, in the laboratory, and in the office. The field segment differs, however, in the paucity of opportunities that are available to gather paleopellet data, and because an archaeologist does not normally go out looking for such data. (In contrast, paleopollen and paleosediments are readily available.) However, because they are so rare, paleopellets are at least never thrown away. Once a collection has been identified, the pellets are taken to a laboratory for identification and counting. When Richard MacNeish's group found fossilized owl pellets in a cave in Oaxaca, Mexico, the first thing they did was collect modern pellets from a nearby cave, identifying 10 species of small mammals; paleopellets could then be compared to them and the prey identified.

Species identification and counting of owl pellet prey are relatively easy tasks. Before the pellet is broken up and the prey identified and counted, it is normally measured and weighed for possible trends in size of the prey species over time. Novices at breaking apart pellets normally use mechanical aids (picks or sticks) to break them open to separate the bones of the prey species, but they soon learn that sticks are not very helpful in separating bones from fur, and once they realize that the pellet is dry and has no odor, they use their hands and fingers to do the sorting (it is still a good idea to wash your hands after handling pellets). Bones are separated from fur and any other extraneous items such as grass or string. Although a barn owl may kill and ingest as many as seven animals in one hunting episode and regurgitate one giant pellet, two or three animals per pellet is the average. Because the aim of this portion of analysis is the identification and counting of the prey species, diagrams of the expected species should be readily at hand for reference purposes. The skulls and mandibles identify the species: one skull and, as the jaws are usually separated, two half-mandibles per animal. Insectivores (shrews), for example, have mandibles with teeth lined up in rows with no spaces between their canines and molars; rodents (voles, mice/rats), in contrast, have large spaces between their canines and molars (see Figure 10.2). The mandibles of a rodent and an insectivore may be the same size, but the teeth indicate to which group they belong. Mice/rats and voles can be separated on the basis of their teeth, though their overall shape is

Figure 10.2
Reference Chart
of Small Mammals

Small mammals can be identified with the naked eye by looking at skulls, mandibles, ▶ and teeth (postcranial bones such as femurs are almost identical). Size is not a distinguishing trait of small mammals, as the ranges overlap, although of course most mice are smaller than most rats and common shrews can be quite small. European and North American small mammals are very similar and can be considered as a single geographic unit.

Rodents
(mice, rats, voles)

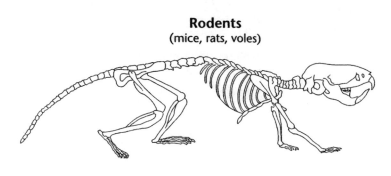

Insectivores
(shrews)

General: gap between incisors and molars; voles have zigzag molars, mice/rats have molars with cusps and roots

Teeth: 16

General: continuous teeth in rows; elongated skulls and jaws

Teeth: 30–32

Water vole

Rat

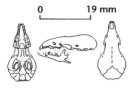

Common shrew

Water shrew

Common vole

Mouse

0   19 mm

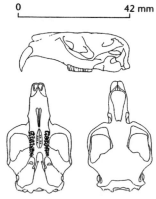

Water vole

0   42 mm

0   48 mm

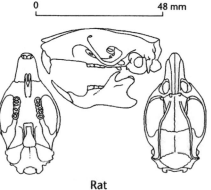

Rat

Common shrew: upper incisor is smooth

Water shrew: upper incisor is bladelike

0   26 mm

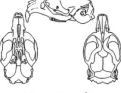

Common vole

0   23 mm

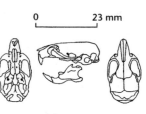

Mouse

Average skull length:

Rat	48 mm
Mouse	23 mm
Common vole	26 mm
Water vole	42 mm
Common shrew	19 mm
Water shrew	22 mm

almost identical. Mice/rats have cusps on three molars in each quadrant, as well as roots that form round holes in the bony area under the teeth. Voles, however, have zigzag-shaped teeth, not cusps, and their three molars have no roots and therefore no holes in the mandibular bone. Because mice/rats indicate quite different environment from voles, it is important to be able to identify them. Once identified and counted, the results are placed on a "master fauna count" for the sample.

A single sample of fossilized owl pellets, no matter how large it is, only suggests the environmental conditions of one time period, as inferred by the relative needs and preferences of the prey species found in the pellets. For owl pellet analysis to be of any help in reconstructing environment over time, numerous samples from different layers in a stratified site are needed. Because owls do not normally regurgitate pellets in the same areas that humans deposit cultural debris, stratified owl pellet sites need to be nearby but will usually not be the same location as archaeology sites. Although the finding of fossilized pellets in different stratigraphic layers in the same area does not happen as often as archaeologists would like, the special conditions under which owl pellets can fossilize tend to remain the same through time, fostering conditions that favor change-through-time studies. If, for example, a sample of owl pellets is found in a particular shallow cave, chances are there will be other owl pellet samples in the same cave but located lower down the stratification, as the cave offered the same owl-roosting area as well as the same special fossilization conditions for a long period of time. Because the climate may have changed considerably over the buildup time of the stratified samples, stratified samples occurring under the same fossilized conditions offer ideal reconstruction conditions. Then, each sample is dated and the frequency of the prey species calculated and arranged chronologically. Whether or not the owl population has changed–and it probably would have, as owls have tolerances and preferences to temperature and moisture conditions as well–doesn't matter, only that the prey change in relative frequencies.

Analysis of Owl Pellets

Once the owl pellets have been identified and counted, the expert can attempt to answer the question, so what? What does it mean that 10,000 years ago at a particular site voles outnumbered mice 10 to 1, whereas 5000 years ago at the same place the opposite was true?

Theoretically, we can infer past ground cover of an area by knowing the preferences and tolerances of the small mammals that scurry around on, over, and under the ground cover. And, theoretically, we can make inferences about temperature and rainfall by knowing what the ground cover of an area was. Unfortunately, there is no necessary one-to-one relationship between a particular species of small mammal and a particular ground cover, past or present, meaning that not all small mammals are good environmental indicators. Lemmings are excellent because they always indicate open terrain and never woods or forests, and wood mice because they are always found in association with woods. Note that the basic inference is relative to ground cover, not to temperature or rainfall. Other small mammals, unfortunately, do quite well in more than one habitat: voles and shrews, for example, are found in both woods and grasslands.

Table 10.1–based on the Taxonomic Habitat Index (THI) devised by Evans, Van Couvering, and Andrews (1981); additional data collected by Peter

Table 10.1   Environmental Indicators of Owl Pellet Prey (EIOPP)

Species	Composite Indications by Habitat		
	Cool (tundra, taiga, steppe; grass)	**Moderate** (boreal forest, deciduous forest, forest steppe; woods)	**Warm** (tropical or semi-Mediterranean)
Common shrews (I)	30	40	30
Water shrews (I)	30	50	20
Water voles (R)	50	45	5
Field voles (R)	45	50	5
Common voles (R)	20	50	30
Mice and rats (R)	10	40	50

Note: Numbers are based on reported relative proportions (given in percentages) of these species in different habitats. I = insectivore, R = rodent.

Andrews for Europe (1990); 12 years of work by David Glue (1974) on 47,865 prey items in England; and cited preferences of three species of voles, two species of shrews, and mice and rats that make up over 90% of a typical owl pellet sample—is a very crude compiled index of Environmental Indicators of Owl Pellet Prey (EIOPP). The THI is a cumulative index of all species that scores for the range of habitats for each species and each habitat, where there are data. For example, a living rodent species might be observed living in what are basically wet habitats today, but in three climatic zones: tundra, boreal forest, and steppe. Out of a possible total 100%, the species scored 40% for tundra, 50% for boreal forest, and 10% for steppe, based on its frequencies in observed contemporary habitats. David Glue's findings, as well as the findings of dozens of ecologists, biologists, and bird-watchers, complement the THI and help form the EIOPP. The EIOPP has one advantage over the THI and that is that it includes considerably more data. The best way to read the EIOPP is to look at each species and see where it does "best" (scores highest). Common shrews appear to do quite well in all three ground cover habitats, whereas mice and rats appear to prefer semitropical over cold habitats, and water voles prefer steppe over tropical habitats.

Although, theoretically, an analysis of owl pellets provides clues to paleoenvironment, a few constraints about this environmental reconstruction tool need to be addressed beyond the total database being very small. As one archaeologist recently stated, he has never run across a fossilized owl pellet in his 20 years of doing archaeology in southeastern states. The first constraint, then, is that microfaunal clues are not ubiquitous; the following are others:

• There is a bias against rare species unless the sample is extremely large. For example, if a real population of small mammals consisted of 98% voles and 2% shrews and probabilistic sampling were done, the chances of a single shrew being found in a sample would be very small. If that population had 20% shrews in it, the chances would be much better that shrews would be found. Often rare species are important climatic indicators, and a large sample would enhance this point. Nonetheless, rare species are not necessarily found even in a relatively large sample.

• Mammals, by definition, may not be good or reliable environmental indicators because, by definition, mammals carry their temperature around with them. While this definition is correct, it is also likely that the small mammal community can adapt to change in environment by either migrating to an environment better suited to its needs, or through natural selection, through which more or less offspring in succeeding generations are produced at the same time that other species in the same habitat are also producing more or less offspring than they did in the past. With either response, the relative frequencies of all species will likely change. It is this change in frequencies of paleospecies relative to each other that allows us to infer change in paleoenvironments.

Because of these constraints–particularly the lack of a large database on which to anchor analysis–most paleofauna experts look at pollen and sediment data first, and hope that their less quantitative and less data-tied faunal evidence fits the general picture. However pessimistic this may sound for paleofaunal reconstruction using small mammals, zooarchaeologist Sandra Olsen (1994) recently characterized the environment of early Bronze Age England via small mammals: "The presence of the western hedgehog, the western mole, and the water vole suggests a wet woodland habitat typical of the fens during this period."

The Microfaunal "Er Curve"

This "er curve" is more qualitative and more difficult for inferring paleoenvironment than are pollen or sediment curves for the preceding reasons cited. However, given enough samples over time, the expert can infer environmental curves. As with pollen "er curves," microfaunal analysis is based on knowledge about the ranges and tolerances of contemporary species, and, as with pollen and sediment curves, the assumption is made that the present predicts the past. In the case of small mammals, it is assumed that ranges and tolerances have not changed very much through time, at least not since the end of the last Ice Age, some 10,000 years ago. Based on these assumptions and on considerable data on rodents in France, Jean Chaline (1976) reconstructed a temperature "er curve" for the entire French Pleistocene, some two million years in duration. This was an amazing piece of climatic inference and stands as a model to be emulated. In another part of the world, Eitan Tchernov (1968) found differential populations of 29 species of rodents in Israeli deposits dating between 120,000 and 40,000 years old. Because different rodent species prefer different ecological niches (swamp, steppe, wood, rock), Tchernov assumed that the differential populations over time reflected environmental change.

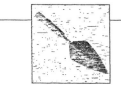

THE EXERCISE

In this exercise, you will play the role of a zooarchaeologist, specializing in the use of microfaunal analysis to reconstruct the environment of a stratified site in a cave in Wales that contains owl pellet remains preliminarily dated as being about 5000 years old. Because this is the time when England–and Wales–were beginning to show evidence of farming, it is a particularly interesting time period for environmental reconstruction, as it will provide the environmental context of British farming. Did the farmers purposely borrow already domesticated crops from the Continent because their environment changed, causing the people to change their food-getting habits, or did they mainly plant the seeds of their own wild plants, with no concomitant change in climate? As a zooarchaeologist, you want to firmly connect the earliest British farming cultures to the environment in which they existed and perhaps to which they had to adapt.

OBJECTIVES

In this exercise, you will

- identify and count by species the prey in one barn owl pellet;
- calculate the proportion of individual prey by species;
- use this and the information on "environmental indicators of owl pellet prey" in Table 10.1 to infer the paleoenvironment for faunal "er curves": temperature, rainfall, ground cover for Wales some 5000 years ago.

DOING THE EXERCISE

1. Measure, take off the foil, and weigh one owl pellet, putting the information in Figure 10.3. Carefully pull apart the pellet and separate bones from fur and other items. Further separate the bones into skulls and mandibles; there should be two half-mandibles for each skull, but even if not, count the largest representation of the bone assemblage. For example, say you sort out three skulls, five half-mandibles, and four femurs of small mammals. Knowing that there is one skull, two half-mandibles, and two femurs per animal, you thus have three animals to identify (because of the three skulls); one half-mandible and two femurs are either missing from the pellet or you overlooked them in your dissection. This is called MNI (Minimal Number of Individuals). Use the reference chart in Figure 10.2 and the reference collection to identify the species of prey in your pellet. Remember that your sample comes from Wales in the western part of Great Britain (see page 141 for geographic clues and species identification). Pay particular attention to tooth position (incisors and molars), and the presence or absence of zigzag molars (voles) or cusps on molars (mice). List and count your prey on the chart in Figure 10.3.

2. Calculate the relative proportion of the prey species in your sample (use Figure 10.3). (Again, the sample is statistically unreliable.) Your sample should add up to 100%.

3. Based on EIOPP information given on page 147, as well as the frequency of each species in your sample, infer the ground cover and, from that, infer both the temperature and rainfall at the time when your sample represented the small mammal community in this specific area in Wales. Draw your three inferences in the appropriate space on Figure 10.4 by filling in zone III, on the "er curves."

Given the very crude nature of the compiled index (EIOPP) and your very small sample, the inferences made will be exceedingly irregular. However, the process of inference is acceptable. If, for example, your sample of three prey includes two mice and one common shrew, you'd conclude by looking at the EIOPP that the environment was relatively warm, wet, and forested, and your "er curve" would reflect this conclusion. If your sample of four includes three water voles and one common vole, you'd conclude that the environment was relatively cool and dry, with no trees, and your "er curve" would reflect this conclusion. (Other inferences may not be so simple.)

4.   In the space indicated in Figure 10.4, write what is happening through time. You need not write the entire sequence, but it would be good practice to write, in qualitative terms, what happened just prior to the data entry on your sample, during the time of your sample, and immediately thereafter.

5.   For each of your environmental reconstruction exercises (Exercises 8, 9, and 10), you have been given a different scenario to work with. In the pollen exercise, your sample was from a 12,000 to 8000-year-old site in upstate New York; in the sediment exercise, your sample was from a 600-year-old site in Zimbabwe; and in the owl pellet exercise, your sample was from a 5000-year-old site in Wales. Obviously, comparing "er curves" from the three different scenarios makes no sense at all. Therefore, you have a brief fourth scenario that will involve all three "er curves": temperature, rainfall, and ground cover, and that will use all three tools: pollen, sediment, and fauna.

As you compare the three "er curves," assume they all came from the same level in an archaeological site in France. There is, in fact, probably more purposefully collaborative scientific research done in France than anywhere else in the world, and French experts report that, in general, the results of one technique of environmental reconstruction has cross-verified the others, with some exceptions. This hypothetical triad "er curve" is therefore commonplace in French archaeology. The three "er curves" in this scenario represent a single layer in a stratified site called Normano in southeast France near the Mediterranean. It is 14C dated as 12,020 years old.

For ease in making your **composite "er curve,"** fill in the entire I–IV zone chronology for pollen (Figure 8.6), sediment (Figure 9.3), and fauna (Figure 10.4). Use a solid line (–) for pollen, a dotted line (···) for sediment, and a dashed line (- - -) for fauna, or use three different colored pens or pencils, one representing pollen, one representing sediment, and one representing fauna. Put these lines in the appropriate spaces on Figure 10.5. Before deciding if the data for zone III cross-verify or not, look at the range of data for zones I, II, IV. If the data in the zones appear to be very close in range but zone III data are not, then you have some basis to judge nonverification. If the three "er curves" for zone III are within the ranges of zones I, II, IV, then they do cross-verify, to some extent at least. Remember that fauna and flora can change quicker than soils; animals can migrate overnight and trees can spread in 50 years, but soils take thousands of years to show change. Be sure to factor this into your decisions. Do your findings cross-verify or is this instance one of those exceptions? Now answer the question in Figure 10.5.

☐   **Check your composite "er curve" with your lab manager for full credit.**

Figure 10.3 Master Fauna Count Chart

Vole	Mouse	Rat	Common shrew	Water shrew	Other

Species	Total Prey	% of Total	Climate Inference
Vole	_____	_____	_____
Mouse	_____	_____	_____
Rat	_____	_____	_____
Common shrew	_____	_____	_____
Water shrew	_____	_____	_____
Other	_____	_____	_____
Total:	_____		

Sample information:

Size (l × w × h) = _____ × _____ × _____ (mm)

Weight   = _____ (g)

Figure 10.4 Faunal "Er Curve"

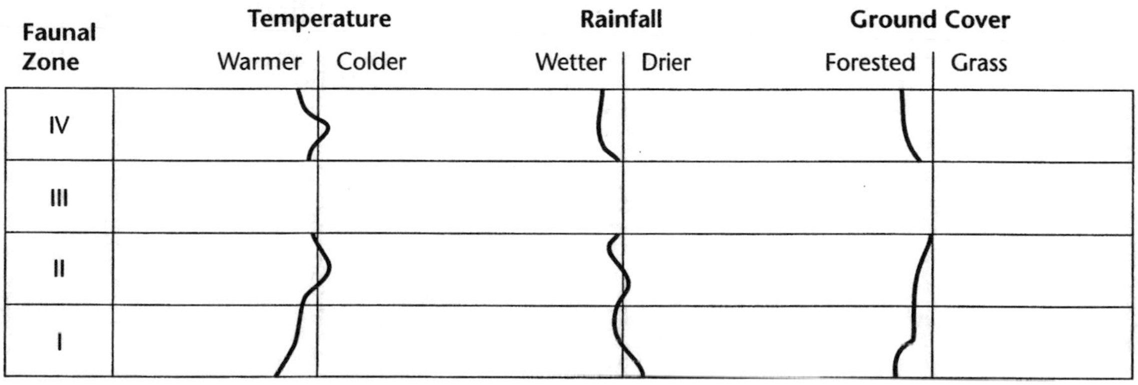

Faunal Zone	Temperature		Rainfall		Ground Cover	
	Warmer	Colder	Wetter	Drier	Forested	Grass
IV						
III						
II						
I						

What is happening through time, as indicated by this faunal "er curve"? _____

_____

_____

_____

_____

_____

_____

Figure 10.5 Composite "Er Curve"

Zone	Temperature		Rainfall		Ground Cover	
	Warmer	Colder	Wetter	Drier	Forested	Grass
IV						
III						
II						
I						

Do the three "er curves" cross-verify? How much is any one out of line with the others? Are you satisfied with the validity of this composite curve? Why or why not? _____

_____

_____

_____

_____

_____

_____

_____

_____

_____

_____

_____

KEY WORDS

paleofauna

zooarchaeology

"er curve"

fauna

owl pellets

environmental indicators of owl pellet prey

composite "er curve"

FOR FURTHER READING

Andrews, Peter. *Owls, Caves, and Fossils.* Chicago: University of Chicago Press, 1990.

Chaline, Jean. "Les Rongeurs." In *La Prehistoire Francaise, Tome 1*, edited by Henry deLumley, 420–24. Paris: Editions du Centre National Recherche Scientifique, 1976.

Davis, Simon. *The Archaeology of Animals.* New Haven, Conn.: Yale University Press, 1987.

Evans, E. M. Nesbit, Judith A. H. Van Couvering, and Peter Andrews. "The Paleoecology of Miocene Sites in Western Kenya." *Journal of Human Evolution* 10 (1981):91–121.

Glue, David. "Food of the Barn Owl in Britain and Ireland." *Bird Study* 21 (1974):200–10.

Klein, Richard, and Kathryn Cruz-Uribe. *The Analysis of Animal Bones from Archaeology Sites.* Chicago: University of Chicago Press, 1984.

MacNeish, R. S., ed. *The Prehistory of the Tehuacan Valley.* 4 vols. Austin, Tex.: University of Texas Press, 1970.

Olsen, Sandra. "Exploitation of Mammals at the Early Bronze Age Site of West Row Fen." *Annals of the Carnegie Museum* 63, no. 2 (1994):115–53.

Taylor, Iain. *Barn Owls.* Cambridge: Cambridge University Press, 1994.

Tchernov, E. *Succession of Rodent Faunas during the Upper Pleistocene of Israel.* Hamburg: Parey, 1968.

West, R. G. *Pleistocene Geology and Biology.* New York: Longman, 1977.

Yalden, D. W. *The Identification of Remains in Owl Pellets.* Reading, England: The Mammal Society, 1977.

11

Differential Recovery Techniques

There's more to dirt than meets the eye. Soil or sediment (the technical terms for dirt) is, in most cases, the most commonly found element in any and all archaeology sites, yet it is what is *in* soil that yields archaeological information that goes beyond merely aiding environmental reconstruction. What is in soil can be macro to micro in size, can be directly or indirectly applied to archaeology, and can be easy or difficult to recover.

What archaeologists are able to recover from soil depends on two factors. First, recovery depends on what has survived between the time of deposition of artifacts/ecofacts and the time of their recovery; in other words, the time between when the original users or makers of cultural items discarded them (knowingly or unknowingly) and when an archaeologist recovers the items. Second, recovery depends on our knowledge about how to recover from the soil what has survived (artifacts/ecofacts).

The term **postdepositional** effects is used to refer to the processes that impact artifacts between deposition and recovery. Most cultural and ecological materials are destroyed through time under normal circumstances, but some are preserved under special circumstances and/or moved from their original provenience. Rodents moving shiny objects from the place where humans deposited them to the rodent's nest; earthquakes moving the lower half of burials feet away from the upper half; simple gravity moving artifacts to lower elevations when conditions are favorable—these are all examples of artifact movement.

PRESERVATION

Understanding the effects of destruction and **preservation** is vital to understanding what can be recovered from archaeological excavations to become the database for prehistory. The following examples show what is recoverable versus what is not.

The recently discovered "Ice Man" on the Austrian/Italian border, in addition to Tollund Man in Denmark and Lindow Man in England, among others, have put preservation in the forefront of eyecatching archaeological concerns. These "special people" are all relatively well preserved, complete with skin, fingernails, hair, and clothing. The question is not so much why did these humans (among several hundred less-publicized cases in both the Old and New World) survive to the present, but rather why not the thousands of other humans who died (or who were killed) in the same time period? What is it about the matrix that surrounded the bodies of these "special people" that preserved them and

154

did not allow the normal biological agents of decay to operate? What do we know of destruction and preservation of artifacts in general?

In a larger perspective, we ask, What part of a past group's behavior, cognition, and emotion—its culture—produces material objects that may become part of the archaeological record? A spear made to hunt a deer can potentially leave material objects behind, such as the spear and the bones from the deer, but does the fact that the hunter (who used the spear) made mother-in-law jokes or divorced each of his four wives or believed in the tooth fairy leave any material objects? Much of a group's "way of life"—its culture—is nonobjectified, meaning much of the behavior, cognition, and emotion never results in any kind of an object. Rules, attitudes, and beliefs by themselves never result in material culture. Clearly, some behavior indirectly results in objects, and some beliefs affect behavior that can result in objects; a group may, for example, decide to use its beliefs about a sun god to build a pyramid toward the sun, decorating both its inside and outside core with sun symbols. This linkage between behavior, cognition, and emotion is assumed to have existed in the past as well. Nonetheless, much past culture was never objectified and could never become part of the archaeological record. Right away, we can talk about the lack of cultural preservation.

And what parts of material culture that were objectified survive biodegradation? Any humanly made or altered object is subject to change in some form, yet all objects are preserved for at least a short period of time and many are preserved for eons. Obviously, a flint arrowhead will be preserved longer and closer to its original condition than a leaf of lettuce, even if both are deposited in the same soil matrix at the same time. Although the edge of the flint arrowhead can be altered by stomping animals or by contact with other hard objects while rolling around in the soil, the leaf of lettuce will probably not survive very long in recognizable form. This is, of course, due to the differential abilities of flint and lettuce to offset the biological forces of decay. Bacteria in the soil will immediately change the lettuce leaf into an unrecognizable glob, whereas, as far as we know, bacteria cannot change flint at all.

Archaeologists have been interested in preservation and decay for a long time. Since the earliest days of excavation, archaeologists have realized that not all objects that were deposited by prehistoric people have survived to become part of the archaeological record. In keeping with modern scientific practices, experimental archaeologists have been successfully demonstrating differential survival rates. For example, experiments have been run under differential soil conditions on buried hair, on different kinds of fabrics, and on different leather-tanning methods. Most experiments concern objects such as flint, pottery, leather, glass, or wood, which have a long life in soil; material items such as food, it is assumed, would quickly biodegrade and have no chance of becoming part of that archaeological record.

OVERTON DOWN

The most energetic and long-term experimental archaeology project yet attempted began in the summer of 1960 on the Wiltshire downs of England as a "turf and ditch" experiment; this is the now-famous Overton Down project. The British Academy for the Advancement of Science commemorated the 100th anniversary of Charles Darwin's *On the Origin of Species*; the project was conceived to give archaeologists knowledge of the long-term effects of preservation, decay, and the movement of objects. Since then, several other projects have been initiated on different parent material to measure the effects of this variable. Morden Bog in Dorset, for example, was built in 1963 on a sandy base but in fairly acidic soil, whereas Overton Down was built on a chalk base.

The earthwork segment was built as a bank of dirt some $69 \times 25 \times 6\frac{1}{2}$ feet high; a ditch was cut into the chalk base next to and parallel to it and along its full length. Seven identical sets of items to be tested for preservation were placed in each of the chalk areas and the turf (soil) areas, with careful notations made as to their positioning. It was suspected that the chalk might act as a preservation agent for some materials. The site was to be excavated in subsequent 2, 4, 8, 16, 32, 64, and 128 years to total seven "slices" of the Overton Down "loaf." After building the earthwork, the bank was left to fill in with silt and the objects in the turf were left to decay. A fence to keep out rabbits, dogs, sheep, cattle, and people did not keep out small burrowers such as moles and worms, but this variable of decay causation and/or movement of artifacts was part of the experiment. Indeed, as was established later, worm activity, as evidenced by worm castings everywhere, pervaded the entire site and was probably responsible for some of the movement of artifacts.

What happened to the ditch in just four years is of interest to archaeologists who have questions concerning the filling in of ditches in this common type of British monument. What is of immediate concern to our focus, however, is the decay or preservation of the various materials thought to have been common in prehistoric societies: flint, pottery, leather, cloth made of different fibers (cotton, linen, wool), wooden tools, and bones of humans and nonhumans. Although no report has been made so far on the human bones, they were buried, interestingly enough, to see if accurate interpretations of known blood types could be made if the bones were buried for a long period of time.

As expected, decay differentially affected the materials: after only two years, some of the fabrics disappeared and some were radically weakened; flint, leather, pottery, and wood showed no change. After four years, all of the fabrics showed signs of decay; the wooden tools had lost one-quarter to one-third of their density; the leather items had stiffened, darkened, and buckled somewhat; the pottery had not changed at all nor had the patina on the flint; and the bone items had hardened somewhat. In 1992, the 32-year excavation showed that the fabrics had completely biodegraded in the turf area but that some pieces remained in the chalk area. Leather had not deteriorated much, nor had wood or bone except for a few cracks. Perhaps the most interesting finding was at Morden Bog, where after only nine years, all ceramics had "disappeared." Due likely to the high acidity of the soil, the finding caused British archaeologists to reassess their belief that parts of England during the Neolithic were without ceramics. Those areas likely had pottery, but it did not survive to the time of the archaeologist's trowel. In summary, items typical of artifacts that were assumed to have been discarded in prehistoric times showed varying degrees of decay in as little as two years, whereas some objects showed no change at all after 32 years.

ORGANIC MATERIALS IN ARCHAEOLOGY SITES

The preservation of inorganic materials (flint, fired ceramics, engravings on rock) is normal; the preservation of most organic materials, such as plant parts, is very rare. Bones, although organic, can become true fossils only if the organic material is replaced by minerals. In order for organic plant material to survive, it must be waterlogged, carbonized, or desiccated. A kernel of wheat provides a good example here. The kernel in question might represent a bit of food or it might tell the archaeologist that grains were domesticated rather than wild; in either case, that kernel of wheat is a valuable piece of data. Of the millions of wheat kernels that have ever existed, the vast majority have been consumed by humans and other animals; fallen to the ground and been stomped on by fast-moving animals; or biodegraded to dust due to rain, air, and bacteria. But a few kernels of wheat have been preserved for archaeologists to recover and study. Some of these kernels became waterlogged in their cultural context in some Belgian swamp; others were carbonized when they were overparched in Turkey; others were totally dried out in an Israeli cave, where they had been stored and forgotten. In addition, fossilized kernels of wheat occasionally are found embedded in clay; this accidental incorporation of kernels can occur when a wet clay pot is set down on a potter's floor or when a worker is resting a loaf-sized mud brick on the floor. In both cases, the wet clay can pick up bits of organic material; in this case, a kernel of wheat. These are examples of the conditions necessary for the preservation of organic materials.

RECOVERY TECHNIQUES

As this discussion has suggested, because the preservation or destruction of objects of archaeological importance is differential, it biases the archaeological record. Additional bias is introduced by differential recovery of artifacts from the soil. One eager young archaeologist-in-training was once heard to say, "You get what's there, no more and no less." As this young archaeologist undoubtedly found out later, what you get depends on how you go about recovering archaeological data, as well as on what has been preserved. A large amount of archaeological material has been lost forever because modern **recovery techniques** to separate artifacts from soil had not yet been discovered. A tremendous amount of information is currently being thrown away because the techniques to recover it have yet to be discovered. Regardless of whether an archaeologist is interested in recovering flint arrowheads or chipping debris, pots or potsherds, or trees or pollen (from the micro to macro size for each category), recovery techniques aim at separating artifacts and ecofacts from their soil matrix.

From the beginning of the relatively unsystematic excavation of sites in the late 1880s in France until the end of the 1960s, archaeologists used a recovery technique we would now call trowel or hand sieving, with the sieving referring to only allowing the soil that did not directly adhere to artifacts to "sieve" through one's fingers. Although we would now cringe at the primitive excavation methods of such famous archaeologists as Lartet and Christy at Laugerie Haute, it was standard practice until fairly recently to recover only the largest and shiniest artifacts and throw away the rest, microartifacts and soil alike. Modern archaeologists advocate that soil should at least be put through a dry sieve, but it is not always done.

Before we judge our archaeology ancestors too harshly in hindsight, it is important to realize that until questions were posed by archaeologists that needed microsized remains to answer them, there was no need to spend the time and effort to do more than manual sieving. The New Archaeology in the 1960s asked new kinds of questions: What was daily life like at site X; how much of each type of food was consumed; how did the people at this site butcher the animals they hunted or herded; what were the steps used by a flint knapper to make a hand ax? To answer these questions, microbones, microflakes, and microplant remains were needed. In addition, archaeologists needed larger samples, whereas in the past, small samples were sufficient to answer such questions as, Did these people domesticate food or not? Hand sieving did not provide the microdata needed.

Screening and Sieving

Of the three basic recovery techniques beyond trowel or hand sieving–**dry screening**/sieving, **wet screening**/sieving, and **flotation**–dry screening is the simplest in equipment and procedure. At many sites today, all soil is dry screened, but only special finds get more elaborate techniques. As the name implies, "screening" uses wire screens as the basis of the technique. Before the 1960s, based on Sir Mortimer Wheeler's excavation methods in the Middle East, a wire screen might be set almost upright a short distance from where excavation was occurring, with dirt tossed at it, the artifacts and chips falling down the front to be at least superficially looked at further, and the soil going through the screen to be part of the "backdirt," never to be looked at again. Today, in dry sieving, the soil is systematically poured from buckets into a sieve, the contents shaken to allow the small soil particles to fall through, leaving the larger clumps of soil and artifacts that were missed in the trowel excavation in the bottom of the screen. Clumps are broken up by hand or by lightly tapping with the handle of the trowel to make sure they contain no hidden objects.

Most archaeologists agree that the *only* trowel for archaeological work is the Marshalltown trowel, manufactured in Marshalltown, Iowa, and immortalized by Kent Flannery in his 1982 spoof in the *American Anthropologist* titled "The Golden Marshalltown." But when it comes to sieves and screens, there has been and continues to be very little agreement as to which shape, size, or mesh is "best." Although commercial sieves are available through scientific supply houses, they are relatively expensive. As most archaeologists make their own sieves, they vary in design and quality: some are handheld, some suspended from swinging bipods or tripods, and some are on rollers. Those that are made on the spot from local materials more often reflect the ingenuity of the maker than any implicit archaeological standards. Archaeologists even disagree on the mesh size, although to some extent this results from attempts to maximize recovery and minimize screen clogging. Window-screen-sized mesh (one-sixteenth inches) will recover most bone fragments, but plant remains other than large nuts or seeds will go through almost all screens.

Wet screening is slightly more complicated than dry screening, as it necessitates pouring soil through a screen as it is immersed in water; the soil dissolves and passes through the screen, leaving small artifacts still in the screen. Variations in size of screen or mesh, as well as in design, are as applicable for wet as for dry screening. The advantage of wet over dry sieving is that it recovers what would have been tossed out in dirt clumps. The first wet sieving was used in the Middle East in 1970 by archaeologist Sebastian Payne, who needed samples of bone that could be recovered by a method that was cheap, simple, efficient, practical, usable anywhere, able to process all of the soil in the excavation, and free from human bias. (In terms of human bias, archaeologists are often biased by what "glitters" in excavations, recovering what is intuitively or purposely looked for rather than recovering what is accurately there.)

To exemplify the recovery efficiency of sieving (dry or wet) over manual troweling, one archaeologist reported that he recovered nine times more bones of large herbivores by sieving the soil than through manual troweling. Another archaeological project in the late 1970s began to use wet sieving using a one-eighth inch screen because they believed their samples were skewed toward large animals. Using water sieving, they recovered additional fish and some plant residue.

Flotation

It was in 1967 at a meeting of the Society for American Archaeology that Stuart Struever reported on a "new technique" of artifact recovery that, in time, revolutionized the archaeological database. In hindsight, it seems remarkable that no one thought to process soil that would maximize recovery of small artifacts and separate heavy- and lightweight artifacts at the same time—think of the amount of microremains that has passed through screens along with the sediment over the years.

The principle of flotation is fairly simple: Items that have lower specific gravity (lighter in weight) than water can be made to float to the top of water, whereas items with higher specific gravity (heavier in weight) will sink. The trick is to "catch" both the light fraction that will float and the heavy fraction that will sink. After using flotation at Apple Creek, a Middle Woodland prefarming site in the lower Illinois River valley, Struever reported recovering large numbers of small seeds, nuts, and bone fragments that would not have been recovered using previously known techniques (in addition, other microartifacts such as flint chips, charcoal, and microsherds are recoverable using flotation). Struever cut the bottoms out of laundry tubs and replaced them with reinforced window screen. The tubs were taken to a shallow stream near the excavation and submerged so that their rims were an inch above the water line. The tubs were then rotated in a circular motion, causing the excavated soil that had been poured from buckets into the tubs to wash out the bottom of the tub into the stream. This caused the light, charred materials (charcoal, carbonized plant materials) to float to the top of the water to be scooped off with a minimeshed tea strainer; heavy rock, ceramic bits, and bone and flint fragments collected on the bottom of the screen and were dumped out on paper or plastic and spread to dry. Similar treatment was given to the scooped-off light fraction materials. This process continued throughout the excavation.

Struever's flotation technique was inexpensive, quick, efficient at recovering small materials, and a sought-after job because volunteers preferred standing in cool water to excavating in the hot Illinois summer sun. The results were phenomenal when compared to using nonflotation methods—Struever calculated that over 90% of plant materials had escaped in manual sieving. By hand troweling at Apple Creek, he found visible plant remains in only one of 600 features; he recovered plant remains in 95% of the 200 features he excavated after inventing and subsequently using the flotation technique. At Apple Creek, he floated 36,000 fragments of hickory nut shell, 42,000 fragments of acorn shell, and over 2000 seeds from three species of wild plant. Flotation worked in the Old World as well: Kent Flannery and his colleagues stated that plant remains were very scarce at Ali Kosh, a site in Iran. Two years and a flotation system later, they recovered over 40,000 seeds.

Struever's initial technique helped eliminate two sources of error inherent in previous recovery attempts: the bias for large over small objects and faunal over floral remains. Before using flotation, Struever hypothesized that the Woodland economy had been based on food gained from hunting, with large to medium-sized fish and plant food of much less importance. By using flotation, he recovered almost double the fish remains, a likely indication that there was more reliance on fish than previously thought. Even more important because of the previous bias against finding floral remains, hickory nuts and acorns emerged as likely staples in the economy, with wild plants widespread. These findings do not necessarily give us an accurate picture of the food/diet of Woodland Native Americans, but they do put fish and plant foods into the picture of what was previously assumed to be an economy based almost entirely on hunting.

During the next 30 years, several variations of flotation were developed in response to what some archaeologists perceived as shortcomings in Struever's technique. For example, his flotation technique required the constant running of water outdoors, a condition that is not common on archaeology sites. Even sites situated near rivers are often far enough away to make carrying every bucket of excavated soil to the river impractical, if not impossible. One variation uses indoor running water for cases where excavation is taking place in conditions that preclude standing in cold running water. Another technique was developed for situations where there is little running water, such as in a desert environment. Here, limited amounts of nonrunning water were used in a double-bucket apparatus that allowed spent sediment to settle in one while the other is in use.

Finally, through the use of chemicals such as zinc chloride, carbonized plant remains (charcoal and seeds) can be separated from bone, even though both are part of the light fraction. Other experiments with chemicals have been successful at separating various parts of either fraction, but considerable care must be taken during the process, as many chemicals are caustic to both human skin and fragile plant parts. Although chemicals and elaborate apparatuses make manual separation of artifact types easier, the more elaborate the technique, the less usable it is in field situations.

Evaluation of Recovery Techniques

Do these elaborate techniques recover enough material that cannot be recovered by any other method to make them worth the time and effort? Are some flotation methods better than others? To test recovery efficiency, archaeologists occasionally test their own techniques by introducing foreign items into their soil samples. Poppy seeds are often used for testing because of their very small size, ease of identification, and because they do not normally occur in archaeological soils. If poppy seeds or some other introduced foreign items are used consistently, efficiency can be compared among sites, not just within a single site. Undamaged foreign items are counted and a known number added to samples before they are screened or put through a flotation system and before subsequent analysis in the laboratory. If the recovery rate percentage is low, something is happening between screening/flotation and the end of the laboratory count; if the items are damaged, some kind of abrasion is occurring during the process. These occurrences serve as warnings to archaeologists, and often the identified problems can be solved. Different techniques do receive different ratings in recovery efficiency tests: Struever's original flotation technique produced an 87% recovery rating, whereas modifications of his system ranged from 84% to 94%. The use of chemicals apparently does not enhance recovery, but it does save time in separating artifacts.

Obviously, then, the largest and most visible objects will be seen and recovered by troweling. Whether a further investment of time and money is warranted depends on the goals of the excavation. If the only interest is in the recovery of projectile points, there is no need to do froth flotation. However, if the reconstruction of diet is the goal (or of environment, or of flint tool technology), then flotation is the only way to get the needed data.

Often, due to lack of time or running water, archaeologists use a combination of recovery techniques. Ideally, they might wish to do flotation or wet sieving on all soil because of each technique's high recovery efficiency, but if there is no running water and if the project is under severe time constraints, it may be possible to do only dry sieving in the field. Under these circumstances, taking carefully chosen samples back to the laboratory for subsequent wet sieving and/or flotation may be the best course of action. Practical considerations often dictate recovery techniques chosen.

POSTRECOVERY PROCEDURES

No matter what technique is used to recover materials—screening or flotation—the small artifacts must be cleaned (washed or rinsed) and dried slowly. Plant residues are particularly prone to damage if they are dried too quickly; residues that shrink and break into smaller pieces hinder identification.

One downside to flotation and its recovery efficiency is the resultant additional amount of artifacts to be sorted and identified; what is lost in additional work, however, is more than made up for in the tremendous amount of data that has already produced considerable new knowledge. Before flotation, archaeological materials were sorted into macrocategories, such as flint, ceramics, bones, and "etcetera." With flotation, there are additional microcategories, such as flint chips, bone fragments, or minisherds, and the "et cetera" becomes charcoal bits and plant parts, which can be further subcategorized into seeds, bark, nuts, and fruit pits. Once small items are sorted, they can be grouped with the appropriate macrospecimens for analysis: microchips with flint tools, bone fragments with entire bones, or minisherds with pottery pieces. Because plant residue is rarely discovered through use of any recovery technique except flotation, there is no macrocategory of plant parts as there is for flint, bone, and pottery. At this point of laboratory analysis, the archaeologist would identify recovered plant parts by species of plant (details on seed and nut identification will be discussed in Exercise 12).

After the materials are sorted into specific categories, including the plant parts that can be identified at the species level, the materials are counted within their categories by raw numbers and/or weighed: plant parts, flint chips, bone fragments, microsherds, charcoal bits.

The recovery of all artifacts, large or small, is not an end in itself; rather, it is a beginning, as it is part of the database for reaching archaeology's many goals. Once the artifacts are recovered, sorted, and identified, analysis gives meaning to data.

THE EXERCISE

In this exercise, you will discover the differences in recovery efficiency using the four basic artifact/ecofact recovery techniques, and you will also be able to measure your individual recovery efficiency to see what kind of an archaeological excavator you would be. The exercise is set up for a two-person team. You can do it alone except for the last technique, flotation; ask your lab manager to help in this part if you are working alone. The following instructions assume this is a two-person exercise. Alternate doing the four techniques, with one "doing" and the other "noting" the first technique; then exchange roles. You will ultimately have the experience of doing two and noting two. Do your analysis individually.

OBJECTIVES

In this exercise, you will

- sieve the contents of the soil from four baggies, using each of the four general recovery techniques: manual troweling, dry sieving, wet sieving, and flotation.
- count the artifacts/ecofacts recovered and assess the technique.

DOING THE EXERCISE

1.   Select a large plastic bag that contains four small baggies of archaeological soil; this constitutes a set of baggies. The large bag has only a letter designation (such as A, B, C), but each of the small baggies is labeled with the same letter designation as well as a number (such as A-1, A-2, and so on). Be sure to keep the set together throughout the exercise and do not mix it up with other sets. Note the number of the four bags (in the first column) on your "Recovery Report" (Figure 11.1). Archaeological soil is the spent backdirt from excavations, sediment that likely has artifact and ecofact materials in it that are "hidden" by the soil itself. Assume that the archaeological soil in the baggies is from a recent excavation and is representative of soil tossed aside. You may assume that because the set of four baggies came from the same specific area in a site that they contain identical materials. It does not matter if the soil is from the Old or the New World, a forager or farming group. For an evaluation of recovery techniques, "dirt is dirt." The volume of soil in each baggie is the same.

2.   One member of your team will do the first technique, manual sieving, and the other will note results. Dump the contents of the baggie onto a plastic tray. Use tweezers, a small card, the end of a pencil—whatever works for you—and separate the artifacts and ecofacts (plant parts, bones) from the soil. Do this separation fairly quickly, as if it were a large sample and you had little time to spend. Return the soil to the baggie, using the brush and scoop. Separate the recovered items on the tray into gross categories: flint, pottery, bone, plant bits, charcoal bits, and "other," as appropriate. (If there were time and we had very sensitive weighing equipment, you would weigh each category of artifact for each recovery technique, but it is more important for you to use your time to do all four techniques and compare results than to weigh each category and have no time to do anything else.) So, given time constraints, you will only *count* items. Record the count numbers for each category of items (as appropriate) under "manual sieving" in Figure 11.1. Return all recovered objects to the baggie with the soil. Do not reuse this small baggie but put it back into the larger bag when the exercise is completed.

3.   Change jobs with your lab partner; the doer is now the recorder and vice versa. Do dry sieving, using your second baggie of archaeological soil in the set. To do dry sieving, put your baggie of soil in a dry sieve (used in sieving excavated materials) and shake the soil through the screen onto a tray. Remove sieved artifacts to a second tray and put sieved soil back into the baggie. Sepa-

rate and count as in manual sieving, noting counts on the "Recovery Report" (Figure 11.1) under "dry sieving."

4. Change jobs and do wet sieving with the contents of the third baggie of archaeological soil. To do wet sieving, take the third baggie of soil and a plastic tray (with a paper towel on the tray) to the wet sieving area and proceed to do the sieving. Use the labeled wet sieve, the square wet-sieve pan, and fill the bottom pan with about 2 inches of water. Set the pan on the floor or table. Pour the contents of your baggie into the sieve. Swish the sieve around and, using your fingers, gently push the soil through the mesh in the sieve. Remove the sieve from the water and transfer the artifactual remains to the paper towel on the tray. One member of your team can spread the artifacts out to dry while the other member cleans the wet sieving equipment. Cleaning the wet sieve means shaking off the water and soil on the sieve (use the sieve brush if needed) and getting rid of the water/soil. Wipe out the pan, if needed, with paper towels. Put the wet sieve back in the pan and return it to where you got it. In the meantime, the second member of the team will sort the recovered objects; count and note them on your "Recovery Report" (Figure 11.1) under "wet sieving." Put the artifacts back into the baggie (the soil is "gone").

5. Alternate jobs and do flotation. Take your last baggie in the set of archaeological soil, along with a plastic tray with a paper towel on it, to the flotation area. Use the labeled flotation buckets, filling the bigger of the two with water to the line marked on the inside. Hold the smaller bucket inside the larger bucket about halfway into the water, and pour the contents of the baggie into the small, inner bucket; immediately rotate the bucket back and forth in a circular fashion, with the water level about an inch above the soil. If you are in doubt about this technique, ask your lab manager to assist you. The agitation of the smaller, inner bucket will cause the soil to go through the screen, the light fraction (seeds, nuts, charcoal) floating to the top of the water, and the heavy fraction (flint, minisherds) sinking to the bottom to be caught by the screen on the smaller, inner bucket. While you or your lab partner is agitating, the other will use a finely meshed tea strainer and scoop off the material that floats. Keep agitating and scooping until there is no more to scoop. Dump the scooped material and the heavy fraction out onto the tray, keeping them separate. While one of you is spreading the materials out on the tray, the other will clean the flotation equipment. Separate into the usual categories and count items, noting them on your "Recovery Report" (Figure 11.1) under "flotation." Clean as you did in (4). Leave all equipment in clean condition. Put the artifacts back into the large bag and give the now used set of baggies to your lab manager (two will contain soil and objects; two will contain objects but no soil). Do not return the baggies to the box, as they cannot be reused by anyone else.

6. Analyze your "Recovery Report." Do this part of the exercise individually, not as a team. Total the flint, pottery, bone, plant bits, and charcoal bits as appropriate and put the number under "Total items" for each recovery technique in Figure 11.1. Based on what you recovered, which is the least and which is the most efficient recovery technique for each individual category of items? Remember that each baggie contained the same number of items. Is there a difference in how much of particular categories of items is recovered; do some categories of artifacts seem to be recovered in higher frequencies (more efficiently) by using one technique over the other? Are some categories not represented using some techniques? Write the answers to these questions in the spaces pro-

vided under "Individual" in Figure 11.2. Based on the total of items you recovered for each recovery technique, what conclusions can you make? Evaluate the four recovery techniques from least to most efficient and write your conclusions in the space provided under "General" in Figure 11.2.

7. Check your "Personal Efficiency Rating" (Figure 11.3). Transfer the totals from Figure 11.1 for each technique onto Figure 11.3 in the spaces provided under "Total counts of items." Ask your lab manager for the known total of items in the archaeological soil baggies. Put these figures under "Known total number of items" column in Figure 11.3. Then calculate percentages for your efficiency for each technique: for example, if you recovered 25 items and the known count is 40, your efficiency rating is 63%; if you recovered a total of 30 items and the known count is 40, your efficiency rating is 75%; if you found 32 items and we told you there were 40, your rating is 80%. Then total your counts and the real counts and do an efficiency rating for all techniques. Are you a budding archaeologist? Did you get an A in recovery techniques?

Finally, write a paragraph in the space indicated on Figure 11.3 on your final conclusions about differential recovery of artifacts based on the relative efficiency of the four techniques. Do this while the details are still fresh.

☐ **Check with your lab manager for full credit.**

KEY WORDS

postdepositional effects

preservation

matrix

recovery techniques

dry screening

wet screening

flotation

FOR FURTHER READING

Bell, M., P. J. Fowler, and S. W. Hillson, eds. "The Experimental Earthwork Project 1960–1992." CBA research report no. 100. York, England, 1996.

Darwin, Charles. *The Formation of Vegetable Mould through the Action of Worms with Observations on Their Habits.* London: Faber and Faber, 1881.

Flannery, Kent. "The Golden Marshalltown." *American Anthropologist* 84 (1982):265–78.

Hastorf, Christine A., and Virginia S. Popper, eds. *Current Paleoethnobotany.* Chicago: University of Chicago Press, 1988.

Payne, Sebastian. "Partial Recovery and Sample Bias: The Results of Some Sieving Experiments." In *Papers in Economic Prehistory,* edited by E. S. Higgs, 49–64. Cambridge: Cambridge University Press, 1972.

Pearsall, Deborah. *Paleoethnobotany: A Handbook of Procedures.* Orlando, Fla.: Academic Press, 1989.

Struever, Stuart. "Flotation Techniques for the Recovery of Small Archaeological Remains." *American Antiquity* 33 (1968):353–62.

Figure 11.1 Recovery Report

Archaeological Soil Baggie #	Recovery Technique	Counts						
		Flint	Pottery	Bone	Plant Bits	Charcoal Bits	Other Bits	Total Items
1. _____	Manual sieving	_____	_____	_____	_____	_____	_____	_____
2. _____	Dry sieving	_____	_____	_____	_____	_____	_____	_____
3. _____	Wet sieving	_____	_____	_____	_____	_____	_____	_____
4. _____	Flotation	_____	_____	_____	_____	_____	_____	_____

Figure 11.2 Recovery Report Findings

General		Individual					
		Flint	Pottery	Bone	Plant Bits	Charcoal Bits	Other Bits
1. _____ (Least)		_____	_____	_____	_____	_____	_____
2. _____		_____	_____	_____	_____	_____	_____
3. _____		_____	_____	_____	_____	_____	_____
4. _____ (Most)		_____	_____	_____	_____	_____	_____

What categories were not recovered by certain techniques? _____

_____

_____

_____

_____

_____

Figure 11.3 Personal Efficiency Rating

	Total Counts of Items	Known Total Number of Items	Technique Efficiency (%)
Hand sieving	_____	_____	_____
Dry sieving	_____	_____	_____
Wet sieving	_____	_____	_____
Flotation	_____	_____	_____
Totals	_____	_____	_____

Overall efficiency rating (total of % found versus % known):_____

Write a short paragraph on differential recovery of artifacts based on the relative efficiency of the four techniques._____

_____

_____

_____

_____

_____

_____

_____

_____

_____

_____

Reconstructing Paleodiets

If we are what we eat, then knowing what we ate should give archaeologists considerable information about what our ancestors were. What people eat—present or past—is important to understanding both human culture and biology. On the cultural side, what we eat has ramifications in technology (we make tools to get food, from spears or digging sticks to tractors); economics (we produce, consume, and distribute food products); social organization (we cook specific foods and present them to people at such special events as weddings or potlatches); political organization (we redistribute food via food stamps, thus giving the federal government use of power); religion (we give symbolic value to many foods, such as Christian bread and wine or Jewish unleavened bread); and worldview (we sing Coca-Cola "friendship" songs while joining hands around a large globe of the world). Food is culturally ubiquitous. On the biological side, many health-conscious Americans avoid foods with heavy fat and cholesterol and instead consume foods with high roughage and protein. Nutritionists tell us there is a direct relationship between what we eat and our resultant biology, our bodies.

The same relationships between culture/biology and food were present in the past as well; how people obtained the food they ate is part of past human behavior, and there is no reason to believe that food constituted any less important a role in economics, social or political organization, or religion in the past. What our ancestors ate not only had an immediate effect on their health during their lifetimes, but in some cases, caused lasting changes in their fossilized bones as well.

If archaeologists can discover what people ate in the past—if prehistoric diet can be reconstructed—a giant step will be taken toward reconstructing paleocultures. What we eat, past or present, can be approached from a behavioral, cognitive, and even emotional perspective, the three major domains of culture. Humans must get food, whether it be by dry farming the top of a mesa or going to the grocery store, so getting food is behavioral. All human groups have very specific rules about what does and does not constitute food, and rules are a cognitive part of culture. Grubs may be regarded as perfectly delightful food in some cultures but not in all; eating dogs may be a luxury in some cultures but repugnant in others; pizza may be high on the valued food list of some cultures, but regarded as nonfood in others. Most cultures have rules about what gender, age, or specific status groups can or cannot eat certain foods: kids don't eat caviar and real men don't eat quiche. And who of us has not gotten a bit emotional at the sight of our favorite food, be it a "death by chocolate" dessert or a juicy steak? For these reasons, it is imperative that archaeologists attempt to reconstruct as fully and accurately as possible what people ate in the past. Only then will those archaeologically important "why" questions be answerable: Why was this food eaten? Why was corn domesticated after beans and squash? Why did this population change so quickly from short to tall?

FOOD VERSUS DIET

Although the two terms **food** and **diet** are often used interchangeably, they are technically different and not always separable in the archaeological record. Food refers to the entire range of edible plants and animals that exists in the world, some of which is selected for eating by reasons of proximity, ease of obtaining, or cultural choice by various human groups. Food, therefore, is potential diet, but what people actually eat is diet. It is easy to note the difference between the two in modern cultures through simple observation, but it is often easier to say what was available as food than what was definitely eaten in the past.

RECONSTRUCTION METHODS

Granted, eating food is a human biological imperative, and it is important to reconstruct past diets, but how do archaeologists go about getting information on food and diet? Luckily, there are a number of different methods of obtaining data on food and diet that, taken together, allow archaeologists to reconstruct what people ate. The inherent biases in the data preclude making definitive statements approximating prehistoric reality; instead, we have to be content with inferences and resultant knowledge.

An Aegean Example

British archaeologist Colin Renfrew suggests that knowledge about a past population's diet comes from three sources: present-day diets of people living in the same area (a kind of ethnoarchaeology), ancient writing about diet and food, and evidence of food/diet from the past, as revealed through archaeological recovery and analysis. This statement is rather specific to Bronze Age Aegeans, and in other situations there may be neither information on relevant present-day diet nor writing. In his reconstruction, Renfrew (1971) began with the diet of modern Greeks because he observed from the archaeological debris that the basic dietary staples of Bronze Age Greeks were the same as modern Greeks, with the exception of potatoes and a few fruits. Modern Greeks cook with olive oil and eat meat, fruit, and fish; the amounts of each food can be observed and calculated as well. Knowing this, Renfrew used a variation of the direct historical approach to obtain the knowledge of what to look for in Aegean excavations. The Greeks wrote about food and diet, including ration allowances (high oil, low meat), and the link between ancient and modern Greek languages is helpful.

Archaeological excavations provided the third component in this reconstruction. Excavations have shown the importance of the olive to Bronze Age Greeks as well as to modern Greeks for cooking, cleaning the body (perfumed oil), and lighting. Olive oil has been found in a Bronze Age jug in a grave, suggesting—as grave goods usually do—the importance of the item, and two marble and ceramic lamps have been excavated as well, both containing residue of olive oil. Archaeologists have excavated remains of all types of modern Greek food (wheat, nuts, animal and fish bones), and they can determine what is wild (some grapes) from what was domesticated (grains). These recovered artifacts are in fairly good harmony with both modern Greek diet and ancient writing.

Not only is this exercise in Greek archaeology a good example of different databases yielding similar results, it additionally suggests that even if writing or use of the direct historical approach (both of which are relatively rare in archaeology) were not available to use in reconstructing diet, the information garnered from only archaeological remains stands a good chance of being correct.

PALEODIET DATA

In addition to Renfrew's third source of **paleodiet**—direct bits of excavated food residue—archaeologists obtain diet information through other sources: through the modeling of existing land-carrying abilities; through the **stomach contents** of Iron Age "bog people" from northern Europe; through bone **paleopathologies** caused by nutritionally deficient diets; through **coprolites;** and through residue on stone tools and the insides of pottery vessels. As Renfrew noted, animal bones and plant parts form the majority of the evidence for paleodiets.

Modeling

One way to look at human paleodiets is to start here: Humans have biological needs that must be satisfied through the extraction of resources (food) from the natural environment. To measure a population's nutritional needs, the archaeologist needs to know its size and demography; only if the demography of a population is abnormal is it potentially a problem. For example, an abnormal number of people of one gender relative to the other might affect extracting behavior; 10 men would find it difficult to hunt for 200 women. Or, an abnormally large population of very old or very young individuals would put a strain on the workforce. A comparison of a population's nutritional needs can then be compared to the estimated resources in the environment to determine if provisioning for the population was easy or difficult, and whether the population had to travel outside its normal area to obtain certain nutritionally necessary items or had to trade. This method of assessing food/diet is very limited, however, because we cannot control many of the necessary variables; we seldom know the real relationship between a population and its land use, or the actual population size at any given time.

Stomach Contents

The 1992 finding of a 5200-year-old man frozen in ice (the "Ice Man") has rekindled interest in a special group of humans, special because of their unusually good preservation. The European "bog people" are noteworthy because preservation of their stomachs and digestive systems provides direct information on their last meals. However, archaeologists are quick to note that there is an inherent bias in stomach content data, because what was eaten may not have been typical of all people at that time, but rather might represent food given to prisoners or sacrificial victims the night before their demise.

Grauballe Man and Tollund Man (Denmark) and Lindow Man (England) are the most well-known bog men, having well-preserved stomach contents. The two Danish bog men had 275 and 610 cubic centimeters of stomach/intestine contents, an amount that gives a good indication of their last meals. Identification of the seeds and nuts was relatively easy because there was no charring to change plant morphology, and in both cases the remains are of well-known domesticated cereals (wheat, rye, barley, linseed) and wild plants (knotweed, weeds, buttercup, goosefoot). Grauballe Man had some meat in his last meal, as small splinters of bone were found in his stomach. The last meal of the most recently found Bog Man, Lindow Man, was very similar to that of the Danish bog men. The "Ice Man's" stomach is devoid of food residue, but the contents of his intestinal tract are currently under analysis.

These last meals did not necessarily duplicate the typical meals of Iron Age peasants in northern Europe, but the range and variety of food items are instructive in attempting to reconstruct their diet. If these meals were representative of their typical diet, the addition of seasonal fruits, vegetables, fish, and a bit more meat would have made the diet fairly nutritious. The British Broadcasting Corporation did a tongue-in-cheek experiment some years ago by boiling up the "bog recipe." It produced a rather oily porridge that appeared rather unappetizing and purple-gray in color, with black and orange flecks. Two well-respected British archaeologists were persuaded to partake of the concoction. Sir Mortimer Wheeler concluded that Tollund Man probably jumped into the bog so he could escape his wife's cooking. Glyn Daniel, a known gourmand who had been accused of studying French menhirs so he could partake of French cooking, claimed it was necessary to wash down the bog recipe with good Danish liquor.

On this side of the ocean, we have our own Native American version of "bog people" at a site called Windover near Cape Canaveral, Florida. In this seventh-century freshwater depression, Native Americans buried at least some of their dead, wrapping the bodies in grass mats, putting them in water, and fastening them to the bottom of the pond with stakes. Peat filled in the pond and preserved the bodies. Based on partial excavation of 160 burials, archaeologists conclude that these Florida natives were hunter-gatherers, who ate a lot of fleshy fruits, mainly wild elderberry, wild grape, and prickly pear cactus. Due to the large number of burials, it is likely that this was normal burial practice and, given the age and gender range of the burials, it is likely that the stomach contents parallel diet reality.

Paleopathologies

Skeletal and dental remains of humans are often good indicators of nutritional status, and are a direct result of food actually eaten. Although the absence of paleopathologies in a skeleton does not necessarily correlate with adequate nutrition during life, many pathologies can point to poor nutrition or stress. Entire populations can suffer from severe dental caries (cavities); society-wide caries usually indicate a diet high in starchy, sticky, soft cereals, as sticky residue from bread or gruel stays on the outside of and between the teeth for bacteria to act on, causing caries. A diet extremely high in starch is normally poor in nutrition, as it often occurs at the expense of fruits, vegetables, and other high-fiber, low-fat food. Additionally, the mean stature of a population can change over a hundred-year period, which suggests nutritional stress, as genetic changes do not occur that quickly. Other indicators of stress in ancient populations have included Harris lines (dense concentrations of bony material on the insides of long bones) and porotic hyperostosis (porous bone found on the forehead and upper surface of eye sockets on skeletal remains). It is usually easier to find indicators of nutritional stress than to assess the indicators' cause. Some nutritional deficiencies leave no skeletal change (pellegra); some deficiencies cause death before bone is affected (beriberi); and single deficiency diseases (porotic hyperostosis) are relatively rare.

Recent work with carbon and nitrogen isotopes and trace elements such as strontium and barium reveals that these chemicals leave "signatures" that record the relative prevalence of large categories of food in diets: marine versus terrestrial foods, arid versus humid-climatic-zone foods, meat versus plant foods. The strontium content of human bone as measured by the ratio of strontium to calcium is used to measure the relative amount of meat versus plant food consumed by a population.

Coprolites

Analyzing fecal remains may not sound like a noble archaeological endeavor, but undigested remains of food (seeds, plant tissues, small bones) that have gone through the digestive system are another direct indicator of what was eaten (if only by a single individual in each case); occasionally, there are latrine deposits that would be treated as group data. In addition, fecal material may contain evidence of parasites or pathogens that can indicate disease or nutritional stress. The preparation of dried fecal material (including that of mummies) from caves in desert areas—the most common places such remains are preserved—separates undigested food from the fecal material. After three days of the material soaking in water in a closed container, food items can be separated, counted, and stored. Seeds such as amaranth, wheat, melon, or squash often come through with little change and are easily identified as to species. Occasionally, feathers or the bones of small animals appear in the residue as well.

The oldest coprolites found, to date, are reported to be a million years old, but many archaeologists are skeptical about assigning human status to the finds. Other "old" likely fecal materials come from Terra Amata, dated at 400,000 years old, and Lazaret, which is a Neandertal site. The coprolites in neither of these cases react well to chemical tests. The classic study of coprolites was done in the early 1970s on over 100 coprolites in the Tehuacan Valley in central Mexico, then dated at about 7000 years old. This analysis was part of the project's broadly based questions concerning early plant domestication in the valley. Closer to modern times, archaeologists at the Middle Woodland Salts Cave site in Kentucky (2000 years old) suggest the following frequencies of plant residue: goosefoot 24%, sunflower 25%, marsh elder 14%, squash 3%, with other minor domesticates and wild foods making up the other third of plant foods. Coprolite analysis of the fecal material remains from the "Ice Man" will be very informative. As there are no stomach contents for this important find, intestinal and fecal material analyses will be the only direct and specific evidence of food ingested.

There are some problems with coprolite analysis, the main one being that it is not always possible to differentiate human from nonhuman remains; archaeologists must use association, context, or chemical tests to assess human coprolites; mummies' and "bog people's" fecal remains are the only true and certain human remains. Coprolite analysis is also biased by preservation. Leaves, roots, and shoots were likely eaten by foragers and farmers alike, but their tissues are quickly and completely digested, and what few fragments do survive to this point are almost impossible to identify. Chemical analysis of food residues—still in its infancy—may alter this picture in the future.

Finally, coprolite data and analysis work best when they are used along with pollen, faunal, and bone chemistry analyses. If an archaeological site happens to show each of these independent clues, and if they cross-verify, then the archaeologist has a reasonably good idea of the represented people's diet. Unfortunately, this is a very rare situation.

Residues

Modern technology has introduced two additional (if limited) tools for assessing direct dietary intake: the assessment of animal-blood residues on flint, and organic residues in ceramics. Although a number of archaeologists have reported finding animal-blood residue on flint tools in both the Old and New World, recent experiments have suggested that blood elements break down in as little as two years; hence, the use of extreme caution in assigning species to these blood remains. Often, sufficient organic residue in ceramics exists to enable archaeologists to come to limited conclusions about food items that are cooked and then become diet items. Dental profiles can be used to identify cholesterol and meat; certain plant waxes indicate vegetables such as cabbage or turnips; another case indicated the cooking of leeks. A dark stain that turned out to be a wine band was recently found in a ceramic jar in Iran; organic elements identified it by its residual acid. Beer has been identified by its barley remains in the same site, causing one archaeologist to comment that the site resembled a 5000-year-old college "block party." These findings of blood and food residue on flint and pottery are so rare that they are mentioned only because of their uniqueness, rather than because of the knowledge they can provide. The finding of horse blood on a knife in central France dating to 20,000 years ago would give us no more information than we already have, and the finding of olive oil residue in bowls from Bronze Age Greece hardly raises an eyebrow.

ARCHAEOLOGICAL EVIDENCE OF DIET

The direct recovery of plant and animal remains in archaeological excavations is the major evidence and source of inference for prehistoric food and diet. Again, we are cautioned that presence of plant and animal remains does not translate directly into dietary use. Animal bones indicate what species were present, not necessarily what was eaten, as animals can be used for other than dietary consumption: bones and antler for tools, sinews for cording, wool, hair, and hides for clothing or shelter. Plant remains also indicate presence of certain species, but not necessarily dietary use; plants can be used for bedding, fish poisons, weaving materials, or medicines, in addition to serving as food. However cautioned, most archaeologists admit that, in the absence of anything for humans to eat other than plants and animals, the remains that are securely tied to cultural debris do indicate "that which was eaten."

Animal Bones as Evidence of Diet

Bones and antlers of animals are often found in archaeology sites, but only in soils that have low acid content. Easily seen macrobones, coupled with the microbones that are recovered by flotation, represent the potential faunal component of human diet. The bones of burrowing animals such as rats and moles must be eliminated from analysis, as they are not likely to have been part of human diet; their bones are due to postdeposition effects.

Identifying species from recovered animal bone is the job of experienced **zooarchaeologists,** who specialize in "archaeological animals." The amount of bone that can be identified to the species level is variable from site to site, ranging from 90% to 10%; teeth and long bones with epiphyseal ends are easily identified, but rib bones are not. Zooarchaeologists either set up their own reference collection or use existing ones at museums, comparing modern bones to their excavated fauna. The counting of animal bones that occurs after identification has changed drastically over the years, from the use of qualitative terms such as "a lot of horse bones and only a few ibex" to quantitative, real counts. Today, most archaeologists count the "minimum numbers of individuals" (MNI) represented by the bones of each species, as this takes into account different animals having different numbers of bones. If you were doing only raw counts and trying to compare them for the relative frequency that they represent, you would run into problems, such as the fact that the major vertebrates have 29–47 skeletal elements, but fish have 2000. Two thousand fish bones may represent one fish in an archaeology site, but 2000 horse bones would represent at least 50 horses. After determining MNI, the numbers must be converted into estimates of food value as, for example, one rabbit does not provide the same amount of potential food as one bison.

Plant Remains as Evidence of Diet

It has always been taken for granted in archaeology that prehistoric people used animals for food, but plant foods have often been ignored, unless domestication becomes involved. This is likely due to several reasons: movie and television images of Native Americans hunting buffalo on the high plains; the Anglo-American dietary emphasis on meat eating; and the fact that until flotation was invented in 1967, plant remains were seldom recovered in an archaeological context. In contrast, how many movies are there showing Native Americans driving mushrooms over cliffs? These factors have biased our perception to favor animal food relative to food eaten in the past. Nonetheless, if ethnoparallels with modern foragers can be used to estimate animal versus plant food in diets, we can expect to find evidence that plant food in the diet of prehistoric foragers has been drastically underestimated.

Although most plant remains quickly biodegrade and are not preserved in soil, in some cases waterlogging, desiccation, or carbonization preserves them. The conditions necessary for waterlogging (water) and desiccation (dry conditions) are geographically more limited than carbonization but less damaging to the residue. Kent Flannery (1986) recovered over 30,000 desiccated nuts, seeds, and pits from six layers at Guilá Naquitz in Oaxaca, Mexico, most of which were residue from wild plants–dry caves in the dry parts of Mexico are excellent preservers of plant materials. In contrast, the conditions necessary for carbonization are found worldwide. When carbonization preserves plant residue, flotation is the only way to recover the seeds and nuts. Carbonization results from the accidental overparching of grains, when grains were coincidentally placed near fires, and/or from true fires where plant parts were near, but not in the fire itself. Actual charring reduces plants to "carbon dust." Many species of grains require heating to remove the edible seeds from the husks; once artificially parched, grains are ground and the husks winnowed out. This process is vital, because humans cannot survive ingesting spiky husks. When grain was accidentally overparched, it was likely tossed in the refuse pile, and archaeologists have recovered at least some of it. Apparently, it was not unusual to overparch in days when heat control was difficult, as large amounts of overparched grain have been found in some refuse pits. Nutshells were probably never purposely parched because they are not food, but they may have become carbonized when tossed into the fire as an additional fuel resource. Those species of grain not needing to be parched may have become carbonized when people kept stored foods too close to fires or when houses or storage areas burned down.

Once recovered, dried, and sorted, various plant remains must be identified to the species level if possible, a job made relatively more difficult if the residue is carbonized, as plant morphology is usually changed under this condition. Although archaeologists and **archaeobotanists** often have access to an herbarium (where samples of "dead" plants from a particular location are kept), herbaria curators are not always willing to lend collections for comparison purposes. Most archaeologists, therefore, build their own collections, beginning with modern types of plants. One way to build a reference collection is to walk a mile or so from the center of a recently excavated site in at least four directions, collecting samples of wild (and domesticated, if pertinent) plants. Back in the laboratory, the collected plant parts are dried and, if carbonization occurred in the archaeological sample, part of the collection of the modern materials would be carbonized to simulate the morphology of paleocarbonization. This becomes the site-specific reference collection to be used for identifying plant parts. Although most nuts are identifiable, and, after practice, most grains as well, seeds—even large seeds such as beans—are often difficult to identify, even by an expert. Lists of morphological traits are not very useful, pictures are somewhat more useful, and the reference collection is the most useful tool in species identification.

The next steps in the laboratory procedure are to sort the recovered plant residue into subcategories, weigh and/or count each, and convert weights/counts into estimates of food value. A thousand seeds of knotgrass will fit into a small thimble, whereas it takes only three lima beans to fill the same amount of space; an acorn is not the same as a grain of wheat, as they differ in size and in what they contribute to the diet.

Once flotation began turning up small "strange" seeds in Midwestern and mid Atlantic sites in the United States that were dated anywhere from 5000 to 2000 years ago, a number of archaeologists have tried to discover if the Native Americans were actually domesticating the seeds in large numbers or gathering them in the wild state. Such seeds as amaranth, marsh elder, maygrass, and lamb's-quarter show botanical change during this time, and it is now generally agreed that Native Americans did domesticate these small seeds. In what is likely the only attempt to estimate the native seed consumption in eastern Native America, Richard Yarnell working in Salts Cave, Kentucky, used 720 grams of human fecal material from 167 samples (referred to previously). Later, he added nutshells and paleobotany remains (not fecal) to this database. Yarnell concluded that the plant part of the diet for those Native Americans was 40% oilseed crops (such as sunflowers); 36% small grains (such as amaranth); 2% weedy greens; 2% fleshy fruits; and 20% nuts (such as hickory). Although this is only an estimate of likely plant foods available for food, rather than true diet, it begins to assess the importance of plant food in prehistoric diet.

PUTTING SOME PIECES TOGETHER: ARROYO HONDO

In most cases, archaeologists find only one diet indication per site—if they are lucky. They may find some desiccated seeds and bones, or some fecal material, or enough human burial fossils to enable them to see systematic paleopathologies, but it is exceedingly rare to find two or more diet indicators for the same situation. In these rare cases, each piece of evidence is evaluated separately and then compared. If they match, they validate the findings of the other evidence; if they do not, it is back to the drawing board.

One such rare situation occurred at Arroyo Hondo, near Pecos, New Mexico, in the 1970s. Arroyo Hondo is a site of a major Native American settlement that existed in A.D. 1400–1500. The Arroyo Hondo project was run for a number of years by the School of American Research in Santa Fe. The project included experts in excavation, experts in bone analyses (paleopathologies), paleobotanists, and zooarchaeologists. The plant specialists identified the species of domesticated and wild materials and quantified their identification, adjusting for various factors. The paleopathology expert looked at 120 skeletons and concluded that there was a high proportion of maize (corn) in the diet, as shown by porotic hyperostosis in the bone. Her evaluation of the strontium levels and bone collagen and nitrogen led to a readjustment of the diet proportions suggested by the excavators and paleobotanists (archaeobotanists), but essentially the two studies were within 20% (total) of each other. Given the problem of sample size, differential preservation bias, and the inability of bone tests to give finely tuned results, perhaps this is as good as we can do at this point.

INTERPRETATION

Once animal bone and plant parts have been converted into estimates of food value, archaeologists can begin to make inferences about prehistoric diets. Two well-respected archaeologists have attempted to go from observing residue to reconstructing paleodiets: Richard MacNeish, at several central Mexican sites in the Tehuacán Valley, and Kent Flannery, at both Ali Kosh in Iran and Guilá-Naquitz in Mexico. MacNeish converted both plant and animal residue to liters of food produced, whereas Flannery converted residue to weight (grams) rather than volume (liters) and, for other purposes, to portions of food (in 100 gram units). Unfortunately, the two systems are only internally comparable (by levels within individual sites), and therefore cannot be used to compare diets of particular populations; however, each did allow the investigator to look at change in diet over time at one particular place, and that *is* comparable information.

Because of preservation bias in the archaeological record for recovering plant materials, many archaeologists are uncomfortable about reconstructing *any* paleodiet. Gayle Fritz (1994, 27) recently commented that though she believes Native Americans in the eastern United States were domesticating local seed plants earlier than previously recognized, most experts "refrain from speculating in print as to percentages of calories or nutrient components derived from these crops." She continues: "Personally, I am unwilling to go on record with a speculation of that sort." Regardless of her pessimism, an analysis of plant and animal residue, if used with caution, allows archaeologists to do gross estimations of paleodiets. When MacNeish attempted to reconstruct the diet of one of the Native American populations in his Mexican study, he postulated a certain amount of domesticated maize in the diet; the expert analyzing the coprolites at the site disagreed with him and claimed that no maize was eaten and only wild resources were exploited. Subsequent isotopic analysis of the bones of 12 individuals from that population supported MacNeish's reconstruction more than it did the coprolite analysis, allowing us a measure of confidence in a process that begins with recovered animal and plant residue and ends with reconstructed paleodiets.

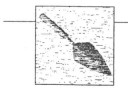

THE EXERCISE

As has been established through the reading, archaeologists are heavy on data about diet, but light on confidence that the data are unbiased. This discrepancy results in less-than-satisfactory conclusions about diet in prehistoric times. Nonetheless, inferences can be made about what people ate and the general nature of the relationship between types of food people and food in the past, as long as we realize the level of confidence—and lack thereof—that is generated by the bias.

This exercise will take you through the basic steps of reconstructing the diet of a prehistoric population, from a sample to identification of specific foods to interpretation and diet. We will concentrate on plant rather than on animal-based food because, with the exception of Eskimos and other Arctic dwellers, foragers in all places and at all times have more likely relied on plant foods rather than on animal foods for the bulk of their diet. With that one exception, up to 80% of the diet of hunter-gatherers today is based on plants, even if most of the people refer to themselves as "hunters." The assumption is that a similar picture was true of prehistoric foragers in the past as well. When domestication occurred 10,000 and 9000 years ago in the Old and New Worlds, plant foods dominated diets, because the production of meat is energy expensive. Pastoral people have lived in a few areas of the Old World for several thousand years; a few groups still practice this basic economy, but as compared with foragers (early) and farmers (later), their numbers are small. Today, however, and probably in the past, meat typically is eaten daily either in small amounts to supplement plant foods, or saved for some special occasion, where it becomes "honored" food. Even in our heavy meat-eating culture, that 4-ounce hamburger is offset daily by several pounds of bread, potatoes, peanut butter, lettuce, and beer—all plant-based foods. We are in that 80/20% plant versus animal bracket as well.

In this exercise, you have a flotation sample from a dry cave in southern Arizona, dating to about 4000 years ago. You can expect to find both wild and domesticated plant residue. Because of the extreme desiccation conditions, the plant residue has survived with a minimum of destruction or modification (comparable plant residue in other parts of the world would have biodegraded or been preserved only if carbonized, which more drastically changes the residue morphology). Extreme aridity will have shrunk the seeds and nuts in your sample, but the general shape is preserved and can be identified.

OBJECTIVES

In this exercise, you will

- separate your sample into subcategories (species).
- identify and count your plant materials; convert the relative counts into food values and food rank orders.
- make inferences about the diet of the prehistoric Arizonians based on these data.
- make inferences about the diet of this group and their predomestication ancestors.

DOING THE EXERCISE

1.   Take a sample and dump it out on a tray. For the purposes of this exercise, assume it is the plant residue that came from a flotation sample from a 4000-year-old site in Arizona. The soil has gone through the flotation system and the heavy fraction has been removed. The plant residue has been dried and is ready to be analyzed. [Note: Because this exercise focuses on plant food—which dominated the diet of prehistoric and historic people—and not on animal food, animal bones were purposely not included in the recovery materials. In real sites, both animal and plant materials are expected and both might be recovered to be identified, counted, and used to establish diet estimates. But there is not time for you to learn to identify animal species (from bone splinters) as well as plants (from seeds and nuts), so for this exercise, the information on meat and fish is simulated and found in Figure 12.1. You will use the fauna figures only in coming to final conclusions about the specific diet of the prehistoric Arizonians.]

Separate your plant materials into individual species, using a pencil, a card, or whatever is easy for you to use. To do this, use morphological clues just as professionals do, but remember that there will be variability even within the same species: size, color, shape, unusual features such as pits, roughened or smooth coat (if the plant residue is carbonized—and black—color would be of no help). Use the flora reference chart. It refers to identified carbonized and uncarbonized plant residue that is apt to be in your sample. The reference chart includes all of the species in your sample, but don't assume that all species on the reference chart are necessarily in your sample. Use the chart to compare and then identify your materials. Once identified, list each plant species by common name in the far left-hand column of your "Diet Evidence Chart" (Figure 12.1). Keep each species separate in a pile on the tray for later counting.

Throughout the reconstruction of paleodiets, it is assumed that the samples, though small, represent food eaten; in all samples, the plant residue was excavated from living floors in archaeology sites. The $64 question is, What is the relationship between recovered food residue and diet? Does the most common species in a site's residue represent the most common species eaten? The answer here is "probably." Does 15% of plant residue identified as species X mean that the diet was composed of 15% of this species? The answer here is "not necessarily," but as Kent Flannery suggests, "We have no basis for assuming anything else" (1986, 305). Plant residues are not wholly comparable, as some are represented by edible parts of the food itself (acorns or onions), some are represented by the inedible parts of a species that are tossed away (fruit seeds or chewed agave cuds), and some foods were eaten raw elsewhere (fruits, berries, nuts) and don't show up in residue at all. Because acorns and onions were both eaten, it is valid to equate them, but it is not valid to equate acorns with seeds that were not eaten. Even though plant residues are not wholly comparable, "fiddling around with the data" and adjusting all figures will probably only compound errors. As Flannery cautions, raw figures (with minor adjustments, in a few cases) at least reflect the activities of the people who left the debris rather than an archaeologist's fantasies. As long as caution is used and only rank orders of food used to infer diet, the noncomparability is less of a problem than it would at first seem.

Specifically, what represents what? How is one acorn equated with one melon seed? Is it one acorn and one seed, or one acorn and one melon, or one oak tree and one vine of melons? Using logic, and Flannery's caution and prece-

Table 12.1   Guilá Naquitz Food

Species and Part	Weight of 1 Edible Part (unit of food—g)	Total Items Recovered	Total Weight of Edible Part (g)	Rank Order
Piñon nuts (pine nuts)	0.167	366	61	7
Onion bulbs	11.0	3	33	8
Agave hearts[a]	2,795.0	368	5,983	3
Acorn nuts	3.2	8,424	26,957	1
Hackberry fruit	0.18	3,112	560	5
Bean seeds	0.125	1,194	149	6
Melonlike fruit	50.0	46	2,300	4
Squash seeds[b]	0.167	150	25	9
Mesquite seeds[c]	1.67	4,603	7,687	2

Source: Data from *Guilá Naquitz: Archaic Foraging and Early Agriculture in Oaxaca* (Flannery 1986).

[a]Agave is a large fibrous century plant with a heart that can be baked and eaten.
[b]Squash seeds, rather than squash pulp, was apparently the eaten part because much of the seed residue appears to have been roasted.
[c]Mesquite is a shrub with pods and beans that are edible.

dents, most experts abide by the principle that one acorn is equivalent to one unit of food, but because melon seeds were apparently not eaten (as squash seeds were), one melon seed is the equivalent of one melon. This principle is used during the exercise.

Table 12.1 shows how Flannery dealt with the data from six layers of debris from Guilá Naquitz in Mexico (at a time that put the people from this area on the brink of domestication). It lists each important species and what part is edible, the weight in grams for each unit of edible food, the total number of items actually recovered in the six stratified layers, the total weight in grams of edible parts, and the resultant rank ordering of food. Only squash is likely to have been domesticated at this time.

To get the final rank orders at Guilá Naquitz, Flannery multiplied the weight of one edible part by the number recovered; for example, a piñon nut weighs 0.167 grams; the team recovered 366 nuts; this totals 61 grams. The "total weight of edible parts" of the agave plant was adjusted because much of the edible heart results in chewed cuds that are not edible, yet part of the heart is completely eaten. This results in mixed evidence: desiccated cuds and "nothing"; hence, Flannery adjusted this figure. Bean pods represent a number of seeds each, so the total items were translated to mesquite seeds and bean seeds. Look carefully at Table 12.1 because you will be using it as a model for your own residue translations.

You have already listed the identified species from your sample on the "Diet Evidence Chart" (Figure 12.1). Use Table 12.2, which lists weights for one unit of food in grams for each species of plant residue that may be in your sample; put the weight of one unit of each species you identified on Figure 12.1 (second column). (There are more items here than you have species.) Your instructor or lab manager may give you a sheet to paste over the space on Table 12.2.

2.   Count the items in each of your piles of plant residue and note the count on Figure 12.1 as "total items recovered." Multiply the unit weight by the

Figure 12.1 Diet Evidence Chart

Plant Species	Weight of 1 Edible Part (unit of food—g)		Total Items Recovered		Total Weight	Rank Order	Diet			
							P	F	C	Fb
_____	_____	x	_____	=	_____	_____	___	___	___	___
_____	_____	x	_____	=	_____	_____	___	___	___	___
_____	_____	x	_____	=	_____	_____	___	___	___	___
_____	_____	x	_____	=	_____	_____	___	___	___	___
_____	_____	x	_____	=	_____	_____	___	___	___	___
_____	_____	x	_____	=	_____	_____	___	___	___	___
_____	_____	x	_____	=	_____	_____	___	___	___	___
_____	_____	x	_____	=	_____	_____	___	___	___	___
_____	_____	x	_____	=	_____	_____	___	___	___	___
			(Subtotal)		(_____)					
Fish[a]	_____	x	2	=	_____	_____	___	___	___	___
Deer	_____	x	1	=	_____	_____	___	___	___	___

P = protein; F = fat; C = carbohydrate; Fb = fiber

[a]Fish are about 85% usable as food, so a 2 lb (average) fish = 771.10 edible g; as deer are about 65% edible, a 40 kg deer = 26,000 edible g. Enter these values in "weight of 1 food unit" and "total weight."

Was this a nutritious diet? Why or why not? _____

_____

_____

_____

_____

_____

_____

_____

Figure 12.2 Change through Time Study

Species	8000-year-old sample (g) % of Total		4000-year-old sample (g) % of Total	
Total plants	__2800__ (g)	_____	Total plants _____ (g)	
Fish (MNI = 5)	_____ (g)	_____	Fish (MNI = 2) _____ (g)	
Deer (MNI = 1)	_____ (g)	_____	Deer (MNI = 1) _____ (g)	

What happened in terms of diet to the group between 8000 and 4000 years ago? _____

_____

_____

_____

_____

_____

_____

□ **Check all figures with your lab manager for full credit.**

Table 12.2   Weight of Residue in Grams

Species	Weight of 1 Unit of Food (g)	Species	Weight of 1 Unit of Food (g)
Acorn (large) (N)	4.2	Pear seed (=1 pear) (F)	140.0
Amaranth seed (C)	0.0002	Peach seed/pit (F) (=1 peach)	60.0
Apple seed (=1 apple) (F)	160.0	Piñon nut seed (N)	0.167
Bean (small, white) (V)	0.125	Piñon nut with wings (N)	0.04
Canary seed (C)	0.008	Rapeseed (C)	0.002
Citrus seed (=1 orange) (F)	150.0	Rye (domestic) (C)	0.03
Flax seed (C)	0.006	Squash seed (V)[a] (=1 squash seed)	0.163
Green pepper seed (V) (=1 green pepper)	100.0	Sunflower seed (C)	0.128
Hickory nut (N)	4.0	Tomato seed (V) (=1 tomato)	120.0
Lentil (V)	0.053	Walnut (N)	1.4
Melon seed (=1 melon) (F)	50.0	Watermelon seed (F) (=1 melon)	100.0
Millet seed (C)	0.004		
Niger seed (C)	0.005	Wheat (domestic) (C)	0.02
Oats (domestic) (C)	0.02	Yucca seed (C)	0.01

N = nut, V = vegetable, C = cereal grain, F = fruit

[a]Cereal grain = various seeds that are presumably roasted and ground and turned into tortilla-type food on a flat griddle or used in gruel/porridge

number of items recovered (as Flannery did), and mark the total weight of each edible plant food. Add the animal and fish data, using the information at the bottom of the figure. Using both the relative weights of the plant residue and the animal weights, do a rank order of food at this site and note it on Figure 12.1 under "rank order." Return the plant materials to the sample baggie and give it to your lab manager.

3.   Although a rank order of food eaten gives us a gross impression of relative amounts of certain foods in a diet, it does not say whether the diet was nutritious or not. Using the following advice of the United States Department of Agriculture (USDA) and the American Heart Association, assess the diet represented by the residue: Food high in fat and cholesterol (meats, nuts, fat) should be kept at a minimum; food high in fiber (cereal grains) should be eaten in large amounts; food high in protein (lean meat, fish, nuts, beans, peas, grains) should be eaten in moderate amounts; foods high in carbohydrates (fruits, vegetables, grains) should be eaten in moderate amounts. Vegetables and fruits have almost no fat; most fish have little fat; vegetables and fruits have little protein; meat has no carbohydrates (at least this is what we believe today). Note that there is an overlap in the "good" and "bad" food: meat is in both the high cholesterol/fat and high-protein categories; one is "bad" and the other is "good."

Using this information, write H(igh), M(edium), or L(ow) for each food for relative amounts of protein, fat, carbohydrates, and fiber in the spaces provided under "Diet" on Figure 12.1. Using the USDA advice previously given, along with the relative amount of each food consumed as noted in your rank orders, assess the diet of these Arizona people some 4000 years ago. Write a short paragraph on the nutritional status of their diet at the bottom of Figure 12.1.

4.   Use the counts of plant and animal residue from Figure 12.1 and compare them to the following data for a change-through-time study; write your data on Figure 12.2. Assume both sets of figures derive from flotation from the same site, but that your sample is radiocarbon dated as 4000 years old and the other sample is radiocarbon dated as 8000 years old. (Get the fish and deer data by multiplying the MNI by the grams as given at the bottom of Figure 12.1.) Total the weight of the plant items in your sample and put the figure on Table 12.2. Put the fish and deer values on the chart for the 8000- and 4000-year-old samples; do a percentage for plants, fish, and deer. As all data are reported in percentages, small and large samples can be compared. Write your assesment of change through time on Figure 12.2

KEY WORDS

food

diet

paleodiet

stomach contents

paleopathologies

coprolites

zooarchaeologist

archaeobotanist

FOR FURTHER READING

Flannery, Kent, ed. *Guilá Naquitz: Archaic Foraging and Early Agriculture in Oaxaca.* Orlando Fla.: Academic Press, 1986.

Ford, Richard. "Paleobotany in American Archaeology." *Advances in Archaeological Method and Theory* 2 (1979):268–336.

Fritz, Gayle. "The Value of Archaeological Plant Remains for Paleodietary Reconstruction." In *Paleonutrition,* edited by Kristin Sobolik. Carbondale, Ill.: Center for Archaeological Investigations, 1994.

Gilbert, Robert I., Jr., and James H. Mielke, eds. *The Analysis of Prehistoric Diets.* Orlando, Fla.: Academic Press, 1985.

Glob, P. V. *The Bog People.* London: Faber and Faber, 1969.

Hole, Frank, Kent Flannery, and J. A. Neely. *The Prehistory and Human Ecology of the Deh Luran Plain.* Ann Arbor: University of Michigan, Museum of Anthropology, 1969.

MacNeish, Richard, ed. *The Prehistory of the Tehuacán Valley.* 4 vols. Austin, Tex.: University of Texas Press, 1970.

Pearsall, Deborah. *Paleoethnobotany: A Handbook of Procedures.* Orlando, Fla.: Academic Press, 1989.

Renfrew, Colin. *Before Civilization.* New York: Knopf, 1971.

Renfrew, Jane. *Paleoethnobotany.* London: Methuen, 1973.

Schoeninger, Margaret. "Reconstructing Prehistoric Human Diet." In *The Chemistry of Prehistoric Human Bones,* edited by T. Douglas Price. New York: Cambridge University Press, 1989.

Sobolik, Kristin, ed. *Paleonutrition.* Carbondale, Ill.: Center for Archaeological Investigations, 1994.

Watson, Patty Jo. *The Prehistory of Salts Cave, Kentucky.* Springfield: Illinois State Museum, 1969.

Wetterstrom, Wilma. *Food, Diet, and Population at Prehistoric Arroyo Hondo Pueblo, New Mexico.* Santa Fe: School of American Research Press, 1986.

Wing, Elizabeth S., and Antoinette B. Brown, eds. *Paleonutrition.* New York: Academic Press, 1979.

13

Dendrochronology

For several hundred years, humans in Western societies have noted and recorded the annual cycle of time through observations of the surrounding natural world, from observing the changing seasonal constellations of the night sky to the keeping of precise records of year length in modern electron clocks. People in the non-Western world made similar observations: the Hohokam, in what is now Arizona, built Casa Grande in the 1300s and likely used it as a lunar and solar observatory, perhaps to predict when the scant (8 inches a year) rainfall would come. For desert farmers, knowledge of when to plant crops would have been vital. Stonehenge, built some 3800 years ago by nonliterate British farmers, was also likely used to note annual celestial occurrences and use them to begin the farming cycle. For a far longer period, some biological organisms—notably trees—have incorporated a permanent record of the earth's annual cycle within their structure, but only recently have humans deciphered how to use this information. Varves, coral, and ibex horns show annual increments as well; even fish grow spine rings, but none is as ubiquitous in nature as trees.

One of archaeology's goals is to date cultural remains. This goal is linked to archaeology's other goals: to reconstruct our cultural past, to explain why cultures were the way they were and why they changed through time, and to explain the archaeological record itself. Implicit in these goals is the organizational principle of time; therefore it is imperative that archaeology be able to date its material. **Relative dating** puts materials in order relative to each other, but does not attempt to assign a calendrical number; so-called **absolute dating** assigns calendar dates. In the **chronometric dating** methods (such as 14C), a number of methodological assumptions must be accepted, and it is sometimes problematic to verify chronometric dates except by cross-dating with other chronometric methods. This is possible only if the methods overlap or have the same approximate range of dating. Only a few methods are both absolute and tied to a calendar: coins, varves, and **dendrochronology.** Because it gives dates that are precise to within a year, and because it can be understood by nonphysicists, dendrochronology will be the focus of this exercise.

Dendrochronology is a dating method that is based on counting the record of growth preserved in the concentric **tree rings** (alternating dark and light bands) visible when a stump or the cut end of a tree is examined (see Figure 13.1). Because *dendro* = tree, *chron* = time, and *-ology* = study, dendrochronology, literally, is the study of tree time. In order for dendrochronology to be used, the wood that is being dated is either the archaeological material itself—a wooden artifact—or is in direct or reasonably close contact with the material being dated and well-preserved enough to use. Noah's Ark, assuming it existed and is eventually found, would be an ideal candidate for dendrochronology; archaeologists would know within a few years when the Ark was built and launched. Although most large ships were built in historical times and written records about them exist, a few fossilized ships need tree-ring dating. Because wood is a popular resource for house building, whether for house frames or floor/ceiling beams, dendrochronology can date a number of housing-related episodes: when they were built, when they were repaired, and when they stopped being built, from individual housing units to entire villages. The famous cliff dwellings in the Southwest are an excellent example of this dating method being directly used on something worth dating. We know a great deal about the Hohokam, Anasazi, and Mogollon because we can date their entire building technology.

Artifacts that are in direct or close to direct association with datable wood can also be dated, if less dramatically. A partially intact fireplace with carbonized, but not fully charred, logs can sometimes date the fire and the people who used it. Or, a collapsed house made of perishable materials may contain one or two precious logs that allow archaeologists to date the episode.

In order for wood to be usable for dendrochronology, it must be preserved until archaeological investigation. But, wood, because it is organic, usually biodegrades when tree cells cease to grow; water, air, bacteria, or animals that gnaw wood start the process of destruction. Wood preservation requires either extremely dry conditions, such as in the desert Southwest; waterlogging, such as at Ozette village in Washington State; or true fossilization, such as in Arizona's Petrified Forest, where tree cells have been replaced by minerals. Unfortunately, fossilization takes millions of years, the process needing to begin long before humans were on Earth.

TREES AS ANNUAL EVENTS

Any use of tree rings as annual events assumes the scientific principle of uniformitarianism. As James Hutton, the eighteenth-century geologist, noted, the present is the key to the past; what we see happening today happened in the past as well, such as trees having annual rings. The use of tree rings further assumes that there were variations in tree growth and weather that had similar effects on trees and that posed limiting factors in the past as they do in the present.

Although we do not have to be plant biologists to understand dendrochronology, it's necessary to know a few basic principles about trees and their growth in order to understand how the dating method works. Figure 13.1 shows a half cross-section of a tree "stem" or trunk. The pith (P) is the center of the stem, the xylem wood makes up the majority of the stem, and the "living" cambium layer separates the xylem wood from the bark. In cross-section, the cambium layer is visible only with a microscope, but it can be seen when a twig is scratched with a fingernail. When a tree is first formed, the primary tissue becomes the pith, and yearly growth in the xylem is laid down on top.

Species of trees differ in details, but the growth principles are similar for all wherever they are found. As dendrochronology studies have been done primarily in midlatitudes (United States and Europe), the following discussion reflects temperate tree growth patterns, where annual growth is generally limited to spring and summer, triggered by longer periods of daylight, higher temperatures, and more moisture. Spring and summer growth produce a new ring each year, followed by a dark brown band that separates individual rings. Under a

Figure 13.1 Half a Tree Trunk in Cross-Section

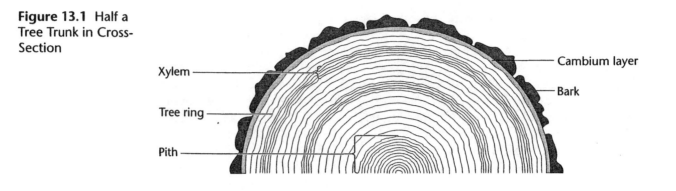

microscope, the size of the cells and the walls and the colors show the growth ring and differentiate one ring from another. It is these yearly rings that form the basis for dendrochronology.

Even if tree rings were identically wide every year, they could still be counted on living, cut, or fossilized trees to assess the age of the tree during its life. Rings on a ceiling beam in a cliff dwelling in New Mexico could be counted and a claim made that the tree used for the beam was 60 years old when it was cut. However, this finding does not indicate *when* the beam was cut, as it is not tied to a modern calendar. This is the point where variation in ring width becomes important. Two famous scientists—da Vinci in the fifteenth century and Linnaeus in the eighteenth century—identified the two major principles of dendrochronology: first, that tree rings vary in width, and second, that temperature and rainfall cause that variability.

The width of rings depends on the amount of temperature and/or moisture during the summer rather than during the spring growth period; temperature and moisture are called "limiting factors" because they limit the possible width of rings. In some areas, such as the Arctic, temperature appears to be the limiting factor, whereas in arid areas, it is the amount of moisture. In midlatitudes, it can be either or both, depending on the particular year. The important point is that the limiting factor in operation during any particular year theoretically affects every tree and every tree ring in a given area in a similar way. Nonclimatic factors such as lack of root minerals, shading by another tree, or tree age also affect ring width, but these effects are noted and affected trees not used.

HISTORY OF DENDROCHRONOLOGY: FROM THE PRESENT TO THE PAST

As early as 1838, a British scientist connected tree rings to dating archaeological material by suggesting that the age of a large tree growing on a burial mound could be determined by counting its growth rings, providing a minimum age for the deposit on which the tree was growing. Four years later, the technique was used in Marietta, Ohio, to date a Native American burial mound as being at least 800 years old, because the oldest tree growing on it had 800 rings.

Although A. E. Douglass, a University of Arizona astronomer, is usually credited with establishing the modern science of dendrochronology shortly after the First World War, it was Clark Wissler of the American Museum of Natural History who recognized the potential for using tree rings to date archaeological materials in the Southwest. He provided Douglass with wooden beams from prehistoric ruins and asked him to date them. Douglass began with a modest chronology on long-lived standing pine trees that could be dated back 500 years; by 1935, the chronology was extended to A.D. 1100, and 40 ruins could be dated to the year they were built. The Laboratory of Tree-Ring Research in Tucson, set up during Douglass's tenure, has continued his work, and at present, tree rings can be dated to 8200 years ago in the Southwest without any gaps in the tree-ring record. Since limiting factors differ regionally, tree-ring dating is only usable within prescribed climatic areas; the 8200-year chronology is exclusive to the desert Southwest in this country.

Although some trees are notoriously long-lived (bristlecone pines are as old as 4000 years), no single tree lives for 8000 years. To establish this long a chronology, scientists had to find a way to bridge the present into the past by connecting modern (live) trees to old (preserved) trees. Douglass invented the method that could do this by finding similar patterns of ring widths in trees. For example, a tree that was cut yesterday but had lived for 50 years has a distinctive tree-ring pattern, representing the limiting factors of the region it grew in for those 50 years. The first 20 rings may match the pattern of the last 20 rings of a tree cut in 1976 that was "born" 30 years earlier. The earlier years of this tree can be matched with an even older tree, and on through as many trees as can be matched.

Before the actual process of matching ring widths can be discussed, three caveats are in order: First, no two trees are identical, although, theoretically, the ring patterns of the same species in the same area will be similar. Again, theoretically, all trees within a certain prescribed area will show similar, but not identical, patterns, because each tree has its own unique history. Second, trees are not biologically uniform in their range. In general, trees in the middle of a range will show less variation (they are more "complacent") than trees on the edges of the range; trees on the edges will be easier to map because their rings show more variation. Finally, not all trees produce one ring every year. Extreme drought may result in no ring, whereas a "false spring" due to a late frost or insect attack might trigger a second ring. Knowing that this can happen, dendrochronologists always cross-check patterns with neighboring areas to make sure that the "one ring equals one year" formula is valid.

DOING AMERICAN DENDROCHRONOLOGY

The basic method of doing dendrochronology has not changed much in almost 80 years. Although the method has not changed, dendrochronology has been extended to other species of trees, to other parts of the country, and to the dating of every beam in every prehistoric ruin in the Southwest. In addition, modern statistical methods and computer technology have improved accuracy and increased information storage.

Data Gathering

Depending on what scientists want to do, data gathering can be done in several ways; three scenarios follow:

- An archaeologist has an undated artifact, so he or she goes to the equivalent of a tree-dating service in the area (a university forestry department, a United States forestry unit, or the Tucson Laboratory of Tree-Ring Research) and asks the dendrochronologist to please date a log that was found next to an artifact.

The specialist would likely take a clean bore sample from the log and attempt to match it to the already established **modern master chronology** (MMC). (The MMC is "modern" because it is tied to a calendar; it is a "master" because it includes the ring data for the area for as long back in time as has been established; and it is a "chronology" because it is in sequential years.) Once the log is matched to the MMC, the specialist tells the archaeologist that the log was cut in the year 1491 and that the tree from which it was cut lived for 29 years. The archaeologist must then interpret this information. Was the log in direct association with the artifact? If, instead of a log, the artifact were a house beam, would the archaeologist then know to a year how old the house was? If people used old wood or recycled beams, there would be a different date for the house-building episode; under these circumstances, the archaeologist could conclude only that the house could not have been built before the tree was cut, but any time afterward.

- An archaeologist brings a log into that same tree-dating service and asks for it to be dated, but the expert cannot match it up with any pattern on the MMC. In this case, all that would be known is that the log is older than the end of the established chronology and that the tree was 29 years old when cut. (The possibility exists that there is something wrong with the MMC.) The archaeologist would likely leave a bore sample and go home not knowing the date the log was cut. In the meantime, more and more fossilized trees will hopefully be located in the area and added to the MMC, and hopefully that undated log will match the pattern of a future-found tree. When a situation occurs in which several logs match but none can be matched to the MMC, it is called a "floating" chronology; it will continue to float until it is bridged by a log that has one end that matches the patterning on the dated MMC and one end that matches the floating example.

- A dendrochronologist decides to go to an area where no tree-ring dating has ever been done and start from scratch, beginning with modern, still-living trees. The boring of modern trees begins the sequence that will eventually establish an MMC for the area.

Data Preparation

Regardless of which scenario we continue, because logs and beams are unwieldy to carry around (particularly when it is time to put them under a microscope), the first thing a specialist would do is to use an increment borer and take several samples of the artifact, log, or sequence of trees, from the bark to the pith; the borer will retract the sample with only minimal damage to the artifact or only momentary damage to the tree. The resultant sample looks a bit like a straw with dark lines on it, but once it is dried and glued to a strip of wood, the expert has a record of the tree's annual growth. The sample is shaved with a sharp razor using an even stroke and then sanded. The artifact is now ready to be "read."

From Skeleton Plots to Composite Patterns to Modern Master Chronologies

Over 50 years ago, Waldo Glock outlined the three major steps that take an investigator from the sample to its date in calendar years: (1) read the rings by judging relative widths of each ring and record the information on graph paper; (2) correlate the ring pattern with other rings in the same area, establishing a

Figure 13.2 Tree Ring Sample and Skeleton Plot

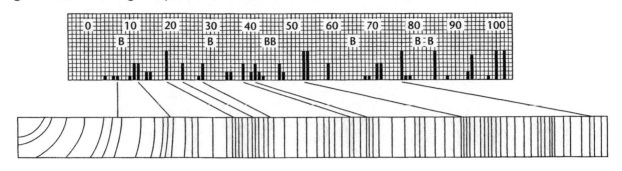

composite pattern (CP) for the sequence; and (3) unite CP sequences to older trees by overlapping matched sequences already in an MMC or to floating chronologies. Calendar dates can then be assigned to each ring.

Reading and Recording the Rings: The Skeleton Plot   A good hand lens is sufficient to read 98% of the rings, but it does take practice and skill to do it accurately. Each ring is identified by the beginning of a ring's dark brown band of demarcation to the next dark band and is usually easy to see. Although ring widths vary in a nonintegral manner, relatively thin and relatively wide rings are noted and medium rings ignored in the Douglass **skeleton plot.** Figure 13.2 shows how a sample would be translated to graph paper. Each ring has one square of graph paper that represents chronological order from the left (the pith) to the right (the bark). Note the vertical line representing the ring is made on the graph line, not in the square itself. Before beginning, 0 is placed at the extreme left representing the innermost ring next to the pith, and every 10th line is numbered, representing every 10 years' duration. For each sample, width assessment is made relative to that sample only, making it relative only to the ring's nearest neighbors. Specifically, the range is very thin to wide, and on paper, the thinner the ring, the taller the line. "Very thin" rings get seven vertical graph paper spaces; "quite thin" rings get four; "thin" rings get one; "medium" rings are ignored; and "wide" rings get B written above the line. Be sure you understand this process before you proceed, as this is the basis for dendrochronology.

Although this appears to be an antiquated, subjective system, it is simple, understandable, and traditional, meaning there are 500,000 or so such skeleton plots in existence. Because relative widths that form a pattern are the only important part of a skeleton plot, the advantage of a skeleton plot is that any age or species of tree can be used as long as it is within the same climate area. (Note, however, that conifers produce rings that are often three times the size of hardwoods, so unless relative measures are used, the two would not be comparable.) Presently, skeleton plots are done by computer in many labs. Figure 13.2 shows the pattern of one set of rings; the figure looks similar to a modern bar code, and could be read as "two thin, one medium, one very thin, one thick, two quite thin," and so on down the plot. Although skeleton plots of the same tree-ring sequence produced by several different workers have been surprisingly similar, computerized plots are even more accurate.

Composite Patterns   To eliminate the variation extremes in skeleton plots in individual samples, correct for any missing or double rings, and eliminate errors due to breakage of bore samples, a composite pattern (CP) is run. It is basically

Figure 13.3 Composite Pattern

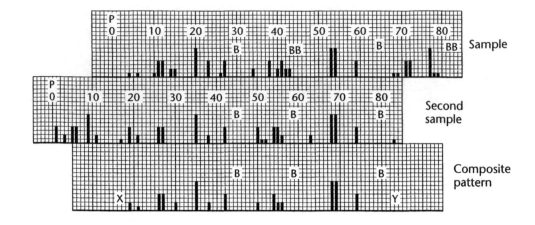

a verification of the information given by a single sample. This is done by finding another sample that at least partially matches the pattern on the original sample. It would be rare to have a second sample the exact same age, but it must overlap one or both ends of the original sample. See Figure 13.3 for this process. In this figure, the pattern of tree rings in the original sample is matched to the second sample, with one pattern overlapping one end and one missing an end; it is in the matched section that CPs are done. Note that on the CP formed at the bottom, the two samples have been averaged and the extreme variations of each eliminated. The diagnostic features of the CP are regarded as typical of the region for that time period. In this case, there were no missing or double rings. How exact must samples be to be considered matched? Douglass noted that no two trees would ever be identical, because the factors that cause rings affect every tree slightly differently. He suggested that "most" rings must match; when pressed for a more definitive answer, he suggested 80%. Computers are used now to attempt validation, but in the long run, it is the skill and experienced eye of the expert who makes the final judgment. In the early days of dendrochronology, when there were only 59 years of tree rings to consider, Douglass was said to be able to look at samples that were ultimately dated between 1845 and 1904 and know exactly where they fit. This is because he memorized the 11 particularly thin ring years (referred to as "pointer years") and the one exceptionally thick year—1863 and 1864 are a unique case of two thin-ringed years in a row. Now that the MMC has so many rings, experts can no longer rely on their memories and must use computers for storing information.

Modern Master Chronology   CPs are either floating or already tied to a calendar date. To bring all composite patterns into the MMC, the expert looks for overlaps or "bridges" in patterns between composites. Ideally, several samples should be found for each bridge, and the overlap should number 30 or more years to eliminate the possibility that there are identical patterns in a long sequence.

Douglass himself provides a good example of chronology building using tree rings. He started out with an idea and 500 years of ring data. Clark Wissler supplied the momentum. By 1923, Douglass had an MMC that went back to A.D. 1284 and a floating chronology of 314 years from wooden beams in Pueblo Bonito, some 230 miles to the east in New Mexico, but no way to tie the float to the Arizona MMC. A National Geographic Society expedition in 1923 collected hundreds of beams from 30 prehistoric and historic sites, adding 585 years to

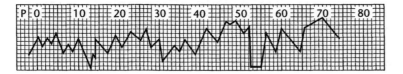

Figure 13.4 Growth Curve

the floating chronology (now it is 899 years), but it still didn't tie in with the MMC. A second expedition in 1928 focused on dwellings on Hopi mesas, some 75 miles north of Flagstaff. A single roof timber, charred from use, was found that bridged one end of the floating chronology and the end of the MMC, which extended the MMC to A.D. 701. Through the addition of more and more bridges (and sequoia and bristlecone pine), the Arizona MMC stands today at 8200 years. Any piece of wood from this area can theoretically be dated to the year it was cut, as long as there are sufficient and variable rings to show a usable, matching pattern with other pieces of wood that were similarly dated.

A Permanent Record: Growth Curves

Although the Douglass method of dating has not changed very much in 80 years, one of the ongoing jobs of the Laboratory of Tree-Ring Research is to make a more permanent and more accurate MMC for the Southwest. The Douglass system is based on ring pattern rather than on precise measurements. Though this has proved to be a very workable method, some scientists feel it is subjective and imprecise. For the system to be more objective, scientists suggest measuring rings in millimeters and turning patterns into **growth curves** (GC). To do this, a microscope with a built-in measurer is normally used. The ring width is measured between the dark bands. This information is either put onto graph paper or automatically entered into a computer program. In the paper method, the width of each ring is measured and marked vertically from the base line using half the actual width of the ring (the oldest year (P) is to the left; each year has one vertical line on the paper). Once plotted, the points are joined to form a GC of jagged lines (see Figure 13.4 for a GC). These can be compared, as patterns, to other GCs, just as skeleton plots are compared to each other. They can also be averaged in a manner similar to averaging CPs.

DOING EUROPEAN DENDROCHRONOLOGY

Because the American system was invented early and was seemingly doing a good job, why was there a necessity for a "European system," especially as Europe has the same basic trees as America? The answer is quite simple: Europeans and Americans wanted to date different things. The American system was invented to date the building resource of the Southwest, the pine tree. Europeans did not normally build with pine but with oak. Therefore, what European archaeologists wanted to date were items made of oak: house beams, doors, frames, roadways, and platforms for activity areas above wetlands.

Until M. G. Baillie started to work on the Irish chronology, it was not known if the entire British Isles were 1 or 10 tree-ring areas. At present, a German team and an Irish team are working independently with oak; the chronology of central Europe is now the longest in the world at 11,494 years, although it was in three parts with two floating chronologies until two bridges were recently discovered. The Irish chronology is now back to 7479 years, and the

English chronology stands at 6989 years. Interestingly, the Irish and German chronologies had to be cross-dated in England to connect the two. The European system differs from the American system in its stronger need for computer verification, because oaks, although they always have annual rings, generally show complacent rings with little variation, making it more difficult to visually identify a pattern to match modern logs with old logs. It has been estimated that 90% of oak rings are statistically complacent. Arctic chronology is dated to A.D. 600, Scandinavian to A.D. 400, French to 6000 years ago, Italian to A.D. 1031, and, on the first try, in Nepal, to A.D. 1557. Pine that existed earlier than oaks and that spans the last glacial period has begun to extend the chronology even farther into the past.

For the rest of the world, not a single chronology has been reported outside of temperate areas, because trees in tropical or semitropical areas grow year-round, leaving no rings to be counted or matched. Temperate South America chronology is dated to 1100 years ago, temperate southern Africa to 400 years ago, and Australia to A.D. 700.

OTHER DENDRO-RELATED STUDIES

One offshoot of dendrochronology is its allied science, **dendroclimatology,** which uses tree rings as proxies for times when no climatic information is available. The limiting factor of temperature or rain and its annual variability provides the data. Tree rings are not, of course, as accurate or precise gauges as thermometers, but the information they provide is still useful in attempts to reconstruct short-term climates of the past. Pollen, faunal, and sediment analyses are usually used for long-term information, but they are not sensitive enough to register short-term changes. Interpretations of climatic change based on tree rings must be made carefully, however, as they represent differences in growth rates, and conditions other than temperature and rainfall may affect growth. As M. G. Baillie (1995) rather cryptically puts it, "We can look at any period in the last 7,000 years and see what trees thought of the conditions."

The calibration or adjustment of another "absolute" archaeological dating technique, **radiocarbon recalibration** (14C), is another use of tree-ring dating. Within the last 25 years, some of the basic assumptions underlying 14C dating have been found to be incorrect. Therefore, an absolute date in "radiocarbon years" often does not correspond to the date of a sample in "real" years, as measured by a calendar. Some successful attempts have been made to link radiocarbon and real dates by the use of tree rings. Because each dated ring in a sequence represents one year's growth, a radiocarbon analysis of that dated ring immediately relates a 14C date to a "real" date. If a sufficient number of rings (one for each year of the absolute sequence) is analyzed in this fashion, a graph may be constructed showing the relationship between radiocarbon and real (also called "dendro") dates for each year for the past 8200 years. Such a graph is shown in Figure 13.5. The vertical scale shows dates based on radiocarbon analyses; the horizontal scale shows real dates based on the dendrochronological scale for the Southwest. There are two lines on the graph: the straight one, marked "concordance line," shows what is expected if every tree dated by dendrochronology had produced exactly the same date by radiocarbon analysis. The curved line shows the actual results. The stippled area indicates years when the radiocarbon dates are younger than the dendrodates; the black areas show the reverse. At only three points do the dendrodates and the radiocarbon dates correspond. At all other points along the curve, the radiocarbon date can be reassigned a real date.

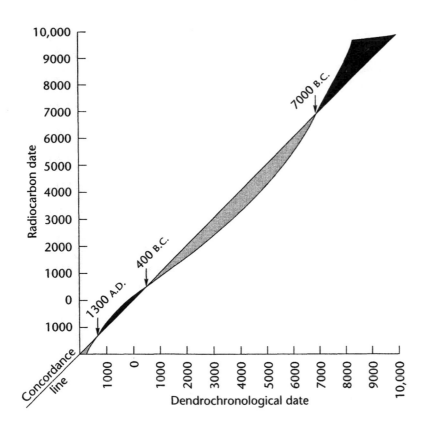

Figure 13.5 Radio-carbon/Dendro-Date Relationship

(Shaded areas show when the 14C dates are younger than the dendro-dates; black areas show when the 14C dates are older than the dendro-dates.)

Although the ability to "recalibrate" radiocarbon dates is possible only for the past 10,000 years, it is expected that recalibration will be extended soon by several thousand years. And because some fossilized logs now radiocarbon date back to 30,000 years, dendrochronology may be extended back into the early Upper Paleolithic. If dendrochronology can be verified to 30,000 years ago, it may be possible to turn the tables and verify radiocarbon dates that are that old.

Interestingly, dendrochronology has needed 14C dating as much as the reverse. When a tree sample is found in a bog and no approximate date can even be guessed at, it would be a formidable job to try to match the tree sample to an MMC that has 10,000 rings in it. By 14C dating a small bit of the tree, an approximate date can be determined, and the scientist can at least begin to search for the matching pattern.

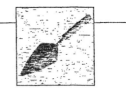

THE EXERCISE

Every archaeologist gets "that phone call" every once in a while, the phone call from the eager and enthusiastic amateur scientist who has "found a bone," or located a Native American campsite, or come across a treasure trove of artifacts of unknown origin while cleaning out Grandma's attic. Unless the bones are human, the modern ones are sent to a biologist; if the bones are very old, fossilized, or just imprints, they are sent to a geologist (particularly anything reported to be a dinosaur bone). Because tradition separates history from prehistory, every artifact of historical note is delegated to a historian. (Professionals in other disciplines reciprocate and send human materials to us as well.) Anthropologists are comfortable only with human bones and cultural artifacts, so the items that end up on our desks are either human bones (rare) or Native American objects (common).

For the duration of this exercise, you are a student doing a paid summer internship with an archaeologist who specializes in Native American prehistory and who has a rather unusual laboratory in that it contains the MMC for your area. However, because it is a small laboratory, it has only basic, not sophisticated, equipment (in other words, it has no computer capabilities for information storage).

The phone rings and it is a farmer in Americus County, who has found a cache of Native American artifacts along with what he thinks are the remains of a campfire. Our archaeological rescue squad goes to the site, does some preliminary scouting, and judges the site to be of potential importance. As it is on private land, we will have to excavate the site ourselves, with the possible help of federal, state, or private grant money. The important things at present are to (1) get permission from the owner/farmer to temporarily seal the site and leave it undisturbed until we get funding to excavate; (2) photograph and map the surface finds, collecting what is on the surface before it disappears; and (3) find a way to date the site. When it comes time to ask for funding, information on the artifacts and the likely date of the site will be necessary for a grant application to be successful.

An initial view of the site reveals signs of fire in the form of darkened rocks in a circle, bits of charcoal, and one fairly large, partially charred (but not carbonized) log. The larger bits of charcoal are picked up with tweezers, placed in a baggie, and sent to the nearest radiocarbon lab. The charred log is removed (using plastic gloves) and placed in a plastic wrap to take to the lab.

Back in the lab, a number of bore samples are taken from the log before it becomes too dry. It is your job to "walk the sample" through the entire dendrochronology process, from bore sampling to dating. You will be using old-fashioned techniques—manual instead of computerized—but all professionals believe beginners must go through the manual process at least once (and this small laboratory has no computer-storage capabilities).

OBJECTIVES

In this exercise, you will

- play the role of an archaeologist dating a partially charred log.
- go through the process of doing dendrochronology in which you will
  - look at a real bore sample under the microscope.
  - do a skeleton plot of a sample.
  - date the sample with the modern master chronology.
  - do a growth curve.

DOING THE EXERCISE

1. Get the equipment necessary for this exercise.

   a. Take a mounted tree sample from the kit and look at it under 10–15× power under the microscope. (If you were doing a real analysis of this sample, you would have taken the sample from its protective straw and shaved and sanded it down, then mounted it for observation. This has been done for you.) Look specifically at individual tree rings; where one begins and ends. If you are having trouble seeing the rings, put a drop of water on the sample and spread the drop with your finger along the area to be viewed.

b. Do a skeleton plot. Use one of the "plastic samples." (They simulate real samples such as the one you looked at under the microscope previously, but are easier to work with, don't bulge up when you glue them down, and don't break.) Put it temporarily in a mount by wrapping both ends with rubber bands to keep it fixed in place. The P on one end indicates the pith, and the shaded area at the other end represents the bark. Tree rings are the spaces between the lines; the extreme ends are not years, as they were not caused by a year's growth. Note the variability in width of the tree rings and the patterns they form.

To read and record the rings, first decide whether you can do this with the naked eye or if you need a hand lens or the low-power microscope. People's eyes differ. Look at the entire length of the sample to begin to identify what is meant by "very thin," "quite thin," "thin," "medium," and "wide" relative to this sample. Starting with the (P)ith end at your left, assess each of the widths of your rings. This begins the skeleton plot for the sample. Make a skeleton plot in Figure 13.6 for this sample, using instructions from page 189 under the "Skeleton Plot" heading. Write in the 0, and note every 10 years before you record your rings, as in Figure 13.2.

At this point, you would normally verify the sample with others from the same area and general time period to eliminate oddities such as double or missing rings. Assume, however, that this has been done (a composite pattern was made) and move on to the next step.

2. Match your skeleton plot with the modern master chronology (MMC) in Figure 13.7 for the immediate area that was done by the archaeologist in charge of the laboratory you are working in. Cut out and slide your sample across the MMC until you find a good match. Note where this occurs, and continue to the end of the MMC just in case there is another match. Answer the questions at the bottom of the figure. Tape your sample back where you cut it.

3. Do a growth curve (GC) as per instructions on page 191 under the "Growth Curves" heading. Prepare another graph in Figure 13.8, mark a 0 at the extreme left-hand, and mark every 10 lines, as in Figure 13.4.

Measure the actual rings on your sample. Measure the first ring by using the dividers (double-pointed instrument) in the kit (the double-pointed instrument); measure the width of the ring on the sample and transfer the width vertically to the first space on your graph paper, one point on the bottom line using the scale of half the ring width on the vertical axis. Two millimeters of width = 1 millimeter on the vertical axis. Mark this on your graph. Continue to mark each year's tree-ring width on your graph, with one square on the bottom line representing each year and vertical squares for that year representing the width of the ring. When you have done all of the widths, connect the dots at the top and you have a growth curve. Write a brief statement about the date of the site that the wood came from on the bottom of the figure.

☐ **Check with your lab manager for full credit.**

KEY WORDS

relative dating

absolute dating

chronometric dating

dendrochronology

tree rings

modern master chronology

composite pattern

skeleton plot

growth curves

dendroclimatology

radiocarbon recalibration

FOR FURTHER READING

Baillie, M. G. *Tree Ring Dating and Archaeology*. Chicago: University of Chicago Press, 1982.

Baillie, M. G. *A Slice through Time: Dendrochronology and Precision Dating*. London: Batsford, 1995.

Fritts, Harold C. *Tree Rings and Climate*. New York: Academic Press, 1976.

Glock, Waldo. "Principles and Methods of Tree-Ring Analysis." Washington, D.C.: Carnegie Institution of Washington, no. 486 (1937):1–113.

Glock, Waldo. *Tree Growth and Rainfall–A Study of Correlation and Methods*. Smithsonian Miscellaneous Collection, vol. 111, no. 18, 1950.

Glock, Waldo. "Uniformity among Growth Layers in Three Ponderosa Pine." Smithsonian Miscellaneous Collection, vol. 145, no. 4 (1963):1–373.

Goksu, H. Y., M. Oberhofer, and D. Regulla. *Scientific Dating Methods*. Dordrecht, Netherlands: Kluwer Academic Press, 1991.

Hughes, M. C., P. M. Kelly, J. R. Pilcher, and V. C. Lamarche. *Climate from Tree Rings*. New York: Cambridge University Press, 1982.

Schweingruber, F. H. *Tree Rings*. Dordrecht, Netherlands: B. Reidel Publishing, 1988.

Schweingruber, F. H. *Trees and Wood in Dendrochronology*. Berlin: Springer Verlag, 1993.

Figure 13.6 Skeleton Plot

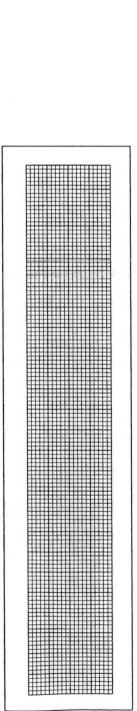

Figure 13.7 Modern Master Chronology

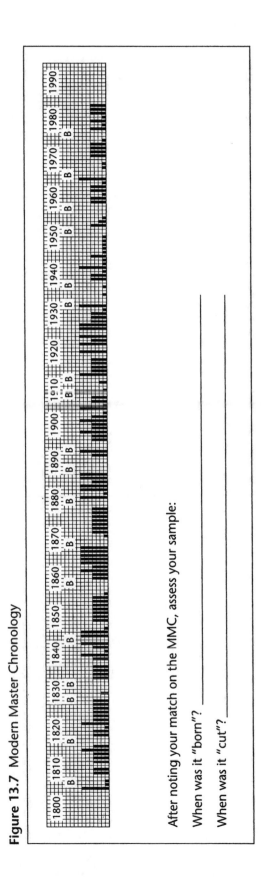

After noting your match on the MMC, assess your sample:

When was it "born"? _____

When was it "cut"? _____

Figure 13.8 Growth Curve

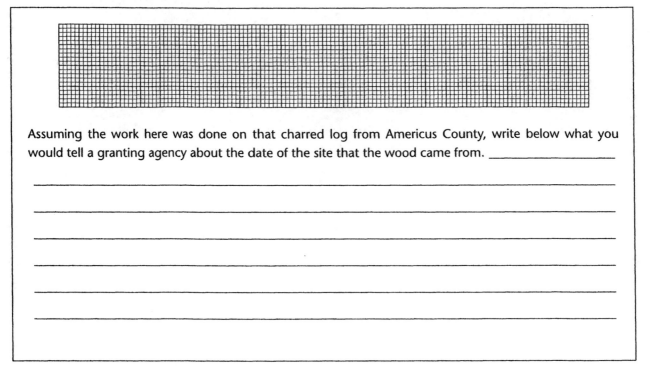

Assuming the work here was done on that charred log from Americus County, write below what you would tell a granting agency about the date of the site that the wood came from. _____

_____

_____

_____

_____

_____

_____

Glossary

absolute dating Dating methods that put the dating of artifacts into calendar years, such as 23,110 ± 70 years ago.

Acheulean A technology or cultural period in the Old World that is characterized by the presence of hand axes; although named for the French site of St. Acheul, the period began in Africa a million years ago and lasted to 60,000 years ago in some areas.

Anasazi This culture is believed to be ancestral to modern pueblo-dwelling Native Americans (Zuni, Hopi), beginning in the Southwest somewhat before A.D. 1.

analogy In archaeology, a process of reasoning that states that if there is an observable link between two items, the other can be assumed in the presence of one item.

anatomically modern human (AMH) Anthropologically refers to the group of humans who were within the range of the modern human species, showing the anatomical traits of moderns such as a cranial capacity of over 1400 cubic centimeters and a chin. When this constellation of traits first occurred is contested.

anther The male sexual organ on the end of a plant stamen that contains and discharges pollen.

anthropology Literally, the study or science of humans, including our past and present, our biology and our culture. Archaeology, physical anthropology, linguistics, and cultural anthropology are its major subfields.

aperturate A grain of pollen having no pores or furrows. Pine, for example, has two sacs around the central area but no pores or furrows.

arboreal pollen Pollen from trees such as pine or oak as opposed to nontree pollen such as sedges.

archaeoculture The totality of past human culture; an extinct group's learned behavior, cognition, and emotion.

archaeofauna Literally, old bones, but in archaeology refers to animal bones found in or near archaeology sites and used to reconstruct diet and environment.

archaeological record That which has survived biodegradation for the archaeologist to recover; may be in situ (rare) or disturbed.

archaeology The study or science of past cultures as revealed by their material remains.

artifact Object made by or in some way altered by humans.

assemblage A collection of artifacts that represents the culture of a prehistoric group.

atlatl A spear-thrower.

backed blade A flint tool that is at least twice as long as it is wide and is backed by secondary retouch on one long edge to blunt it; likely function was to cut.

beaker culture The farming people who used bell-shaped ceramic beakers (and copper technology as well) in western Europe between 4700 and 4000 years ago.

behaviorally modern humans (BMH) Anthropologically refers to the group of humans who had the capabilities and showed the range of behavior of modern humans, including the ability to use symbolic behavior (art and supernaturalism). When this occurred is contested.

Bergmann's law The law that states that when a species inhabits a territory with varying environmental conditions, those members in the coldest areas will show body shapes that are compact whereas bodies will be more angular in the warmest areas.

blind test As in archaeology, refers to one archaeologist doing an experiment and another archaeologist doing the analysis of that experiment; the classic blind test is the Keeley-Newcomer project on use-wear and function of tools.

bog people A name given to Iron Age "victims" found in bogs in northern Europe, dating from 2000 to 1500 years ago. Tollund Man in Denmark and Lindow Man in England are examples.

bore sample (also called core sample) In dendrochronology, the archaeologist uses an increment borer to remove a straw-sized core from the bark to the pith of a tree so each tree ring can be noted and counted.

beriberi A disease caused by thiamin (vitamin B) deficiency that attacks the peripheral nervous system and causes partial paralysis, emaciation, and anemia.

biodegradation The opposite of preservation in archaeology; all organic matter is subject to biodegradation unless fossilized.

blade Flint piece, usually Upper Paleolithic in date, that is at least twice as long as it is wide and usually narrow; can be blank (unretouched) or retouched by secondary percussion to form a tool.

bucket-urn tradition A ceramic tradition in Britain from about 5000 to 3000 years ago that was indigenous to Britain and identified by urn-shaped ceramics.

burin A flint tool, usually an Upper Paleolithic blade, wherein at least one burin facet is driven off the top of the prepared blade while held perpendicular rather than parallel to the

ground; assumed function is to whittle or scrape wood or bone.

burnishing To make ceramics smooth and somewhat shiny by rubbing before firing.

calibrations As used in archaeology, methods of adjusting the standardization of graduations of quantitative measures, such as with 14C and dendrochronology.

cambium layer The layer of cells just under a tree's bark that becomes the annual "ring" in a tree-ring sequence.

carbon 14 (14C) A chronometric dating method of organic materials (charcoal, bone, shell, and so forth) that uses the principle that radioactive carbon ceases to be absorbed at the death of an organism and disintegrates into nitrogen at an assumed known, steady, and measurable rate.

carbonization The process by which organic materials such as small seeds "fossilize" by being partially burned.

ceramics A technical term for pottery.

chest punch (also called crutch) A device proposed to remove flutes from Clovis and Folsom tools.

chronometric dating Any dating that ties the object being dated to the Western calendar, such as 429 years ago; some examples are 14C, thermoluminescence, dendrochronology.

clan A group of kin related in a consanguineal fashion (genetics, "blood") to an assumed common ancestor/tress that acts as a corporate unit because of this relationship. Can be related by male or female relatives, resulting in patriclans or matriclans.

Clovis blade Large, elegant type of spear blade primarily found in the high plains; associated with woolly mammoths and dated from 12,000 to 11,000 years ago.

coil A method of making pottery whereby the potter forms a base and then uses long "ropes" of clay to build up the sides, usually smoothing the surface.

collagen The fibrous part of bone.

colpate   A furrow on a pollen grain, as on oak.

complacent ring   When the tree rings from particular species of trees (such as oak) show no visible difference in ring patterns, they are called complacent.

compass map   A preliminary sketch map of an archaeology site and its surroundings made from the perspective of the individual making the map.

composite curve   When all of the gradient curves (called "er curves") are completed, a composite curve is constructed from the data. All independent curves can be shown in one chart or they can be reduced to one collective curve.

concordance line   A line of agreement, such as between dendrodates and 14C dates.

conifer   Cone-bearing evergreen trees, such as pine and spruce.

coprolite   Fossilized fecal material.

core   A nodule of flint from which flakes or blades are struck, as well as the used-up, often pyramidal-shaped piece that can also be used as a tool.

Cro-Magnon   A collective term for Upper Paleolithic Europeans; in actuality, a hill near the modern French town of Les Eyzies where several Upper Paleolithic fossils were recovered.

cross-dating   A method of dating objects or sites by way of other sites or objects that are similar.

cultural anthropology   That branch of anthropology that studies modern people usually in non-Western societies for knowledge of their behavior, cognition, and emotions (that is, their culture).

culture   The patterned (learned and taught) ways of behaving, thinking, and feeling that characterize named human groups.

cuneiform   The wedge-shaped symbols stamped into soft clay by the Sumerians; that is, the first writing using particular iconographic pictographs.

deduction   A process of argument that begins with a specific hypothesis and uses data to support or reject the hypothesis.

dendrochronology   Literally, the science of dating by trees (tree rings); tree rings are counted and the pattern of the width of their individual rings matched with trees of known age.

deposition   A geologic term that refers to the process of soil settling.

direct historical approach   This archaeological tool uses direct analogies from the present to link to the past when modern people show a basic similarity to the same phenomenon in the past, such as kivas in the present and the past.

dry screening   In archaeology, excavated soil and sediment should be sieved in some way. In dry screening, soil is put through usually a $\frac{1}{4}$ inch mesh to recover artifacts not discovered during excavation.

dumpy   An instrument used by archaeologists (and surveyors) that uses a small telescope on a fixed platform to measure the depth of artifacts by sighting onto a stadia rod.

earthenwear   A ceramic paste that is relatively coarse and porous; used for dishes and domestic jobs.

eboulis   French for rock materials.

econiche   Refers to the ecological area a species or population "does best" in according to reproduction measurement.

ecofact   Information about the environment being reconstructed, usually derived from pollen, soil, or fauna.

edge damage   The result of use-wear on flint; edge damage shows where a tool was used.

emic   An "insider" approach in studying culture; in this approach, the anthropologist or archaeologist attempts to discover how individuals in particular societies view happenings, rules, and the world in general.

environmental indicators   Rainfall, temperature, and ground cover can be inferred from analyzing pollen, sediment/soil, and faunal debris to provide an environmental context for archaeological events.

epiphyseal ends   Refers to the ends of long bones that often can be used to identify the species of animals.

"er curve"   A gradient between extremes of ranges of temperature (hotter, colder), moisture (wetter, dryer), and ground cover (treed, nontreed) as used by archaeologists to reconstruct the environment during archaeological events.

ethnoarchaeology   Also called "living archaeology," it is the study of modern people for insights into the culture of past people.

ethnoculture   Literally, the way of life of modern people, as opposed to archaeoculture, the culture of people in the past.

ethnography   The study of the way of life of a particular group of people, such as the Mbuti pygmies or the Navajo.

ethnology   The study or science of human culture.

ethnoparallels   In archaeology, using observation or knowledge of present-day people to interpret archaeological findings.

etic   An "outsider" approach in studying culture; in this approach, the anthropologist or archaeologist attempts to discover the rules behind the behavior and belief systems based on his or her own training and knowledge.

exine   The outer shell of pollen that is very resistant to soil biodegradation, allowing pollen to survive for thousands of years.

experimental archaeology   One of the main subfields of archaeology and a major component of middle-range theory; archaeologists use analogies with the present and do experiments using techniques and materials known to have been used in the past to try to explain the past.

fauna   Refers to animals in archaeology, usually when reconstructing diet or environment.

femur   The bone in the upper leg of many animals, including all mammals; in humans, it is the largest bone in the body.

flake (tool)   A stone, usually flint, made by knocking off a piece of flint from a nodule with direct percussion (a rock or base of an antler) and then retouched or used.

flint   A very hard, finely grained quartz that comes in nodular or tabular form and can be made into many different sized and shaped tools. Because they are not known to biodegrade, flint tools form the basis of many archaeological chronologies and traditions.

floating chronology   As used in dendrochronology, a partial chronology not fixed at either end to the Western calendar.

flora   Refers to plants in archaeology, usually when reconstructing diet or environment.

flotation   A kind of sieving using water and pails where one pail is agitated while the excavated soil is poured through and the floating materials scooped off the top of the water.

flute   The long and slender piece of flint removed from the basal end of a bifacially made Clovis or Folsom spearpoint. The function is debated: as an aid in hafting? To improve the spear aerodynamically? Or for bloodletting?

folk taxonomy   How people themselves classify items as opposed to how scientists classify items.

Folsom blade   Large, elegant spear blade ranging from the high plains to the far western, far eastern, and southeastern United States; associated with bison killing and dated from 11,000 to 10,000 years ago.

forager   Same as hunter-gatherer, wherein the entire basic economy (food getting) is based on nondomesticated foods.

fossil   A substitution of organic material in cells by minerals that occur generally in water.

FUN dating   Refers to relative techniques of dating that include fluorine, uranium, and nitrogen analysis.

Gallo-Belgic culture   A ceramic tradition in France and Belgium about 3000 years ago that diffused as far west as Britain.

gestalt   A word from the German language that refers to observing or analyzing something as a whole unit rather than looking at its component parts.

glacial till A geological term referring to the heterogeneous and unconsolidated mixture of boulders, gravel, clay, and sand caused by glacial action.

glaze A thin coat of colored or clear clay material applied to ceramics before firing to produce a smooth and shiny appearance.

goosefoot A New World herb that was likely domesticated in the mid-Atlantic region before the corn/bean/squash complex diffused from Mexico. Also called *lamb's quarter*.

gourd A plant related to squash and pumpkin, gourds are usually grown for use in storage.

Harris lines Dense concentrations of bony material that form on long bones that look like lines around the circumference of the bone under x rays.

heavy fraction The heavyweight materials that sink to the bottom of flotation equipment mesh such as pottery sherds, large seeds, and flint chips.

herbarium The place where dried specimens of plants are stored for reference use.

herbivore Any animal that eats plant food; the term is usually used for large grazing animals in the Old and New Worlds, such as in the cattle, horse, or deer families.

hieroglyphics Early writing used in Egypt and middle America that used pictographic (iconographic) symbols.

Hohokam A cultural tradition in southern Arizona and northern Mexico beginning before 300 B.C. and lasting until around A.D. 1500 that depended on corn/beans/squash farming.

Ice Age A geological term for the cold period in Eurasia and the North American continent; the last Ice Age ended 15,000 to 10,000 years ago.

igneous rock Rock formed from a molten state as from a volcano.

incisors Front teeth; in each quadrant of the mouth, humans have two incisors.

inclusions In archaeology, refers to the unusu-

ally colored and different textured foreign bodies enclosed in flint; used to identify refits.

insectivore Any group of mammal that feeds on insects, such as shrews.

in situ Literally, "in place"; in archaeology, it refers to the status of an artifact or a living floor relative to its original position when deposited. If a floor has not been altered since its deposition, its artifacts can be said to be "in situ."

induction A process of argument that begins with data or facts; a hypothesis explaining the data emerging from the data.

inference A process of reasoning based on evidence that goes beyond physical evidence. One could infer tailored clothing during the Upper Paleolithic based on evidence of bone buttons, bone needles, and deer bones, in the absence of tangible clothing.

intuitive map Same as compass map and used as a preliminary map for quick reference.

Jomon A prefarming early ceramic culture in Japan dated to 12,500 years ago.

Kalinga A modern group of farmers living in the Philippines who make distinctive round-bottomed cooking and storing pots for their own, not commercial, use.

kitchen middens Refers to the refuse of basically food materials, such as shells and bones of fish and seafood on the Danish coast, and dated as Mesolithic.

Kiva A medium to large circular pit likely used for ritual and other group activities begun by the Anasazi in A.D. 500 in the Southwest and continuing until modern times among pueblo-dwelling Native Americans.

knapping The technical term for the act of making/replicating flint tools.

La Tene culture A prehistoric Iron Age people who also worked bronze and gold in woodland and temperate northern Europe from 400 B.C. until the Roman conquest.

law of stratigraphy A geological principle that states that due to gravity and the breakdown of earth materials, deposited soil, sediment, and rock stratify into layers that are often morphologically distinctive, with earlier layers at the bottom and later layers at the top of the stratification.

law of gravity   As used in geology and archaeology, a principle that states that gravity brings soil and rock to the lowest levels, where they stratify into chronologically determinable layers.

law of uniformitarianism   As first noted by James Hutton in 1784, this law states that forces of nature observed today (gravity, uplifting of mountains, river formation, and so on) are the same forces that operated in the past.

lemming   A northern European rodent noted for its periodic mass migrations.

light fraction   The lightweight materials that float to the top of flotation equipment during agitation, such as seeds, shells, or microchips of flint.

limiting factors   In environmental reconstruction, limiting factors affect the minimum end of a range of temperature, rainfall, or ground cover.

lineage   A group of kin related by known links through either males or females that acts as a corporate group because of these relationships; can be patrilineages or matrilineages.

loess   A very fine-grained, light-colored, and wind-deposited soil.

mandible   The lower jaw.

marsh elder   A shrub thought to be domesticated for its seeds in middle America about 4000 years ago.

material culture   That part of human behavior, cognition, and emotion that leaves material objects behind that form the basis of the archaeological record and its investigation.

matriclan   A corporate group of people who claim descent through females to an assumed common ancestress.

matrilineage   A corporate group of people who claim descent through females to a known common ancestress.

matrilocal residence   The cultural rule in societies whereby couples live with or near the bride's family after marriage.

matrix   The physical material that surrounds an artifact during excavation; usually the matrix is soil or sediment, but it can be water or ice.

megalith   Literally, large stone, as at Stonehenge and other northern European sites.

menhir   A single tall, upright megalith found in Britain and northern France and dating to about 5000 years ago.

mental template   The mental "picture" in the human head of what a human-made artifact will look like, such as the shape of a hand ax.

Mesolithic   Literally, the middle Stone Age, recognized in the Middle East as a transition between the Upper Paleolithic and the advent of farming in the Neolithic which occurred about 15,000–10,000 years ago and in Europe between 10,000 and 8,000 years ago. In both cases, the period is preceramic and preagricultural.

metamorphic rock   Rock formed by great heat or pressure from inside the earth.

microwear   Same as use-wear, whereby archaeologists attempt to discover the function or use of tools (usually flint) by looking for clues in edge damage, striations, and gloss.

middle-range theory   As postulated by Lewis Binford in the 1960s, this New Archaeology credo is an attempt to find skills, techniques, or ideas that span particular sites and times to provide ways to discover knowledge about the past.

minimal number of individuals (MNI)   A way of counting animal bones in archaeology sites to obtain information on what a sample of bone represents.

Mogollon   A cultural tradition in southern New Mexico and northern Mexico beginning at A.D. 100 and lasting until it merged with the Anasazi; associated with farming and foraging.

molars   Back teeth; humans have two premolars and three molars in each quadrant of the mouth.

monoporate   A grain of pollen having but one pore; for example, grass.

morphology   Literally, the outer shape of some object.

Natufian   A Mesolithic sedentary cultural tradition in the Near East related to exploitation of wild emmer wheat and barley.

Neandertal   The 125,000–38,000-year-old members of the genus *Homo* who lived in Europe and the Middle East and who had distinctive traits such as a very large cranial capacity. Whether they were in our direct lineage or contributed even in a minor way to our biological or cultural heritage is contested.

Neo-Indian   The cultural period that began with domestication in the New World, now put at 7500 years ago for squash in Mexico, and ended in various parts of the New World with "civilization"; the Meso-American Olmecs were the first to have cities some 3500 years ago.

Neolithic   Literally, the new Stone Age. A cultural period in the Old World that began with domestication of cereal grains about 10,000 years ago in the Middle East, and somewhat later in Asia and Africa.

New Archaeology   The name given to the post-1960 school of archaeology that focused on middle-range theory as its main paradigm.

nonarboreal pollen   Pollen from nontree plants such as from sedges and grasses.

occupation floor   Ideally, the excavated debris of an archaeological event, such as a two-week camp while hunting and gathering, that has been only minimally altered by natural or cultural events.

optical stimulated luminescence   The method of using a laser to attempt to date ceramic vessels and burned hearths.

owl pellet   What is regurgitated after an owl ingests small mammals and its harsh stomach acids reduce it to bones and fur; the pellet is small, brown to black, and has no odor. Pellets are used to reconstruct environments.

paleodiet   The diet of humans in the past; what people actually ate rather than what was available to be eaten.

paleofauna   Literally, old animals, but in archaeology, it refers to animal bones found in or around archaeology sites. Analyses can be used to reconstruct diet or environment at the time of deposition.

Paleo-Indian   The New World cultural period that began when the first Native Americans stepped foot on the North American continent (contested dates range from 25,000 to 15,000 years ago) to about 8,000 years ago and characterized by the hunting of large game and the collection of wild fruits and berries.

Paleolithic   Literally, old Stone Age. An Old World tradition in Africa; the first remains of human culture, the Oldowan chopper, date back to some 2 ½ million years ago. The tradition was taken to Asia and Europe and lasted until about 15,000 years ago. It is characterized by hunting and gathering.

paleopathology   Evidence of abnormalities in fossilized human bones that shows deficiencies in diet and other bone problems.

paleopollen   Literally, old pollen, but in archaeology, it refers to pollen found in soil and sediment that represents past pollen records; used primarily to reconstruct ancient diet and environment.

paleovegetation   In archaeology, it refers to the ground cover in the past as inferred by pollen, sediment, and faunal remains.

palynology   In botanical and archaeological terms, it refers to pollen analysis, primarily for environmental and diet reconstruction.

particle size analysis (PSA)   A test using a set of different meshed sieves to recover and report percentage of sizes of sediment or soil grains.

pathogen   Anything that causes disease.

patina   A glossy shine on flint that occurs under varing conditions.

peat   Classified as soil by geologists, peat contains a high amount of leaves and other organic matter.

Pecos   Refers to the classic 1916 excavation by A.V. Kidder at Pecos Pueblo in the Southwest that eventually yielded a regional sequence of pottery for the area.

pellagra   A niacin deficiency disease characterized by digestive and nervous disturbances and eventual mental deterioration.

phytolith   Minute silica crystals originally in plant cells that resist biodegradation and that can be identified to the family level.

pistil   The female, seed-bearing organ of a flowering plant.

pith   The soft, spongy substance in the middle of plant stems and trees.

pollen   The small, usually airborne, male sexual element produced by the anthers of flowering plants.

porate   A type of pollen, as identified by openings in the axis of the grain; birch has three pores.

porotic hyperostosis   Porous bone located on the forehead and upper surface of eye sockets on skeletal remains due to nutritional deficiencies.

porcelain   The finest-textured clay made into ceramic figurines and domestic wares; usually glazed.

postdeposition   Literally, after deposit; it refers to what can and does happen to artifacts between the time they were discarded by past people and excavation by archaeologists.

potsherds   Often referred to as *sherds,* they are the broken pieces of any kind of pottery.

potter's wheel   A moving, circular device that often has a foot pedal; used by potters in the Old World to make pottery.

prairie   A flat to rolling grassland.

prehistory   Literally, before history, that is, before writing, which occurred first in the Old World about 5400 years ago (the Sumerians) and in the New World about 2150 years ago (the Mayans).

prey species   Species preyed upon for food by meat-eating animals. Can be large animals, such as dik-diks in Africa, preyed upon by lions or small mice or voles, preyed upon by owls.

provenience   Literally, the location of artifacts in space; usually involves the proper horizontal and vertical measurement of each artifact.

pueblo   A multistoried adobe brick, communal "apartment" dwelling dating from about 2000 years ago in the Southwest to the modern pueblo-dwelling Hopi in Arizona.

radiocarbon dating   The most widely used chronometric dating method in archaeology

that theoretically dates organic materials up to 40,000 years old.

reactivity phenomenon   The principle that the knowledge that one's behavior is being monitored causes behavioral change.

"r strategy"   Refers to animal species that reproduce in large, "gross" numbers but, due to poor parenting or high predation, the net reproduction keeps the species in check.

refits   In archaeology, refers to putting flint tools or pottery sherds back together as in a puzzle, when there are enough pieces to do so.

relative dating   A technique of putting artifacts into chronological order in terms of which item occurred first, followed by another item, and so forth. Some examples of relative dating are stratigraphy, fluorine, and ceramic seriation.

salt lick   A naturally occurring outcrop of salt that animals go to for their sodium needs.

sampling column   In geology and archaeology, used to predict and/or verify geological and/or archaeological levels in a site; the column is normally a vertical shaft.

scalar   Refers to the shape of edge damage on flint tools—the shape looks like fish scales.

scientific method   The method used to find knowledge in science by using hypotheses, data, and testing to come to conclusions.

sedentism   The state of being sedentary. In anthropology and archaeology, it refers to groups of people who have more or less permanent housing and lifestyles as opposed to people who are mobile and move camp every week or two; associated with farming.

sedimentary rock   Rock formed by sedimentation, meaning formed by material settling to the bottom of lakes or rivers, where in time and under pressure, it forms rock.

SEM (scanning electron microscope)   An electronic (as opposed to a mechanical) microscope that records images by scanning.

seriation   A technique used to give relative dates to objects of a single category, such as pottery, by use of the principle of popularity of styles.

sherds   Pieces of pottery; also called *potsherds.*

shrew A small, insect-eating mammal, identified by contiguous teeth.

sibling exchange The cultural practice of a man and his sister marrying a woman and her brother; same as a woman and her brother marrying a man and his sister.

signature In archaeology, refers to distinctive and identifiable characteristics, such as particular scratches on flint to identify motion, area of use, or raw material.

silica gloss The sheen or polish that occurs on flint when it is used to cut grass.

site A place where artifacts (and assumed human behavior) are located.

SSS (site surface survey) map A systematic and accurate map of an archaeology site and its surroundings, indicating all important physical and cultural features.

skeuomorphs The result of changing raw materials for an item but keeping the basic shape, such as early pottery in gourd shape.

slip A thin layer of clay put over the finished pot to give it a smooth coat.

spall The small, usually long and thin flint piece removed from a burin, that is, a "burin spall."

species A group of plants or animals that interbreed among themselves but do not interbreed with other groups; modern humans (*Homo sapiens*) are an example of a species.

spore The asexual reproductive organ found in nonflowering plants.

stadia rod A measured and marked pole used for depth measurement of artifacts.

stratigraphy A geological term that refers to strata (layers) of rock and soil and their placement relative to each other.

striations Scratch marks or elongated abrasions as on flint (from small bits of flint scratching the surface as the tool is moved in use) or pottery (by metal spoons in stirring), for example.

surface map Also called *preliminary surface map*. A systematic but preliminary map of an archaeology site and its surroundings.

taiga A thinly forested subarctic landscape of deciduous or evergreen trees in Siberia and Canada.

temper Material added to pottery for strength, color, consistency in firing, and so forth, such as straw or ground pottery sherds.

template A pattern used to accurately make something else. A mental template is a vision in the mind that tells the artisan what a stone ax is to look like, and a pottery template is used to accurately measure a rim, for example.

terra-cotta A low-fired, usually dark red clay used in making pottery for cooking or decoration.

TGP (The Garbage Project) A project initiated by William Rathje in Tucson, Arizona, to study the waste and waste habits of Americans.

theodolite Similar to a transit, a telescopic instrument used with a stadia rod by archaeologists and surveyors to measure depths of artifacts.

thermal spall The small, shallow, roundish pits removed from pottery resulting from high heat and escaping moisture; often occurs at rims of cooking pots.

thermoluminescence A chronometric dating technique that measures the light given off by clay and baked hearths when reheated.

tool kit The collection of usually different kinds of tools used by a group of people that either represents a minimal activity or the general technology of a group.

traceology The term used by Semenov for describing the principles of use-wear.

transit A measuring instrument similar to a theodolite, used to measure depths of artifacts.

tree ring The annual demarcation between spring/summer and fall/winter growth that appears on a cross section of most trees.

trizonocolpate A grain of pollen having three furrows equidistant around the circumference (axis) of the grain, as in oak, for example.

trizonoporate A grain of pollen having three pores equidistant around the circumference (axis) of the grain, as in birch, for example.

tuber A root crop, such as potato.

tundra A treeless land surface between the northern ice cap and the treed taiga, characterized by low-growing shrubs and mosses.

typology A classification, usually used for flint or sherds.

xylem The woody tissue of a tree between the pith and the cambium layer.

Upper Paleolithic A cultural period in the Old World beginning about 40,000 years ago in Europe and characterized by flint blades and burins, bone tools, and art.

use-wear Same as *microwear* or *traceology*. The term refers to the "signatures" left on flint by using tools: edge damage, striations, and polish.

varves The annual rings found around glacial lakes caused by a winter freeze followed by a quick spring thaw and the resulting reoccurrence of rock settlement.

Venus In archaeology, as opposed to astronomy, mythology, or art, Venuses are small statuettes of the female body that date to about 25,000 years ago in Europe.

vole A small rodent with a short tail.

waterlogged As used in archaeology, a medium of preservation. Truly waterlogged organic materials may not biodegrade as quickly as other materials, due to a low amount of oxygen in the water.

wet sieving A technique of artifact recovery wherein soil is passed through a sieve that is then swished in water to dissolve soil and leave archaeological residue.

ziggurat A large terraced, pyramid-shaped edifice with a temple on the top, as built by the Sumerians beginning about 5000 years ago.

zooarchaeology A subfield of archaeology that specializes in analyzing animal bones in or near archaeology sites for information relating to diet and environment.

Index

FUTURE
English for Results

INTRO

Yvonne Wong Nishio

Series Consultants

Beatriz B. Díaz

Ronna Magy

Federico Salas-Isnardi

PEARSON
Longman

Future Intro
English for Results

Pearson Education, 10 Bank Street, White Plains, NY 10606

Staff credits: The people who made up the **Future Intro** team, representing editorial, production, design, and manufacturing, are Rhea Banker, Maretta Callahan, Elizabeth Carlson, Aerin Csigay, Dave Dickey, Nancy Flaggman, Irene Frankel, Shelley Gazes, Mike Kemper, Katie Keyes, Melissa Leyva, Linda Moser and Liza Pleva.

Cover design: Rhea Banker
Cover photo: Kathy Lamm/Getty Images
Text design: Elizabeth Carlson
Text composition: Word and Image Design, Inc.
Text font: Helvetica Neue

Nishio, Yvonne Wong.
    Future: english for results / Yvonne Wong Nishio ... [et al.].
      p. cm.
    ISBN 978-0-13-240876-9 (student bk. intro)—ISBN 978-0-13-199144-6 (student bk.1)—ISBN 978-0-13-199148-4 (student bk. 2)—ISBN 978-0-13-199152-1 (student bk. 3)—ISBN 978-0-13-199156-9 (student bk. 4)—ISBN 978-0-13-240875-2 (student bk. 5)
    1. English language—Textbooks for foreign speakers. I. Title.
    PE1128.N56 2009
    428.0076--dc22

                                                                    2008021069

ISBN-13: 978-0-13-240876-9
ISBN-10: 0-13-240876-7

1 2 3 4 5 6 7 8 9 10—WC—14 13 12 11 10 09

The author would like to thank her beginning level ESL students. Their cultural backgrounds, challenges, hopes, and aspirations have inspired this book. The author also wishes to recognize Pearson Longman's dedicated staff: **Joanne Dresner** for providing the initial opportunity to publish, **Irene Frankel** for her insightful guidance throughout the *Future* project, and **Maretta Callahan** for her unfailing support and enthusiasm.

Yvonne Wong Nishio
Author of Student Book Intro

Contents

Acknowledgments

The authors and publisher would like to extend special thanks to our Series Consultants whose insights, experience, and expertise shaped the course and guided us throughout its development.
Beatriz B. Díaz Miami-Dade County Public Schools, Miami, FL
Ronna Magy Los Angeles Unified School District, Los Angeles, CA
Federico Salas-Isnardi Texas LEARNS, Houston, TX

We would also like to express our gratitude to the following individuals. Their kind assistance was indispensable to the creation of this program.

Consultants

Wendy J. Allison Seminole Community College, Sanford, FL
Claudia Carco Westchester Community College, Valhalla, NY
Maria J. Cesnik Ysleta Community Learning Center, El Paso, TX
Edwidge Crevecoeur-Bryant University of Florida, Gainesville, FL
Ann Marie Holzknecht Damrau San Diego Community College, San Diego, CA
Peggy Datz Berkeley Adult School, Berkeley, CA
MaryAnn Florez D.C. Learns, Washington, D.C.
Portia LaFerla Torrance Adult School, Torrance, CA
Eileen McKee Westchester Community College, Valhalla, NY
Julie Meuret Downey Adult School, Downey, CA
Sue Pace Santa Ana College School of Continuing Education, Santa Ana, CA
Howard Pomann Union County College, Elizabeth, NY
Mary Ray Fairfax County Public Schools, Falls Church, VA
Gema Santos Miami-Dade County Public Schools, Miami, FL
Edith Uber Santa Clara Adult Education, Santa Clara, CA
Theresa Warren East Side Adult Education, San Jose, CA

Piloters

MariCarmen Acosta American High School, Adult ESOL, Hialeah, FL
Resurrección Ángeles Metropolitan Skills Center, Los Angeles, CA
Linda Bolognesi Fairfax County Public Schools, Adult and Community Education, Falls Church, VA
Patricia Boquiren Metropolitan Skills Center, Los Angeles, CA
Paul Buczko Pacoima Skills Center, Pacoima, CA
Matthew Horowitz Metropolitan Skills Center, Los Angeles, CA
Gabriel de la Hoz The English Center, Miami, FL
Cam-Tu Huynh Los Angeles Unified School District, Los Angeles, CA
Jorge Islas Whitewater Unified School District, Adult Education, Whitewater, WI
Lisa Johnson City College of San Francisco, San Francisco, CA
Loreto Kaplan Collier County Public Schools Adult ESOL Program, Naples, FL
Teressa Kitchen Collier County Public Schools Adult ESOL Program, Naples, FL
Anjie Martin Whitewater Unified School District, Adult Education, Whitewater, WI
Elida Matthews College of the Mainland, Texas City, TX
Penny Negron College of the Mainland, Texas City, TX
Manuel Pando Coral Park High School, Miami, FL
Susan Ritter Evans Community Adult School, Los Angeles, CA
Susan Ross Torrance Adult School, Torrance, CA
Beatrice Shields Fairfax County Public Schools, Adult and Community Education, Falls Church, VA
Oscar Solís Coral Park High School, Miami, FL
Wanda W. Weaver Literacy Council of Prince George's County, Hyattsville, MD

Reviewers

Lisa Agao Fresno Adult School, Fresno, CA
Carol Antuñano The English Center, Miami, FL
Euphronia Awakuni Evans Community Adult School, Los Angeles, CA
Jack Bailey Santa Barbara Adult Education, Santa Barbara, CA
Robert Breitbard District School Board of Collier County, Naples, FL
Diane Burke Evans Community Adult School, Los Angeles, CA
José A. Carmona Embry-Riddle Aeronautical University, Daytona Beach, FL
Veronique Colas Los Angeles Technology Center, Los Angeles, CA
Carolyn Corrie Metropolitan Skills Center, Los Angeles, CA
Marti Estrin Santa Rosa Junior College, Sebastopol, CA
Sheila Friedman Metropolitan Skills Center, Los Angeles, CA
José Gonzalez Spanish Education Development Center, Washington, D.C.
Allene G. Grognet Vice President (Emeritus), Center for Applied Linguistics
J. Quinn Harmon-Kelley Venice Community Adult School, Los Angeles, CA
Edwina Hoffman Miami-Dade County Public Schools, Coral Gables, FL
Eduardo Honold Far West Project GREAT, El Paso, TX
Leigh Jacoby Los Angeles Community Adult School, Los Angeles, CA
Fayne Johnson Broward County Public Schools, Ft. Lauderdale, FL
Loreto Kaplan, Collier County Public Schools Adult ESOL Program, Naples, FL
Synthia LaFontaine Collier County Public Schools, Naples, FL
Gretchen Lammers-Ghereben Martinez Adult Education, Martinez, CA
Susan Lanzano Editorial Consultant, Briarcliff Manor, NY
Karen Mauer ESL Express, Euless, TX
Rita McSorley North East Independent School District, San Antonio, TX
Alice-Ann Menjivar Carlos Rosario International Public Charter School, Washington, D.C.
Sue Pace Santa Ana College School of Continuing Education, Santa Ana, CA
Isabel Perez American High School, Hialeah, FL
Howard Pomann Union County College, Elizabeth, NJ
Lesly Prudent Miami-Dade County Public Schools, Miami, FL
Valentina Purtell North Orange County Community College District, Anaheim, CA
Mary Ray Fairfax County Adult ESOL, Falls Church, VA
Laurie Shapero Miami-Dade Community College, Miami, FL
Felissa Taylor Nause Austin, TX
Meintje Westerbeek Baltimore City Community College, Baltimore, MD

Thanks also to the following teachers, who contributed their ideas for the Persistence Activities:

Dave Coleman Los Angeles Unified School District, Los Angeles, CA
Renee Collins Elk Grove Adult and Community Education, Elk Grove, CA
Elaine Klapman Venice Community Adult School, Venice, CA (retired)
Yvonne Wong Nishio Evans Community Adult School, Los Angeles, CA (retired)
Daniel S. Pittaway North Orange County Community College District, Anaheim, CA
Laurel Pollard Educational Consultant, Tucson, AZ
Eden Quimzon Santiago Canyon College, Division of Continuing Education, Orange, CA

About the Series Consultants and Author

SERIES CONSULTANTS

Dr. Beatriz B. Díaz has taught ESL for more than three decades in Miami. She has a master's degree in TESOL and a doctorate in education from Nova Southeastern University. She has given trainings and numerous presentations at international, national, state, and local conferences throughout the United States, the Caribbean, and South America. Dr. Díaz is the district supervisor for the Miami-Dade County Public Schools Adult ESOL Program, one of the largest in the United States.

Ronna Magy has worked as an ESL classroom teacher and teacher-trainer for nearly three decades. Most recently, she has worked as the ESL Teacher Adviser in charge of site-based professional development for the Division of Adult and Career Education of the Los Angeles Unified School District. She has trained teachers of adult English language learners in many areas, including lesson planning, learner persistence and goal setting, and cooperative learning. A frequent presenter at local, state and national, and international conferences, Ms. Magy is the author of adult ESL publications on life skills and test preparation, U.S. citizenship, reading and writing, and workplace English. She holds a master's degree in social welfare from the University of California at Berkeley.

Federico Salas-Isnardi has worked for 20 years in the field of adult education as an ESL and GED instructor, professional development specialist, curriculum writer, and program administrator. He has trained teachers of adult English language learners for over 15 years on topics ranging from language acquisition and communicative competence to classroom management and individualized professional development planning. Mr. Salas-Isnardi has been a contributing writer or consultant for a number of ESL publications, and he has co-authored curriculum for site-based workforce ESL and Spanish classes. He holds a master's degree in applied linguistics from the University of Houston and has completed a number of certificates in educational leadership.

AUTHOR

Yvonne Wong Nishio has been an adult school teacher, curriculum coordinator, counselor, and resource/demonstration teacher over the past 37 years in the Los Angeles Unified School District (LAUSD). She has taught all six ESL levels at Evans Community Adult School, one of the largest adult learning centers in the country. Ms. Nishio developed curriculum as well as materials for the Division of Adult and Career Education of LAUSD, including the *Asian Project*, which pioneered ESL materials culturally relevant to Asian Pacific immigrants; *Holidays in the U.S.*, which highlighted the multicultural roots of American holidays and customs; and *Places to See in the Los Angeles Area*. Ms. Nishio prepared a video program on domestic violence, *To Ensure Domestic Tranquility*, through a grant from the American Bar Association. Ms. Nishio's extensive work in ESL literacy includes contributions to the ESL Language Model Standards for Adult Education Programs established by the California Department of Education as well as the successful books *Longman ESL Literacy*, now in its third edition, and *Longman ESL Literacy Teacher's Resource Book*.

Scope and Sequence

UNIT	VOCABULARY AND PHONICS	LISTENING	SPEAKING	GRAMMAR	
Pre-Unit Getting Started *page 2*	• Activities in the classroom • The alphabet • Numbers 1–10	• Understand the letters in the alphabet • Understand numbers 1–10	• Say your name • Say the letters of the alphabet • Say numbers 1–10	• *My name is . . .* ◦ Introduction to imperatives	
1 Nice to meet you. *page 8*	• Countries • Alphabet • Numbers 0–9 • The sounds of *m* and *n*	• Listen to people introduce themselves • Listen and write letters, words, and names • Listen and write telephone numbers • Listen and identify student ID numbers	• Introduce yourself and say where you are from • Ask where someone is from • Ask for someone's name and confirm the spelling • Introduce your classmates	◦ *Wh-* questions with *be* ◦ Possessive pronouns: *my, your* • *Wh-* questions: *What is your . . . ?* • *Be* simple present: full forms and contractions • Subject pronouns	
2 Welcome to class! *page 28*	• Classroom objects • Classroom instructions • Places in a school • The sounds of *p* and *b*	• Listen to and follow classroom instructions • Listen to and follow directions for places in a school	• Ask for classroom objects • Give classroom instructions • Identify places in a school • Give directions for places in a school	◦ Questions with *Do* and short answers: *Yes, I do. No, I don't.* • Imperatives: affirmative and negative ◦ *Wh-* questions: *Where is . . . ?* • Prepositions of place: *in, across from, next to* ◦ *How do you . . . ?* • Simple present affirmative statements with *I, you, we, they*	
3 On Time *page 46*	• Numbers 0–59 • Clock time • Daily activities • Days of the week • The sounds of *d* and *t*	• Listen to and write numbers • Listen to and write clock time • Listen to a conversation about a student's schedule	• Ask for and say clock time • Talk about daily activities • Talk about your weekly schedule	• Prepositions of time: *at, on, from / to* ◦ *Wh-* questions: *What, When* • Simple present: third person singular	
4 Family and Friends *page 62*	• Family members • Household chores • Months and dates • Ordinal numbers 1st–31st • The sounds of *d* and *th*	• Listen to a conversation about family members • Listen to and write dates	• Say who is in your family • Say who does household chores in your home • Ask for and say dates	◦ *Who's that?* ◦ Questions with *Do* • Singular and plural nouns • Questions with *Who* • Simple present: affirmative statements	

LIFE SKILLS	READING	WRITING	NUMERACY	PERSISTENCE
• Introduce yourself • Identify upper and lower case letters • Understand course numbers and room numbers for school	• Read the alphabet • Read numbers 1–10 • Read student IDs	• Write the alphabet • Write numbers 1–10	• Numbers 1–10	
• Say and write the alphabet • Say and write numbers 0–9 • Say and spell first and last names • Say and write your telephone number • Ask for and write telephone numbers • Identify gender	• Read a paragraph about a student and a teacher • Read a personal information form • Read a story about different ways to greet people	• Start first and last names with capital letters • Start country names with capital letters • Start sentences with capital letters; end sentences with periods • End questions with question marks • Fill out a personal information form • Write about how people say hello in your country • Write sentences about yourself using personal information	• Cardinal numbers 0–10 • Telephone numbers • Student ID numbers	• Team Project: Meet Your Class
• Understand classroom instructions • Learn about places in a school • Talk about study skills • Use appropriate titles: Mr., Ms., Mrs., Miss	• Read a paragraph about how someone studies • Read a personal information form • Read a cross-cultural story about different classrooms	• Fill out a personal information form • Write about classrooms in your country • Write sentences about yourself with personal information	• Counting	• Team Project: Places in the School
• Write numbers as words • Understand clock time • Understand A.M. (morning) and P.M. (afternoon, evening) • Say, read, and write days of the week	• Read schedules • Read a paragraph about someone's schedule • Read a story about being on time	• Write about time in your culture • Write about your schedule • Write sentences about your weekly schedule	• Cardinal numbers 0–59 • Clock time • Schedules	• Team Project: Time to Get Up
• Talk about household chores • Say, read, and write months of the year • Read and write dates in words and numbers • Say and write dates of birth	• Read a paragraph about a family • Read a personal information form • Read a story about household chores	• Fill out a personal information form • Write about household chores and jobs in your country • Write sentences about your English program	• Ordinal numbers 1st –31st • Calendars • Dates	• Team Project: Birthdays

° Indicates a grammar point that appears in context, but not explicitly taught
Text in red = Civics and American culture

UNIT	VOCABULARY AND PHONICS	LISTENING	SPEAKING	GRAMMAR	
5 **How much is it?** *page 80*	• U.S. coins • U.S. bills • Drugstore items • The sounds of *g* and *c*	• Listen to a conversation about an item on sale • Listen to information about the location of drugstore items • Listen to and write prices	• Ask for and give change • Ask where things are in a store • Ask for and say prices	○ Questions with *Do* • *Where is / Where are* ○ *How much is . . . ?*	
6 **Let's eat!** *page 96*	• Fruits and vegetables • Quantities and containers • Food and prices on a menu • Breakfast, lunch, dinner foods • The sounds of *f* and *v*	• Listen to a conversation about likes and dislikes • Listen and understand what someone needs from the store • Listen to and write prices	• Say what you like and don't like • Say what someone likes and doesn't like • Talk about shopping for food • Say the quantity of food you need	○ *Do you like . . . ?* ○ Simple present: *like* ○ Simple present: *need, have* ○ *I'd like* for ordering food	
7 **Apartment for Rent** *page 114*	• Rooms • Words to describe rooms • Furniture and appliances • *Street, drive, avenue, road, lane, boulevard* • The sounds of *l* and *r*	• Listen to a conversation about an apartment for rent • Listen to and write a street address • Listen to information about an apartment for rent	• Say what rooms are in your home • Say what furniture and appliances are in your home • Ask for and give a street address • Ask for information about an apartment for rent	• *There is / There are* • Yes / No questions: *Is there / Are there*	
8 **Let's go shopping.** *page 130*	• Clothes • Colors • Problems with clothing • The sounds of *s* and *sh*	• Listen to a conversation about clothes and sizes • Listen and say why someone is returning clothing items	• Say the clothes you want • Ask for the sizes you need • Say what someone is wearing • Return clothing to a store and say the problem(s)	• *This / That, These / Those* • Adjective + noun ○ *I need to return . . .*	

LIFE SKILLS	READING	WRITING	NUMERACY	PERSISTENCE
• Make change with U.S. coins and bills • Read price tags • Read a shopping receipt • Write a personal check	• Read a store directory • Read a store receipt • Read a cross-cultural story about shopping	• Write a personal check • Write about shopping in your country • Write sentences about how you shop	• U.S. money • Prices • Shopping receipts	• Team Project: Coins and Bills
• Read grocery ads • Understand quantities and containers • Write a shopping list • Read a menu • Order meals in a restaurant	• Read a paragraph about making soup • Read a shopping list • Read a grocery ad • Read a menu • Read a cross-cultural story about different ways to eat	• Write a shopping list • Write about how people eat • Find out what a classmate needs and write his/her shopping list	• Prices • Quantities	• Team Project: Plan a Party
• Talk about rooms, furniture, and appliances • Ask about an apartment for rent • Say and write your street address • Address an envelope	• Read a paragraph about an apartment • Read addresses on an envelope • Read a cross-cultural story about single people	• Address an envelope • Write about single people in your country • Write an ad	• Street addresses • Cost of housing	• Team Project: What's your home like?
• Identify basic clothing • Read size labels • Describe what someone is wearing • Ask for and give prices • Return clothing to a store	• Read a paragraph about two friends and shopping • Read store ads • Read a cross-cultural story about the colors of clothes	• Write about the colors of clothes in your country • Write a conversation between a customer and a sales assistant	• Clothing sizes • Regular prices and sale prices	• Team Project: A Clothing Sale

º Indicates a grammar point that appears in context, but not explicitly taught
Text in red = Civics and American culture

UNIT	VOCABULARY AND PHONICS	LISTENING	SPEAKING	GRAMMAR	
9 **Our Busy Lives** *page 146*	• Free-time activities • Household chores • Workplace activities • The sounds of *a* (*date*) and *e* (*yes*)	• Listen to a conversation about free-time activities • Listen to a conversation about household chores • Listen to a conversation about workplace activities	• Talk about your free-time activities • Say how often you do something • Say what you are doing now • Say what someone is doing now	○ *How often. . . ?* • Present continuous: affirmative statements • Present continuous: *Yes / No* questions and short answers • Present continuous: negative statements	
10 **Where's the bus stop?** *page 162*	• Places in the community • Types of transportation • Traffic signs • Directions • The sounds of *a* (*bank*) and *i* (*library*)	• Listen to a conversation about the location of a place • Listen to someone giving directions • Listen to directions and find the place on a map	• Ask where places are • Give directions • Ask about types of transportation	• Prepositions of place: *on, between, across from* ○ *Wh-* questions: *Where* ○ Review: Imperatives ○ *How do you get to . . . ?*	
11 **Get well soon!** *page 178*	• Parts of the body • Medical instructions • Common health problems • Medicine and dosages • The sounds of *e* (*sleep*) and *i* (*in*)	• Listen to a phone call to 911 • Listen to instructions during a medical exam and do the actions	• Make a doctor's appointment • Describe symptoms of a health problem • Offer suggestions when someone doesn't feel well • Call 911	○ *I'd like to* + verb ○ Suggestions with *should*	
12 **What do you do?** *page 194*	• Occupations • Job skills • Abbreviations for job ads • The sounds of *o* (*hospital*) and *u* (*bus*)	• Listen to someone applying for a job • Listen to a job interview	• Say your occupation • Ask about someone's occupation • Talk about job skills	• *Where do / Where does . . . ?* • *Can* for ability: questions and short answers	

LIFE SKILLS	READING	WRITING	NUMERACY	PERSISTENCE
• Identify free-time activities, household chores, workplace activities • Say who does household chores in your home • Understand and write phone messages	• Read a paragraph about a phone call. • Read telephone messages • Read a cross-cultural story about a family's activities	• Write telephone messages • Write about your family's activities • Write sentences about your weekly activities	• *once, twice, three times*	• Team Project: Free-Time Activities
• Ask for directions • Give directions • Identify forms of transportation • Read traffic signs	• Read a map • Read a paragraph about how a student gets to school • Read a story about someone's new business	• Write about your dream business • Write places on a map	• Map directions	• Team Project: Places in the Neighborhood
• Make a doctor's appointment • Follow medical instructions during a medical exam • Call 911 • Read a medicine label	• Read a paragraph about someone's checkup • Read a cross-cultural story about going to the doctor	• Write about going to the doctor • Write about directions on a medicine label	• Medicine dosages	• Team Project: Give Health Tips
• Read job ads • Talk about your job skills in an interview	• Read a paragraph about someone's job interview • Read a story about someone's first job interview in the U.S.	• Write about job interviews • Write a dialogue for a job interview • Fill out a job application	• Phone numbers • Work schedule	• Team Project: Talk About Jobs

° Indicates a grammar point that appears in context, but not explicitly taught
Text in red = Civics and American culture

Correlations

UNIT	CASAS Reading Basic Skill Content Standards	CASAS Listening Basic Skill Content Standards	
Pre-Unit	**L1:** 2.2; **L2:** 1.1, 1.2, 2.4; **L3:** 1.2, 1.3, 2.6, 4.1	**L1:** 2.1, 4.1; **L2:** 1.1, 2.2; **L3:** 1.3, 2.1, 2.3	
1	**L1:** 2.4, 3.1; **L2:** 1.1, 1.2, 1.3; **L3:** 4.1; **L4:** 3.1; **L5:** 3.10; **L6:** 3.10; **L7:** 3.1, 4.6; **L8:** 3.11; **SWYK Review:** 1.1, 1.2, 1.3, 1.4, 3.11; **SWYK Expand:** 4.6	**L1:** 1.1, 3.1; **L2:** 1.2, 2.1, 3.1; **L3:** 1.2, 3.1; **L4:** 1.2, 3.1; **L5:** 1.2, 3.1; **L6:** 1.2, 3.1; **L7:** 1.2, 3.1; **L8:** 1.2; **SWYK Review:** 1.3, 3.1; **SWYK Expand:** 1.1, 1.2, 3.1	
2	**L1:** 2.2; **L2:** 3.6, 3.8; **L3:** 2.2, 3.6, 3.8; **L4:** 4.9; **L5:** 4.6; **L6:** 3.3; **L7:** 3.3; **SWYK Review:** 1.1, 1.2, 1.3, 1.4; **SWYK Expand:** 4.6, 4.9	**L1:** 1.1, 1.2, 3.3; **L2:** 1.1, 1.2, 2.1, 3.2; **L3:** 1.1, 1.2; **L5:**1.1, 1.2, 1.3; **L6:** 1.1; **SWYK Review:** 1.3, 1.4, 3.3; **SWYK Expand:** 1.1, 3.1, 3.4	
3	**L1:** 4.1, 4.2; **L2:** 3.12, 4.1, 4.2; **L3:** 3.12, 4.1, 4.2; **L4:** 2.3, 4.1, 4.2, 4.6; **L5:** 4.1; **L6:** 3.3, 3.11, 3.12; **SWYK Review:** 1.2, 1.3, 1.4, 2.3, 4.1; **SWYK Expand:** 4.1, 4.2, 4.6	**L1:** 1.1; **L2:** 1.1; **L3:** 1.1, 1.4; **L4:** 1.1, 1.4; **L6:** 1.1, 1.4, 3.3; **SWYK Review:** 1.3; **SWYK Expand:** 1.3	
4	**L1:** 3.2, 3.12; **L2:** 3.3, 3.11, 3.12, 4.6; **L3:** 3.11, 3.12; **L4:** 4.1, 4.3, 4.8; **L5:** 4.3; **L6:** 3.11, 4.6; **L7:** 3.3, 3.11, 3.12; **SWYK Review:** 1.2, 1.3, 1.4, 1.6; **SWYK Expand:** 2.6, 3.11, 3.12, 4.6	**L1:** 1.1, 1.2; **L2:** 1.2, 3.3; **L3:** 1.2, 3.3; **L4:** 1.2; **L6:** 1.2; **L7:** 1.2, 1.4, 3.1, 3.3; **SWYK Review:** 1.3, 3.4; **SWYK Expand:** 1.4, 3.1	
5	**L1:** 2.1, 3.12, 4.4; **L2:** 2.1, 3.12, 4.4; **L3:** 3.12, 4.9; **L4:** 4.1, 4.4; **L5:** 3.11, 3.12, 4.4, 4.6; **L6:** 3.11, 3.12, 4.4; **SWYK Review:** 1.1, 1.2, 1.3, 1.6, 2.1, 4.1, 4.4; **SWYK Expand:** 2.7, 4.1, 4.6	**L1:** 1.1, 1.2, 3.3; **L2:** 1.1, 1.2, 3.3; **L4:** 1.1, 3.3; **L6:** 1.4, 3.3, 4.2; **SWYK Review:** 1.1, 2.5, 3.3; **SWYK Expand:** 1.3	
6	**L1:** 3.3, 3.11, 3.12; **L2:** 3.11, 3.12; **L3:** 3.2, 4.6; **L4:** 3.11, 3.12; **L5:** 3.11, 3.12, 4.1, 4.4; **L6:** 3.2, 3.8, 4.1, 4.4, 4.6, 4.10; **L7:** 3.2, 3.8, 3.11, 3.12; **SWYK Review:** 1.2, 1.3, 1.4; **SWYK Expand:** 3.3, 3.11, 3.12, 4.1, 4.4	**L1:** 1.1, 1.2, 3.2, 3.3; **L2:** 1.2, 3.2, 3.3; **L3:** 1.1, 1.2, 3.2, 3.3; **L4:** 3.3; **L6:** 1.1, 1.2, 1.4, 2.5; **SWYK Review:** 1.3; **SWYK Expand:** 2.5	
7	**L1:** 3.11, 3.12, 4.9; **L2:** 3.8, 3.11, 3.12, 4.9; **L3:** 3.8, 3.11, 3.12, 4.9; **L4:** 3.8, 3.11, 3.12, 4.1, 4.4, 4.9; **L5:** 2.4, 2.6, 4.5, 4.1; **L6:** 3.11, 3.12, 7.8; **SWYK Review:** 1.1, 1.2, 1.3, 1.4, 1.6, 3.11, 3.12; **SWYK Expand:** 3.11, 4.1, 4.4	**L1:** 1.1, 1.2, 4.1; **L2:** 1.1, 1.2, 4.1; **L3:** 1.1, 1.2. 3.3; **L4:** 1.1, 3.5; **L6:** 3.3; **SWYK Review:** 1.3, 4.1; **SWYK Expand:** 3.3, 3.4	
8	**L1:** 3.2, 3.3, 3.11, 3.12; **L2:** 3.2, 3.3, 4.1; **L3:** 3.11, 3.12; **L4:** 3.8, 3.11, 3.12; **L5:** 3.11, 3.12, 4.1, 4.3, 4.4; **L6:** 3.11, 3.12, 6.2, 7.8; **SWYK Review:** 1.2, 1.3, 1.4; **SWYK Expand:** 3.11, 3.12	**L1:** 1.1, 1.2, 2.1, 4.1, 4.4; **L2:** 1.1, 1.2, 2.1, 4.1; **L3:** 1.1, 1.2, 3.3; **L4:** 1.1, 1.2; **L5:** 4.2; **L6:** 4.2, 4.4; **SWYK Review:** 1.1, 1.2, 1.3, 4.1; **SWYK Expand:** 4.1	
9	**L1:** 3.2, 3.8; **L2:** 3.1, 3.2, 3.3, 3.8; **L3:** 3.2, 3.3, 3.8, 3.11, 3.12; **L4:** 3.2, 3.3, 3.8, 3.11, 3.12; **L5:** 4.1, 4.3, 4.5, 4.6; **L6:** 3.11, 7.8; **SWYK Review:** 1.2, 1.3, 1.4; **SWYK Expand:** 3.11, 3.12, 4.8	**L1:** 1.1, 1.2; **L2:** 4.3; **L3:** 1.1, 1.2, 3.2; **L4:** 1.1, 1.2, 3.2; **L5:** 5.2; **SWYK Review:** 1.3; **SWYK Expand:** 3.3	
10	**L1:** 2.3, 2.5, 3.2, 3.8; **L2:** 2.3, 2.5, 3.2, 3.8; **L3:** 2.3, 2.5, 3.2, 3.8; **L4:** 2.3, 2.5, 3.2, 3.8, 4.9; **L5:** 2.1; **L6:** 3.3, 3.11, 3.12; **SWYK Review:** 1.1, 1.2, 1.3, 1.4; **SWYK Expand:** 4.9	**L1:** 1.1, 1.2, 1.4, 2.1, 2.5; **L2:** 1.1, 1.2, 1.4, 2.1, 2.5; **L3:** 1.1, 1.2, 1.4, 2.1, 2.5; **L4:** 1.1, 1.2, 1.4, 2.1, 2.5, 3.4; **L5:** 1.1, 1.2, 1.4, 2.1, 2.5, 2.6; **SWYK Review:** 3.3, 3.4; **SWYK Expand:** 2.5	
11	**L1:** 3.2, 3.8, 3.12; **L2:** 3.2, 3.6, 3.8, 3.11, 3.12; **L3:** 3.2, 3.6, 3.8; **L4:** 3.2, 3.8, 3.12; **L5:** 2.3, 3.3, 3.6, 4.1, 4.10; **L6:** 3.11, 3.12, 7.8; **SWYK Review:** 1.2, 1.3, 1.4, 3.12; **SWYK Expand:** 2.3, 3.6, 4.1	**L1:** 1.1, 1.2, 1.4; **L2:** 1.1, 1.2, 1.4, 3.4; **L3:** 1.1, 1.2, 1.4, 2.5; **L4:** 2.2; **L5:** 1.1, 1.2, 2.5; **SWYK Review:** 1.1, 1.2, 2.5, 3.4; **SWYK Expand:** 2.5, 3.4	
12	**L1:** 3.2, 3.8, 3.12; **L2:** 3.2, 3.8, 3.12; **L3:** 3.2, 3.8, 3.12; **L4:** 3.2, 3.8, 3.12; **L5:** 2.7, 2.12, 4.1; **L6:** 3.11; **SWYK Review:** 1.2, 1.3, 1.4, 3.2; **SWYK Expand:** 2.7, 4.6	**L1:** 1.1, 1.2; **L2:** 1.1, 1.2; **L3:** 1.1, 1.2; **L4:** 3.2, 3.4, 4.2; **SWYK Expand:** 1.1, 3.4	

CASAS Competencies	LAUSD ESL Beginning Low Competencies	Florida Adult ESOL Course Standards
L1: 0.1.1, 1.1.4, 1.1.5; **L2:** 0.1.1; **L3:** 0.1.1, 0.1.2, 6.0.1	4; 58a	1.01.01, 1.01.02, 1.04.01
L1: 0.1.1, 0.1.2, 0.1.4, 0.1.5, 0.1.6, 0.2.1; **L2:** 0.1.1, 0.1.2, 0.1.4, 0.1.5; **L3:** 0.1.1, 0.1.2, 0.2.1, 2.1.8, 6.0.1; **L4:** 0.1.4, 0.1.5; **L5:** 0.1.2, 0.1.5; **L6:** 0.1.2, 0.1.5, 0.2.1; **L7:** 0.1.1, 0.2.2; **L8:** 0.1.1, 0.1.5, 2.7.2; **SWYK Review:** 0.1.5, 0.2.1; **SWYK Expand:** 0.1.4, 0.2.2, 2.1.8	1; 4; 5; 9a; 9b; 9c; 58a; 58b	1.01.01, 1.01.02, 1.01.03, 1.02.11, 1.02.12, 1.04.01
L1: 0.1.1, 0.1.4, 0.1.5; **L2:** 0.1.1, 0.1.2, 0.1.7; **L3:** 0.1.1, 0.1.5, 0.1.6, 2.2.1, 2.8.3; **L4:** 0.1.5, 2.8.3; **L5:** 0.1.1, 0.1.2, 2.8.5; **L6:** 2.8.2, 7.4.1, 7.4.2, 7.4.3, 7.4.4, 7.4.5, 7.4.7, 7.4.9; **L7:** 2.7.2, 2.7.9; **SWYK Review:** 0.1.2, 0.1.5; **SWYK Expand:** 0.1.5, 2.8.3, 2.8.5	9d; 12; 15; 17; 59a	1.01.03, 1.06.03
L1: 0.1.1, 6.0.1; **L2:** 0.1.1, 0.1.5, 0.1.6, 2.3.1; **L3:** 0.1.1, 0.1.5; **L4:** 0.1.1, 2.3.2, 7.1.4; **L5:** 2.3.1, 6.0.1, 6.0.2, 6.0.3; **L6:** 2.7.2; **SWYK Review:** 0.1.5, 6.0.2; **SWYK Expand:** 2.3.2, 2.3.4, 7.1.4	25; 26; 59a	1.01.03, 1.01.05, 1.03.09, 1.03.10, 1.04.01
L1: 0.1.1, 0.1.2, 0.1.5, 0.1.6; **L2:** 0.1.5, 0.1.7, 7.1.4; **L3:** 0.1.6, 8.1.4, 8.2.1, 8.2.2, 8.2.3, 8.2.4, 8.2.5, 8.2.6, 8.3.1; **L4:** 0.1.1, 0.2.4, 2.3.2, 2.3.4, 6.0.1; **L5:** 0.2.2, 2.3.4; **L6:** 0.2.2; **L7:** 2.7.2, 2.7.9; **SWYK Review:** 0.1.5, 2.3.4; **SWYK Expand:** 2.8.5, 8.2.1, 8.2.3, 8.2.4, 8.2.5, 8.2.6	6; 7; 26; 59a	1.01.03, 1.01.05, 1.02.07, 1.04.01
L1: 0.1.1, 0.1.2, 0.1.4, 0.1.5, 1.1.6; **L2:** 0.1.1, 0.1.2, 0.1.4, 1.1.6, 6.0.1, 6.0.2, 6.0.3, 6.0.4; **L3:** 0.1.1, 1.2.1, 1.2.6, 1.2.7; **L4:** 0.1.1, 0.1.4, 1.2.2; **L5:** 1.3.1, 1.6.4, 2.3.2; **L6:** 2.7.2; **SWYK Review:** 0.1.1, 0.1.5, 1.1.6; **SWYK Expand:** 1.2.7, 1.6.4	9d; 30a; 30b; 31; 32; 59a	1.04.02, 1.04.06, 1.04.07, 1.04.09, 1.05.05
L1: 0.1.1, 0.1.5, 1.2.8; **L2:** 0.1.2, 0.1.5; **L3:** 0.1.1, 1.2.8, 7.4.8; **L4:** 0.1.1, 1.1.4, 1.1.7, 6.0.2, 6.0.3; **L5:** 0.1.1, 1.2.1, 1.2.2, 1.2.4; **L6:** 0.1.1, 0.1.4, 2.6.4; **L7:** 0.1.5, 2.7.2; **SYWK Review:** 1.2.8, 2.6.4; **SYWK Expand:** 0.1.5, 2.6.4	9a; 19; 35; 37; 59a	1.01.03, 1.04.02, 1.05.06
L1: 0.1.1, 0.1.2, 1.4.1; **L2:** 0.1.1, 1.4.1, 1.4.2; **L3:** 0.1.1, 0.1.2, 1.4.1, 1.4.2; **L4:** 0.1.1, 1.4.1, 1.4.2; **L5:** 0.2.3, 0.2.4; **L6:** 0.1.8, 0.2.4, 2.1.8, 2.7.2; **SWYK Review:** 0.1.1, 1.4.1; **SWYK Expand:** 0.1.5, 1.4.1, 1.4.2, 1.7.6	1; 2; 4; 8; 38; 39; 59a	1.01.03, 1.02.07, 1.02.10, 1.04.01, 1.04.04
L1: 0.1.1, 0.1.5, 1.2.9; **L2:** 0.1.1, 0.1.2, 1.2.7, 1.3.7; **L3:** 0.1.1, 0.1.4, 0.1.5, 0.1.6; **L4:** 0.1.1, 1.3.3; **L5:** 0.2.4, 1.1.6, 1.2.1, 1.2.2, 1.2.3, 1.2.4; **L6:** 2.7.2, 2.7.9; **SWYK Review:** 1.2.9, 1.3.1; **SWYK Expand:** 0.1.5, 1.2.7	33; 34; 59a	1.01.03, 1.04.02, 1.04.03
L1: 0.1.1, 0.1.5, 2.3.2; **L2:** 0.1.2, 0.1.6, 7.2.2, 7.2.3, 7.2.5; **L3:** 0.1.1, 0.1.2, 8.2.1, 8.2.2, 8.2.3, 8.2.4, 8.2.5, 8.2.6; **L4:** 0.1.1, 0.1.2, 4.6.2, 4.8.1, 4.8.3; **L5:** 2.1.7; **L6:** 0.2.4, 2.7.2; **SWYK Review:** 8.2.1, 8.2.2, 8.2.3, 8.2.4, 8.2.5, 8.2.6; **SWYK Expand:** 0.1.2, 2.8.3, 7.1.4	2; 4; 9a; 55; 59a	1.01.03, 1.01.05, 1.01.07
L1: 0.1.1, 0.1.4, 0.1.5, 0.1.6, 2.2.5; **L2:** 0.1.1, 2.5.1, 2.5.8, 3.1.3; **L3:** 0.1.2, 0.1.5, 2.2.3, 7.1.4; **L4:** 2.2.5; **L5:** 0.1.1, 0.1.5, 2.2.2; **L6:** 0.1.5, 2.7.2; **SWYK Review:** 0.1.5, 0.1.6; **SWYK Expand:** 0.1.5, 2.2.5	9d; 22; 23a; 23b; 49; 59a	1.02.01, 1.02.02, 1.03.01, 1.03.14, 1.06.01, 1.06.02, 1.06.03
L1: 0.1.1, 0.1.2, 0.1.5, 3.1.1, 3.1.2, 3.6.1, 3.6.4; **L2:** 0.1.1, 0.1.2, 3.6.4; **L3:** 0.1.1, 0.1.5, 0.1.6, 3.6.3; **L4:** 0.1.1, 2.1.2; **L5:** 3.3.1, 3.3.2, 3.3.3, 3.3.4, 3.4.1; **L6:** 2.7.2, 2.7.9; **SWYK Review:** 0.1.1, 3.6.1, 3.6.4; **SWYK Expand:** 3.3.1, 3.3.2, 3.3.4, 3.6.4	9a; 20; 43; 44; 46; 59a	1.01.03, 1.01.09, 1.04.01, 1.05.01, 1.05.02, 1.05.03, 1.05.04, 1.07.02
L1: 0.1.1, 0.1.5, 0.1.6, 0.2.4, 7.1.4; **L2:** 0.1.1, 0.1.2, 0.1.5; **L3:** 0.1.1, 4.1.3, 4.1.5, 4.1.6, 4.1.8; **L4:** 0.1.5, 4.1.2, 4.1.3; **L5:** 4.1.3; **L6:** 2.2.3, 2.7.9, 4.1.5; **SWYK Review:** 0.1.2; **SWYK Expand:** 4.1.2, 4.1.3, 4.1.5, 4.1.8	7; 9a; 50; 51; 52; 53; 54; 59a	1.01.02, 1.01.03, 1.01.04, 1.03.01, 1.03.02, 1.03.03, 1.03.04, 1.03.06, 1.03.15

All units of *Future* meet most of the **EFF Content Standards**. For details, as well as for correlations to other state standards, go to www.pearsonlongman.com/future.

To the Teacher

Welcome to *Future*
English for Results

Future is a six-level, four-skills course for adults and young adults correlated to state and national standards. It incorporates research-based teaching strategies, corpus-informed language, and the best of modern technology.

KEY FEATURES

Future provides everything your students need in one integrated program.

In developing the course, we listened to what teachers asked for and we responded, providing six levels, more meaningful content, a thorough treatment of grammar, explicit skills development, abundant practice, multiple options for state-of-the-art assessment, and innovative components.

Future serves students' real-life needs.

We began constructing the instructional syllabus for *Future* by identifying what is most critical to students' success in their personal and family lives, in the workplace, as members of a community, and in their academic pursuits. *Future* provides outstanding coverage of life skills competencies, basing language teaching on actual situations that students are likely to encounter and equipping them with the skills they need to achieve their goals. Grammar and other language elements in each lesson are taught and practiced in realistic contexts, enabling students to use language meaningfully, from the beginning.

Future grows with your students.

Future takes students from absolute beginner level through low-advanced proficiency in English, addressing students' abilities and learning priorities at each level. As the levels progress, the curricular content and unit structure change accordingly, with the upper levels incorporating more academic skills, more advanced content standards, and more content-rich texts.

Level	Description	CASAS Scale Scores
Intro	True Beginning	Below 180
1	Low Beginning	181–190
2	High Beginning	191–200
3	Low Intermediate	201–210
4	High Intermediate	211–220
5	Low Advanced	221–235

Future is fun!

Humor is built into each unit of *Future*. Fun and lively illustrations at the end of lessons provide speaking models for students. In addition, many activities have students interacting in pairs and groups. Not only does this make classroom time more enjoyable, it also creates an atmosphere conducive to learning in which learners are relaxed, highly motivated, and at their most receptive.

Future puts the best of 21st-century technology in the hands of students and teachers.

In addition to its expertly developed print materials and audio components, *Future* goes a step further.

- Every **Student Book comes with a Practice Plus CD-ROM** for use at home, in the lab, or wherever students have access to a computer. The Practice Plus CD-ROM can be used both by students who wish to extend their practice beyond the classroom and by those who need to "make up" what they missed in class. The CD-ROM also includes the entire class audio program as MP3 files so students can get extra listening practice at their convenience.
- The **Workbook with Audio CD** gives students access to more listening practice than ever before possible.
- The **Tests and Test Prep** book comes with the *Future Exam View® Assessment Suite*, enabling teachers to print ready-made tests, customize these tests, or create their own tests for life skills, grammar, vocabulary, listening, and reading for students at three levels—on-level, pre-level, or above-level.
- The **Teacher Training DVD** provides demo lessons of real teachers using *Future* with their classes. Teachers can select from the menu and watch a specific type of lesson, such as a grammar presentation, or a specific type of activity, such as an information gap, at their own convenience.
- The **Companion Website** provides a variety of teaching support, including a pdf of the Teacher's Edition and Lesson Planner notes for each unit in the Student Book.

Future provides all the assessment tools you need.

- The **Placement Test** evaluates students' proficiency in all skill areas, allowing teachers and program administrators to easily assign students to the right classes.
- The **Tests and Test Prep** book for each level provides:
  o **Printed unit tests** with accompanying audio CD. These unit tests use standardized testing formats, giving students practice "bubbling-in" responses as required

for CASAS and other standardized tests. In addition, reproducible test prep worksheets and practice tests provide invaluable help to students unfamiliar with such test formats.

o The *Future* **Exam***View®* *Assessment Suite* is a powerful program that allows teachers to create their own unique tests or to print or customize already prepared tests at three levels: pre-level, on-level, and above-level.

- **Performance-based assessment:** Lessons in the Student Book end with a "practical assessment" activity called Show What You Know. Each unit culminates with role-play activities, which require students to demonstrate their oral competence in a holistic way. The **Teacher's Edition and Lesson Planner** provides speaking rubrics to make it easy for teachers to evaluate students' oral proficiency.
- **Self-assessment:** For optimal learning to take place, students need to be involved in monitoring their own progress. *Future* has addressed this in the Student Book with end-of-unit reviews that allow students to see their progress in vocabulary, grammar, and writing. In addition, the CD-ROM provides students with continuous feedback (and opportunities for self-correction) as they work through each lesson, and the Workbook contains the answer keys, so that students can check their own work outside of class.

Future addresses multilevel classes and diverse learning styles.

Using research-based teaching strategies, *Future* provides teachers with creative solutions for all stages of lesson planning and implementation, allowing them to meet the needs of all their students.

- The **Multilevel Communicative Activities Book** provides an array of reproducible activities and games that engage students through different modalities. Teachers' notes provide multilevel options for pre-level and above-level students, as well as extension activities for additional speaking and writing practice.
- The **Teacher's Edition and Lesson Planner** offers pre-level and above-level variations for every lesson plan as well as numerous optional and extension activities designed to reach students at all levels.
- The **Transparencies and Reproducible Vocabulary Cards** include picture and word cards that will help kinesthetic and visual learners acquire and learn new vocabulary. Teachers' notes include ideas for multilevel classes.

- The **Practice Plus CD-ROM** included with the Student Book is an extraordinary tool for individualizing instruction. It allows students to direct their own learning, working on precisely what they need and practicing what they choose to work on as many times as they like. In addition, the CD-ROM provides all the audio files for the book, enabling students to listen as they wish to any of the material that accompanies the text.
- The **Workbook with Audio CD**, similarly, allows students to devote their time to the lessons and specific skill areas that they need to work on most. In addition, students can replay the audio portions they want to listen to as many times as necessary, choosing to focus on the connections between the written and spoken word, listening for grammar pronunciation, and/or listening for general comprehension.
- The **Tests and Test Prep** book, as noted on page xiv, includes the *Future* **Exam***View®* *Assessment Suite*, which allows teachers to print out prepared tests at three levels (pre-level, on-level, and above-level) and to customize existing tests or create their own tests using the databank.

Future's persistence curriculum motivates students to continue their education.

Recent research about persistence has given us insights into how to keep students coming to class and how to keep them learning when they can't attend. Recognizing that there are many forces operating in students' lives—family, jobs, childcare, health—that may make it difficult for them to come to class, programs need to help students:

- Identify their educational goals
- Believe that they can successfully achieve them
- Develop a commitment to their own education
- Identify forces that can interfere with school attendance
- Develop strategies that will help them try to stay in school in spite of obstacles
- Find ways to continue learning even during "stopping out" periods

Future addresses all of these areas with its persistence curriculum. Activities found throughout the book and specific persistence activities in the back of the book help students build community, set goals, develop better study skills, and feel a sense of achievement. In addition, the Practice Plus CD-ROM is unique in its ability to ensure that even those students unable to attend class are able to make up what they missed and thus persist in their studies.

Future supports busy teachers by providing all the materials teachers need, plus the teacher support.

The **Student Book, Workbook with Audio CD, Multilevel Communicative Activities Book,** and **Transparencies and Reproducible Vocabulary Cards** were designed to provide teachers with everything they need in the way of ready-to-use classroom materials so they can concentrate on responding to their students' needs. The **Future Teacher Training DVD** gives teachers tips and models for conducting various activity types in their classroom.

Future provides ample practice, with flexible options to best fit the needs of each class.

The Student Book provides 60–100 hours of instruction. It can be supplemented in class by using:
- Teacher's Edition and Lesson Planner expansion ideas
- Transparencies and Reproducible Vocabulary Cards
- Workbook exercises
- Multilevel Communicative Activities
- Tests
- CD-ROM activities
- Activities on the Companion Website (longmanusa.com/Future)

TEACHING MULTILEVEL CLASSES

Teaching tips for pair and group work

Using pair and group work in an ESL classroom has many proven benefits. It creates an atmosphere of liveliness, builds community, and allows students to practice speaking in a low-risk environment. Many of the activities in *Future* are pair and small-group activities. Here are some tips for managing these activities:
- Limit small groups to three or four students per group (unless an activity specifically calls for larger groups). This maximizes student participation.
- Change partners for different activities. This gives students a chance to work with many others in the class and keeps them from feeling "stuck."
- If possible, give students a place to put their coats when they enter the classroom. This allows them to move around freely without worrying about returning to their own seats.
- Move around the classroom as students are working to make sure they are on task and to monitor their work.

- As you walk around, try to remain unobtrusive, so students continue to participate actively, without feeling they are being evaluated.
- Keep track of language points students are having difficulty with. After the activity, teach a mini-lesson to the entire class addressing those issues. This helps students who are having trouble without singling them out.

Pairs and groups in the multilevel classroom

Adult education ESL classrooms are by nature multilevel. This is true even if students have been given a placement test. Many factors—including a student's age, educational background, and literacy level—contribute to his or her ability level. Also, the same student may be at level in one skill, but pre-level or above-level in another.

When grouping students for a task, keep the following points in mind:
- *Like-ability* groups (in which students have the same ability level) help ensure that all students participate equally, without one student dominating the activity.
- *Cross-ability* groups (in which students have different ability levels) are beneficial to pre-level students who need the support of their at- or above-level classmates. The higher-level students benefit from "teaching" their lower-level classmates.

For example, when students are practicing a straightforward conversation substitution exercise, like-ability pairings are helpful. The activity can be tailored to different ability levels, and both students can participate equally. When students are completing the more complex task of creating their own conversations, cross-ability pairings are helpful. The higher-level student can support and give ideas to the lower-level student.

The *Future* Teacher's Edition and Lesson Planner, the Teacher's Notes in the Multilevel Communicative Activities Book, and the Teacher's Notes in the Transparencies and Reproducible Vocabulary Cards all provide specific suggestions for when to put students in like-ability versus cross-ability groups, and how to tailor activities to different ability levels.

Unit Opener

Each unit starts with new vocabulary, which is presented in picture dictionary format and includes audio.

Short **model conversations** present the core competency and language of the lesson.

Students practice the conversation **in pairs**. They then practice the conversation **substituting** new vocabulary.

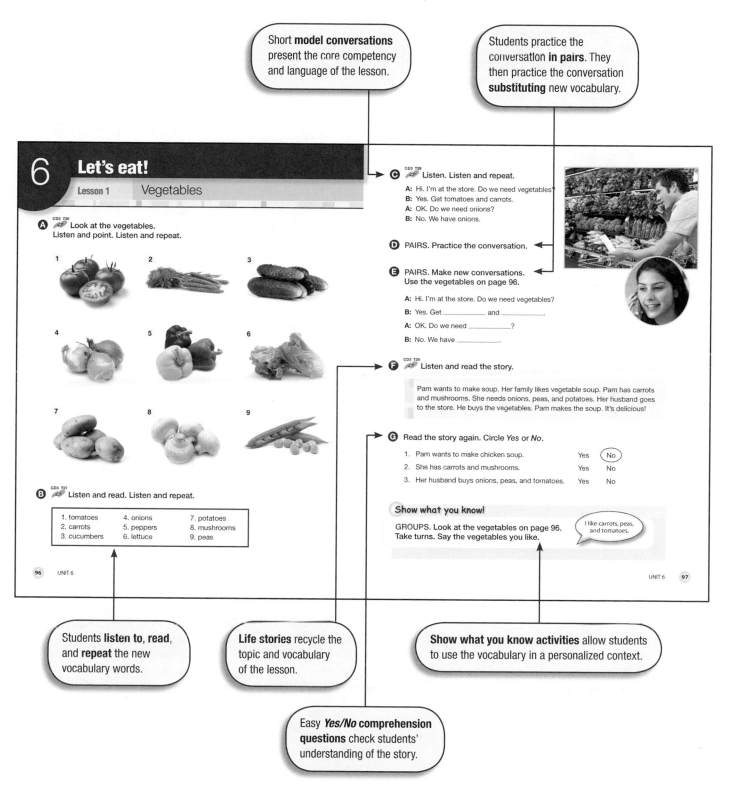

6 **Let's eat!**

Lesson 1   Vegetables

A CD3 T26 Look at the vegetables.
Listen and point. Listen and repeat.

1
2
3

4
5
6

7
8
9

B CD3 T27 Listen and read. Listen and repeat.

1. tomatoes	4. onions	7. potatoes
2. carrots	5. peppers	8. mushrooms
3. cucumbers	6. lettuce	9. peas

96   UNIT 6

C CD3 T28 Listen. Listen and repeat.

A: Hi. I'm at the store. Do we need vegetables?
B: Yes. Get tomatoes and carrots.
A: OK. Do we need onions?
B: No. We have onions.

D PAIRS. Practice the conversation.

E PAIRS. Make new conversations.
Use the vegetables on page 96.

A: Hi. I'm at the store. Do we need vegetables?

B: Yes. Get _____ and _____.

A: OK. Do we need _____?

B: No. We have _____.

F CD3 T29 Listen and read the story.

Pam wants to make soup. Her family likes vegetable soup. Pam has carrots and mushrooms. She needs onions, peas, and potatoes. Her husband goes to the store. He buys the vegetables. Pam makes the soup. It's delicious!

G Read the story again. Circle *Yes* or *No*.

1. Pam wants to make chicken soup.	Yes	No
2. She has carrots and mushrooms.	Yes	No
3. Her husband buys onions, peas, and tomatoes.	Yes	No

Show what you know!

GROUPS. Look at the vegetables on page 96. Take turns. Say the vegetables you like.

I like carrots, peas, and tomatoes.

UNIT 6   97

Students **listen to, read**, and **repeat** the new vocabulary words.

Life stories recycle the topic and vocabulary of the lesson.

Show what you know activities allow students to use the vocabulary in a personalized context.

Easy *Yes/No* **comprehension questions** check students' understanding of the story.

Grammar

Grammar lessons introduce and practice target grammar step-by-step.

Target grammar is presented in context in model conversations.

Simple questions check students' **listening comprehension** of the conversation.

An easy-to-read **grammar chart** provides examples of the **target grammar** related to the conversation.

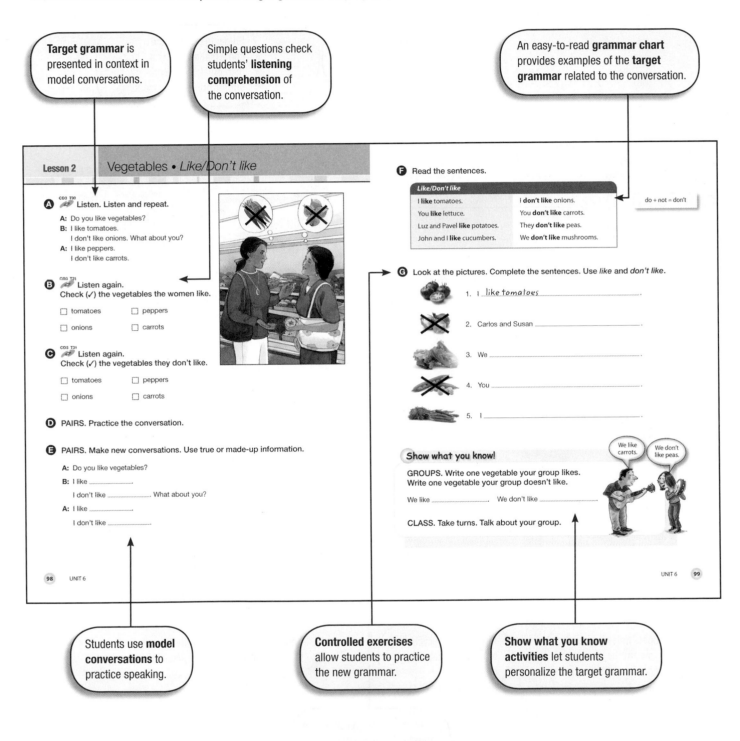

Students use **model conversations** to practice speaking.

Controlled exercises allow students to practice the new grammar.

Show what you know activities let students personalize the target grammar.

Life Skills

The Life Skills lesson in each unit focuses on functional language, practical skills, and printed materials such as personal forms, store ads, and medicine labels.

Simple **writing activities** recycle language from the unit. Students practice helpful **life skills** such as filling out forms, writing lists, and writing telephone messages.

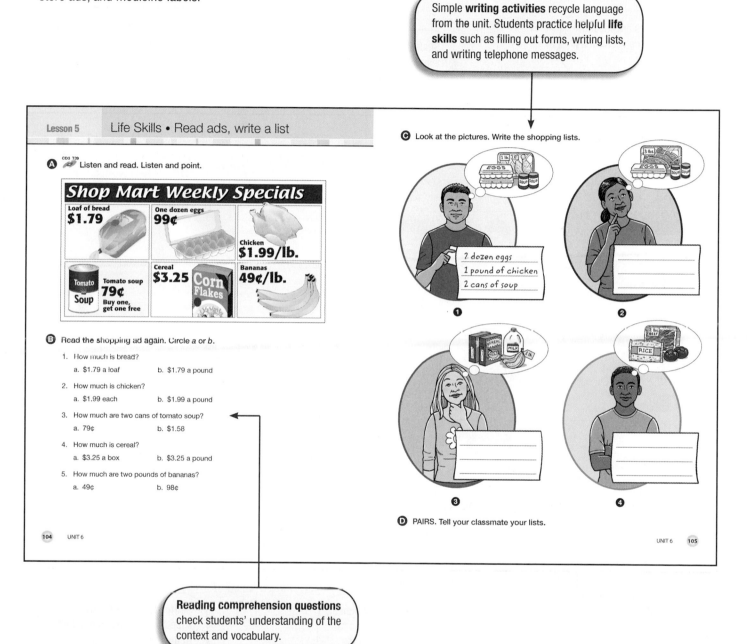

Reading comprehension questions check students' understanding of the context and vocabulary.

Reading

Beautiful illustrations present a story in graphic novel format. The stories engage students with cross-cultural topics that are interesting and relevant to their lives.

The pictures are used to pre-teach the **vocabulary** for the story.

Students **read to learn** while learning to read in English.

Easy *Yes/No* **comprehension questions** check students' understanding of the story.

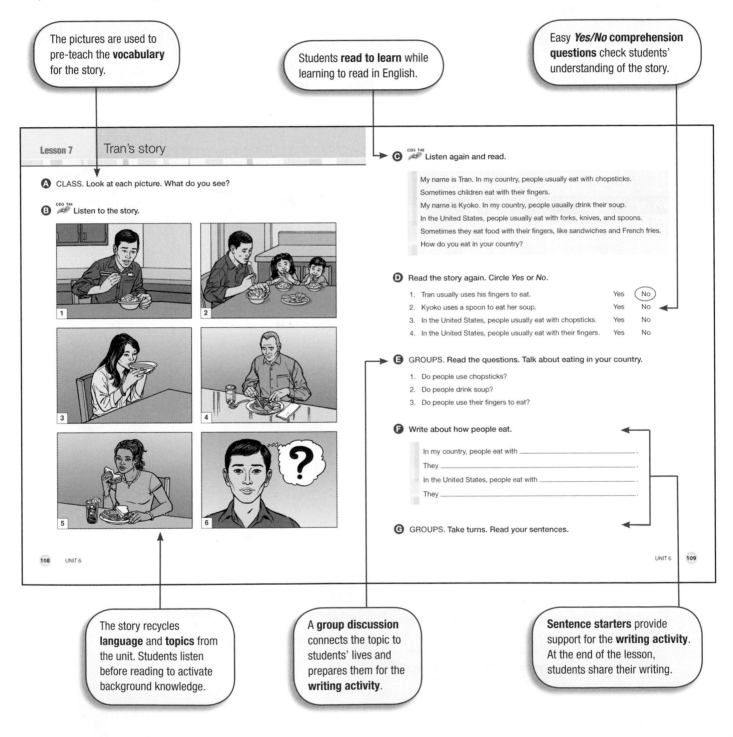

The story recycles **language** and **topics** from the unit. Students listen before reading to activate background knowledge.

A **group discussion** connects the topic to students' lives and prepares them for the **writing activity**.

Sentence starters provide support for the **writing activity**. At the end of the lesson, students share their writing.

Review

The Review lesson recycles unit vocabulary in the form of phonics activities and vocabulary exercises. Students also review speaking competencies.

Phonics activities focus on two sounds. Students read and pronounce words recycled from the unit, then listen to check their pronunciation.

Vocabulary activities include listening and repeating, categorizing, labeling, and matching exercises.

REVIEW Show what you know!

1 THE SOUNDS OF *F* AND *V*

A Read the words out loud softly.

fruit	favorite	Friday
food	fish	beef

B CD3 T46 Listen and repeat.

C Read the words out loud softly.

vegetables	very	live
favorite	five	have

D CD3 T47 Listen and repeat.

E CD3 T48 Listen. Write *f* or *v*. Listen again and repeat.

1. ____ood
2. ____egetables
3. ____ish
4. fi____e
5. ____ery
6. bee____
7. ha____e
8. ____ruit
9. ____a____orite

F DICTATION. PAIRS. Student A, say three words from Exercise A. Student B, listen and write.

_____ _____ _____

G DICTATION. SAME PAIRS. Student B, say three words from Exercise C. Student A, listen and write.

_____ _____ _____

2 VOCABULARY

A Circle the word that does not belong in each group.

1. apples   (cucumbers)   pears
2. lettuce   carrots   oranges
3. chicken   ground beef   lemons
4. rice   bread   apples
5. mushrooms   milk   onions
6. cherries   eggs   grapes
7. cereal   potatoes   tomatoes
8. peas   mangoes   strawberries

D PAIRS. Use the words in Exercise A. Write one word for each quantity.

1. a pound of _____
2. a bag of _____
3. a box of _____
4. a loaf of _____
5. a dozen _____

3 SPEAKING

You are reading a menu. The waitress asks: *May I help you? What do you say?*

a. We need carrots and onions.
b. I'd like a hamburger and a green salad.
c. I like apples and pears.

Go to the CD-ROM for more practice.

Students **listen** and **distinguish** between sounds by writing missing letters.

Students practice the focused sounds by **dictating** words to each other and **writing** the words.

Students review **speaking competencies** by completing a conversation.

Expand

The activities on the Expand lesson synthesize the language, themes, and competencies of the unit.

Students hear a **model conversation** that reviews the language and competency.

Role plays give students the opportunity to show what they know through fun, lively activities.

A **writing activity** allows students to build their writing skills by using the unit vocabulary.

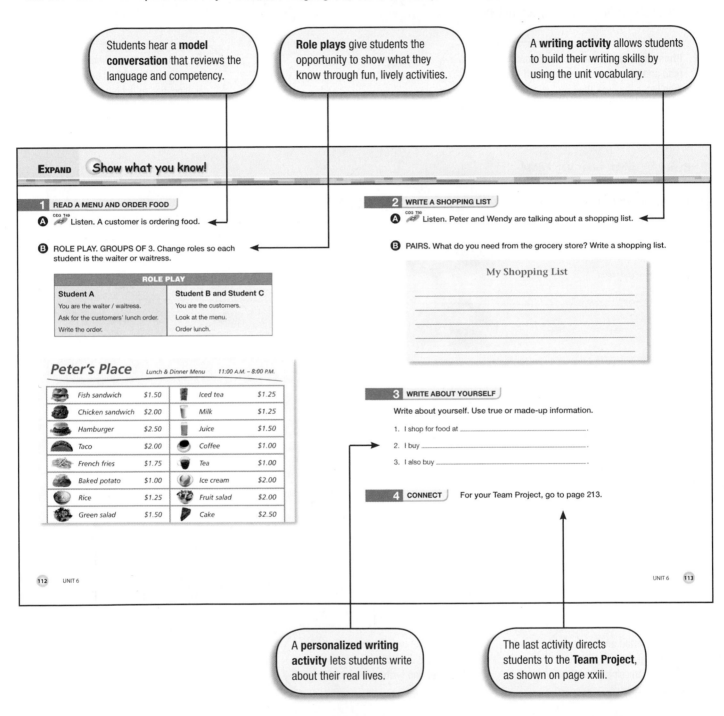

EXPAND Show what you know!

1 READ A MENU AND ORDER FOOD

A CD3 T49 Listen. A customer is ordering food.

B ROLE PLAY. GROUPS OF 3. Change roles so each student is the waiter or waitress.

ROLE PLAY	
Student A	**Student B and Student C**
You are the waiter / waitress.	You are the customers.
Ask for the customers' lunch order.	Look at the menu.
Write the order.	Order lunch.

Peter's Place Lunch & Dinner Menu 11:00 A.M. – 8:00 P.M.

Fish sandwich	$1.50		Iced tea	$1.25
Chicken sandwich	$2.00		Milk	$1.25
Hamburger	$2.50		Juice	$1.50
Taco	$2.00		Coffee	$1.00
French fries	$1.75		Tea	$1.00
Baked potato	$1.00		Ice cream	$2.00
Rice	$1.25		Fruit salad	$2.00
Green salad	$1.50		Cake	$2.50

2 WRITE A SHOPPING LIST

A CD3 T50 Listen. Peter and Wendy are talking about a shopping list.

B PAIRS. What do you need from the grocery store? Write a shopping list.

My Shopping List

_____
_____
_____
_____
_____

3 WRITE ABOUT YOURSELF

Write about yourself. Use true or made-up information.

1. I shop for food at _____ .
2. I buy _____ .
3. I also buy _____ .

4 CONNECT   For your Team Project, go to page 213.

A **personalized writing activity** lets students write about their real lives.

The last activity directs students to the **Team Project**, as shown on page xxiii.

Team Projects

Each unit includes a collaborative project that integrates lesson themes, language, and competencies, and supports community-building.

> Students **work in teams** to discuss and collect information related to the unit theme.

> Each student on the team is assigned **a role**.

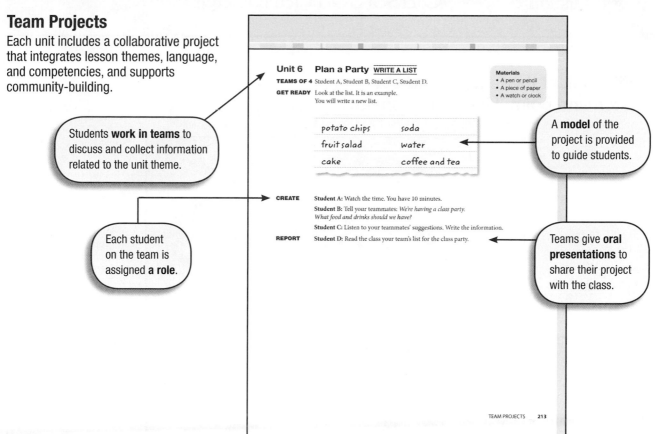

Unit 6   Plan a Party   WRITE A LIST

TEAMS OF 4 Student A, Student B, Student C, Student D.

GET READY Look at the list. It is an example.
You will write a new list.

potato chips	soda
fruit salad	water
cake	coffee and tea

Materials
- A pen or pencil
- A piece of paper
- A watch or clock

CREATE   Student A: Watch the time. You have 10 minutes.

Student B: Tell your teammates: *We're having a class party. What food and drinks should we have?*

Student C: Listen to your teammates' suggestions. Write the information.

REPORT   Student D: Read the class your team's list for the class party.

TEAM PROJECTS   213

> A **model** of the project is provided to guide students.

> Teams give **oral presentations** to share their project with the class.

Writing Practice

Writing practice pages provide models of upper and lowercase letters in print and cursive styles.

Writing Practice

A A   N N
B B   O O
C C   P P
D D   Q Q
E E   R R
F F   S S
G G   T T
H H   U U
I I   V V
J J   W W
K K   X X
L L   Y Y
M M   Z Z

236   WRITING PRACTICE   WRITING PRACTICE   237

A CD1 T2   Look at the teacher and student.
Listen and point. Listen and repeat.

B   PAIRS. Practice the conversation. Use your name.

C Look at the actions.
Listen and point. Listen and repeat.

1	2	3	4
look	listen	point	repeat
5	6	7	8
read	write	open	close

D PAIRS. Point to a picture in Exercise C. Say the action.

E Your teacher will say each sentence. Listen and point.

Work alone.   Work in pairs.   Work in groups.

A　 Look at the alphabet.
Listen and read. Listen and repeat.

CD1 T4

B capital letter
b lowercase letter

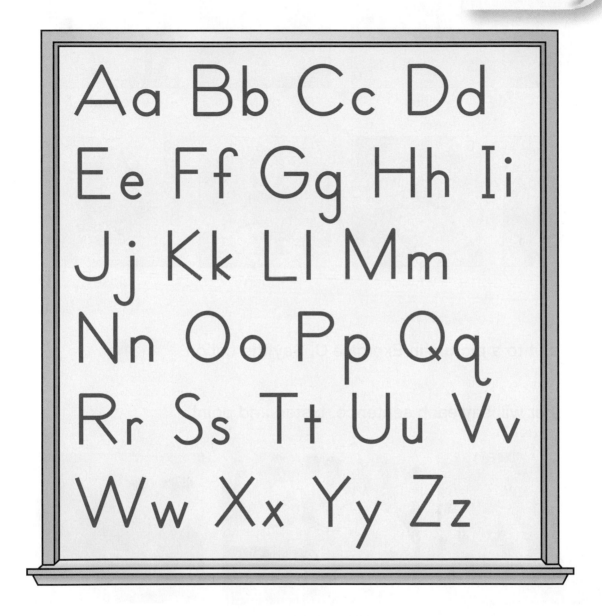

B　PAIRS. Point to a letter. Say the letter.

C Circle the capital letters.

a   f   Ⓥ   q   P   R   o   z   T   L

CD1 T5

D 💿 Listen. Write the capital letters.

1. __S__   6. _____

2. _____   7. _____

3. _____   8. _____

4. _____   9. _____

5. _____   10. _____

> See pages 236–243 for writing practice.

E Circle the lowercase letters.

ⓑ   S   m   v   K   C   p   e   H   j

CD1 T6

F 💿 Listen. Write the lowercase letters.

1. __c__   6. _____

2. _____   7. _____

3. _____   8. _____

4. _____   9. _____

5. _____   10. _____

G Write your name.

> Start names with a capital letter.

_____

Say and write numbers

A CD1 T7 Look at the numbers.
Listen and point. Listen and repeat.

B PAIRS. Point to a number. Say the number.

C CD1 T8 Listen for the number. Circle.

a. ③ 6   d. 1   10   g. 7   6

b. 2   7   e. 5   6   h. 8   9

c. 4   8   f. 1   9   i. 4   5

D CD1 T9 Listen. Write the number.

a. __6__   d. _____   g. _____

b. _____   e. _____   h. _____

c. _____   f. _____   i. _____

E **Listen and read. Listen and repeat.**

ID = identification

My name is ___Alba___.

My student ID number is _7281_.

I'm in ___English 1A___.

My class is in Room ___4___.

Name: Alba Monte

Class: English 1A
Room: 4

F **Read the student ID and schedule. Write the information.**

My name is ___Hong___.

My student ID number is _____.

I'm in English _____.

My class is in Room _____.

Name: Hong Chin

Class: English 1A
Room: 4

G **Complete the sentences. Use true information.**

My name is _____.

My student ID number is _____.

I'm in English _____.

My class is in Room _____.

CD1 T11

A Look at the map.
Listen and point. Listen and repeat.

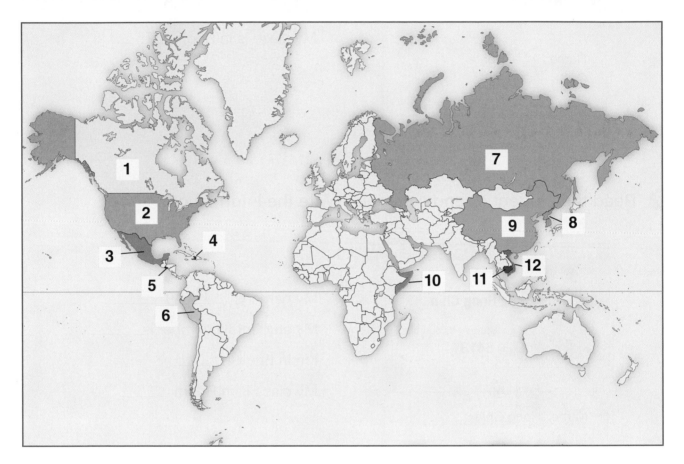

CD1 T12

B Listen and read. Listen and repeat.

1. Canada	5. El Salvador	9. China
2. the United States	6. Peru	10. Somalia
3. Mexico	7. Russia	11. Cambodia
4. Haiti	8. Korea	12. Vietnam

See page 234
for more
countries.

C PAIRS. Point to your country. Say the name.

D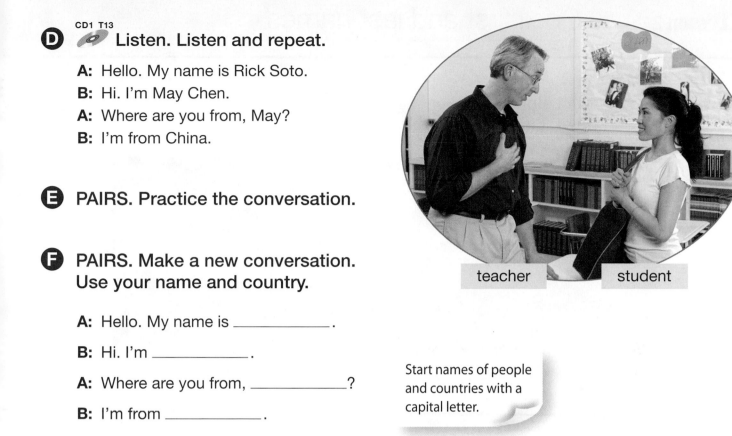

CD1 T13

Listen. Listen and repeat.

A: Hello. My name is Rick Soto.

B: Hi. I'm May Chen.

A: Where are you from, May?

B: I'm from China.

E PAIRS. Practice the conversation.

teacher　　student

F PAIRS. Make a new conversation.
Use your name and country.

A: Hello. My name is _____ .

B: Hi. I'm _____ .

A: Where are you from, _____?

B: I'm from _____ .

Start names of people
and countries with a
capital letter.

Show what you know!

CLASS. Walk around the room.
Ask three classmates: *What's your name? Where are you from?*
Write the information.

	Name	Country
	May	China
1.		
2.		
3.		

CLASS. Take turns. Talk about your classmates.

May is
from China.

Spell first and last names

CD1 T14

A Look at the alphabet.
Listen and point. Listen and repeat.

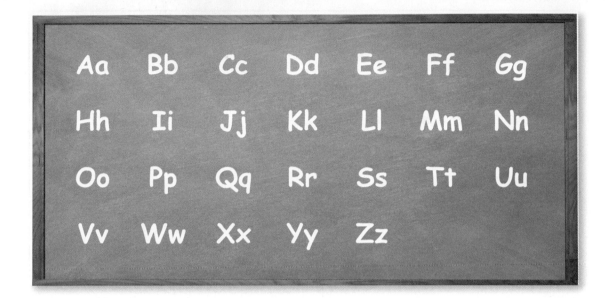

Aa	Bb	Cc	Dd	Ee	Ff	Gg
Hh	Ii	Jj	Kk	Ll	Mm	Nn
Oo	Pp	Qq	Rr	Ss	Tt	Uu
Vv	Ww	Xx	Yy	Zz		

CD1 T15

B Listen. Write the capital letters.

B capital letter
b lowercase letter

1. _C_   5. ___   9. ___

2. ___   6. ___   10. ___

3. ___   7. ___   11. ___

4. ___   8. ___   12. ___

C PAIRS. Say a letter. Write the letter.

___   ___   ___   ___   ___

CD1 T16

D Listen. Write the words.

1. _h_ _e_ _l_ _l_ _o_   4. ___ ___ ___ ___

2. ___ ___   5. ___ ___ ___

3. ___ ___ ___ ___   6. ___ ___ ___ ___

E   Listen. Listen and repeat.

A: What's your name, please?

B: Ana Sol.

A: Spell your first name.

B: A-N-A.

A: Spell your last name.

B: S-O-L.

F   PAIRS. Practice the conversation.

G   PAIRS. Make a new conversation. Use your name.

A: What's your name, please?

B: _____

A: Spell your first name.

B: _____

A: Spell your last name.

B: _____

Show what you know!

GROUPS OF 4. Take turns.
Ask: *What's your name? Spell your first name. Spell your last name.*
Write the information.

	First Name	Last Name
	Ana	Sol
1.		
2.		
3.		

This is Ana Sol.

CLASS. Take turns. Introduce your classmates.

A   CD1 T18   Listen and point to the numbers. Listen and repeat.

0	1	2	3	4	5	6	7	8	9
zero	one	two	three	four	five	six	seven	eight	nine

B   CD1 T19   Listen. Write the numbers.

a. ____   b. ____   c. ____   d. ____   e. ____   f. ____

C   CD1 T20   Listen. Listen and repeat.

A: What's your student ID number?
B: 83241.
A: 83241?
B: That's right.

D   PAIRS. Practice the conversation.

E   CD1 T21   Listen for the student ID. Circle *a* or *b*.

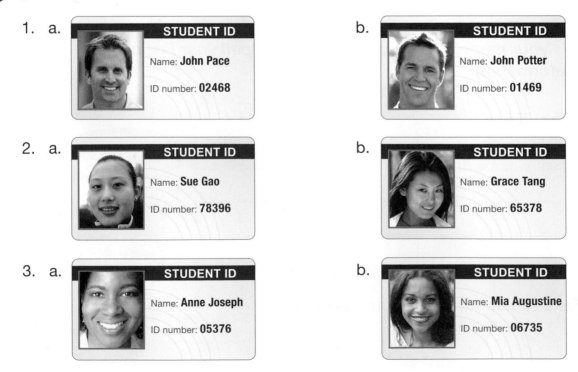

1. a. STUDENT ID   Name: **John Pace**   ID number: **02468**
   b. STUDENT ID   Name: **John Potter**   ID number: **01469**

2. a. STUDENT ID   Name: **Sue Gao**   ID number: **78396**
   b. STUDENT ID   Name: **Grace Tang**   ID number: **65378**

3. a. STUDENT ID   Name: **Anne Joseph**   ID number: **05376**
   b. STUDENT ID   Name: **Mia Augustine**   ID number: **06735**

F 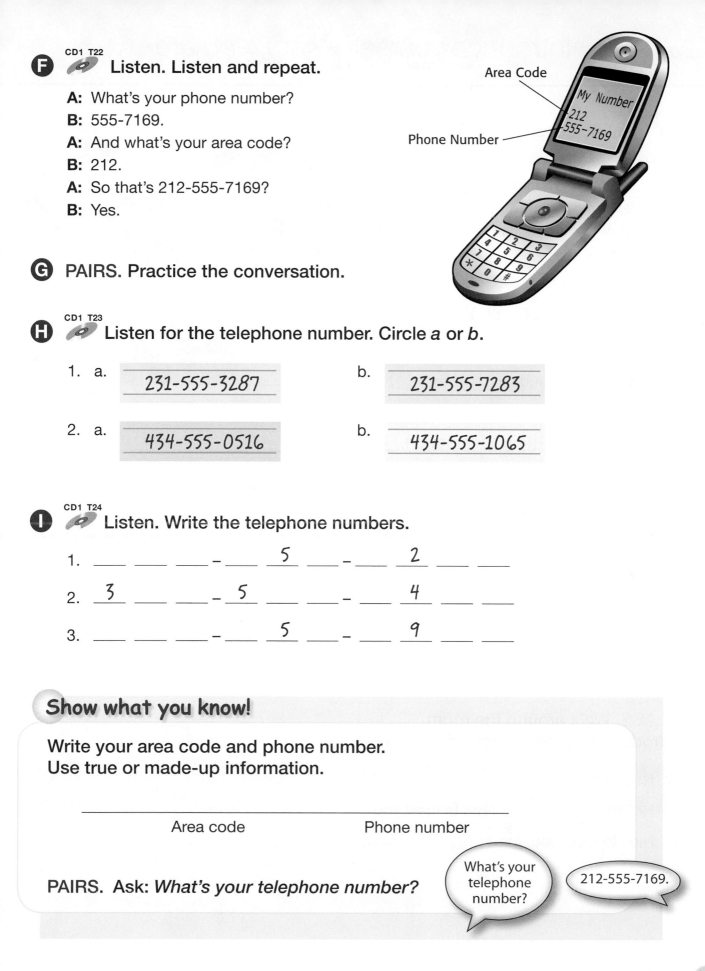 **Listen. Listen and repeat.**

CD1 T22

A: What's your phone number?
B: 555-7169.
A: And what's your area code?
B: 212.
A: So that's 212-555-7169?
B: Yes.

Area Code

My Number
212
555-7169

Phone Number

G PAIRS. Practice the conversation.

H 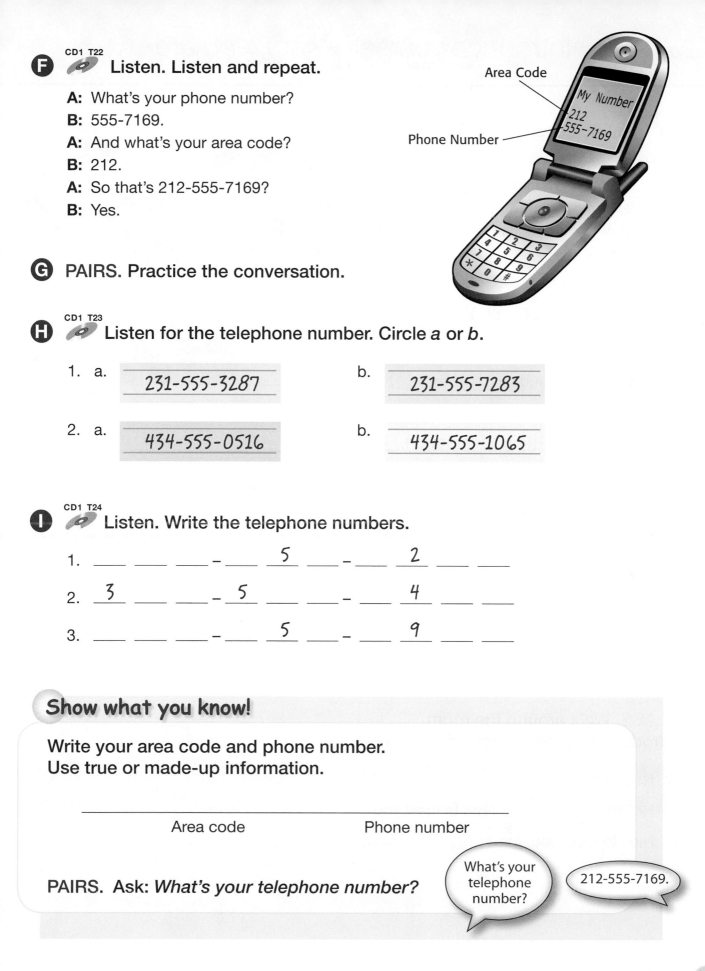 **Listen for the telephone number. Circle *a* or *b*.**

CD1 T23

1. a. 231-555-3287   b. 231-555-7283

2. a. 434-555-0516   b. 434-555-1065

I 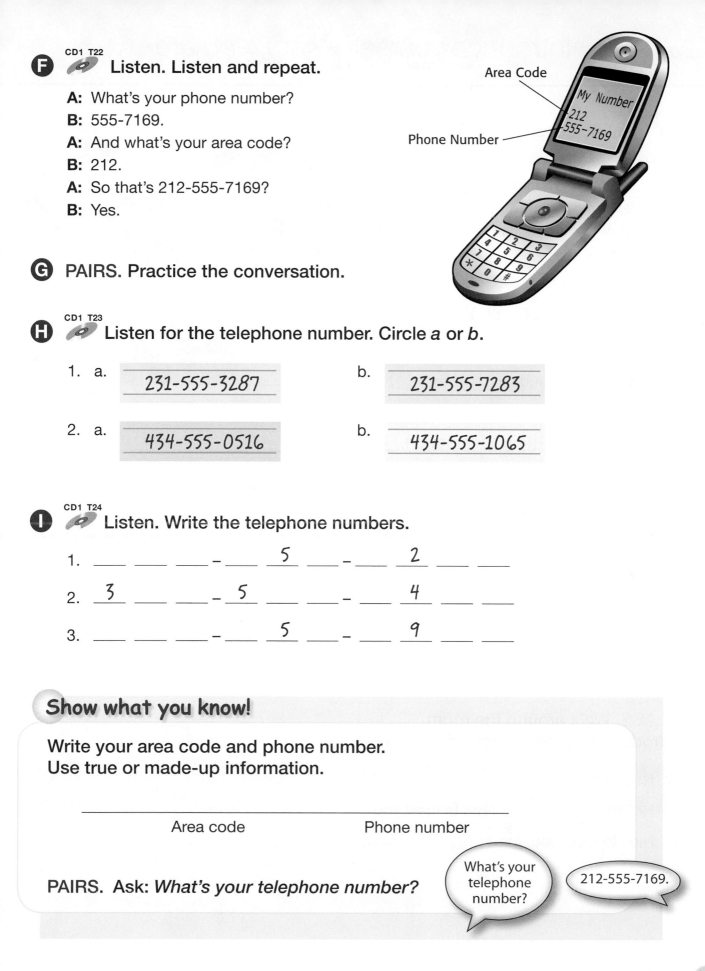 **Listen. Write the telephone numbers.**

CD1 T24

1. ___ ___ ___ – ___ 5 ___ – ___ 2 ___ ___

2. 3 ___ ___ – 5 ___ ___ – ___ 4 ___ ___

3. ___ ___ ___ – ___ 5 ___ – ___ 9 ___ ___

Show what you know!

Write your area code and phone number.
Use true or made-up information.

_____
        Area code   Phone number

PAIRS. Ask: *What's your telephone number?*

What's your telephone number?

212-555-7169.

A 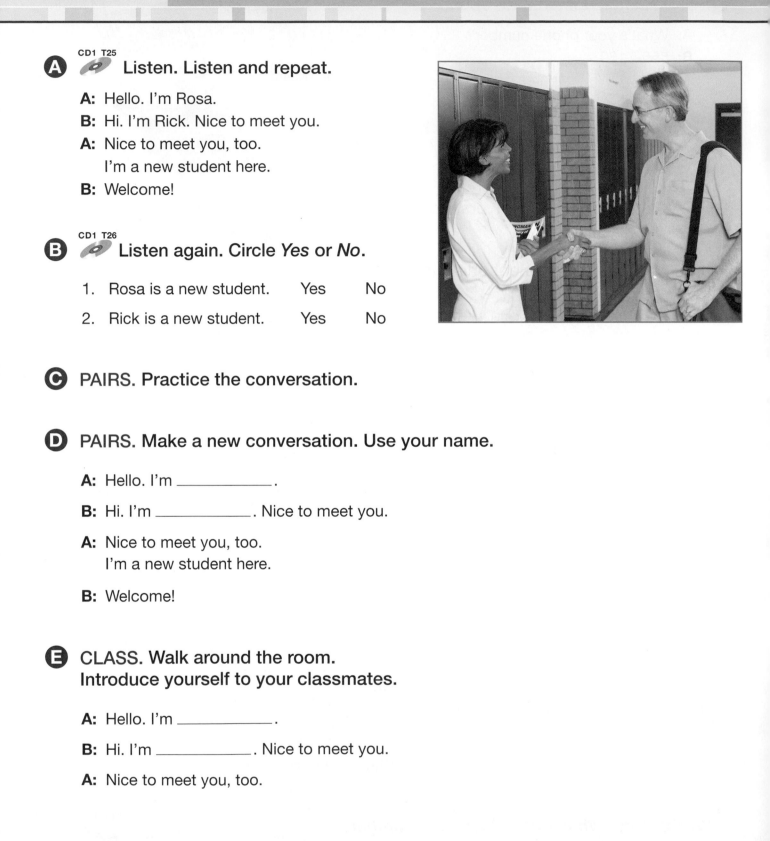 **CD1 T25** Listen. Listen and repeat.

A: Hello. I'm Rosa.

B: Hi. I'm Rick. Nice to meet you.

A: Nice to meet you, too.
I'm a new student here.

B: Welcome!

B **CD1 T26** Listen again. Circle *Yes* or *No*.

1. Rosa is a new student.   Yes   No

2. Rick is a new student.   Yes   No

C PAIRS. Practice the conversation.

D PAIRS. Make a new conversation. Use your name.

A: Hello. I'm _____.

B: Hi. I'm _____. Nice to meet you.

A: Nice to meet you, too.
I'm a new student here.

B: Welcome!

E CLASS. Walk around the room.
Introduce yourself to your classmates.

A: Hello. I'm _____.

B: Hi. I'm _____. Nice to meet you.

A: Nice to meet you, too.

F Read the sentences.

I am, you are

I am Rosa.
I'm Rosa.

You are the teacher.
You're the teacher.

G Write *am* or *are*.

1. I ___*am*___ a new student.

2. You _____ my English teacher.

3. You _____ a good teacher.

4. I _____ in the classroom.

5. I _____ from Russia.

6. You _____ my classmate.

H Rewrite the sentences in Exercise G. Use *I'm* and *You're*.

1. ___I'm a new student.___

2. _____

3. _____

4. _____

5. _____

6. _____

> Start a sentence with a capital letter.
>
> End a sentence with a period.

I CD1 T27 Listen and check your answers. Listen and repeat.

Show what you know!

You're Ahmed.

You're right!

CLASS. Walk around the room.
Talk to five classmates.
Say each classmate's name. Are you correct?

Read the sentences.

He is a student.

She is a teacher.

CD1 T28

 Listen and read the story.

Jin Su is a new student. He is from Korea. He is in a beginning English class. Lora is from the United States. She is a teacher. She is Jin Su's teacher!

C **Read the story again. Circle *Yes* or *No*.**

1. Jin Su is from Korea.   (Yes)   No

2. He is a new student.   Yes   No

3. Lora is from Korea.   Yes   No

4. She is a teacher.   Yes   No

D **Write *he* or *she*.**

1. _____   2. _____   3. _____

4. _____   5. _____   6. _____

E Read the sentences.

He is, she is

Jin Su **is** from Korea.	Lora **is** from the United States.
He **is** from Korea.	She **is** from the United States.
He**'s** from Korea.	She**'s** from the United States.

Start a sentence with a capital letter.

End a sentence with a period.

F Write three sentences for each picture.
Use *he, she, he's, she's*.

1.  Carla / my friend

   Carla is my friend.
   She is my friend.
   She's my friend.

2.  Mariam / from Somalia

   _____
   _____
   _____

3. Gloria / a new student

   _____
   _____
   _____

4. Mr. Lane / the teacher

   _____
   _____
   _____

Show what you know!

GROUPS. Take turns.
Ask: *Who's that? Where is he/she from?*
Use *he's* and *she's* in your answers.

Who's that?

Mariam.

Where is she from?

She's from Somalia.

A Read the sentences.

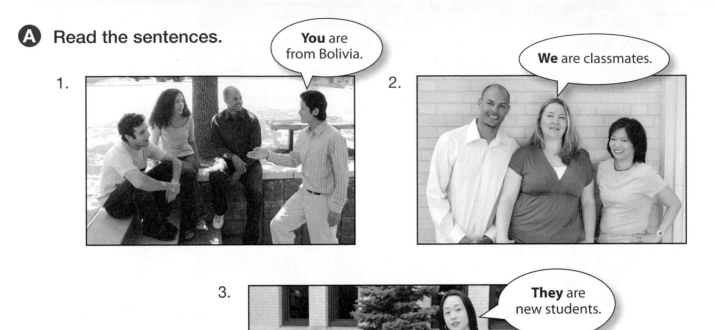

1.

You are
from Bolivia.

2.

We are classmates.

3.

They are
new students.

B CD1 T29 Listen. Listen and repeat.

A: Who are they?
B: Oscar and Carlos.
     They're my classmates.
A: Where are they from?
B: They're from Brazil.

C PAIRS. Practice the conversation.

D Read the sentences.

> **You are, we are, they are**
>
> You **are** from Bolivia.   We **are** from Peru.   They **are** new students.
> You**'re** from Bolivia.   We**'re** from Peru.   They**'re** new students.

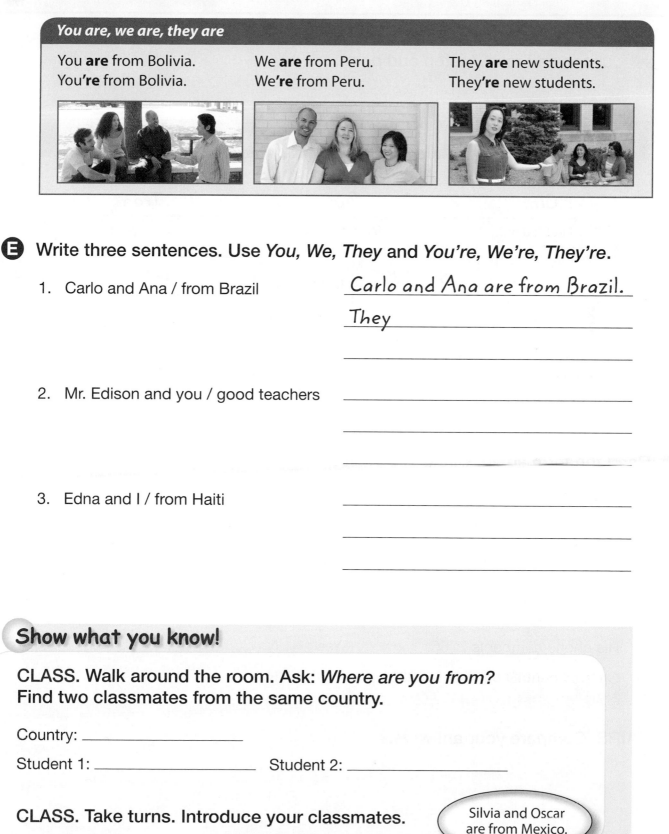

E Write three sentences. Use *You, We, They* and *You're, We're, They're.*

1. Carlo and Ana / from Brazil

   Carlo and Ana are from Brazil.
   They _____

2. Mr. Edison and you / good teachers

3. Edna and I / from Haiti

Show what you know!

CLASS. Walk around the room. Ask: *Where are you from?*
Find two classmates from the same country.

Country: _____

Student 1: _____   Student 2: _____

CLASS. Take turns. Introduce your classmates.

> Silvia and Oscar are from Mexico.

A CD1 T30 Listen and read. Listen and point.

last name = family name

Adult Education Center

Chi	Bu	Tran
First Name	Middle Name	Last Name

Telephone 760 – 555 – 7765   **Place of Birth** Vietnam

Area Code   Phone Number   Country

Student Identification Number 78031

B Read the form again. Circle *Yes* or *No*.

1. This is Chi's form.   (Yes)   No

2. His middle name is Tran.   Yes   No

3. His last name is Bu.   Yes   No

4. Chi is a student.   Yes   No

5. He is from China.   Yes   No

6. His phone number is 7765.   Yes   No

7. Chi's student ID number is 78031.   Yes   No

C PAIRS. Compare your answers.

D Complete the sentences. Use true or made-up information.

1. My first name is _____.

2. My middle name is _____.

3. My last name is _____.

4. My area code is _____.

5. My phone number is _____.

6. I'm from _____.

7. My student ID number is _____.

E Fill out the form. Use your information in Exercise D.

Adult Education Center

First Name	Middle Name	Last Name

Telephone [   ] – [   ]   **Place of Birth** [   ]
Area Code   Phone Number   Country

Student Identification Number [   ]

F PAIRS. Read your classmate's form. Is the form complete?

A CLASS. Look at each picture. What do you see?

CD1 T31
B Listen to the story.

C Listen again and read.

> My name is Ivan. I'm a student.
>
> I say hello to a classmate and I smile.
>
> In my school, some students say hello and shake hands.
>
> Some students say hello and hug.
>
> Some students say hello and bow.
>
> Other students say hello and kiss.
>
> How do you say hello?

D Read the story again. Write five ways people say hello.

1. People _____ *smile* _____ .

2. They _____ .

3. They _____ .

4. They _____ .

5. They _____ .

E GROUPS. Ask your classmates: *How do people say hello in your country?*

F Write about how people say hello.

> My name is _____ .
>
> In my country, people say hello and _____ .
>
> In the United States, people _____ .

G GROUPS. Take turns. Read your sentences.

Show what you know!

1 THE SOUNDS OF *M* AND *N*

A Read the words out loud softly.

map	**m**y	**m**eet
nu**m**ber	welco**m**e	fro**m**

CD1 T33

B Listen and repeat.

C Read the words out loud softly.

name	**n**umber	**n**ice
a**n**swer	pho**n**e	liste**n**

CD1 T34

D Listen and repeat.

CD1 T35

E Listen. Write *m* or *n*. Listen again and repeat.

1. ___ice

2. fro___

3. ___ap

4. ___u___ber

5. pho___e

6. ___eet

7. a___swer

8. liste___

9. welco___e

F DICTATION. PAIRS. Student A, say three words from Exercise A. Student B, listen and write.

_____ _____ _____

G DICTATION. SAME PAIRS. Student B, say three words from Exercise C. Student A, listen and write.

_____ _____ _____

2 VOCABULARY

A CD1 T36 **Listen. Listen and repeat.**

Cambodia	hug	place of birth	telephone number
eight	kiss	shake hands	three
first name	middle name	smile	the United States
five	nine	Somalia	Vietnam

B **Circle four countries in Exercise A. Write the words.**

____________ ____________ ____________ ____________

C **Underline four ways to say hello in Exercise A. Write the words.**

____________ ____________ ____________ ____________

D **Check (✓) four numbers in Exercise A. Write the words.**

____________ ____________ ____________ ____________

3 SPEAKING

A **Maria is a new student in your class.**
What do you say?

a. Where is the office?
b. She's the teacher.
c. Hi. I'm ____. Nice to meet you.

B **Your teacher asks: *Where are you from?***
What do you say?

a. He's from ____.
b. We're from ____.
c. I'm from ____.

Go to the CD-ROM for more practice.

1 INTRODUCE YOURSELF

A CD1 T37
Listen. Two people are introducing themselves.

B CLASS. Walk around the room. Introduce yourself to five classmates.

2 SAY AND WRITE NAMES AND TELEPHONE NUMBERS

A CD1 T38
Listen. A student is giving information.

B PAIRS. Use true or made-up information.
Ask your classmate for information. Fill out the form.

▶ Name: ☐☐☐☐☐☐☐☐☐☐☐☐☐☐☐☐
FIRST

☐☐☐☐☐☐☐☐☐☐☐☐☐☐☐☐
LAST

▶ Telephone number: ☐☐☐ – ☐☐☐ – ☐☐☐☐
AREA CODE   PHONE NUMBER

C SAME PAIRS. Read your classmate's form. Is the form complete?

3 FILL OUT A FORM

Fill out the form. Use true or made-up information.

Adult Education Center

Student Information Form

Name _____
First   Middle   Last

Telephone _____ - _____   Place of Birth _____
Area Code   Phone Number   Country

Student Identification Number _____

---

4 WRITE ABOUT YOURSELF

Write about yourself. Use true or made-up information.

1. My name is _____.

2. My telephone number is _____.

3. I'm from _____.

4. My student ID number is _____.

5 CONNECT   For your Team Project, go to page 210.

A CD1 T39 Look at the classroom objects.
Listen and point. Listen and repeat.

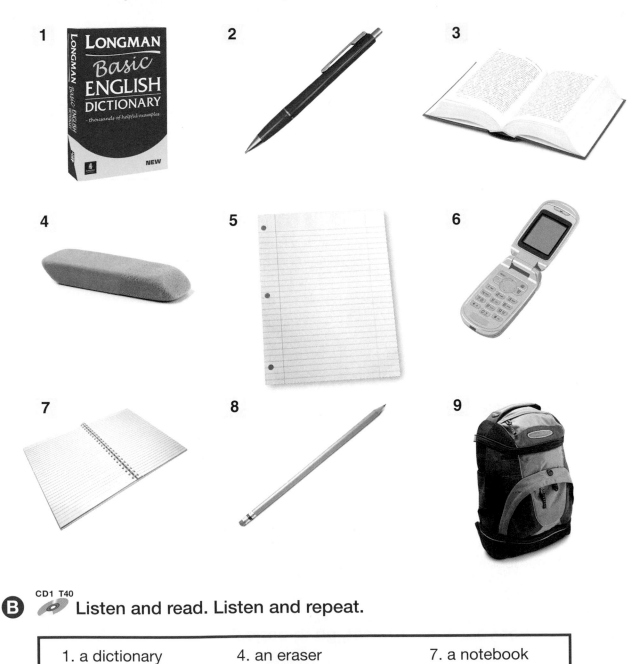

B CD1 T40 Listen and read. Listen and repeat.

1. a dictionary	4. an eraser	7. a notebook
2. a pen	5. a piece of paper	8. a pencil
3. a book	6. a cell phone	9. a backpack

C 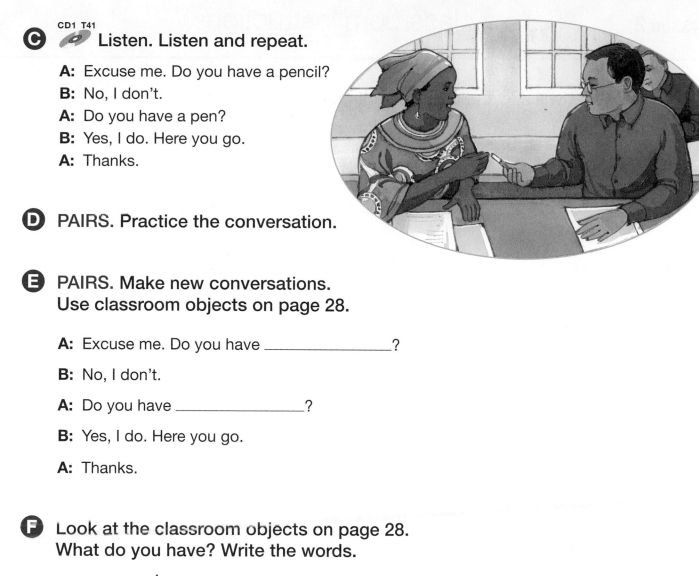 Listen. Listen and repeat.

CD1 T41

A: Excuse me. Do you have a pencil?

B: No, I don't.

A: Do you have a pen?

B: Yes, I do. Here you go.

A: Thanks.

D PAIRS. Practice the conversation.

E PAIRS. Make new conversations.
Use classroom objects on page 28.

A: Excuse me. Do you have _____?

B: No, I don't.

A: Do you have _____?

B: Yes, I do. Here you go.

A: Thanks.

F Look at the classroom objects on page 28.
What do you have? Write the words.

_____ book _____   _____

_____   _____

_____   _____

Show what you know!

GROUPS. Take turns.
Tell your classmates your words in Exercise F.

I have a pen, a notebook, and a book.

A Your teacher will say and do each action. Listen and watch.

B Your teacher will say and do each action.
Do each action with your teacher.

C Your teacher will say each action.
Say and do each action.

D CD1 T42 Listen and read. Listen and repeat.

1. Turn on the light.	4. Turn off the light.
2. Take out your pencil.	5. Put away your book.
3. Open your book.	6. Close your dictionary.

E 📀 Listen. Listen and repeat.

A: OK, everyone. Get ready for a test.
B: OK.
A: Use a pencil. Don't use a pen.

F Read the sentences.

Imperatives: affirmative and negative	
Use a pencil.	**Don't use** a pencil.
Put away your dictionary.	**Don't put away** your dictionary.

don't = do + not

G Write negative sentences.

Start a sentence with a capital letter.

End a sentence with a period.

1. Open your book. _Don't open your book._

2. Use a dictionary. _____

3. Put away your notebook. _____

4. Turn off your cell phone. _____

5. Take out your dictionary. _____

6. Close the door. _____

H 📀 Listen and check your answers. Listen and repeat.

Close your book.

Show what you know!

GROUPS. Look at the actions on page 30.
Take turns. Student A, give an instruction.
Your classmates do the action.

A CD1 T45 Look at the places in a school.
Listen and point. Listen and repeat.

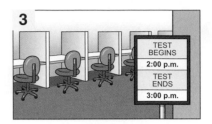

B CD1 T46 Listen and read. Listen and repeat.

1. library	4. cafeteria	7. classroom
2. office	5. men's room	8. bookstore
3. testing room	6. women's room	9. computer lab

C Look at the words in Exercise B. What places are in your school?

office

_____   _____

_____   _____

D PAIRS. Tell your classmate your words in Exercise C.

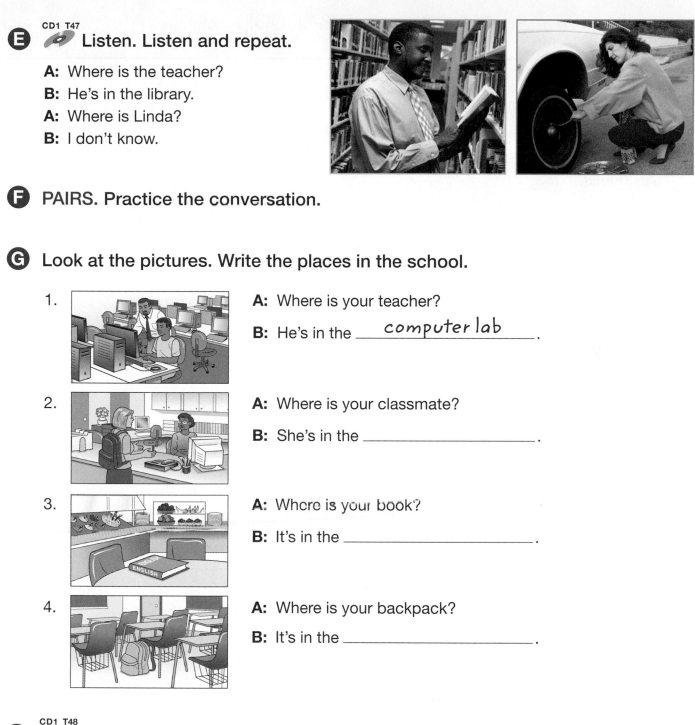

E CD1 T47 💿 **Listen. Listen and repeat.**

A: Where is the teacher?
B: He's in the library.
A: Where is Linda?
B: I don't know.

F **PAIRS. Practice the conversation.**

G **Look at the pictures. Write the places in the school.**

1.
   A: Where is your teacher?
   B: He's in the ___computer lab___ .

2.
   A: Where is your classmate?
   B: She's in the _____ .

3.
   A: Where is your book?
   B: It's in the _____ .

4.
   A: Where is your backpack?
   B: It's in the _____ .

H CD1 T48 💿 **Listen and check your answers. Listen and repeat.**

Show what you know!

PAIRS. Ask and answer the questions in Exercise G. Use true information.

Where is your teacher?

She's in the classroom.

A CD1 T49 Listen. Listen and repeat.

A: Excuse me. Where is the bookstore?
B: It's next to the testing room.
A: Thanks.

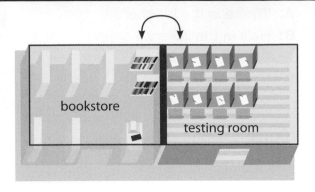

bookstore

testing room

B PAIRS. Practice the conversation.

C PAIRS. Look at the maps. Make new conversations. Use *next to*.

Conversation 1

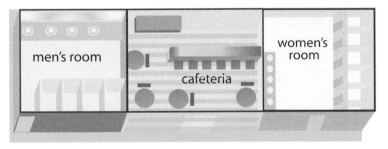

men's room

cafeteria

women's room

Conversation 2

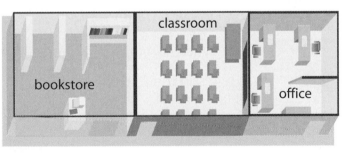

classroom

bookstore

office

Conversation 3

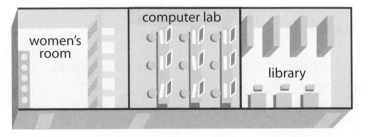

women's room

computer lab

library

D 🎧 **Listen. Listen and repeat.**

> **A:** Excuse me. Where is the library?
> **B:** It's across from the office.
> **A:** Thanks.

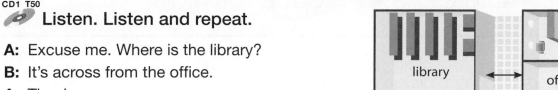

E PAIRS. Practice the conversation.

F PAIRS. Look at the map. Make new conversations. Use *across from*.

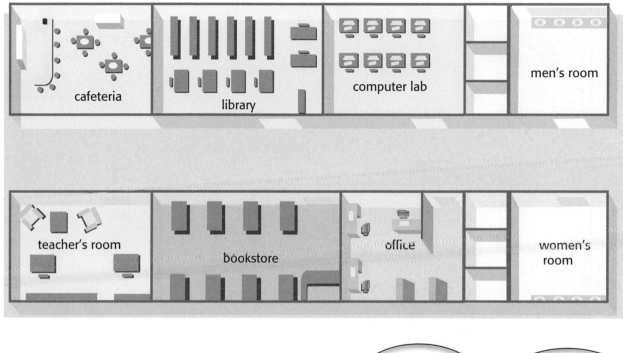

Show what you know!

GROUPS. Take turns.
Talk about places in your school.
Use *next to* and *across from*.

The cafeteria is next to the library.

The library is across from the bookstore.

A CD1 T51 Listen and point. Listen and repeat.

Mr.   Mrs.   Ms.   Miss   Ms.   Mr.

married   single

male

female

B CD1 T52 Listen and read. Listen and point.

Vista Learning Center

PLEASE PRINT.

☐ Mr.
☑ Mrs.
☐ Miss
☐ Ms.

Lopez
Last Name

Mexico
Place of Birth

English 100
Class

Alexa
First Name

☑ Female   ☐ Male

Mr. Chen
Teacher

C Read the form again. Circle *Yes* or *No*.

1. Alexa is married.   (Yes)   No

2. Alexa is from England.   Yes   No

3. Alexa is a man.   Yes   No

4. Alexa is in English 100.   Yes   No

5. Alexa's teacher is Mr. Lopez. Yes   No

D Read the questions. Write your information.

1. What is your first name? _____

2. What is your last name? _____

3. Are you *Mr.*, *Mrs.*, *Miss*, or *Ms.*? _____

4. What English class are you in? _____

5. What is your teacher's name? _____

6. Where are you from? _____

7. Are you a woman (female)
   or a man (male)? _____

E Fill out the form. Use your information in Exercise D.

Vista Learning Center

PLEASE PRINT.

☐ Mr.		
☐ Mrs.	Last Name	First Name
☐ Miss		☐ Female ☐ Male
☐ Ms.	Place of Birth	
	Class	Teacher

F PAIRS. Read your classmate's form. Is the form complete?

A CD1 T53 🔘 Listen. Listen and repeat.

A: How do you study English?
B: I talk to people and I write new words.
A: That's great!

B CD1 T54 🔘 Listen again.
How does the woman study English?
Circle Yes or No.

1. The woman talks to people.   Yes   No

2. The woman reads books.   Yes   No

C PAIRS. Practice the conversation.

D CD1 T55 🔘 Listen and point. Listen and repeat.

1

use a dictionary

2

go to class

3

ask the teacher questions

4

read signs

5

write in my notebook

6

practice with my classmates

E PAIRS. Look at the pictures in Exercise D. Say how you study English.

F Read the sentences.

Simple present: *I, you, we, they*	
I **practice** with my classmates.	We **write** new words.
You **use** a dictionary.	They **ask** the teacher questions.

G Read the story. Write the correct verb.

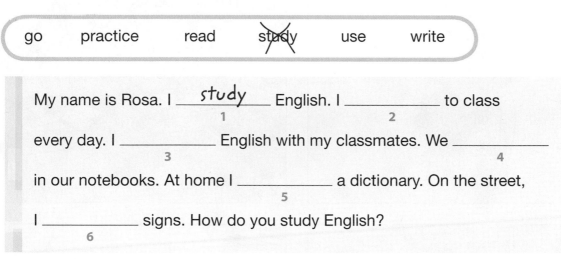

go   practice   read   ~~study~~   use   write

My name is Rosa. I ___*study*___ English. I _____ to class
                        1   2

every day. I _____ English with my classmates. We _____
                3   4

in our notebooks. At home I _____ a dictionary. On the street,
                                5

I _____ signs. How do you study English?
    6

H Read the story again. Circle *Yes* or *No*.

1. Rosa goes to class every day.   (Yes)   No

2. She practices with her classmates.   Yes   No

3. Rosa writes in her dictionary.   Yes   No

4. She reads signs on the street.   Yes   No

Show what you know!

GROUPS. Ask your classmates: *How do you study English?*
Check (✓) the information about your group.

☐ We go to class.   ☐ We write in our notebooks.

☐ We ask the teacher questions.   ☐ We use a dictionary.

☐ We practice with our classmates.   ☐ We read signs.

CLASS. Take turns. Talk about how your group studies English.

> We ask the teacher questions. We read signs.

Lan's story

A CLASS. Look at each picture. What do you see?

B CD1 T56 Listen to the story.

C Listen again and read.

> My name is Lan.
>
> In my country, students don't talk in class.
>
> They listen to the teacher.
>
> In the United States, students talk in groups.
>
> In my class, students ask many questions.
>
> My teacher listens to the students.

D Read the story again. Circle *Yes* or *No*.

1.	Lan is from the United States.	Yes	(No)
2.	In Lan's country, students talk in class.	Yes	No
3.	In the United States, students ask questions.	Yes	No
4.	The teacher listens to the students.	Yes	No

E GROUPS. Read the questions. Talk about students in your country.

1. Do students talk in class?

2. Do students ask a lot of questions in class?

F Write about students.

> In my country, students _____.
>
> They _____.
>
> In the United States, students _____.
>
> They _____.

G GROUPS. Take turns. Read your sentences.

REVIEW Show what you know!

1 THE SOUNDS OF *P* AND *B*

A Read the words out loud softly.

pen	**p**ractice	**p**encil
paper	back**p**ack	o**p**en

CD1 T58

B Listen and repeat.

C Read the words out loud softly.

book	**b**irth	**b**ackpack
num**b**er	note**b**ook	li**b**rary

CD1 T59

D Listen and repeat.

CD1 T60

E Listen. Write *p* or *b*. Listen again and repeat.

1. num____er
2. ____ractice
3. ____ook

4. ____ack____ack
5. o____en
6. li____rary

7. ____a____er
8. ____en
9. ____irth

F DICTATION. PAIRS. Student A, say three words from Exercise A. Student B, listen and write.

_____   _____   _____

G DICTATION. SAME PAIRS. Student B, say three words from Exercise C. Student A, listen and write.

_____   _____   _____

A 🎧 **CD1 T61** Listen. Listen and repeat.

book	computer lab	office	pen	take out
cafeteria	library	open	pencil	turn on
close	notebook	paper	put away	women's room

B Circle four things you need for class in Exercise A. Write the words.

_____ _____ _____ _____

C Underline four places in a school in Exercise A. Write the words.

_____ _____ _____ _____

D Check (✓) four classroom instructions in Exercise A. Write the words.

_____ _____ _____ _____

3 SPEAKING

A You have a test. You need a pencil.
What do you say?

a. Do you have a pencil?
b. Here you go.
c. Where is the pencil?

B A new student asks: *Excuse me, where is the office?*
What do you say?

a. Where is the classroom?
b. It's next to the library.
c. Nice to meet you.

💻 Go to the CD-ROM for more practice.

Show what you know!

1 FOLLOW CLASSROOM INSTRUCTIONS

A CD1 T62 Listen. A teacher is giving instructions.

B GROUPS. Take turns. Give classroom instructions. Do the actions.

2 ASK ABOUT PLACES IN A SCHOOL

A CD1 T63 Listen. Emma is helping a new student.

B ROLE PLAY. PAIRS.

ROLE PLAY 1	
Student A	**Student B**
Ask about the library and the computer lab.	Help Student A. Look at the map. Use *across from* and *next to*.

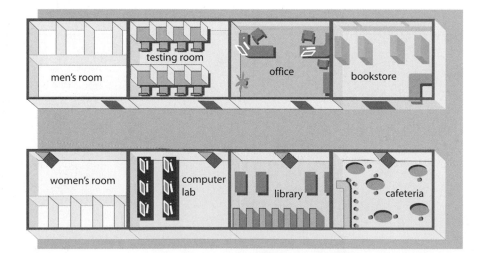

ROLE PLAY 2	
Student B	**Student A**
Ask about the testing room and the office.	Help Student B. Look at the map. Use *across from* and *next to*.

3 FILL OUT A FORM

Fill out the form. Use true or made-up information.

Student Information Form

Vista **L**earning **C**enter

☐ Mr.　☐ Mrs.　☐ Miss　☐ Ms.

Name _____
　　　　First　　　　　　　　　　　　Last

Class _____ Teacher _____

Place of Birth _____ Female ☐　Male ☐

4 WRITE ABOUT YOURSELF

Write about yourself. Use true or made-up information.

1. My name is _____.

2. I am in _____.

3. My teacher's name is _____.

4. I'm from _____.

5 CONNECT　　For your Team Project, go to page 210.

3 On Time

CD2 T2

A Look at the numbers.
Listen and point. Listen and repeat.

0	1	2	3	4	5	6	7	8	9
10	11	12	13	14	15	16	17	18	19

20	21	22	23	24	25	26	27	28	29
30	31	32	33	34	35	36	37	38	39

40	41	42	43	44	45	46	47	48	49
50	51	52	53	54	55	56	57	58	59

B PAIRS. Point to a number in Exercise A. Say the number.

CD2 T3

C Listen for the number. Circle *a* or *b*.

1. a. 10   (b.) 20   5. a. 15   b. 50

2. a. 17   b. 19   6. a. 42   b. 14

3. a. 24   b. 14   7. a. 26   b. 36

4. a. 30   b. 13   8. a. 27   b. 47

D Listen and point to the clocks. Listen and repeat.

E Listen. Listen and repeat.

A: What time is it?
B: It's 1:00.

F PAIRS. Look at each clock. Write the time.

1. _8:05_

2. _____

3. _____

4. _____

5. _____

6. _____

7. _____

8. _____

Show what you know!

GROUPS. Look at the clocks in Exercise F.
Take turns. Point to a clock. Ask: *What time is it?*

A Read the sentences. Draw the hands on the clocks.

1. Taka's class starts at 9:00.

2. Taka's class is over at 12:30.

B CD2 T6 **Listen. Listen and repeat.**

A: What time is your English class?

B: It's from 9:00 to 12:30.

A: What time is your break?

B: It's from 10:45 to 11:15.

C CD2 T7 **Listen again. Circle *Yes* or *No*.**

1. The class starts at 9:00.   Yes   No

2. The class is over at 12:00.   Yes   No

3. The break starts at 10:45.   Yes   No

D PAIRS. Practice the conversation.

E PAIRS. Make a new conversation. Use true information.

A: What time is your English class?

B: It's from _____ to _____.

A: What time is your break?

B: It's from _____ to _____.

F Read the sentences.

From/to, at	
My class is **from** 9:00 **to** 12:30.	My class starts **at** 9:00.
My break is **from** 10:45 **to** 11:15.	My break is over **at** 11:15.

G Write sentences. Use *from/to* and *at*.

1. The computer class is / 8:00 / 10:00 _The computer class is from 8:00 to 10:00._

2. My English class starts / 6:30 _____

3. The break is / 8:00 / 8:15 _____

4. My class is over / 9:30 _____

5. The class is over / 10:00 _____

H CD2 T8 Look at the signs.
Listen and point. Listen and repeat.

6:00 A.M. = in the morning
2:00 P.M. = in the afternoon
6:00 P.M. = in the evening
10:00 P.M. = at night

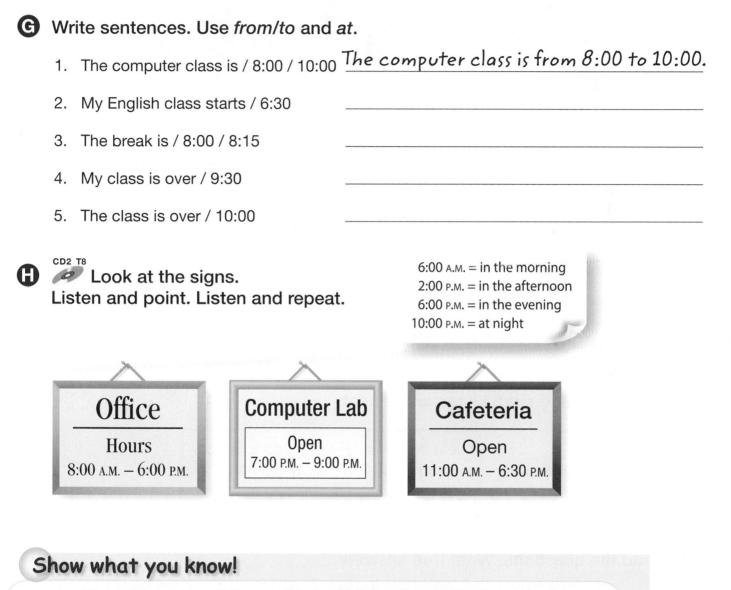

Office
Hours
8:00 A.M. – 6:00 P.M.

Computer Lab
Open
7:00 P.M. – 9:00 P.M.

Cafeteria
Open
11:00 A.M. – 6:30 P.M.

Show what you know!

GROUPS. Take turns. Use true or made-up information.
Ask: *When is the _____ open?*
Use *from/to* and *at* in your answers.

When is the office open?

The office is open from 8:00 to 5:00.

CD2 T9

A Look at the daily activities.
Listen and point. Listen and repeat.

CD2 T10

B Listen and read. Listen and repeat.

1. get up	4. eat breakfast	7. go to school
2. take a shower	5. go to work	8. get home
3. get dressed	6. eat lunch	9. go to sleep

C Read the questions. Write true answers.

1. What time do you get up?   _I get up at_ _____

2. What time do you eat lunch?   _____

3. What time do you get home?   _____

4. What time do you go to sleep? _____

D PAIRS. Ask your classmate the questions in Exercise C.

E **Listen. Listen and repeat.**

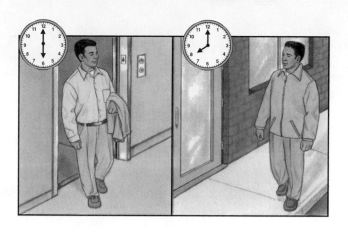

A: Tam goes to work at 6:00 in the morning.
B: That's early!
A: He gets home at 8:00 at night.
B: That's late!

F PAIRS. Practice the conversation.

G Read the sentences.

Third person singular	
Tam **goes** to work at 6:00.	He **gets** home at 8:00.

go → goes

H Write the correct form of the verb.

1. Silvia (get up) _____ at 6:00. She (eat) _____ breakfast at 6:30.

2. Tim (go) _____ to work at 8:00. He (get) _____ home at 5:00.

3. Li (take) _____ a shower at 7:00. He (get) _____ dressed at 7:15.

4. Kyung (get) _____ home at 9:00. She (go) _____ to bed at 10:30.

Show what you know!

PAIRS. Ask: *What time do you _____?*
Write the time.

get up _____   go to school _____

eat breakfast _____   get home _____

go to work _____   go to bed _____

Metta gets up at 5:30.
She eats breakfast at 5:45.

Metta

CLASS. Take turns.
Talk about your classmate's daily activities.

Days of the week • *From/to,on*

CD2 T12

A **Look at the days of the week.**
Listen and point. Listen and repeat.

Sunday	Monday	Tuesday	Wednesday	Thursday	Friday	Saturday
	Work 9 – 5	Work 8 – 12	Work 9 – 5	Work 10 – 4	Work 9 – 5	Class 10 – 2

CD2 T13

B **Listen. Listen and repeat.**

A: When do you work, Nora?
B: I work from Monday to Friday.
A: When do you go to school?
B: I go to school on Saturday.
A: You're really busy!

> Start days of
> the week with a
> capital letter.

C PAIRS. Practice the conversation.

CD2 T14

D **Listen and read the story.**

Nora is very busy. She works from Monday to Friday.
Nora studies English. She goes to school on Saturday.
The class is from 10:00 to 2:00. On Sunday Nora goes to the library.
She studies from 12:00 to 3:00.

E Read the story again. Circle *Yes* or *No*.

1. Nora is very busy.   (Yes)   No

2. She works five days a week.   Yes   No

3. Nora goes to English class two days a week.   Yes   No

4. Her class starts at 10:00.   Yes   No

5. Nora studies in the library on Saturday.   Yes   No

F Read the sentences.

From/to, on	
I work **from** Monday **to** Friday.	I go to school **on** Monday and Wednesday.

G Complete the sentences. Use *from/to* and *on*.

1. I get up at 7:00 _*from*_ Monday _*to*_ Thursday.

2. I go to school _____ 6:00 _____ 9:00 in the evening.

3. I play soccer _____ Tuesday.

4. I get home late _____ Friday.

5. I eat lunch at home _____ Sunday.

Schedule
Monday
  Work: 9:00 – 5:00
  English: 6:00 – 9:00
Tuesday
  Work: 9:00 – 5:00
  Soccer: 6:00 – 8:00
Wednesday
  Work: 8:00 – 4:00
  English: 6:00 – 9:00
Thursday
  Work: 10:00 – 4:00
Friday
  Work: 2:00 – 9:00

CD2 T15

H 💿 Listen and check your answers. Listen and repeat.

Show what you know!

PAIRS. Ask: *When do you* _____?
Write the information on the schedule.
Use true or made-up information.

	Sunday	Monday	Tuesday	Wednesday	Thursday	Friday	Saturday
Work							
Go to school							

CLASS. Take turns.
Talk about your classmate's schedule.
Use *from/to* and *on*.

Nora works from Monday to Friday.

She goes to school from 10:00 to 2:00 on Saturday.

A Read the words. Write the numbers.

_10_ ten		_____ twenty		_____ thirty	
_11_ eleven		_____ twenty-one		_____ forty	
_____ twelve		_____ twenty-two		_____ fifty	
_____ thirteen		_____ twenty-three		_60_ sixty	
_____ fourteen		_____ twenty-four		_70_ seventy	
_____ fifteen		_____ twenty-five		_80_ eighty	
_____ sixteen		_____ twenty-six		_90_ ninety	
_____ seventeen		_____ twenty-seven		_100_ one hundred	
_____ eighteen		_____ twenty-eight			
_____ nineteen		_____ twenty-nine			

B CD2 T16 Look at the numbers in Exercise A. Listen and repeat.

C Read the schedules. Write the answers.

Ivan's Schedule

Class 9:00 A.M.–12:00 P.M.

Break 10:15 A.M.–10:30 A.M.

Yun's Schedule

Class 6:00 P.M.–9:00 P.M.

Break 7:30 P.M.–7:45 P.M.

1. How long is Ivan's class? It's _three_ hours.

2. How long is Ivan's break? It's _____ minutes.

3. How long is Yun's class? It's _____ hours.

4. How long is Yun's break? It's _____ minutes.

D Write the numbers.

fifty-nine ___59___   seventy-two _____

ninety-one _____   eighty-six _____

thirty-three _____   sixty-eight _____

forty _____   ninety-seven _____

eighty-five _____   fifty-four _____

E Write the words.

12 ___twelve___   53 _____

17 _____   58 _____

21 _____   62 _____

24 _____   77 _____

33 _____   84 _____

46 _____   95 _____

CD2 T17

F 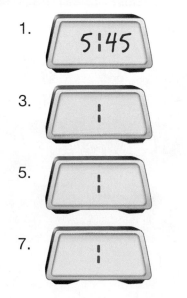 Listen. Write the time.

1. 5:45   2.

3.   4.

5.   6.

7.   8.

A CLASS. Look at each picture. What do you see?

CD2 T18

B Listen to the story.

C 🎧 **Listen again and read.**

> Carlo likes to be on time.
>
> He gets up early and gets ready for work.
>
> He gets to work at 6:50. He starts work at 7:00.
>
> Carlo goes to school after work.
>
> He is always early for class.
>
> On weekends, Carlo meets friends. He is always late!

D **Read the story again. Circle Yes or No.**

1. Carlo likes to be on time. (Yes)   No

2. He starts work on time.   Yes   No

3. Carlo goes to school late.   Yes   No

4. He goes to parties early.   Yes   No

E **GROUPS. Read the questions. Talk about time in your country.**

1. Do people go to work on time?

2. Do people go to school on time?

3. Do people go to parties on time?

F **Complete the sentences. Use early, on time, or late.**

> In my country, people go to work _____.
>
> They go to school _____.
>
> They go to parties _____.

G **GROUPS. Take turns. Read your sentences.**

Show what you know!

1 THE SOUNDS OF *D* AND *T*

A Read the words out loud softly.

dinner	**d**o	**d**on't
day	Mon**d**ay	rea**d**

CD2 T20

B Listen and repeat.

C Read the words out loud softly.

two	**T**uesday	**t**ime
ge**t** up	ea**t**	breakfas**t**

CD2 T21

D Listen and repeat.

CD2 T22

E Listen. Write *d* or *t*. Listen again and repeat.

1. ea____   4. ____ime   7. ____wo

2. ____ay   5. Mon____ay   8. rea____

3. ____inner   6. ge____ up   9. breakfas____

F DICTATION. PAIRS. Student A, say three words from Exercise A. Student B, listen and write.

_____   _____   _____

G DICTATION. SAME PAIRS. Student B, say three words from Exercise C. Student A, listen and write.

_____   _____   _____

2 VOCABULARY

A Write the numbers.

1. forty-six   _46_
2. sixteen   ____
3. eighty-one   ____
4. twenty-five   ____
5. thirty-eight   ____

6. seventy-three   ____
7. two   ____
8. fifty-seven   ____
9. eleven   ____
10. ninety-nine   ____

B Look at the numbers in Exercise A. Write them in the correct order.

_2_   _11_   ____   ____   ____   ____   ____   ____   ____   ____

C Write the days of the week in the correct order.

1. _Sunday_
2. ____
3. ____
4. ____
5. ____
6. ____
7. ____

> Tuesday
> Saturday
> Wednesday
> S~~u~~nday
> Monday
> Friday
> Thursday

3 SPEAKING

A new classmate asks: *When is the break?*
What do you say?

a. Mondays and Wednesdays.
b. Class starts at 8:30.
c. It's from 10 to 10:30.

Go to the CD-ROM for more practice.

1 SAY THE TIME

A PAIRS. Student A, say a time.
Student B, draw the time on the clock.

B SAME PAIRS. Student B, say a time.
Student A, draw the time on the clock.

2 DAILY ACTIVITIES

A CD2 T23 Listen. Ali is talking about his daily activities.

B Choose a day. What are your daily activities?
Write sentences. Use true or made-up information.

Day: _____

_____

_____

_____

_____

_____

C PAIRS. Tell your classmate about your daily routine.

3 TALK ABOUT YOUR SCHEDULE

Answer the questions.
Write your information in the schedule.

1. When do you work?

2. When do you go to class? When is the break?

3. When do you study English?

4. When do you meet friends?

| My Schedule | | | | | | |
SUNDAY	MONDAY	TUESDAY	WEDNESDAY	THURSDAY	FRIDAY	SATURDAY

4 WRITE ABOUT YOURSELF

Write about yourself. Use true or made-up information.

1. I work _____.

2. I go to class _____.

3. The break is _____.

4. I study English _____.

5. I meet friends _____.

5 CONNECT   For your Team Project, go to page 211.

Family and Friends

A CD2 T24 Look at the families.
Listen and point. Listen and repeat.

B CD2 T25 Listen and read. Listen and repeat.

1. sister	5. mother	9. grandfather
2. brother	6. father	10. daughter
3. wife	7. parents	11. son
4. husband	8. grandmother	12. children

C Listen. Listen and repeat.

A: Who's that?
B: That's my brother.
A: Who's that?
B: That's my sister.

D PAIRS. Practice the conversation.

E Take out pictures of your family or draw a picture of your family.

Show what you know!

GROUPS. Take turns. Show your pictures. Your classmates point and ask: *Who's that?*

Who's that? That's my father.

Say who is in your family • Singular/Plural

A **Listen. Listen and repeat.**

A: Do you have any sisters or brothers?
B: Yes. I have two sisters and one brother.
A: That's nice. Do you have any children?
B: No, I don't.

B **Listen again. Circle _Yes_ or _No_.**

1. Olga has two sisters.   Yes   No
2. Olga has two brothers.   Yes   No
3. Olga has children.   Yes   No

C PAIRS. Practice the conversation.

D 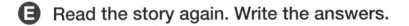 **Listen and read the story.**

This is Marta and her family. Her husband is Pedro. Her parents are Linda and Roberto. Marta has two sons. Their names are Ernesto and Tino. She has one daughter. Her name is Ana.

Pedro   Marta   Linda   Roberto

Tino   Ernesto   Ana

E Read the story again. Write the answers.

1. Pedro is Marta's _____.

2. Ana is Tino's _____.

3. Linda is Marta's _____.

4. Ernesto and Tino are Marta's _____.

5. Roberto and Linda are Ana's _____.

F Listen and read. Listen and repeat.

Singular	Plural
one brother	two brothers
a sister	three sisters
one son	two sons
a daughter	three daughters
one parent	two parents
a grandparent	four grandparents

one child → two children

G Match.

1. my brother Tom and my brother Mark ___b___

2. my son and daughter ____

3. my grandmother and grandfather ____

4. my mother and father ____

5. my sister Sue and my sister Mary ____

a. my grandparents

b. my brothers

c. my sisters

d. my children

e. my parents

Show what you know!

GROUPS OF 4. Take turns. Ask: *Do you have any _____?*
Write the information.

	Name	Sisters	Brothers	Children
	Olga	2	1	0
1.				
2.				
3.				

CLASS. Take turns. Talk about your classmates.

Olga has two sisters and one brother.

She doesn't have any children.

A CD2 T31
 Look at the household chores.
Listen and point. Listen and repeat.

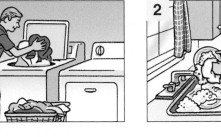

B CD2 T32
 Listen and read. Listen and repeat.

1. do the laundry	3. make dinner	5. vacuum
2. wash the dishes	4. clean the house	6. take out the garbage

C What household chores do you do?
Read the sentences. Circle *Yes* or *No*.

1.	I vacuum.	Yes	No
2.	I do the laundry.	Yes	No
3.	I make dinner.	Yes	No
4.	I wash the dishes.	Yes	No
5.	I clean the house.	Yes	No
6.	I take out the garbage.	Yes	No

D PAIRS. Tell your classmate your answers from Exercise C.

66   UNIT 4

E  Listen. Listen and repeat.

A: Who vacuums at your house?
B: My father vacuums.
A: Who makes dinner?
B: My grandmother makes dinner.

F PAIRS. Practice the conversation.

G Read the sentences.

Questions with *Who*	
Who vacuum**s**?	My father vacuum**s**.
Who make**s** dinner?	My grandmother make**s** dinner.

do → does
wash → washes

H Write the questions.

End a question with a question mark.

1. Who / vacuum   _Who vacuums?_____

2. Who / do the laundry _____

3. Who / make dinner   _____

4. Who / wash the dishes _____

5. Who / clean the house _____

6. Who / take out the garbage _____

Show what you know!

PAIRS. Ask your classmate the questions in Exercise H.

CLASS. Take turns. Talk about your classmates.

Min's father does the dishes.

Tam's sister does the laundry

CD2 T34

A Look at the calendars.
Listen and point. Listen and repeat.

January						
S	M	T	W	T	F	S
	1	2	3	4	5	
6	7	8	9	10	11	12
13	14	15	16	17	18	19
20	21	22	23	24	25	26
27	28	29	30	31		

February						
S	M	T	W	T	F	S
					1	2
3	4	5	6	7	8	9
10	11	12	13	14	15	16
17	18	19	20	21	22	23
24	25	26	27	28		

March						
S	M	T	W	T	F	S
					1	2
3	4	5	6	7	8	9
10	11	12	13	14	15	16
17	18	19	20	21	22	23
24/31	25	26	27	28	29	30

April						
S	M	T	W	T	F	S
	1	2	3	4	5	6
7	8	9	10	11	12	13
14	15	16	17	18	19	20
21	22	23	24	25	26	27
28	29	30				

May						
S	M	T	W	T	F	S
			1	2	3	4
5	6	7	8	9	10	11
12	13	14	15	16	17	18
19	20	21	22	23	24	25
26	27	28	29	30	31	

June						
S	M	T	W	T	F	S
						1
2	3	4	5	6	7	8
9	10	11	12	13	14	15
16	17	18	19	20	21	22
23/30	24	25	26	27	28	29

July						
S	M	T	W	T	F	S
	1	2	3	4	5	6
7	8	9	10	11	12	13
14	15	16	17	18	19	20
21	22	23	24	25	26	27
28	29	30	31			

August						
S	M	T	W	T	F	S
				1	2	3
4	5	6	7	8	9	10
11	12	13	14	15	16	17
18	19	20	21	22	23	24
25	26	27	28	29	30	31

September						
S	M	T	W	T	F	S
1	2	3	4	5	6	7
8	9	10	11	12	13	14
15	16	17	18	19	20	21
22	23	24	25	26	27	28
29	30					

October						
S	M	T	W	T	F	S
		1	2	3	4	5
6	7	8	9	10	11	12
13	14	15	16	17	18	19
20	21	22	23	24	25	26
27	28	29	30	31		

November						
S	M	T	W	T	F	S
					1	2
3	4	5	6	7	8	9
10	11	12	13	14	15	16
17	18	19	20	21	22	23
24	25	26	27	28	29	30

December						
S	M	T	W	T	F	S
1	2	3	4	5	6	7
8	9	10	11	12	13	14
15	16	17	18	19	20	21
22	23	24	25	26	27	28
29	30	31				

CD2 T35

B Listen for the month. Circle *a* or *b*.

1. a. November   (b.) December
2. a. July   b. June
3. a. October   b. November
4. a. January   b. July
5. a. March   b. May
6. a. August   b. April

> Start months with
> a capital letter.

CD2 T36

C Listen. Listen and repeat.

A: What's your favorite month?
B: July. What's your favorite month?
A: September.

D PAIRS. Make a new conversation for Exercise C.
Use true information.

E 🔘 Listen. Listen and repeat.

A: When is your birthday?
B: October 1.

> Write *October 1.*
> Say *October first.*

F 🔘 Listen and point. Listen and repeat.

October 🍁🎃🍂🍃

Sunday	Monday	Tuesday	Wednesday	Thursday	Friday	Saturday
	1 first	**2** second	**3** third	**4** fourth	**5** fifth	**6** sixth
7 seventh	**8** eighth	**9** ninth	**10** tenth	**11** eleventh	**12** twelfth	**13** thirteenth
14 fourteenth	**15** fifteenth	**16** sixteenth	**17** seventeenth	**18** eighteenth	**19** nineteenth	**20** twentieth
21 twenty-first	**22** twenty-second	**23** twenty-third	**24** twenty-fourth	**25** twenty-fifth	**26** twenty-sixth	**27** twenty-seventh
28 twenty-eighth	**29** twenty-ninth	**30** thirtieth	**31** thirty-first			

G PAIRS. Point to a date on the calendar. Say the date.

When is your birthday?

October first.

Show what you know!

CLASS. Walk around the room.
Ask your classmates: *When is your birthday?*

Say and write dates

CD2 T39

A Listen and point to the dates. Listen and repeat.

Date of birth:
February 13, 1972

Date of birth:
July 4, 1995

Date of birth:
November 23, 2007

B Write your date of birth. Use true or made-up information.

_____ _____ _____
month   day   year

CD2 T40

C Listen for the dates. Circle *a* or *b*.

1. a. January 1, 2006   b. January 1, 2007
2. a. April 12, 2089   b. April 12, 1989
3. a. May 15, 1993   b. May 15, 1983
4. a. August 27, 2006   b. August 27, 2016
5. a. December 8, 2000   b. December 8, 2010

D PAIRS. Point to a date. Say the date.

January 20, 1986   March 12, 1995   October 1, 2012

E Write the answers.

1. What's today's date?   _____ _____, _____

2. What's tomorrow's date? _____ _____, _____

F 🔘 Listen and point to the dates. Listen and repeat.

September 28, 1994 9/28/94	January 2, 2000 1/2/00	June 20, 2010 6/20/10

G PAIRS. Put the months in the correct order. Write the number. Then write the words.

___ November   ___ December   _1_ January   ___ March

___ April   ___ July   _2_ February   ___ August

___ October   ___ May   ___ September   ___ June

1. _January_   7. _____

2. _February_   8. _____

3. _____   9. _____

4. _____   10. _____

5. _____   11. _____

6. _____   12. _____

H Write the dates. Use numbers.

1. February 16, 2001 _2/16/01_   3. August 30, 1996 _____

2. May 2, 2010 _____   4. October 12, 2005 _____

April second
two thousand eight.

Show what you know!

GROUPS. Take turns.
Think of a date and say it to your classmates.
Write the date in words and numbers.

Life Skills • Fill out a form

A CD2 T42

 Listen and read. Listen and point.

Adult Education Center

Adult
Education
Center

Name | Viktor   Oleg   Popov
      First   Middle   Last

Date of Birth | 10/30/84   Place of Birth | Russia

Class | ESL-3   Teacher | Mrs. Brown

Class Schedule | Monday, Wednesday   2:30 p.m. – 5:30 p.m.   14
                 Day/s   Time   Room

B Read the sentences. Then read the form again.
Circle the mistake. Write the correct information.

1. Viktor is a (teacher). _student_____

2. Viktor's last name is Oleg. _____

3. He is from Poland. _____

4. Viktor was born on March 30, 1984. _____

5. His teacher is Miss Brown. _____

6. Viktor is in ESL-2. _____

7. He goes to class on Monday and Tuesday. _____

8. Viktor's English class ends at 2:30 p.m. _____

C Answer the questions. Use true or made-up information.

1. What is your first name? _____

2. What is your middle name? _____

3. What is your last name? _____

4. What is your date of birth? _____

5. Where are you from? _____

6. What class are you in? _____

7. What is your teacher's name? _____

8. What day is your class? _____

9. What time is your class? _____

10. What room is your class in? _____

D Fill out the form. Use your information in Exercise C.

Adult Education Center

Adult
Education
Center

Name			
First	Middle	Last	

Date of Birth		Place of Birth	

Class		Teacher	

Class Schedule			
Day/s	Time	Room

E PAIRS. Read your classmate's form. Is the form complete?

A CLASS. Look at each picture. What do you see?

B **Listen to the story.**

CD2 T43

C Listen again and read.

> Ernesto and Maria are married.
>
> In their country, men go to work.
>
> In their country, women stay at home. They do all the household chores.
>
> In the United States, both Maria and Ernesto go to work.
>
> Ernesto helps at home. He does the dishes.
>
> Sometimes Ernesto goes to the supermarket, too.

D Read the story again. Circle *Yes* or *No*.

1. In their country, both Ernesto and Maria go to work.   Yes   (No)
2. In the United States, Maria goes to work.   Yes   No
3. In the United States, Ernesto stays at home.   Yes   No
4. In the United States, Ernesto goes to the supermarket.   Yes   No

E GROUPS. Read the questions. Talk about men and women in your country.

1. Do women go to work? Do they do the household chores?
2. Do men help at home? What household chores do they do?

F Write about household chores and work.

> In my country, men _____ .
>
> Women _____ .
>
> In the United States, men _____ .
>
> Women _____ .

G GROUPS. Take turns. Read your sentences.

1 THE SOUNDS OF *D* AND *TH*

A Read the words out loud softly.

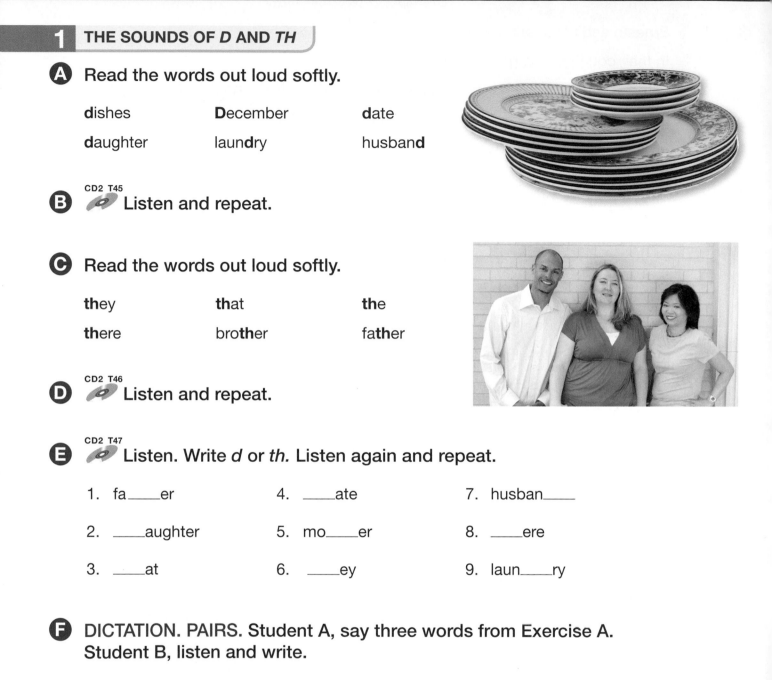

dishes	**D**ecember	**d**ate
daughter	laun**d**ry	husban**d**

CD2 T45

B 🎧 Listen and repeat.

C Read the words out loud softly.

they	**th**at	**th**e
there	bro**th**er	fa**th**er

CD2 T46

D 🎧 Listen and repeat.

CD2 T47

E 🎧 Listen. Write *d* or *th*. Listen again and repeat.

1. fa____er   4. ____ate   7. husban____

2. ____aughter   5. mo____er   8. ____ere

3. ____at   6. ____ey   9. laun____ry

F DICTATION. PAIRS. Student A, say three words from Exercise A. Student B, listen and write.

_____   _____   _____

G DICTATION. SAME PAIRS. Student B, say three words from Exercise C. Student A, listen and write.

_____   _____   _____

2 VOCABULARY

A Write the months of the year in the correct order.

1. _____January_____   7. _____

2. _____   8. _____

3. _____   9. _____

4. _____   10. _____

5. _____   11. _____

6. _____   12. _____

CD2 T48

B Listen and check your answers.

C Read the calendar. Write the dates in words and numbers.

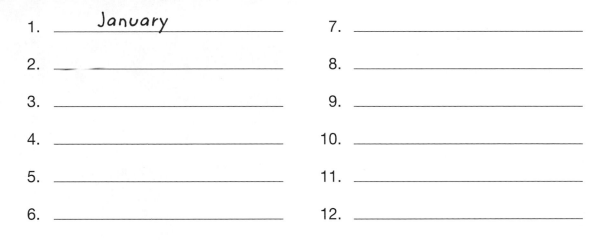

April 5, 2009
4/5/09

April 2009

S	M	T	W	T	F	S
			1	2	3	4
5	6	7	8	9	10	11
12	13	14	15	16	17	18
19	20	21	22	23	24	25
26	27	28	29	30		

3 SPEAKING

Your classmate asks: *When is your birthday?*
What do you say?

a. 1988
b. March 3
c. January

Show what you know!

1 SAY WHO IS IN YOUR FAMILY

A Look at Marta's family tree. Find Marta.

B CD2 T49
Listen.
Marta is talking about her family.

C Draw a family tree.
Write the names of your family.

D PAIRS. Talk about your family. Say:
That's my _____. These are my _____.

2 TALK ABOUT HOUSEHOLD CHORES

A CD2 T50
Listen. Kato is talking about household chores.

B Who does the housework in your family?
Use the words in the box. Write complete sentences.

My mother cleans the house.

1. _____

2. _____

3. _____

4. _____

5. _____

6. _____

clean the house
do the laundry
make dinner
take out the garbage
vacuum
wash the dishes

C PAIRS. Tell your classmate your information.

3 FILL OUT A FORM

Fill out the form. Use true or made-up information.

Student Information Form

The **L**anguage **C**enter

☐ Mr. ☐ Mrs. ☐ Miss ☐ Ms.

Name _____
        First   Middle   Last

Date of Birth _____   Place of Birth _____

Class _____   Teacher _____

Class Schedule _____
            Day/s   Time   Room

4 WRITE ABOUT YOURSELF

Write about yourself. Use true or made-up information.

1. My name is _____ .

2. I'm from _____ .

3. I'm in _____ .

4. My teacher is _____ .

5. I go to English class on _____ .

6. Class starts at _____ .

5 CONNECT   For your Team Project, go to page 211.

How much is it?

Make change with U.S. coins

A CD3 T2 **Look at the coins.**
Listen and point. Listen and repeat.

B CD3 T3   **Listen and read. Listen and repeat.**

1. a penny	3. a dime	5. a half-dollar
2. a nickel	4. a quarter	6. a dollar coin

1 penny
2 pennies

C  **CD3 T4**

Listen. Listen and repeat.

A: Excuse me. Do you have change for a dollar?
B: Yes. I have two quarters and five dimes.
Here you go.
A: Thanks.

D **PAIRS. Practice the conversation.**

E **Look at the pictures. Complete the sentences.**

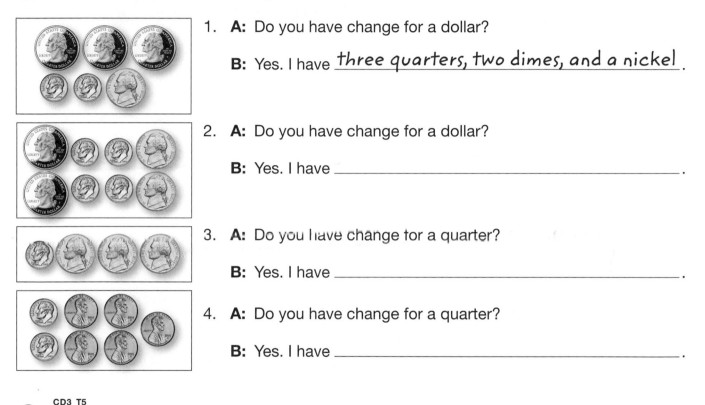

1. **A:** Do you have change for a dollar?

   B: Yes. I have _three quarters, two dimes, and a nickel_.

2. **A:** Do you have change for a dollar?

   B: Yes. I have _____.

3. **A:** Do you have change for a quarter?

   B: Yes. I have _____.

4. **A:** Do you have change for a quarter?

   B: Yes. I have _____.

F **CD3 T5**

Listen and check your answers. Listen and repeat.

Show what you know!

GROUPS. Take out your coins. Count the coins. Tell your classmates.

____ pennies   ____ nickels   ____ dimes

____ quarters   ____ half-dollars   ____ dollar coins

I have two pennies, three nickels, and two quarters.

Make change with U.S. bills

CD3 T6

A Look at the bills.
Listen and point. Listen and repeat.

1

2

3

4

5

6

CD3 T7

B Listen and read. Listen and repeat.

1. one dollar
2. five dollars
3. ten dollars
4. twenty dollars
5. fifty dollars
6. one hundred dollars

a single = a one-dollar bill
a ten = a ten-dollar bill

C Listen. Listen and repeat.

A: Excuse me. Do you have change for a ten?
B: Yes. I have a five and five singles.
Here you go.
A: Great.

D PAIRS. Practice the conversation.

E Look at the pictures. Complete the sentences.

1. **A:** Do you have change for a five?

   B: Yes. I have ___five singles_____.

2. **A:** Do you have change for a twenty?

   B: Yes. I have _____.

3. **A:** Do you have change for a fifty?

   B: Yes. I have _____.

4. **A:** Do you have change for a hundred?

   B: Yes. I have _____.

F Listen and check your answers. Listen and repeat.

Show what you know!

GROUPS. Take turns.
Ask: *Do you have change for a ten?*
Do you have change for a twenty?

A CD3 T10 Look at the drugstore items.
Listen and point. Listen and repeat.

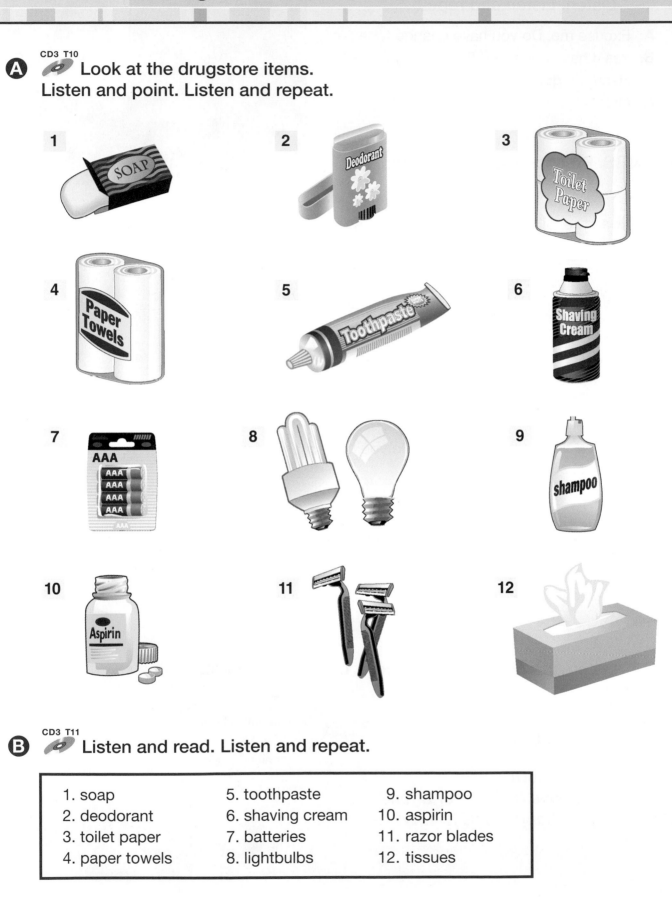

1. SOAP

2. Deodorant

3. Toilet Paper

4. Paper Towels

5. Toothpaste

6. Shaving Cream

7. AAA

8.

9. shampoo

10. Aspirin

11.

12.

B CD3 T11 Listen and read. Listen and repeat.

1. soap	5. toothpaste	9. shampoo
2. deodorant	6. shaving cream	10. aspirin
3. toilet paper	7. batteries	11. razor blades
4. paper towels	8. lightbulbs	12. tissues

C Read the sentences.

Where is/Where are	
Where is the soap?	**Where are** the razor blades?
Where is the aspirin?	**Where are** the tissues?

D Write *is* or *are*.

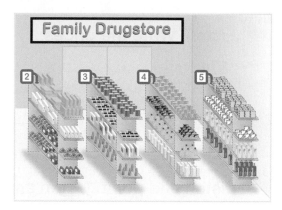

Family Drugstore

1. Where ____is____ the shampoo?

2. Where _____ the paper towels?

3. Where _____ the shaving cream?

4. Where _____ the lightbulbs?

5. Where _____ the batteries?

CD3 T12

E 💿 Listen and check your answers. Listen and repeat.

F Read the sign.

Family Drugstore

Aspirin	Aisle 1	Paper towels	Aisle 3	Soap	Aisle 2
Batteries	Aisle 3	Razor blades	Aisle 4	Tissues	Aisle 3
Deodorant	Aisle 2	Shampoo	Aisle 5	Toilet paper	Aisle 3
Lightbulbs	Aisle 3	Shaving cream	Aisle 4	Toothpaste	Aisle 4

Show what you know!

GROUPS. Read the directory in Exercise F.
Take turns. Ask: *Where is _____? Where are _____?*

Where is the shampoo?

Aisle 5.

Ask for and give prices

A 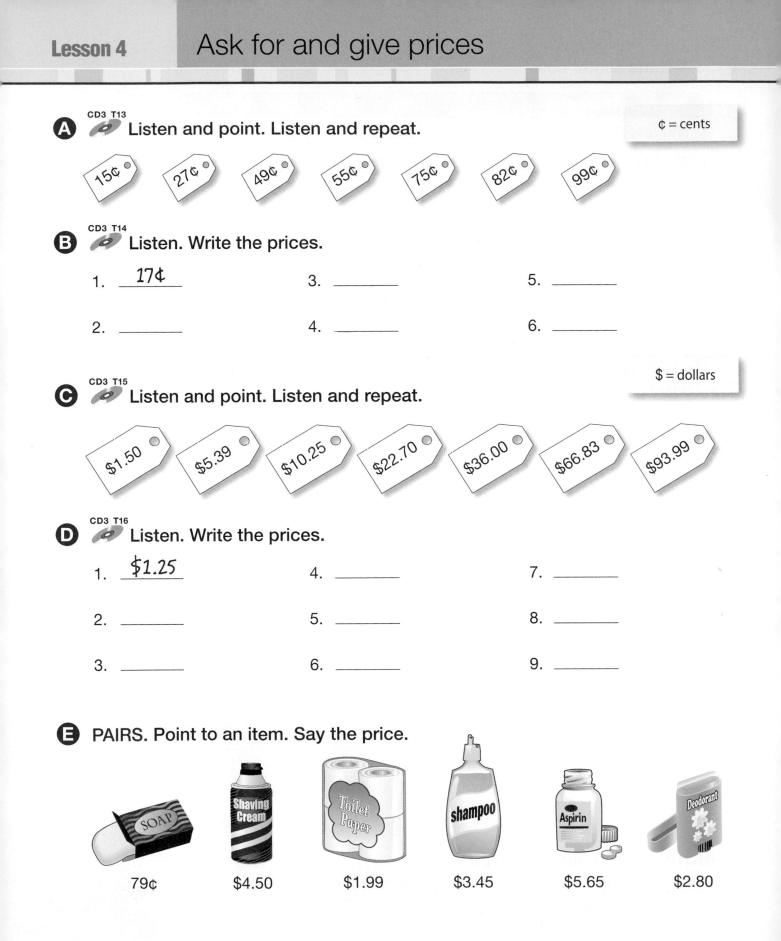 Listen and point. Listen and repeat.

¢ = cents

15¢   27¢   49¢   55¢   75¢   82¢   99¢

CD3 T14

B Listen. Write the prices.

1. __17¢__   3. _____   5. _____

2. _____   4. _____   6. _____

$ = dollars

CD3 T15

C Listen and point. Listen and repeat.

$1.50 $5.39 $10.25 $22.70 $36.00 $66.83 $93.99

CD3 T16

D Listen. Write the prices.

1. __$1.25__   4. _____   7. _____

2. _____   5. _____   8. _____

3. _____   6. _____   9. _____

E PAIRS. Point to an item. Say the price.

SOAP   Shaving Cream   Toilet Paper   shampoo   Aspirin   Deodorant

79¢ $4.50 $1.99 $3.45 $5.65 $2.80

86   UNIT 5

F **Listen. Listen and repeat.**

CD3 T17

A: Excuse me. Is toothpaste on sale?
B: Yes, it is.
A: How much is it?
B: It's $1.99.
A: Thanks.

G  **Listen again. Circle *Yes* or *No*.**

CD3 T18

1. The toothpaste is on sale.   Yes   No
2. The toothpaste is $2.99.   Yes   No

H PAIRS. Practice the conversation.

I PAIRS. Look at the pictures in Exercise E. Make new conversations.

A: Excuse me. Is _____ on sale?
B: Yes, it is.
A: How much is it?
B: It's _____.
A: Thanks.

Show what you know!

GROUPS. Write a new price for each item.

1. deodorant	$3.29	4. shaving cream	
2. soap		5. aspirin	
3. shampoo		6. batteries	

CLASS. Walk around the room.
Ask about each item: *How much is _____?*

How much is deodorant?

Three twenty-nine.

A Read the receipt.

```
Family Drugstore

        Date: 03/04/10

1 Shampoo              $2.79
1 Soap                  .99
1 Tissues              1.79
1 Razor blades         3.99
1 Shaving cream        4.25
1 Batteries            4.99


Transaction Total:

6 items      Subtotal  $18.80
             Tax        1.55
             Total     $20.35


Paid by: Cash          $30.00
Change                  $9.65
```

.99 = 99¢

B Read the receipt again. Write the answers.

1. The shampoo is ___$2.79___.

2. The tissues are _____.

3. The razor blades are _____.

4. The tax is _____.

5. The total is _____.

6. The change is _____.

C Read the receipt again. Circle *Yes* or *No*.

1. The name of the store is Drugstore.   Yes   (No)

2. The date on the receipt is March 4, 2010.   Yes   No

3. The person is buying five drugstore items.   Yes   No

4. The person is paying cash.   Yes   No

D Read the check.

Daniel Jones
17 Riverside Drive
New York, NY 10024

100

March 4, 2009

PAY TO THE
ORDER OF *ABC Drugstore* $ *30.79*

Thirty dollars and $\frac{79}{100}$ —————————————— DOLLARS

City Bank
1001 Main Street
New York, NY 10001

Daniel Jones

FOR ——————————————

⑈ 1 2 3 4 5 6 7 ⑈ ⑆ 0 0 1 2 3 ⑈ 4 5 6 ⑆ 1 0 0

E Read the check again. Circle *a* or *b*.

1. Who is writing the check?

   a. Daniel Jones   b. ABC Drugstore

2. How much money is the check?

   a. March 4, 2007   b. $30.79

3. Who is the check for?

   a. Daniel Jones   b. ABC Drugstore

F Write a check for $33.45.
Use today's date. Sign your name.

101

PAY TO THE
ORDER OF *ABC Drugstore* $

—————————————————————————————— DOLLARS

City Bank
1001 Main Street
New York, NY 10001

FOR ——————————————

⑈ 1 2 3 4 5 6 7 ⑈ ⑆ 0 0 1 2 3 ⑈ 4 5 6 ⑆ 1 0 1

Edna's story

A CLASS. Look at each picture. What do you see?

B CD3 T19 Listen to the story.

C 🔘 **Listen again and read.**

> My name is Edna. In my country, I shop at markets.
>
> I talk to the salespeople about the prices.
>
> I get good bargains.
>
> In the United States, I shop in big stores.
>
> I pay the price on the price tag.
>
> How do I get good bargains? I buy things on sale!

D **Read the story again. Circle *Yes* or *No*.**

1.	In her country, Edna shops at big stores.	Yes	(No)
2.	In her country, Edna pays the price on the price tag.	Yes	No
3.	In the United States, Edna shops at big stores.	Yes	No
4.	In the United States, Edna gets bargains.	Yes	No

E **GROUPS. Read the questions. Talk about shopping in your country.**

1. Do people shop at markets? Do they shop in big stores?

2. Do people pay the price on the price tags?

3. Do people ask the salespeople for different prices?

4. Do people get good bargains?

F **Write about shopping.**

In my country, people _____.

They _____.

In the United States, people _____.

They _____.

G **GROUPS. Take turns. Read your sentences.**

1 THE SOUNDS OF G AND C

A Read the words out loud softly.

go	**g**et	**g**ood
bi**g**	dru**g**store	price ta**g**

CD3 T21

B Listen and repeat.

C Read the words out loud softly.

coin	**c**ount	**c**ash
country	**c**omputer	shaving **c**ream

CD3 T22

D Listen and repeat.

CD3 T23

E Listen. Write *g* or *c*. Listen again and repeat.

1. ____o
2. dru____store
3. ____ash

4. ____omputer
5. bi____
6. shaving ____ream

7. ____ount
8. ____et
9. ____ountry

F DICTATION. PAIRS. Student A, say three words from Exercise A. Student B, listen and write.

_____   _____   _____

G DICTATION. SAME PAIRS. Student B, say three words from Exercise C. Student A, listen and write.

_____   _____   _____

A PAIRS. Point to a coin. Say the amount.

B PAIRS. Point to a bill. Say the amount.

Your classmate asks: *Do you have change for a dollar?*
What do you say?

a. No, I can't.
b. Yes. I have two quarters and five dimes.
c. Yes. I have three quarters and three nickels.

Go to the CD-ROM for more practice.

1 ASK WHERE THINGS ARE IN A STORE

A CD3 T24 Listen. A customer is asking for information.

B PAIRS. Ask where the item is. Say the aisle number.

| Aisle 5 | Aisle 4 | Aisle 2 | Aisle 3 | Aisle 2 | Aisle 6 |

2 ASK FOR AND GIVE CHANGE

A  CD3 T25 Listen. Someone is asking for change.

B ROLE PLAY. PAIRS.

ROLE PLAY 1	
Student A	**Student B**
Ask for change for a quarter.	Use true or made-up information.
Ask for change for a ten.	Tell your classmate the change.

ROLE PLAY 2	
Student B	**Student A**
Ask for change for a dollar.	Use true or made-up information.
Ask for change for a twenty.	Tell your classmate the change.

3 READ A RECEIPT, WRITE A CHECK

A Read the receipt.
How much is the total? _____

CDS Drugstore

Date: 08/11/10

1	Shampoo	$2.79
1	Soap	.89
1	Tissues	1.99
1	Razors	3.50
1	Paper towels	2.25

Transaction Total:

5 items	Subtotal	$11.42
	Tax	.94
	Total	$12.36

Paid by: Check	$12.36
Change	$0.00

B Write a check for the total.

```
                                                        102
                                  _____

PAY TO THE    CDS Drugstore                        $ [        ]
ORDER OF  _____

_____ DOLLARS

City Bank
1001 Main Street
New York, NY 10001

FOR _____    _____

  ⑈1234567⑈  ⑈00123⑈456⑈ 102
```

4 WRITE ABOUT YOURSELF

Write about yourself. Use true or made-up information.

1. My name is _____ .

2. I shop at _____ .

3. I buy _____ .

4. I pay with _____ .

5 CONNECT   For your Team Project, go to page 212.

6 Let's eat!

CD3 T26

A Look at the vegetables.
Listen and point. Listen and repeat.

CD3 T27

B Listen and read. Listen and repeat.

1. tomatoes	4. onions	7. potatoes
2. carrots	5. peppers	8. mushrooms
3. cucumbers	6. lettuce	9. peas

C CD3 T28 Listen. Listen and repeat.

A: Hi. I'm at the store. Do we need vegetables?
B: Yes. Get tomatoes and carrots.
A: OK. Do we need onions?
B: No. We have onions.

D PAIRS. Practice the conversation.

E PAIRS. Make new conversations.
Use the vegetables on page 96.

A: Hi. I'm at the store. Do we need vegetables?

B: Yes. Get _____ and _____.

A: OK. Do we need _____?

B: No. We have _____.

F CD3 T29 Listen and read the story.

Pam wants to make soup. Her family likes vegetable soup. Pam has carrots and mushrooms. She needs onions, peas, and potatoes. Her husband goes to the store. He buys the vegetables. Pam makes the soup. It's delicious!

G Read the story again. Circle *Yes* or *No*.

1.	Pam wants to make chicken soup.	Yes	(No)
2.	She has carrots and mushrooms.	Yes	No
3.	Her husband buys onions, peas, and tomatoes.	Yes	No

Show what you know!

GROUPS. Look at the vegetables on page 96.
Take turns. Say the vegetables you like.

I like carrots, peas, and tomatoes.

A CD3 T30

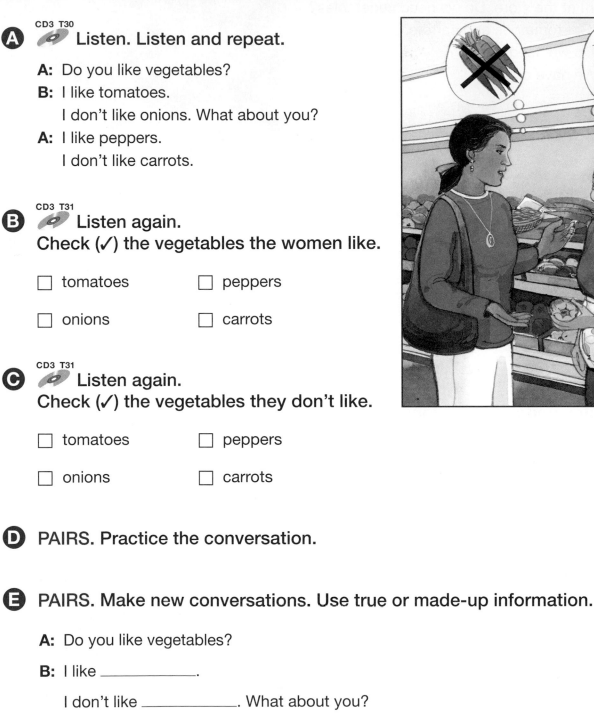

Listen. Listen and repeat.

A: Do you like vegetables?

B: I like tomatoes.
I don't like onions. What about you?

A: I like peppers.
I don't like carrots.

B CD3 T31

Listen again.
Check (✓) the vegetables the women like.

☐ tomatoes   ☐ peppers

☐ onions   ☐ carrots

C CD3 T31

Listen again.
Check (✓) the vegetables they don't like.

☐ tomatoes   ☐ peppers

☐ onions   ☐ carrots

D PAIRS. Practice the conversation.

E PAIRS. Make new conversations. Use true or made-up information.

A: Do you like vegetables?

B: I like _____.

I don't like _____. What about you?

A: I like _____.

I don't like _____.

F Read the sentences.

Like/Don't like	
I **like** tomatoes.	I **don't like** onions.
You **like** lettuce.	You **don't like** carrots.
Luz and Pavel **like** potatoes.	They **don't like** peas.
John and I **like** cucumbers.	We **don't like** mushrooms.

do + not = don't

G Look at the pictures. Complete the sentences. Use *like* and *don't like*.

1. I _like tomatoes_ .

2. Carlos and Susan _____ .

3. We _____ .

4. You _____ .

5. I _____ .

Show what you know!

GROUPS. Write one vegetable your group likes.
Write one vegetable your group doesn't like.

We like _____. We don't like _____.

CLASS. Take turns. Talk about your group.

We like carrots.

We don't like peas.

CD3 T32

A Look at the fruit.
Listen and point. Listen and repeat.

CD3 T33

B Listen and read. Listen and repeat.

1. apples	4. oranges	7. bananas
2. cherries	5. pears	8. peaches
3. mangoes	6. strawberries	9. grapes

C Look at the words in Exercise B. Write three fruits you like.

_____ _____ _____

D PAIRS. Tell your classmate your words in Exercise C.

E  Listen. Listen and repeat.

   A: Does your daughter like fruit?

   B: She likes apples.

      She doesn't like pears.

F Read the sentences.

Likes/Doesn't like	
My daughter **likes** apples.	She **doesn't like** pears.
My son **likes** oranges.	He **doesn't like** bananas.

does + not = doesn't

G Complete the sentences.

1. My mother (like) _____*likes*_____ grapes.

2. My teacher (not / like) _____ peaches.

3. He (not / like) _____ apples.

4. Dan's sister (not / like) _____ mangoes.

5. She (like) _____ bananas.

Show what you know!

GROUPS OF 4. Say one fruit you like. Say one fruit you don't like.
Write your classmates' information.

Name	Likes	Doesn't like
Olga	apples	pears
1.		
2.		
3.		

CLASS. Take turns. Talk about one classmate.

> Olga likes apples.
> She doesn't like pears.

A  CD3 T35

A Listen and point. Listen and repeat.

bananas
99¢/lb.

grapes
$1.79/lb.

fish
$6.99/lb.

ground beef
$2.89/lb.

chicken
$3.39/lb.

avocados
$1.99 each

lb. = pound
lbs. = pounds

B CD3 T36

B Listen. Listen and repeat.

A: Do you need anything from the store?

B: Yes. I need one pound of grapes and two pounds of ground beef.

C PAIRS. Practice the conversation.

D PAIRS. Look at the shopping lists. Make new conversations.

A: Do you need anything from the store?

B: Yes. I need _____ and _____.

Conversation 1

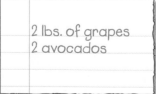

2 lbs. of grapes
2 avocados

Conversation 2

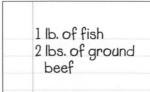

1 lb. of fish
2 lbs. of ground
　beef

Conversation 3

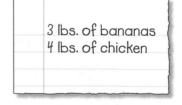

3 lbs. of bananas
4 lbs. of chicken

E 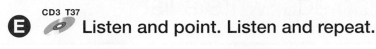 Listen and point. Listen and repeat.

Singular		Plural
gallon	→	gallons
loaf	→	loaves
box	→	boxes
a dozen	→	two dozen
a bag	→	two bags
can	→	cans

a gallon of milk

a loaf of bread

a box of cereal

a dozen eggs

a bag of rice

a can of soup

F 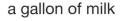 Listen. Listen and repeat.

A: What do we need from the store?

B: We need a bag of rice and two dozen eggs.

G PAIRS. Practice the conversation.

H PAIRS. Look at the pictures. Make new conversations.

A: What do we need from the store?

B: We need _____ and _____.

Conversation 1

Conversation 2

Conversation 3

A   CD3 T39   Listen and read. Listen and point.

B   Read the shopping ad again. Circle *a* or *b*.

1. How much is bread?

    a. $1.79 a loaf   b. $1.79 a pound

2. How much is chicken?

    a. $1.99 each   b. $1.99 a pound

3. How much are two cans of tomato soup?

    a. 79¢   b. $1.58

4. How much is cereal?

    a. $3.25 a box   b. $3.25 a pound

5. How much are two pounds of bananas?

    a. 49¢   b. 98¢

C Look at the pictures. Write the shopping lists.

1. 2 dozen eggs
   1 pound of chicken
   2 cans of soup

2.

3.

4.

D PAIRS. Tell your classmate your lists.

Read a menu and order a meal

CD3 T40

A **Listen and point to the menu. Listen and repeat.**

── Marie's Café ── Breakfast Menu ──

Served from 6:00 A.M. to 11:00 A.M.

Pancakes..........................$2.50	Juice..................................$1.50
Eggs and toast....................$2.00	Coffee...............................$1.00
	Tea....................................$1.00
Cereal...............................$2.00	Milk...................................$1.25

CD3 T41

B **Listen. Listen and repeat.**

A: Good morning! Can I take your order?
B: Hi. I'd like pancakes and coffee.
A: Anything else?
B: No, thank you.

C **PAIRS. Practice the conversation.**

D **PAIRS. Make new conversations. Use the menu in Exercise A.**

A: Good morning! Can I take your order?

B: Hi. I'd like _____ and _____.

A: Anything else?

B: No, thank you.

E Listen and point to the menu. Listen and repeat.

Peter's Place
Lunch & Dinner Menu   11:00 A.M. – 8:00 P.M.

	Fish sandwich	$1.50		Iced tea	$1.25
	Chicken sandwich	$2.00		Milk	$1.25
	Hamburger	$2.50		Juice	$1.50
	Taco	$2.00		Coffee	$1.00
	French fries	$1.75		Tea	$1.00
	Baked potato	$1.00		Ice cream	$2.00
	Rice	$1.25		Fruit salad	$2.00
	Green salad	$1.50		Cake	$2.50

F Listen. Listen and repeat.

A: Are you ready to order?

B: I'd like a fish sandwich, a green salad, and iced tea.

G PAIRS. Practice the conversation.

H PAIRS. Make new conversations. Use the menu in Exercise E.

A: Are you ready to order?

B: I'd like _____, _____, and _____.

- **a** fish sandwich
- **a** chicken sandwich
- **a** hamburger
- **a** taco
- **a** baked potato
- **a** green salad

Show what you know!

GROUPS. Take turns.
Ask: *What do you eat for breakfast? What do you eat for lunch?*

A CLASS. Look at each picture. What do you see?

CD3 T44

B  Listen to the story.

1

2

3

Picture 4

4

5

Picture 6

6

C 📀 **Listen again and read.**

> My name is Tran. In my country, people usually eat with chopsticks.
>
> Sometimes children eat with their fingers.
>
> My name is Kyoko. In my country, people usually drink their soup.
>
> In the United States, people usually eat with forks, knives, and spoons.
>
> Sometimes they eat food with their fingers, like sandwiches and French fries.
>
> How do you eat in your country?

D **Read the story again. Circle _Yes_ or _No_.**

1. Tran usually uses his fingers to eat.	Yes	(No)
2. Kyoko uses a spoon to eat her soup.	Yes	No
3. In the United States, people usually eat with chopsticks.	Yes	No
4. In the United States, people usually eat with their fingers.	Yes	No

E **GROUPS. Read the questions. Talk about eating in your country.**

1. Do people use chopsticks?
2. Do people drink soup?
3. Do people use their fingers to eat?

F **Write about how people eat.**

> In my country, people eat with _____.
>
> They _____.
>
> In the United States, people eat with _____.
>
> They _____.

G **GROUPS. Take turns. Read your sentences.**

1 THE SOUNDS OF *F* AND *V*

 A Read the words out loud softly.

fruit	favorite	Friday
food	fish	beef

CD3 T46

 B Listen and repeat.

C Read the words out loud softly.

vegetables	very	live
favorite	five	have

CD3 T47

D Listen and repeat.

CD3 T48

E Listen. Write *f* or *v*. Listen again and repeat.

1. ___ood

2. ___egetables

3. ___ish

4. fi___e

5. ___ery

6. bee___

7. ha___e

8. ___ruit

9. ___a___orite

F DICTATION. PAIRS. Student A, say three words from Exercise A. Student B, listen and write.

_____   _____   _____

G DICTATION. SAME PAIRS. Student B, say three words from Exercise C. Student A, listen and write.

_____   _____   _____

2 VOCABULARY

A Circle the word that does not belong in each group.

1. apples	(cucumbers)	pears
2. lettuce	carrots	oranges
3. chicken	ground beef	lemons
4. rice	bread	apples
5. mushrooms	milk	onions
6. cherries	eggs	grapes
7. cereal	potatoes	tomatoes
8. peas	mangoes	strawberries

B PAIRS. Use the words in Exercise A. Write one word for each quantity.

1. a pound of _____

2. a bag of _____

3. a box of _____

4. a loaf of _____

5. a dozen _____

3 SPEAKING

You are reading a menu. The waitress asks: *May I help you?*
What do you say?

a. We need carrots and onions.
b. I'd like a hamburger and a green salad.
c. I like apples and pears.

 Go to the CD-ROM for more practice.

1 READ A MENU AND ORDER FOOD

A CD3 T49 Listen. A customer is ordering food.

B ROLE PLAY. GROUPS OF 3. Change roles so each student is the waiter or waitress.

ROLE PLAY	
Student A	**Student B and Student C**
You are the waiter / waitress.	You are the customers.
Ask for the customers' lunch order.	Look at the menu.
Write the order.	Order lunch.

Peter's Place   *Lunch & Dinner Menu*   *11:00 A.M. – 8:00 P.M.*

	Fish sandwich	$1.50		Iced tea	$1.25
	Chicken sandwich	$2.00		Milk	$1.25
	Hamburger	$2.50		Juice	$1.50
	Taco	$2.00		Coffee	$1.00
	French fries	$1.75		Tea	$1.00
	Baked potato	$1.00		Ice cream	$2.00
	Rice	$1.25		Fruit salad	$2.00
	Green salad	$1.50		Cake	$2.50

2 WRITE A SHOPPING LIST

A 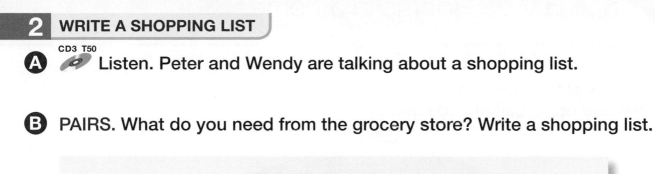 **CD3 T50** Listen. Peter and Wendy are talking about a shopping list.

B PAIRS. What do you need from the grocery store? Write a shopping list.

My Shopping List

_____

_____

_____

_____

_____

3 WRITE ABOUT YOURSELF

Write about yourself. Use true or made-up information.

1. I shop for food at _____.

2. I buy _____.

3. I also buy _____.

4 CONNECT   For your Team Project, go to page 213.

A CD4 T2 Look at the rooms in the home.
Listen and point. Listen and repeat.

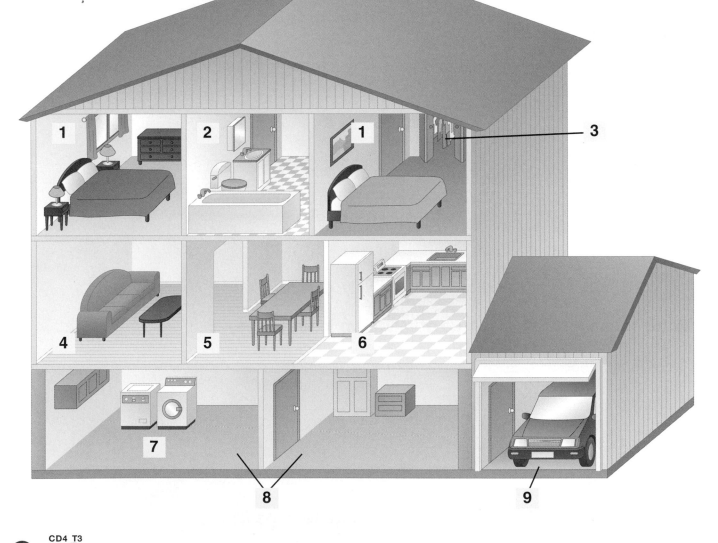

B CD4 T3 Listen and read. Listen and repeat.

1. bedroom	4. living room	7. laundry room
2. bathroom	5. dining room	8. basement
3. closet	6. kitchen	9. garage

C  Listen. Listen and repeat.

A: Guess what? I have a new apartment.
B: Really? What's it like?
A: It has a kitchen, a living room, and one bedroom.
B: It sounds great!

D PAIRS. Practice the conversation.

E PAIRS. Look at the apartments. Make new conversations.

A: Guess what? I have a new apartment.

B: Really? What's it like?

A: It has _____.

B: It sounds great!

Conversation 1

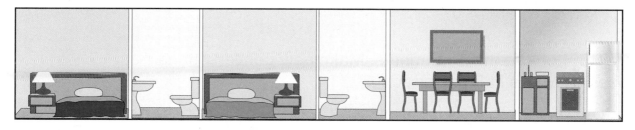

Conversation 2

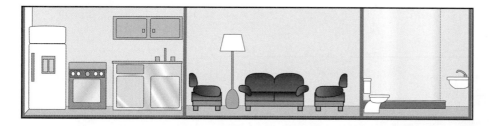

Show what you know!

GROUPS. Take turns.
Talk about your apartment or house. Say the rooms.

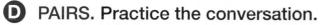

My apartment has one kitchen, one bedroom, and one bathroom.

Ask about apartments • *There is/There are*

A **Listen and point to the rooms. Listen and repeat.**

sunny

modern

large

small

B **Listen. Listen and repeat.**

A: Can you tell me about the apartment for rent?

B: There is a sunny bedroom, a modern kitchen, and a large living room.

A: It sounds nice.

C PAIRS. Practice the conversation.

D PAIRS. Look at the apartments. Make new conversations. Use the words in Exercise A.

A: Can you tell me about the apartment for rent?

B: There is a _____, a _____, and a _____.

A: It sounds nice.

Conversation 1

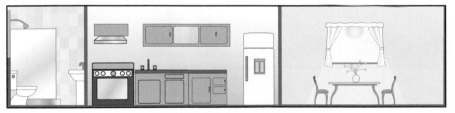

Conversation 2

E Look at the home. Read the sentences.

There is / There are	
There is a modern kitchen.	**There are** two bedrooms.

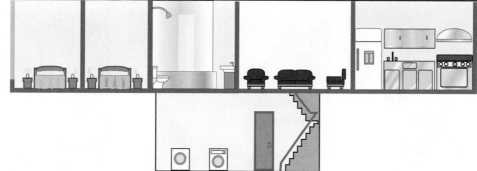

F Read the story. Write *There is* and *There are*.

I like my home. _There are_ six rooms. _____ two small
                        1   2

bedrooms. _____ a living room. _____ a modern kitchen.
              3   4

_____ a large bathroom. _____ a laundry room in the basement.
    5   6

G Read the story again. Circle *Yes* or *No*.

1. There are three rooms.   Yes   (No)

2. The bedrooms are small.   Yes   No

3. The kitchen is old.   Yes   No

4. There is a laundry room.   Yes   No

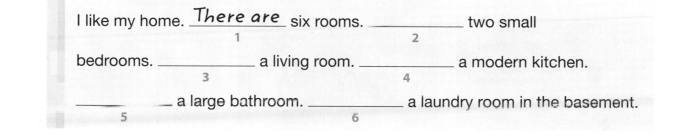

My dream house is large. There are five sunny bedrooms. There is a modern kitchen.

Show what you know!

GROUPS. Take turns.
Talk about your dream apartment or house.
Use *there is* and *there are*.
Use *sunny, small, large,* and *modern*.

A Look at the furniture and appliances. Listen and point. Listen and repeat.

CD4 T7

 B Listen and read. Listen and repeat.

CD4 T8

1. refrigerator	4. dishwasher	7. lamp	10. table
2. stove	5. bed	8. sofa	11. washing machine
3. sink	6. dresser	9. chair	12. dryer

C Look at the words in Exercise B.
What do you have in your apartment or house?

_____   _____   _____

_____   _____   _____

D PAIRS. Tell your classmate your words in Exercise C.

E 🎵 **Listen. Listen and repeat.**
CD4 T9

A: I have some questions about the apartment.
Is there a sofa?

B: Yes, there is.

A: Are there any lamps?

B: No, there aren't.

tenant   landlord

F **Read the sentences.**

Is there / Are there			
Is there a dishwasher?	Yes, **there is.**	No, **there isn't.**	
Are there any beds?	Yes, **there are.**	No, **there aren't.**	

isn't = is + not
aren't = are + not

G **Write the questions and the answers.**

1. **A:** _____Is there_____ a stove?

   B: Yes, _____.

2. **A:** _____ any chairs?

   B: Yes, _____.

3. **A:** _____ any lamps?

   B: No, _____.

4. **A:** _____ a washing machine?

   B: No, _____.

H 🎵 **Listen and check your answers. Listen and repeat.**
CD4 T10

Show what you know!

Is there a stove in your apartment?

Yes, there is.

PAIRS. Ask the questions in Exercise G.
Use true or made-up information about your home.

A   CD4 T11   Look at the addresses.
Listen and point. Listen and repeat.

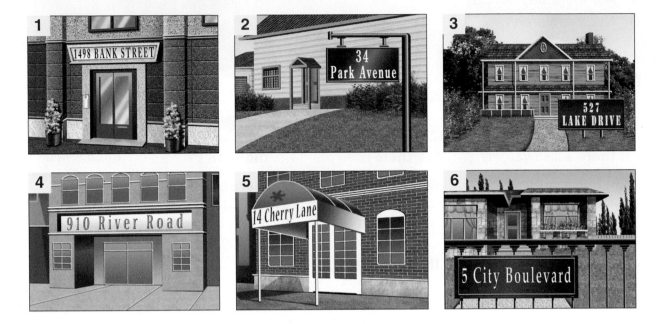

B   CD4 T12   Listen for the address. Circle *a* or *b*.

1. a. 207 John Lane   b. 270 John Lane

2. a. 15 City Street   b. 51 City Street

3. a. 1460 Third Avenue   b. 1640 Third Avenue

4. a. 40 Park Drive   b. 60 Park Drive

5. a. 309 Sun Boulevard   b. 319 Sun Boulevard

C   CD4 T13   Listen. Complete the addresses.

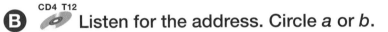

1. _____75_____ Sandy Boulevard   4. _____ Jones Road

2. _____ West Avenue   5. _____ North Drive

3. _____ Main Street   6. _____ Town Lane

D

CD4 T14
Listen. Listen and repeat.

A: I'm looking for an apartment.
B: Oh! There's an apartment for rent on my block.
A: What's the address?
B: It's 1630 River Street.
A: How much is the rent?
B: It's $700 a month.

E CD4 T15
Listen again. Circle *Yes* or *No*.

1. There is an apartment for rent on the woman's block.   Yes   (No)
2. The address is 1260 River Street.   Yes   No
3. The rent is $700 a month.   Yes   No

F PAIRS. Practice the conversation.

G PAIRS. Read the ads. Make new conversations.

A: I'm looking for an apartment.

B: Oh! There's an apartment for rent on my block.

A: What's the address?

B: It's _____.

A: How much is the rent?

B: It's _____ a month.

Conversation 1

1 bedroom
658 River Drive
$475/month

Conversation 2

3 bedrooms
1920 Park Lane
$975/month

Conversation 3

2 bedrooms
19 Bank Street
$750/month

Show what you know!

PAIRS. Ask: *What's your address?*
Use true or made-up information.

What's your address?   64 School Street.

Life Skills • Address an envelope

A Write the abbreviation.

Apt.   Ave.   Blvd.   Dr.   Ln.   Rd.   ~~St.~~

1. Street _____St._____   5. Road _____

2. Avenue _____   6. Boulevard _____

3. Drive _____   7. Apartment _____

4. Lane _____

B Read the envelope.

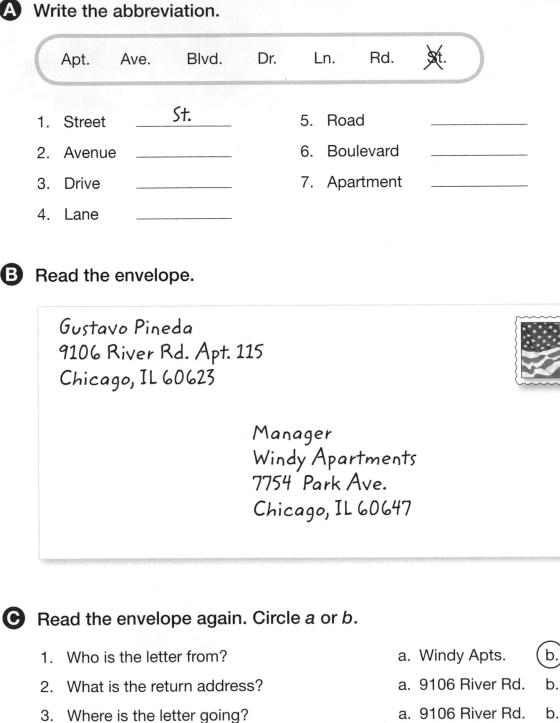

Gustavo Pineda
9106 River Rd. Apt. 115
Chicago, IL 60623

Manager
Windy Apartments
7754 Park Ave.
Chicago, IL 60647

C Read the envelope again. Circle *a* or *b*.

1. Who is the letter from?   a. Windy Apts.   (b.) Gustavo Pineda

2. What is the return address?   a. 9106 River Rd.   b. 7754 Park Ave.

3. Where is the letter going?   a. 9106 River Rd.   b. 7754 Park Ave.

4. What is the zip code for Windy Apartments?   a. 60647   b. 60326

5. What is Mr. Pineda's zip code?   a. 60623   b. 60547

D Write your answers. Use true or made-up information.

1. What's your first and last name? _____

2. What's your street address? _____

3. What's your city and state? _____

4. What's your zip code? _____

E PAIRS. Ask your classmate. Write your classmate's information.

1. What's your first and last name? _____

2. What's your street address? _____

3. What's your city and state? _____

4. What's your zip code? _____

F Address the envelope to your classmate.
Write your address for the return address.

A   CLASS. Look at each picture. What do you see?

CD4 T16

B   Listen to the story.

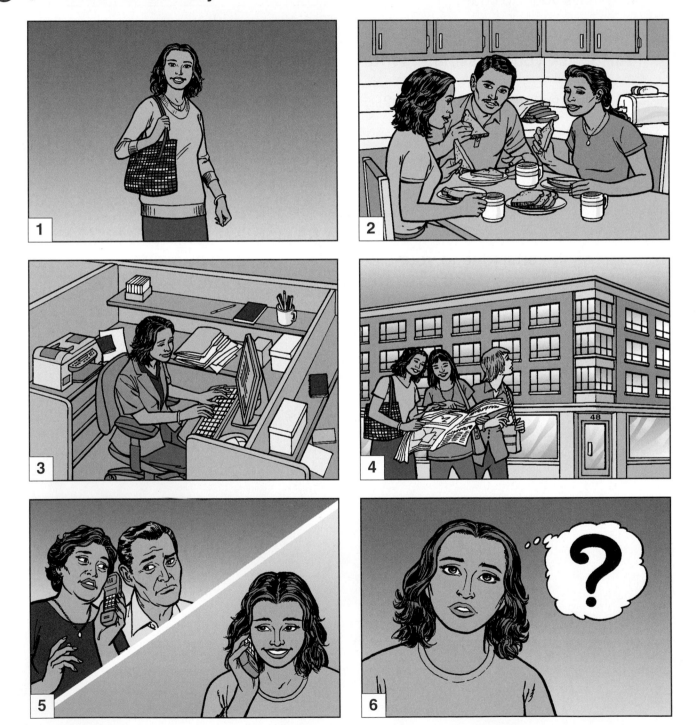

C Listen again and read.

> Alicia is 21 years old. She is single. Alicia lives with her older sister and her brother-in-law in California. Alicia has a good job. Now she wants to move to an apartment with her friends.
>
> But Alicia's parents are not happy. In their country, single people live with their families. In the United States, single people often live alone or with friends. What should Alicia do?

D Read the story again. Circle *Yes* or *No*.

1. Alicia lives with her parents and sister.   Yes   No
2. Alicia wants her sister to move to an apartment.   Yes   No
3. Alicia wants to live with her friends.   Yes   No
4. Alicia's parents want Alicia to live with her sister.   Yes   No
5. In the United States, single people live alone.   Yes   No

E GROUPS. Read the questions.
Talk about single people in your country.

1. Do single people live with their families?
2. Do single people live alone or with friends?

F Write about single people.

In my country, single people live _____.

They _____.

In the United States, single people live _____ _____.

They _____.

G GROUPS. Take turns. Read your sentences.

1 THE SOUNDS OF L AND R

A Read the words out loud softly.

lamp	living room	large
closet	boulevard	table

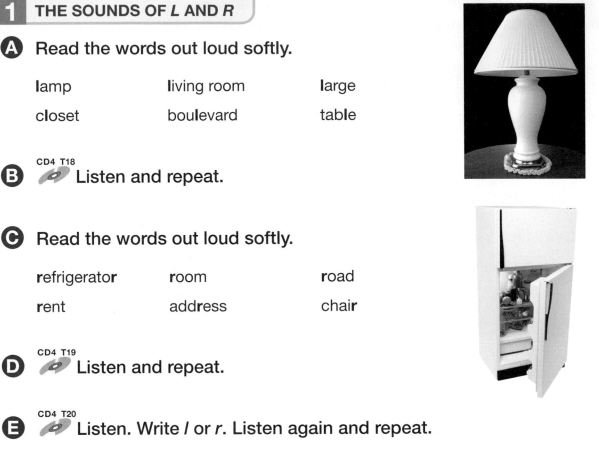

CD4 T18

B 🔊 Listen and repeat.

C Read the words out loud softly.

refrigerator	room	road
rent	address	chair

CD4 T19

D 🔊 Listen and repeat.

CD4 T20

E 🔊 Listen. Write *l* or *r*. Listen again and repeat.

1. ___arge
2. ___ent
3. ___amp
4. c___oset
5. chai___
6. ___efrigerato___
7. tab___e
8. add___ess
9. ___iving ___oom

F DICTATION. PAIRS. Student A, say three words from Exercise A. Student B, listen and write.

_____   _____   _____

G DICTATION. SAME PAIRS. Student B, say three words from Exercise C. Student A, listen and write.

_____   _____   _____

CD4 T21

A Listen. Listen and repeat.

bathroom	chair	kitchen	refrigerator	stove
bed	dining room	lamp	sink	table
bedroom	dryer	living room	sofa	washing machine

B Look at the picture. Write the five rooms. Use the words in Exercise A.

1. _____   2. _____

3. _____

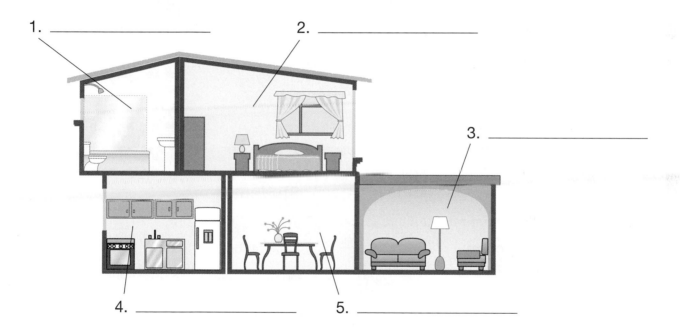

4. _____   5. _____

C PAIRS. Look at the picture.
Point to the furniture and appliances in each room. Say the words.

3 **SPEAKING**

Your classmate tells you: *I have a new apartment!*
What do you say?

a. There are two bedrooms.
b. What's new?
c. What's it like?

Show what you know!

1 TALK ABOUT ROOMS IN A HOME

A CD4 T22
Listen. Two friends are talking about an apartment.

B Draw the floor plan of a house or an apartment.
Write the names of the rooms.

C PAIRS. Show your classmate your floor plan. Say the name of each room.

2 ASK ABOUT AN APARTMENT

A CD4 T23
Listen. A woman is asking for information.

B ROLE PLAY. PAIRS.

ROLE PLAY 1	
Student A	**Student B**
There is an apartment with furniture for rent.	You are the landlord.
Ask about the kitchen:	Look at the apartment.
a stove, a refrigerator, a table and chairs	Answer Student A's questions.

ROLE PLAY 2	
Student B	**Student A**
There is an apartment with furniture for rent.	You are the landlord.
Ask about the living room:	Look at the apartment.
a sofa, a table, a chair, lamps	Answer Student B's questions.

3 READ AN AD FOR AN APARTMENT

A Read the ads.

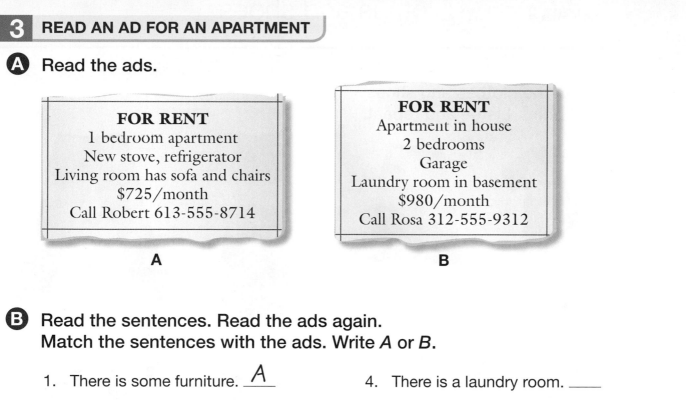

FOR RENT
1 bedroom apartment
New stove, refrigerator
Living room has sofa and chairs
$725/month
Call Robert 613-555-8714

A

FOR RENT
Apartment in house
2 bedrooms
Garage
Laundry room in basement
$980/month
Call Rosa 312-555-9312

B

B Read the sentences. Read the ads again.
Match the sentences with the ads. Write *A* or *B*.

1. There is some furniture. _A_

2. There are two bedrooms. ____

3. There is a new stove. ____

4. There is a laundry room. ____

5. The rent is $725 a month. ____

6. There is a garage. ____

4 WRITE ABOUT YOURSELF

Write an ad for your apartment or house.
Use true or made-up information.

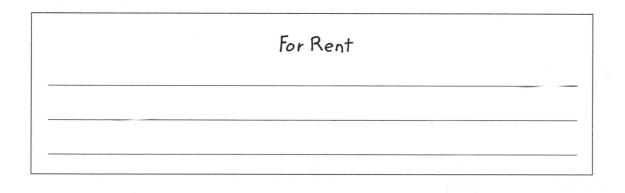

For Rent

_____

_____

_____

5 CONNECT   For your Team Project, go to page 214.

Let's go shopping.

8

Lesson 1   Clothes and shoes

CD4 T24

A   Look at the clothes and shoes.
Listen and point. Listen and repeat.

CD4 T25

B   Listen and read. Listen and repeat.

1. a T-shirt	4. jeans	7. socks	10. a sweater
2. a skirt	5. a jacket	8. shoes	11. pants
3. a dress	6. a blouse	9. a shirt	12. sneakers

C  Listen. Listen and repeat.

A: Let's go shopping!
I need a new jacket.
B: OK. I need shoes and pants.

D PAIRS. Practice the conversation.

E Listen and read the story.

> Aisha and Helen are classmates. They are on Third Avenue.
> The department store has a sale today. Aisha needs a new jacket.
> Helen needs new shoes. She wants a pair of pants, too.

F Read the story again. Circle *Yes* or *No*.

1. Aisha and Helen are classmates.   (Yes)   No
2. They are in school.   Yes   No
3. Aisha needs a new dress.   Yes   No
4. Helen needs shoes.   Yes   No
5. Helen wants a pair of socks.   Yes   No

Show what you know!

GROUPS. Play a game.
Say the clothes your classmates need.
Say the clothes you need.

I need a dress.

Silvia needs a dress. I need a jacket.

Silvia needs a dress. Adam needs a jacket. I need socks.

Silvia   Adam   Manuel

A CD4 T28
 Listen and point. Listen and repeat.

small   medium   large   extra large

B CD4 T29
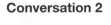 **Listen. Listen and repeat.**

A: Can I help you?

B: Do you have this shirt in a large?

A: Yes. Here you go.

B: Do you have these pants in a size 12?

A: No, I'm sorry. We don't.

C PAIRS. Practice the conversation.

D PAIRS. Look at the pictures.
Make new conversations.

A: Can I help you?

B: Do you have this _____ in a large?

A: Yes. Here you go.

B: Do you have these _____ in a size 12?

A: No, I'm sorry. We don't.

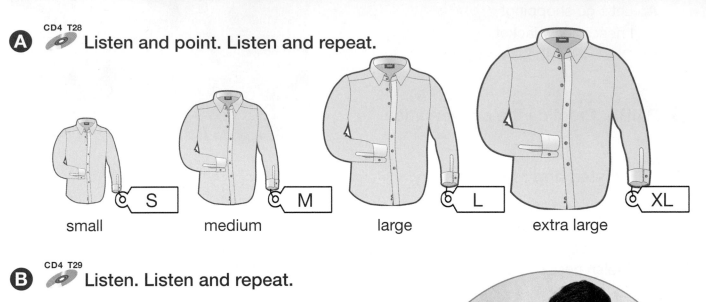

Conversation 1   **Conversation 2**   **Conversation 3**

E Read the sentences.

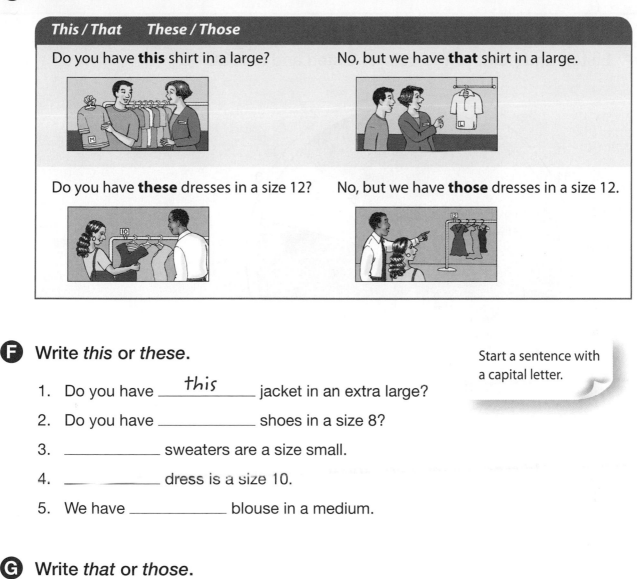

This / That   These / Those

Do you have **this** shirt in a large?   No, but we have **that** shirt in a large.

Do you have **these** dresses in a size 12?   No, but we have **those** dresses in a size 12.

F Write *this* or *these*.

> Start a sentence with a capital letter.

1. Do you have _____this_____ jacket in an extra large?

2. Do you have _____ shoes in a size 8?

3. _____ sweaters are a size small.

4. _____ dress is a size 10.

5. We have _____ blouse in a medium.

G Write *that* or *those*.

1. Do you have _____those_____ socks in a small?

2. Do you have _____ skirt in a large?

3. _____ shirt is a medium.

4. We have _____ T-shirts in an extra large.

5. _____ jeans are a size 12.

Show what you know!

PAIRS. Practice the conversations in Exercise E.

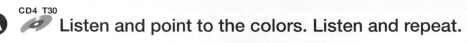

A   CD4 T30   Listen and point to the colors. Listen and repeat.

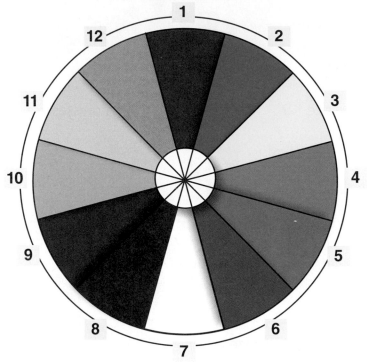

B   CD4 T31   Listen and read. Listen and repeat.

1. red	4. green	7. white	10. pink
2. blue	5. orange	8. black	11. beige
3. yellow	6. brown	9. purple	12. gray

C Write your answers.

1. What color is your favorite jacket?   _____

2. What color are your favorite pants?   _____

3. What color are your favorite shoes?   _____

4. What color is your favorite T-shirt?   _____

5. What is your favorite color?   _____

D PAIRS. Ask your classmate the questions in Exercise C.

E CD4 T32 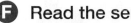 **Listen. Listen and repeat.**

A: Is Nina here?
B: Yes. She's over there.
   She's wearing a red blouse and black pants.
A: OK. Thanks.

F **Read the sentences.**

> **Adjective + noun**
>
> He's wearing a **white shirt**.
>
> She's wearing a **red blouse** and **black pants**.

G **Look at the pictures. Complete the sentences.**

| **Rob** | **Tina** | **Ling** | **Ed** |

1. Rob is wearing ___*a white shirt, gray pants, and black shoes*___.

2. Tina is wearing _____.

3. Ling is wearing _____.

4. Ed is wearing _____.

Show what you know!

CLASS. Take turns.
Say what one classmate is wearing.
Ask your classmates: *Who is it?*

She's wearing
a yellow T-shirt
and blue jeans.
Who is it?

Clara!

A CD4 T33 Listen and point. Listen and repeat.

  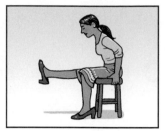

| It's too small. | It's too long. | They're too short. | They're too big. |

B CD4 T34 Listen for the problem. Circle *a* or *b*.

1. a. too small   (b.) too big   4. a. too small   b. too big

2. a. too short   b. too long   5. a. too short   b. too long

3. a. too small   b. too long   6. a. too small   b. too big

C CD4 T35 Listen. Listen and repeat.

A: I need to return a suit and some shoes.

B: What's the problem?

A: The suit is too big and the shoes are too small. Here's my receipt.

D CD4 T36 Listen again. Circle *Yes* or *No*.

1. The man is buying a suit and shoes.   Yes   No

2. The suit is too small.   Yes   No

3. The shoes are too small.   Yes   No

E   PAIRS. Practice the conversation.

F PAIRS. Look at the pictures. Make new conversations.

A: I need to return a _____ and some _____.

B: What's the problem?

A: The _____ is too _____ and the _____ are too _____.

Here's my receipt.

Conversation 1

Conversation 2

Show what you know!

GROUPS. Take turns.
Point to each picture. Say the problem.

The skirt is too small.

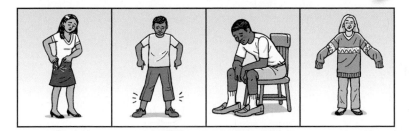

A Read the store ad.

Clothes Mart **Sale April 22–29**

$25.00 on sale

$39.00
on sale $25.50

all dresses on sale

$28.99
on sale $20.00

all men's suits
on sale

$49.99
on sale $39.99

B Read the ad again. Circle *a* or *b*.

1. When is the sale?   a. April 20–27   b. April 22–29

2. What is the regular price of the shoes?   a. $39.00   b. $25.50

3. How much are the shirts on sale?   a. $25.00   b. $20.00

4. How much can you save on pants?   a. $9.99   b. $8.99

5. How much can you save on jackets?   a. $10.00   b. $20.00

C Listen and read the ad. Listen again and write the information.

Dan's Clothing Store
Sale February 16-18

Regular price $25.99
ON SALE $15.99

Regular price $19.00
ON SALE _____

Regular price $12.50
ON SALE _____

Regular price $32.99
ON SALE _____

Regular price $30.99
ON SALE _____

Regular price $75.00
ON SALE _____

D Read the ad again. Circle *Yes* or *No*.

1. The sale starts on February 18.   Yes   (No)

2. Dresses are $25.99 on sale.   Yes   No

3. Pants are regularly $19.00.   Yes   No

4. On sale, T-shirts are $12.50.   Yes   No

5. Shoes and sneakers are on sale now.   Yes   No

6. Jackets are on sale until February 18.   Yes   No

A CLASS. Look at each picture. What do you see?

B CD4 T38 Listen to the story.

C 🔊 Listen again and read.

> My name is Yun. My wedding is in August. I want to wear a long white dress.
>
> In my country, people wear white for funerals. Women wear a red and green dress on their wedding day. My mother and grandmother want me to wear a red and green dress. What should I do?

D Read the story again. Circle *Yes* or *No*.

1. Yun's mother is getting married.	Yes	(No)
2. Yun is getting married in August.	Yes	No
3. She wants to wear a long white dress.	Yes	No
4. In Yun's country, women wear red and green wedding dresses.	Yes	No
5. Yun's grandmother wants Yun to wear a white dress.	Yes	No

E GROUPS. Read the questions.
Talk about the color of clothes in your country.

1. What color do people wear at funerals?
2. What color dress does a woman wear at her wedding?

F Write about clothes for funerals and weddings.

At weddings in my country, women wear _____.

They _____.

At funerals in my country, people wear _____.

They _____.

G GROUPS. Take turns. Read your sentences.

1   THE SOUNDS OF *S* AND *SH*

A Read the words out loud softly.

suit	**s**ize	dre**ss**
sale	**s**mall	pant**s**

CD4 T40

B Listen and repeat.

C Read the words out loud softly.

shoes	**sh**irt	**sh**ould
she	**sh**ort	**sh**opping

CD4 T41

D Listen and repeat.

CD4 T42

E Listen. Write *s* or *sh*. Listen again and repeat.

1. ___ize   4. ___irt   7. pant___

2. ___mall   5. ___opping   8. dre___ ___

3. ___e   6. ___ort   9. ___ale

F DICTATION. PAIRS. Student A, say three words from Exercise A. Student B, listen and write.

_____   _____   _____

G DICTATION. SAME PAIRS. Student B, say three words from Exercise C. Student A, listen and write.

_____   _____   _____

CD4 T43

A 🔘 **Listen. Listen and repeat.**

beige	brown	jacket	pink	skirt	sweater
black	dress	jeans	purple	shoes	T-shirt
blouse	gray	orange	red	sneakers	yellow
blue	green	pants	shirt	socks	white

B **PAIRS. Look at the picture. What colors do you see?**
Write the colors and the clothes.

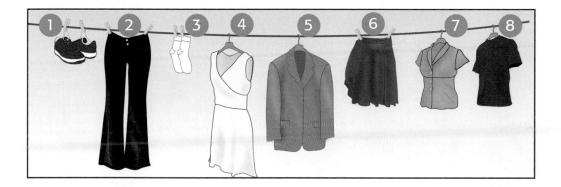

1. _red sneakers_

2. _____

3. _____

4. _a yellow dress_

5. _____

6. _____

7. _____

8. _____

3 **SPEAKING**

A sales assistant asks: *Can I help you?*
What do you say?

a. Do you have this shirt in a medium?

b. Thank you.

c. I'm wearing a red shirt and black pants.

🖥 **Go to the CD-ROM for more practice.**

Show what you know!

1 ASK ABOUT CLOTHING SIZE AND COLOR

CD4 T44

A Listen. A sales assistant is helping a customer.

B ROLE PLAY. PAIRS.

ROLE PLAY 1	
Student A	**Student B**
You are the customer.	You are the sales assistant.
Ask for:	Look at the picture.
a pair of blue sneakers	Help the customer.
an orange T-shirt, size large	

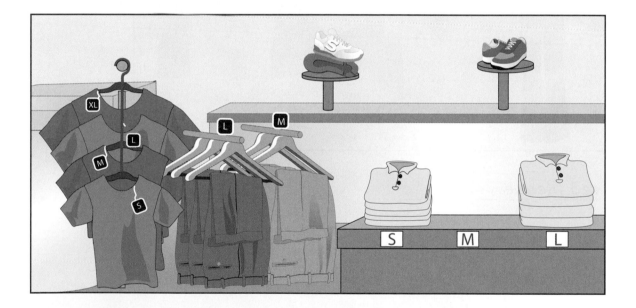

ROLE PLAY 2	
Student B	**Student A**
You are the customer.	You are the sales assistant.
Ask for:	Look at the picture.
beige pants, size medium	Help the customer.
a yellow sweater, size medium	

2 ASK A SALES ASSISTANT FOR HELP

A CD4 T45

Listen. A customer and a sales assistant are talking.

B PAIRS. Look at the pictures. The customer is asking about size and color. Write a conversation. Use *this, that, these,* or *those.*

A: _____

B: _____

A: _____

B: _____

A: _____

B: _____

C CLASS. Take turns. Role-play your conversation for the class.

3 CONNECT   For your Team Project, go to page 215.

9 Our Busy Lives

A CD5 T2
Look at the free-time activities.
Listen and point. Listen and repeat.

1

2

3

4

5

6

7

8

9

B CD5 T3
Listen and read. Listen and repeat.

1. use e-mail	4. play soccer	7. visit friends
2. play the guitar	5. exercise	8. go to the movies
3. listen to music	6. watch TV	9. read the newspaper

CD5 T4

C 🔘 Listen and point. Listen and repeat.

February						
Sunday	Monday	Tuesday	Wednesday	Thursday	Friday	Saturday
1	2	3	4	5	6	⑦
8	9	10	11	12	13	⑭
15	16	17	18	19	20	㉑
22	23	24	25	26	27	㉘

every Saturday
once a week

February						
Sunday	Monday	Tuesday	Wednesday	Thursday	Friday	Saturday
1	②	3	④	5	6	7
8	⑨	10	⑪	12	13	14
15	⑯	17	⑱	19	20	21
22	㉓	24	㉕	26	27	28

every Monday and Wednesday
twice a week

February						
Sunday	Monday	Tuesday	Wednesday	Thursday	Friday	Saturday
1	②	3	④	5	⑥	7
8	⑨	10	⑪	12	⑬	14
15	⑯	17	⑱	19	㉠	21
22	㉓	24	㉕	26	㉗	28

every Monday, Wednesday, and Friday
three times a week

CD5 T5

D 🔘 Listen. Listen and repeat.

A: What do you do in your free time?
B: I listen to music. What do you do?
A: I play soccer.
B: How often?
A: Once a week.

E PAIRS. Practice the conversation.

F PAIRS. Make new conversations.
Use the free-time activites on page 146.

A: What do you do in your free time?

B: I _____. What do you do?

A: I _____.

B: How often?

A: _____.

Show what you know!

GROUPS. Take turns.
Ask: *What do you do in your free time?*
How often?

What do you do in your free time?

I play soccer.

How often?

Once a week.

A Listen. Listen and repeat.

A: Hello?
B: Hi, Sara. It's Bill. Are you busy?
A: I'm watching a movie. Can I call you later?
B: No problem. Bye.
A: Goodbye.

B Listen again. Circle *Yes* or *No*.

1.	Sara and Bill are on the phone.	(Yes)	No
2.	Sara is busy now.	Yes	No
3.	Sara is reading the newspaper now.	Yes	No
4.	Bill is busy now.	Yes	No

C PAIRS. Practice the conversation.

D Listen and read the story.

It's Wednesday evening. Sara is home. She has free time now. She wants to talk to Bill. She calls his cell phone. Bill's cell phone is off. He is in English class. Sara needs to call him later.

E Read the story again. Circle *Yes* or *No*.

1.	Sara is at work.	Yes	(No)
2.	Sara is busy.	Yes	No
3.	Bill is calling Sara.	Yes	No
4.	Bill is in English class.	Yes	No
5.	Sara needs to call Bill later.	Yes	No

F Read the sentences.

Present continuous	
I **am** watch**ing** a movie.	I**'m** watch**ing** a movie.
You **are** watch**ing** a movie.	You**'re** watch**ing** a movie.
He **is** watch**ing** a movie.	He**'s** watch**ing** a movie.
She **is** watch**ing** a movie.	She**'s** watch**ing** a movie.
We **are** watch**ing** a movie.	We**'re** watch**ing** a movie.
They **are** watch**ing** a movie.	They**'re** watch**ing** a movie.

G Write the answers. Use contractions.

> Start a sentence with a capital letter.
>
> End a sentence with a period.

1. **A:** What are you doing?

   B: (I / listen to music) _I'm listening to music._

2. **A:** What is Mrs. White doing?

   B: (she / go to the library) _____

3. **A:** What are you doing?

   B: (we / visit my sister) _____

4. **A:** What's Rob doing?

   B: (he / watch a movie on TV) _____

5. **A:** What are Sheena and David doing?

   B: (they / read the newspaper) _____

H ^{CD5 T9} Listen and check your answers. Listen and repeat.

Show what you know!

You're exercising!

GROUPS. Look at page 146.
Take turns.
Student A, choose an activity. Do the actions.
Your classmates say: *You're _____!*

A CD5 T10   Listen and point to the household chores. Listen and repeat.

B CD5 T11 Listen and read. Listen and repeat.

1. walk the dog	4. pay bills	7. do homework
2. make dinner	5. clean the house	8. take out the garbage
3. do the laundry	6. talk on the phone	9. wash the car

C Look at the words in Exercise B. What do you do at home?

_____   _____   _____

_____   _____   _____

D PAIRS. Tell your classmate your words in Exercise C.

E CD5 T12 Listen. Listen and repeat.

A: Hello?

B: Hi, Mom. Are the kids helping you?

A: Well . . .

B: Is Alex doing the laundry?

A: Yes, he is.

B: Is Tina washing the car?

A: No, she isn't. She's talking on the phone!

F Read the sentences.

Present continuous: *Yes/No* questions and short answers		
Are you do**ing** the laundry?	Yes, **I am**.	No, **I'm not**.
Is Alex do**ing** the laundry?	Yes, **he is**.	No, **he isn't**.
Is Tina do**ing** the laundry?	Yes, **she is**.	No, **she isn't**.
Are the kids do**ing** the laundry?	Yes, **they are**.	No, **they aren't**.

isn't = is + not
aren't = are + not

End a question with a question mark.

G Write the questions.

1. (your mother / make dinner) *Is your mother making dinner?*

2. (Tom and his friend / play soccer) _____

3. (you / wash the car) _____

4. (Ana / do homework) _____

5. (your friends / talk on the phone) _____

Show what you know!

GROUPS OF 3. Look at page 150.
Take turns.
Student A, choose an activity. Do the actions.
Your classmates ask *Yes/No* questions.

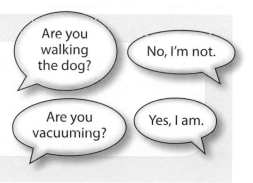

Are you walking the dog?

No, I'm not.

Are you vacuuming?

Yes, I am.

Present continuous negative

A Look at the workplace activities.
Listen and point. Listen and repeat.

B Listen and read. Listen and repeat.

1. work on the computer	4. take orders	7. answer the phone
2. help a customer	5. count money	8. drive a truck
3. take a break	6. look for something	9. fix cars

C PAIRS. Point to a picture in Exercise A. Say the workplace activity.

D 🔊 **CD5 T15** Listen. Listen and repeat.

A: Where is John? Is he helping a customer?
B: No, he's not helping a customer.
   He's looking for something.
A: OK. I'll see him later.

E Read the sentences.

Present continuous negative
I'**m not** help**ing** a customer.
He'**s not** help**ing** a customer.
She'**s not** help**ing** a customer.
We'**re not** help**ing** a customer.
They'**re not** help**ing** a customer.

I'm not = I am not
She's not = She is not
We're not = We are not

Start a sentence with a capital letter.

F Complete the sentences. Write the correct verb form.

1. (he / not fix) _He's not fixing_ a car. He's counting money.

2. (I / not work) _____ on the computer. I'm on the phone.

3. (they / not take) _____ a break. They're helping customers.

4. (she / not take) _____ orders. She's looking for something.

5. (we / not drive) _____ trucks today. We're taking orders.

G 🔊 **CD5 T16** Listen and check your answers. Listen and repeat.

Show what you know!

GROUPS. Look at page 152. Take turns.
Student A, point to a picture.
Ask about a different action.
Your classmates say the correct action.

Picture 3.
Is she answering
the phone?

She's not
answering the
phone. She's
taking a break.

A   CD5 T17   Listen and read the message.

Message

For   Mr. Green   Date   June 9

Caller   Victor Mata   Phone   917-555-9876

Message   He's not coming to work today.

B   Read the message again. Circle *Yes* or *No*.

1. The message is for Mr. Green.   Yes   No

2. Victor is calling Mr. Green.   Yes   No

3. Victor is coming to work today.   Yes   No

C   CD5 T18   Listen and read the message.

Message

For   Ms. Lark   Date   October 1

Caller   Jane Black   Phone

Message   She's not coming to her appointment today.
Please call her at 212-555-4366.

D   Read the message again. Circle *Yes* or *No*.

1. The message is for Ms. Black.   Yes   No

2. Jane Black is calling Ms. Lark.   Yes   No

3. Jane Black is coming to her appointment today.   Yes   No

E 🔘 Listen. Write the message.

Message

For _Dave_____   **Date** _January 15_____

Caller _Carlos_____   **Phone** _212- 555-0123_____

Message _____

_____

_____

F PAIRS. Compare your messages.

G 🔘 Listen. Write the message.

Message

For _Mr. Cohen_____   **Date** _November 15_____

Caller _Mira Lopez_____   **Phone** _did not give number_

Message _____

_____

_____

H PAIRS. Compare your messages.

Alfonso's story

A CLASS. Look at each picture. What do you see?

CD5 T21

B Listen to the story.

C 🎧 Listen again and read.

My name is Alfonso. I have two children. They are busy every weekend with their friends. They talk on the phone and go shopping. They play sports and watch TV.

On weekends, my wife and I eat alone. Our children don't sit down with us to eat. In my country families eat together on weekends. Then they spend time relaxing and talking.

What do you do on weekends? Do you spend time with your family or friends?

D Read the story again. Circle *Yes* or *No*.

1. Alfonso's two children are busy every weekend.	(Yes)	No
2. On weekends, his family eats together.	Yes	No
3. In Alfonso's country, families eat together on weekends.	Yes	No
4. Alfonso spends a lot of time with his children on weekends.	Yes	No

E GROUPS. Read the questions. Talk about families in your country.

1. Are children busy on weekends? What do they do?

2. When do families eat together?

3. When do families relax together?

F Write about what families do on weekends.

In my country, children _____.

They _____.

In my country, families _____.

They _____.

G GROUPS. Take turns. Read your sentences.

1   THE SOUNDS OF *A* (*DATE*) AND *E* (*YES*)

 A Read the words out loud softly.

date	make	take
play	name	later
late	today	newspaper

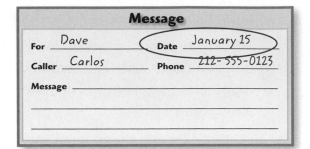

Message
For ___Dave___   Date ___January 15___
Caller ___Carlos___   Phone ___212- 555-0123___
Message _____

CD5 T23
 B 💿 Listen and repeat.

 C Read the words out loud softly.

exercise	every	Wednesday
yes	spend	message
hello	help	sentence

CD5 T24
 D 💿 Listen and repeat.

CD5 T25
 E 💿 Listen. Write *a* or *e*. Listen again and repeat.

1. __very
2. l__ter
3. n__me

4. m__ssage
5. d__te
6. newsp__per

7. h__lp
8. W__dnesday
9. t__ke

F DICTATION. PAIRS. Student A, say three words from Exercise A. Student B, listen and write.

_____   _____   _____

G DICTATION. SAME PAIRS. Student B, say three words from Exercise C. Student A, listen and write.

_____   _____   _____

CD5 T26

A Listen. Listen and repeat.

clean the house	help a customer	take a break
do homework	listen to music	take orders
drive a truck	make dinner	take out the garbage
exercise	pay bills	visit friends
go to the movies	play soccer	work on the computer

B Circle three free-time activities in Exercise A. Write the words.

_____   _____   _____

C Underline three workplace activities in Exercise A. Write the words.

_____   _____   _____

D Check (✓) three household chores in Exercise A. Write the words.

_____   _____   _____

3 SPEAKING

Your classmate asks: *What household chores do you do at home?*
What do you say?

a. I use e-mail.
b. I take out the garbage.
c. I visit friends.

Go to the CD-ROM for more practice.

Show what you know!

1 SAY WHAT SOMEONE IS DOING

PAIRS. Find the differences.
Ask *Yes/No* questions.
Student A, cover Student B's picture.
Student B, cover Student A's picture.

Is Fang taking an order?

Fang isn't taking an order. She's working on the computer.

Student A, look at this picture.

Mario   Fang   Alice   Alex

Student B, look at this picture.

Mario   Fang   Alex   Alice

2 TALK ABOUT YOUR SCHEDULE

A 🎧 Listen. Barbara is talking about her weekly activities.

Monday	Tuesday	Wednesday	Thursday	Friday	Saturday	Sunday
Work	Work	Work	Work	Work	Soccer 9:00 - 11:00	
						Lunch with family 1:00
English class 6:00 - 9:00		English class 6:00 - 9:00		Movies 8:00		

B What do you do every week? Write your activities.

Monday	Tuesday	Wednesday	Thursday	Friday	Saturday	Sunday

C PAIRS. Tell your classmate about your activities.

3 WRITE ABOUT YOURSELF

Write about yourself. Use true or made-up information.

1. My name is _____.

2. Once a week I _____.

3. Every _____ I _____.

4. On weekends I _____.

4 CONNECT   For your Team Project, go to page 216.

CD5 T28

A   Look at the places.
Listen and point. Listen and repeat.

CD5 T29

B   Listen and read. Listen and repeat.

1. a bank	4. a restaurant	7. a supermarket
2. a drugstore	5. an ATM	8. a computer store
3. a gas station	6. a hospital	9. a parking lot

C Listen and look at the map. Listen and point to the streets.

Bank	Drugstore	Hospital

FIRST STREET

CENTRAL AVENUE

Gas station

MAIN AVENUE

Restaurant

GRAND AVENUE

Parking lot

SECOND STREET

Supermarket

Computer store

ATM

THIRD STREET

D Listen. Listen and repeat.

A: Excuse me. Is there a bank near here?

B: Yes. There's a bank on the corner of First Street and Central Avenue.

A: Thank you.

E PAIRS. Practice the conversation.

F PAIRS. Look at the map. Make a new conversation. Ask about the ATM.

A: Excuse me. Is there an _____ near here?

an ATM

B: Yes. There's an _____ on the corner of _____

and _____.

A: Thank you.

Show what you know!

GROUPS. Take turns. Ask about places on the map.

Is there a bank?

There's a bank on the corner of First Street and Central Avenue.

A CD5 T32 Listen and point to the places. Listen and repeat.

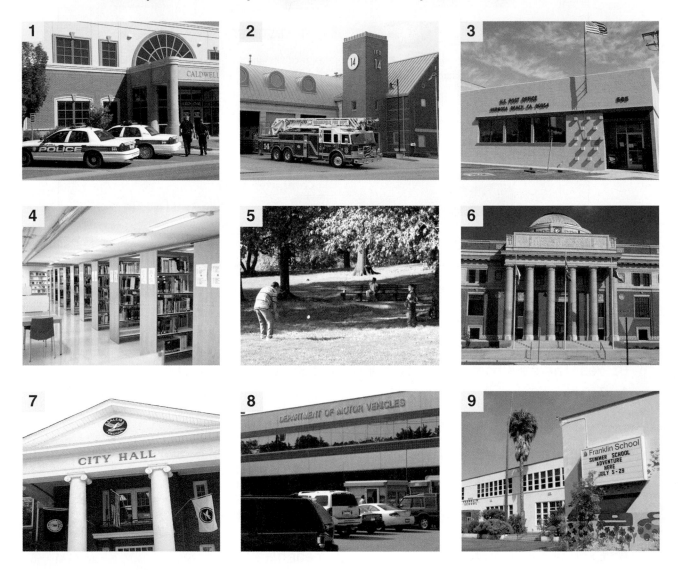

B CD5 T33 Listen and read. Listen and repeat.

1. police station
2. fire station
3. post office
4. library
5. park
6. court house
7. City Hall
8. Department of Motor Vehicles (DMV)
9. school

C PAIRS. Point to a place in Exercise A. Say the place.

CD5 T34

D Listen. Listen and repeat.

A: Excuse me. Where is City Hall?

B: It's between the police station and the DMV.

A: Between the police station and the DMV?

B: Yes. And it's across from the park.

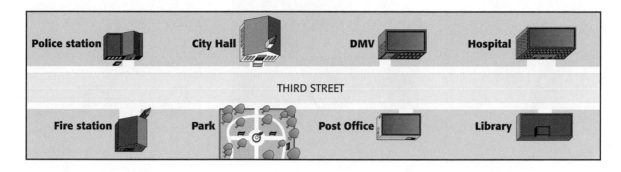

E Read the sentences.

Between/Across from	
City Hall is **between** the police station and the DMV.	It's **across from** the park.
The post office is **between** the park and the library.	It's **across from** the DMV.

F Look at the map in Exercise D. Complete the sentences.

1. The DMV is between _the hospital and City Hall_ .

2. The hospital is across from _____ .

3. The park is between _____ .

4. The fire station is across from _____ .

Show what you know!

GROUPS. Look at the map in Exercise D.
Take turns. Ask: *Where is the _____?*
Use *between* and *across from* in your answers.

Where is the park?

It's across from City Hall.

Types of transportation

A Look at the types of transportation.
Listen and point. Listen and repeat.

B Listen and read. Listen and repeat.

1. walk	4. ride a bike	7. take the subway
2. drive	5. take the bus	8. take a taxi
3. carpool	6. take the train	9. take a ferry

C PAIRS. Point to a picture in Exercise A. Say the type of transportation.

D Listen. Listen and repeat.

A: Hi, Ed. Where are you going?
B: I'm going to my English class.
A: Oh. How do you get to school?
B: I take the bus.

E PAIRS. Practice the conversation.

F CD5 T38

Listen and read the story.

Ed is a student. He studies English. He goes to school on Monday and Wednesday morning. Ed's school is on the corner of White Street and Second Avenue. He takes the bus to school.

G Read the story again. Circle *Yes* or *No*.

1. Ed is a student.   (Yes)   No

2. He studies Spanish.   Yes   No

3. Ed goes to school on Monday.   Yes   No

4. He takes the subway to school.   Yes   No

Show what you know!

PAIRS. Ask: *How do you get to _____?* Write the information.

Place	Type of Transportation
1. school	
2. the supermarket	
3. the post office	

Manny takes a bus to school. He rides a bike to work.

CLASS. Talk about your classmate.

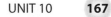

Life Skills • Ask for and give directions

A Listen to your teacher say the directions. Listen again and repeat.

Turn left. Go straight. Turn right.

CD5 T39

B Listen. Check (✓) the directions you hear.

1. ☐ Go straight.
   ☐ Turn left.
   ☐ Turn right.

2. ☐ Go straight.
   ☐ Turn left.
   ☐ Turn right.

3. ☐ Go straight.
   ☐ Turn left.
   ☐ Turn right.

4. ☐ Go straight.
   ☐ Turn left.
   ☐ Turn right.

5. ☐ Go straight.
   ☐ Turn left.
   ☐ Turn right.

6. ☐ Go straight.
   ☐ Turn left.
   ☐ Turn right.

CD5 T40

C Listen for the directions. Write each place on the map.

~~gas station~~   hospital   drugstore   post office   school

a. _____ Bank Street
b. _____
c. _____
d. gas station
Church Street
First Avenue
Second Avenue
Third Avenue
YOU ARE HERE
e. _____
White Street

D **Listen. Listen and repeat.**

A: Excuse me. Where is the train station?

B: It's on Park Street. Go straight for one block.
Then turn left on Park Street.

A: Thanks a lot!

CD5 T42

E **Listen again. Circle *Yes* or *No*.**

1. The woman is going to the gas station.   Yes   (No)

2. The woman should go straight for one block.   Yes   No

3. The woman should turn right on Park Street.   Yes   No

F **PAIRS. Practice the conversation.**

G **PAIRS. Look at the maps. Make new conversations. Ask about the police station and the post office.**

A: Excuse me. Where is the _____?

B: It's on _____. Go straight for _____.

Then turn _____.

A: Thanks a lot!

Conversation 1

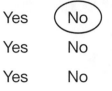

Bank Street

Police Station

White Street

First Avenue

Second Avenue

YOU ARE HERE

Main Street

Conversation 2

YOU ARE HERE

Bank Street

White Street

First Avenue

Post Office

Second Avenue

Main Street

CD5 T43

A 🔘 Look at the traffic signs.
Listen and point. Listen and repeat.

1
stop sign

2
no left turn

3
walk / don't walk

4
train crossing

5
no parking

6
no U-turn

7
one-way street

8
speed limit
25 miles per hour

9
yield

B PAIRS. Point to a sign. Read the sign.

C Listen. Write *1, 2, 3, 4, 5, 6* in the order you hear.

a. _____

b. _____

c. ___1___

d. _____

e. _____

f. _____

D PAIRS. Compare your answers.

E Listen for the sign. Circle *a* or *b*.

1. (a.) ONE WAY   b. [no U-turn sign]

2. a. [walk sign]   b. [hand sign]

3. a. [no parking sign]   b. STOP

4. a. ONE WAY   b. SPEED LIMIT 25

5. a. [railroad crossing sign]   b. YIELD

A CLASS. Look at each picture. What do you see?

B CD5 T46 Listen to the story.

C 💿 Listen again and read.

My name is Hong. In my country, I worked in a restaurant. I was a cook. Here in the United States, I'm a cook, too.

I have a dream. I want to open my own restaurant here. I need to go to City Hall for a business license. I need to go to the bank for a loan. I need to show the bank my business plan.

Soon my family and friends can eat at my new restaurant!

D Read the story again. Circle *Yes* or *No*.

1.	Hong wants to open his own supermarket.	Yes	No
2.	He needs to go to the police station for a license.	Yes	No
3.	Hong needs money.	Yes	No
4.	He has a business plan.	Yes	No

E GROUPS. Read the questions. Talk about dreams.

1. What is your dream job?

2. Do you want to have your own business? What is your dream?

F Write about your dream job or your dream business.

My dream is to _____.

I need to _____.

I need to _____.

G GROUPS. Take turns. Read your sentences.

1   **THE SOUNDS OF A (BANK) AND I (LIBRARY)**

A   Read the words out loud softly.

bank	gas	taxi
answer	thanks	family

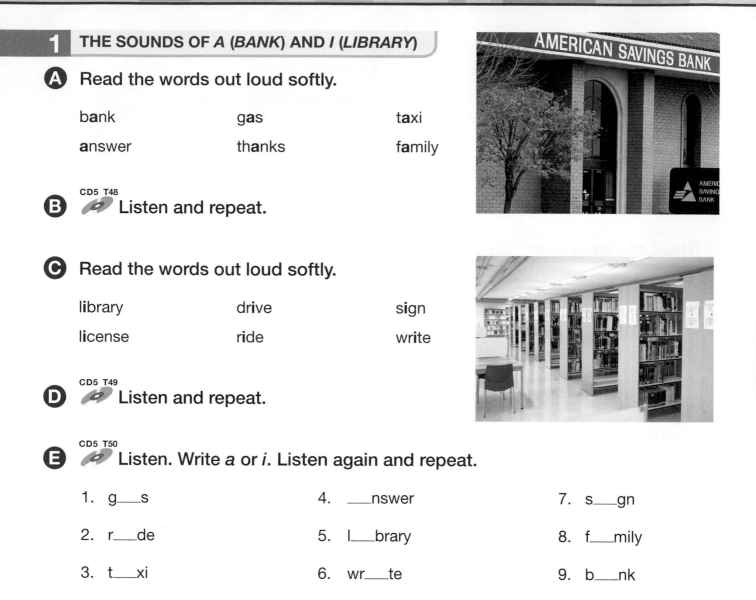

CD5 T48

B   Listen and repeat.

C   Read the words out loud softly.

library	drive	sign
license	ride	write

CD5 T49

D   Listen and repeat.

CD5 T50

E   Listen. Write *a* or *i*. Listen again and repeat.

1. g___s

2. r___de

3. t___xi

4. ___nswer

5. l___brary

6. wr___te

7. s___gn

8. f___mily

9. b___nk

F   DICTATION. PAIRS. Student A, say three words from Exercise A.
Student B, listen and write.

_____   _____   _____

G   DICTATION. SAME PAIRS. Student B, say three words from Exercise C.
Student A, listen and write.

_____   _____   _____

A  CD5 T51 Listen. Listen and repeat.

ATM	drugstore	hospital	school
DMV	gas station	library	supermarket

B Complete the sentences. Use the words in Exercise A.

1. **A:** I need money.

   B: Go to the _____ATM_____.

2. **A:** I need food.

   B: Go to the _____.

3. **A:** I need gas.

   B: Go to the _____.

4. **A:** I need a driver's license.

   B: Go to the _____.

5. **A:** I need soap.

   B: Go to the _____.

6. **A:** I need some books.

   B: Go to the _____.

C Write the type of transportation.

1. _____   2. _____   3. _____   4. _____

3 | **SPEAKING**

Your classmate asks: *How do you get to work?*
What do you say?

a. Go straight.
b. It's next to the school.
c. I drive.

Go to the CD-ROM for more practice.

1 GIVE DIRECTIONS TO PLACES

A CD5 T52 Listen. A woman is giving directions.

B ROLE PLAY. PAIRS.

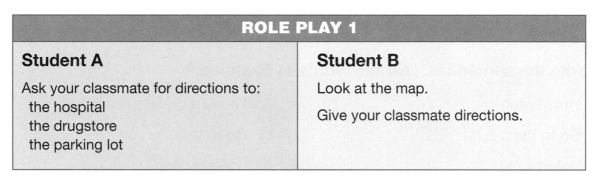

ROLE PLAY 1	
Student A	**Student B**

Ask your classmate for directions to:
  the hospital
  the drugstore
  the parking lot
	Look at the map.
	
	Give your classmate directions.

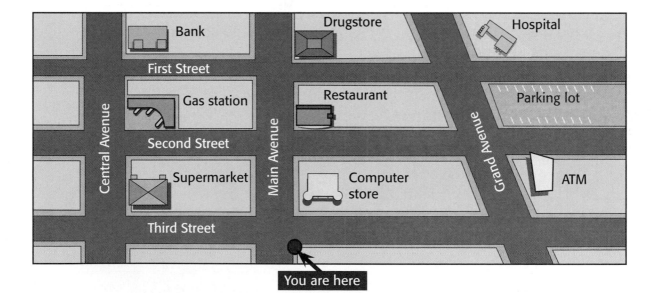

ROLE PLAY 2	
Student B	**Student A**

Ask your classmate for directions to:
  the bank
  the gas station
  the computer store
	Look at the map.
	
	Give your classmate directions.

READ AND UNDERSTAND MAPS

A Look at the map.
Find the hospital, the bank, the parking lot, and the park.

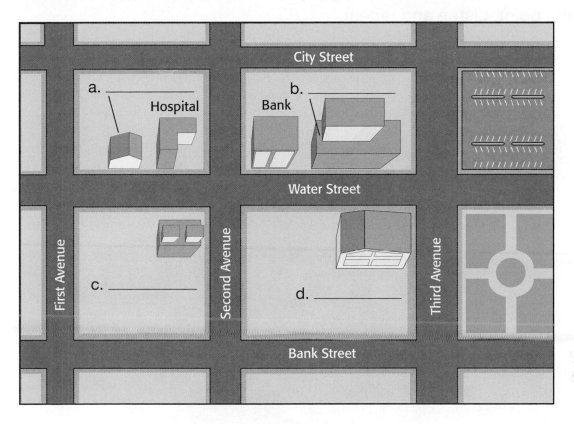

B Read the sentences. Write the places on the map.

1. The **police station** is next to the hospital.
2. The **school** is across from the parking lot and next to the bank.
3. The **drugstore** is across from the hospital.
4. The **library** is across from the school and across from the park.

C PAIRS. Compare answers.

3 CONNECT   For your Team Project, go to page 217.

A CD6 T2 Look at the parts of the man's body.
Listen and point. Listen and repeat.

B CD6 T3 Listen and read. Listen and repeat.

1. ear	5. stomach	9. hand
2. eye	6. knee	10. arm
3. nose	7. foot / feet	11. chest
4. neck	8. leg	12. shoulder

C **Listen. Listen and repeat.**

A: Hello. Westside Health Clinic.
B: I'd like to make an appointment, please.
A: What's the problem?
B: My back hurts.
A: Can you come in at 4:00?
B: Yes, I can.

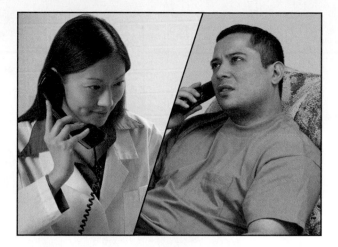

D PAIRS. Practice the conversation.

E PAIRS. Make new conversations.
Use the words on page 178.

A: Hello. Westside Health Clinic.

B: I'd like to make an appointment, please.

A: What's the problem?

B: My _____ hurts.

A: Can you come in at 4:00?

B: Yes, I can.

Your neck hurts.

Show what you know!

GROUPS. Play a guessing game.
Take turns.
Student A, touch the part of your body that hurts.
Your classmates say: *Your _____ hurts.*

A Your teacher will say and do each action. Listen and watch.

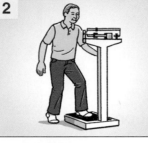

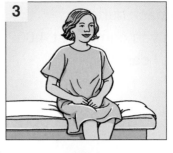

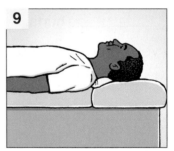

B Your teacher will say and do each action.
Do each action with your teacher.

C Your teacher will say each action.
Say and do each action.

D CD6 T5 Listen and read. Listen and repeat.

1. Take off your jacket.	4. Breathe in.	7. Open your mouth.
2. Step on the scale.	5. Breathe out.	8. Roll up your sleeves.
3. Sit on the table.	6. Look straight ahead.	9. Lie down.

E **Listen. Listen and repeat.**

    A: Hello. I'm Dr. Medina. Why are you here today?
    B: I'm here for a checkup.
    A: OK. Sit on the table. Look straight ahead.

F **PAIRS. Practice the conversation.**

CD6 T7

G **Listen and read the story.**

> Sonia gets a checkup every year. She has an appointment
> on Monday. She goes to the health clinic. The doctor
> checks her. Sonia follows the doctor's instructions. The
> doctor says, "You are in good health."

H **Read the story again. Circle *Yes* or *No*.**

1. Sonia gets a checkup every year.	(Yes)	No
2. Sonia has a doctor's appointment on Tuesday.	Yes	No
3. Her appointment is at the school.	Yes	No
4. The doctor gives Sonia instructions.	Yes	No
5. She has health problems.	Yes	No

Please sit on
the table.

Show what you know!

GROUPS. Look at page 180.
Take turns.
Student A, you are the doctor. Give instructions.
Your classmates are the patients. They do the actions.

Common health problems • *Should*

A Look at the health problems.
Listen and point. Listen and repeat.

B Listen and read. Listen and repeat.

1. a headache	4. a toothache	7. a fever
2. a backache	5. a cold	8. the flu
3. a stomachache	6. a cough	9. a sore throat

C PAIRS. Take turns. Point to a picture. Say the problem.
Use *She has* _____. and *He has* _____.

D Listen. Listen and repeat.

CD6 T10

A: What's the matter?
B: I have a cold.
A: You should drink a lot of liquids.
B: OK.
A: Get well soon!

E Read the sentences.

1

You should drink a lot of liquids.

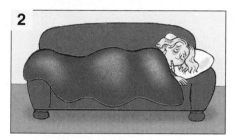

2

You should get a lot of rest.

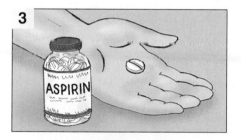

3

You should take an aspirin.

4

You should stay home from work.

F PAIRS. Make new conversations.
Use the suggestions in Exercise E.

Show what you know!

GROUPS. Look at the problems on page 182.
Take turns.
Student A, say a problem.
Your classmates give a suggestion.

I have a headache.

You should take an aspirin.

CD6 T11

A Look at the emergencies.
Listen and point. Listen and repeat.

CD6 T12

B Listen and read. Listen and repeat.

> 1. My friend is having a heart attack.
> 2. There was a car accident.
> 3. There is a building on fire.
> 4. Someone robbed my house.

C PAIRS. Take turns. Point to a picture. Say the emergency.

D  Listen. Listen and repeat.

A: 911. What's your emergency?
B: My friend is having a heart attack.
A: Where are you?
B: 1038 Park Avenue in Circle City.
A: What's the cross street?
B: River Road.

CD6 T14
E Listen again. Circle *Yes* or *No*.

1. There is an emergency.   (Yes)   No
2. Someone is having a heart attack.   Yes   No
3. The men are on Circle Avenue.   Yes   No
4. The men are in Park City.   Yes   No

F PAIRS. Practice the conversation.

G PAIRS. Make new conversations. Use the emergencies on page 184.
Use real or made-up street names.

A: 911. What's your emergency?

B: _____

A: Where are you?

B: _____

A: What's the cross street?

B: _____

Show what you know!

CLASS. Take turns.
Perform one of your conversations in Exercise G.

911. What's your emergency?

There was a car accident.

A CD6 T15 **Listen and point. Listen and repeat.**

cough syrup

aspirin

prescription medicine

1 teaspoon

tablets

capsules

every 4 hours

every 6 hours

twice a day

B CD6 T16 **Listen for the information about each medicine. Circle *a* or *b*.**

Conversation 1

1. The woman is taking ____.

   a. aspirin

   b. cough syrup

2. She should take ____.

   a. 2 teaspoons every hour

   b. 2 teaspoons every 4 hours

Conversation 2

3. The man is taking ____.

   a. prescription medicine

   b. cough syrup

4. The directions say take 1 capsule ____.

   a. two times a day with food

   b. every hour with food

C Read the directions on the label.

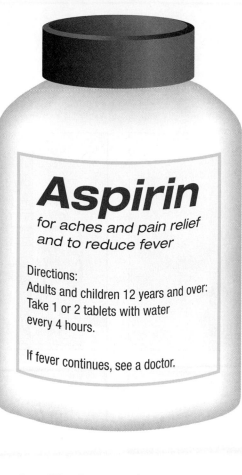

Aspirin
*for aches and pain relief
and to reduce fever*

Directions:
Adults and children 12 years and over:
Take 1 or 2 tablets with water
every 4 hours.

If fever continues, see a doctor.

D Read the directions again. Circle *a* or *b*.

1. The medicine is for _____.

   a. coughs   b. pain and fever

2. Ben has a headache and a fever. He should _____.

   a. take some aspirin   b. take some cough syrup

3. Ben is 25 years old. He should _____.

   a. take 2 tablets   b. take 3 tablets

4. Ben should take the aspirin _____.

   a. every 2 hours   b. every 4 hours

5. After five days, Ben still has a fever. He should _____.

   a. take more aspirin   b. see a doctor

Mariam's story

A CLASS. Look at each picture. What do you see?

B CD6 T17 Listen to the story.

C 🔊 **Listen again and read.**

My name is Mariam. I'm 45 years old. In my country, people go to a doctor when they are sick.

Now my family and I are in the United States. My daughter is 23 years old. She says that women here have a checkup every year. She says it's important.

But I feel healthy. I don't feel sick. Why should I go to a doctor?

D **Read the story again. Circle _Yes_ or _No_.**

1.	Mariam is 40 years old.	Yes	**No**
2.	In Mariam's country, healthy people go to a doctor.	Yes	No
3.	In the U.S., women have a checkup every year.	Yes	No
4.	Mariam is sick and wants to go to a doctor.	Yes	No

E **GROUPS. Read the questions.**
Talk about going to a doctor in your country.

1. How often do people go to a doctor?

2. Why do they go to a doctor?

F **Write about going to a doctor.**

In my country, people go to the doctor _____ .

They _____ .

In the United States, people _____ .

They _____ .

G **GROUPS. Take turns. Read your sentences.**

1   THE SOUNDS OF *E* (*SLEEP*) AND *I* (*IN*)

A   Read the words out loud softly.

sleep	week	feel
knee	teeth	feet
see	sleeves	street

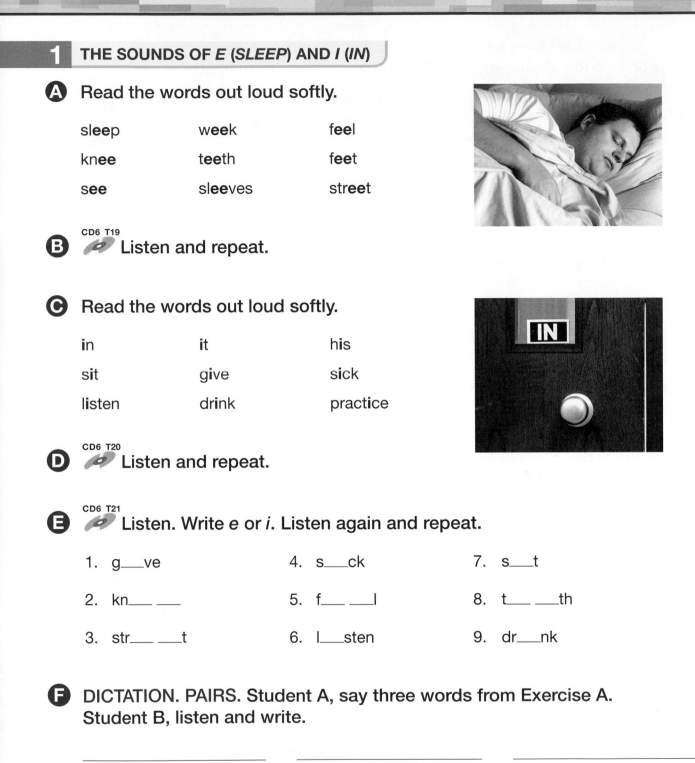

CD6 T19

B   Listen and repeat.

C   Read the words out loud softly.

in	it	his
sit	give	sick
listen	drink	practice

CD6 T20

D   Listen and repeat.

CD6 T21

E   Listen. Write *e* or *i*. Listen again and repeat.

1. g__ve
2. kn__ __
3. str__ __t
4. s__ck
5. f__ __l
6. l__sten
7. s__t
8. t__ __th
9. dr__nk

F   DICTATION. PAIRS. Student A, say three words from Exercise A.
Student B, listen and write.

_____   _____   _____

G   DICTATION. SAME PAIRS. Student B, say three words from Exercise C.
Student A, listen and write.

_____   _____   _____

CD6 T22

A 🔊 Listen. Listen and repeat.

arm	ear	foot / feet	knee	neck	shoulder
chest	eye	hand	leg	nose	stomach

B PAIRS. Point to each part of the body. Say the name.

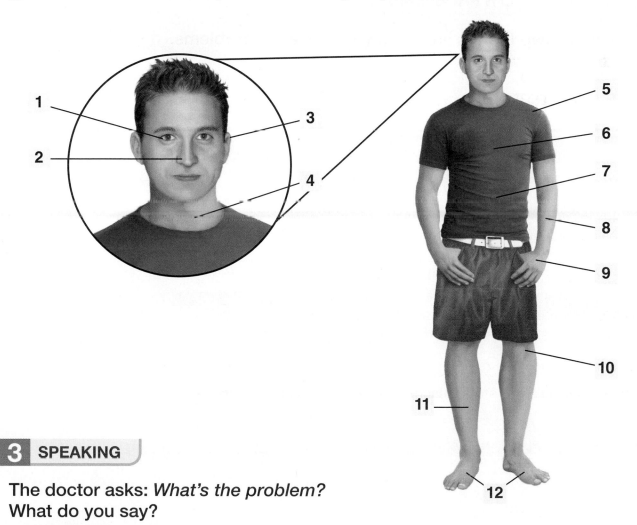

3   **SPEAKING**

The doctor asks: *What's the problem?*
What do you say?

a. Breathe out.
b. I can come in at 10:00.
c. I have a sore throat.

1 FOLLOW MEDICAL INSTRUCTIONS

A CD6 T23 Listen. A doctor is talking to a patient.

B GROUPS. Review the actions on page 180.
Take turns. Give medical instructions. Do the actions.

2 TALK ABOUT HEALTH PROBLEMS

A CD6 T24 Listen. Two friends are talking about health problems.

B ROLE PLAY. PAIRS.

ROLE PLAY 1	
Student A	**Student B**
You don't feel well.	You are Student A's friend.
You have a headache and a cough.	Give your friend suggestions.

ROLE PLAY 2	
Student B	**Student A**
You don't feel well.	You are Student B's friend.
You have the flu and a stomachache.	Give your friend suggestions.

A Read the directions on the label.

Cough Syrup

Take for coughs, not for fevers.

Directions:
Adults: Take 2 teaspoons every 4-6 hours.

Children 6-12 years: Take 1 teaspoon every 4-6 hours.

Children under 6: See a doctor for instructions.

B Read the directions again.
Use the information in the box. Write the answers.

2 teaspoons	cough syrup	see a doctor
1 teaspoon	every 4–6 hours	

1. What kind of medicine is it? _____

2. How much medicine should an adult take? _____

3. How often should an adult take this medicine? _____

4. How much medicine should a 12-year-old child take? _____

5. How often should a 12-year-old child
    take this medicine? _____

6. Your child is 5. What should you do? _____

4 CONNECT   For your Team Project, go to page 218.

A Look at the jobs.
Listen and point. Listen and repeat.

CD6 T25

B Listen and read. Listen and repeat.

CD6 T26

1. a mechanic	4. a construction worker	7. a dentist
2. a homemaker	5. a teacher's assistant	8. a housekeeper
3. a painter	6. a sales assistant	9. a bus driver

C 🖭 CD6 T27 Listen. Listen and repeat.

A: Let's get coffee.
B: I'm sorry. I can't. I have to go to work.
A: Oh. What do you do?
B: I'm a mechanic.

D PAIRS. Practice the conversation.

E PAIRS. Make new conversations.
Use the jobs on page 194.

A: Let's get coffee.

B: I'm sorry. I can't. I have to go to work.

A: Oh. What do you do?

B: I'm _____.

Show what you know!

GROUPS OF 4. Use real or made-up information.
Write your name and job.
Ask your classmates: *What do you do?*
Write the information.

Name	Job
Rodrigo	mechanic
1.	
2.	
3.	
4.	

CLASS. Take turns. Talk about your classmates.

Rodrigo is a mechanic.

A CD6 T28

Look at the jobs.
Listen and point. Listen and repeat.

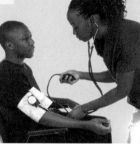

B CD6 T29

Listen and read. Listen and repeat.

1. a cashier	4. a cook	7. a security guard
2. a doctor	5. a nurse	8. a waiter / a waitress
3. a factory worker	6. an office assistant	9. a custodian

C PAIRS. Point to a picture in Exercise A. Say the job.

D  Listen. Listen and repeat.

CD6 T30

A: Who's that?

B: That's Ilhan. He's a nurse.

A: Where does he work?

B: He works at Valley Hospital.

E Read the sentences.

Where do / Where does	
Where do you work?	**Where does** he work?
Where do they work?	**Where does** she work?

F Write *do* or *does*.

1. **A:** Where _____ Gino work?

   B: He works at Corner Café.

2. **A:** Where _____ you work?

   B: I work at a restaurant.

3. **A:** Where _____ Ana work?

   B: She works at home.

4. **A:** Where _____ Ivan work?

   B: He works at ABC Mechanics.

5. **A:** Where _____ Katrina and Sasha work?

   B: They work at City Hotel.

Show what you know!

CLASS. Take turns.
Ask: *What do you do? Where do you work?*

What do you do?

Where do you work?

I'm a cashier.

I work at Family Drugstore.

A CD6 T31 Look at the job skills.
Listen and point. Listen and repeat.

Hello. 你好

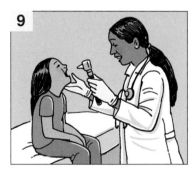

B CD6 T32 Listen and read. Listen and repeat.

1. speak two languages	4. use a computer	7. fix cars
2. use a cash register	5. use office machines	8. drive a truck
3. help customers	6. build houses	9. help sick people

C PAIRS. Say a job skill in Exercise B. Point to the picture.

D Listen. Listen and repeat.

A: What are your job skills?
B: I use a computer.
   And I use a cash register.
A: What other skills do you have?
B: I speak two languages.

E PAIRS. Practice the conversation.

F CD6 T34
 Listen and read the story.

Grace is looking for a new job. She has an interview at a
department store on Third Avenue. Grace has many skills.
She uses a computer and a cash register. Grace also
speaks two languages.

G Read the story again. Circle *Yes* or *No*.

1. Grace has a job.   (Yes)   No
2. Grace wants a new job.   Yes   No
3. She wants to work in a supermarket.   Yes   No
4. Grace uses a cash register.   Yes   No
5. She speaks three languages.   Yes   No

Show what you know!

CLASS. Walk around the room.
Ask: *What are your job skills?*

Apply for a job

A  **CD6 T35**
 **Listen. Listen and repeat.**

A: Hello. I'd like to apply for the office assistant job.
B: OK. Can you use a computer?
A: Yes, I can.
B: Please fill out the application.
A: Thank you.

B **CD6 T36**
Listen again. Circle *Yes* or *No*.

1. The man wants the mechanic job.   Yes   (No)
2. The man can use a computer.   Yes   No
3. The man should fill out the application.   Yes   No

C **PAIRS. Practice the conversation.**

D **PAIRS. Read the job ads. Make new conversations.**

A: Hello. I'd like to apply for the _____ job.
B: OK. Can you _____?
A: Yes, I can.
B: Please fill out the application.
A: Thank you.

Conversation 1

**Mechanic needed
to fix cars**

Conversation 2

**Sales assistant needed
to help customers**

Conversation 3

**Construction
worker needed
to build houses**

E Read the sentences.

Can: Yes / No questions and short answers		
Can you **use** a computer?	**Yes**, I **can**.	**No**, I **can't**.
Can Mr. Vega **use** a computer?	**Yes**, he **can**.	**No**, he **can't**.
Can Nancy **use** a computer?	**Yes**, she **can**.	**No**, she **can't**.
Can Alex and Chris **use** a computer?	**Yes**, they **can**.	**No**, they **can't**.

End a question with a question mark.

F Write the questions and answers.

1. **A:** _Can Miss Tang wait on tables?_____ (can / Miss Tang / wait on tables)

   B: Yes, _she can_____.

2. **A:** _____ (can / Mr. Black / use a computer)

   B: No, _____.

3. **A:** _____ (can / you / build houses)

   B: Yes, _____.

4. **A:** _____ (can / Marina and Pedro / help customers)

   B: Yes, _____.

5. **A:** _____ (can / Mrs. Daniels / speak two languages)

   B: No, _____.

CD6 T37

G 💿 Listen and check your answers. Listen and repeat.

Show what you know!

PAIRS. Ask: *Can you* _____? Check (✓) the job skills.

- ☐ speak two languages
- ☐ take care of sick people
- ☐ use a computer
- ☐ use office machines
- ☐ use a cash register
- ☐ fix cars

CLASS. Take turns. Talk about your classmate.

> Trina can use a cash register and a computer. She can speak two languages.

A   PAIRS. Complete the sentences. Circle *a* or *b*.

1. I work 15 hours a week. I work _____.

   a. full-time   (b.) part-time

2. I work 40 hours a week. I work _____.

   a. full-time   b. part-time

3. I work on Saturdays and Sundays. I work _____.

   a. weekends   b. week days

4. I work Monday to Friday. I work _____.

   a. weekends   b. week days

5. I have to go to the office for my interview. I have to _____.

   a. go in person   b. send an e-mail

6. I need to have experience for this job. Experience is _____.

   a. not needed   b. required

B   Read the job ads.

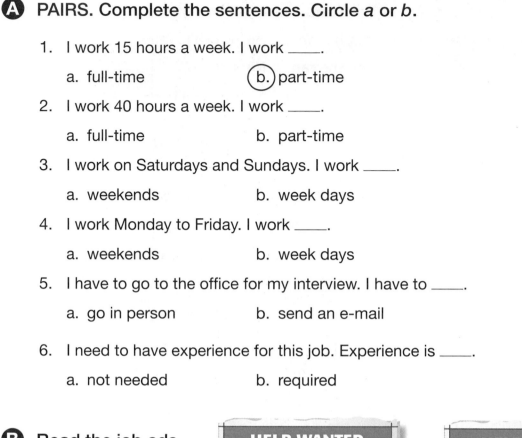

HELP WANTED
City Hotel
Part-time housekeeper
Experience required
Weekends
Apply in person

A

HELP WANTED
TG Factory
Office assistant
Full-time Monday–Friday
Call 603-555-1919 for
interview appointment

B

C   Read the sentences. Read the ads again.
Match the sentences with the ads. Write *A* or *B*.

1. The job is an office assistant. _B_

2. It is a full-time job. _____

3. The person needs to work on weekends. _____

4. The person should have experience. _____

5. You should call for an interview. _____

D PAIRS. Match.

1. full-time _d_   a. PT
2. part-time ____   b. &
3. hours a week ____   c. req
4. Monday to Friday ____   ~~d.~~ FT
5. required ____   e. wknds
6. experience ____   f. exp
7. weekends ____   g. hrs/wk
8. and ____   h. M–F

E Read the job ads.

Help Wanted
Sales Assistant
1 yr exp req
FT evenings
& wknds
Call 555-2434

A

Job Available
CASHIER
No exp req
PT 25 hrs/wk
See Sam Lee
6703 Lake Road

B

DRIVER NEEDED
FT 35 hrs/wk
M–F
2 yrs exp req
Apply in person
ABC Company
300 Plaza Ave.

C

F Read the sentences. Read the ads again.
Match the sentences with the ads. Write A, B, or C.

1. This job is full-time evenings and weekends. _A_
2. You need two years experience. ____
3. This job is part-time. ____
4. You need to call to apply. ____
5. You do not need experience. ____
6. This job is 35 hours a week. ____

A   **CLASS. Look at each picture. What do you see?**

B   **CD6 T38**   Listen to the story.

C 💿 **Listen again and read.**

> My name is Monika. I have my first job interview in the United States on Thursday. I feel confident. I practiced my interview skills in my English class.
>
> I need to remember three important things. I need to get to the interview early. I need to remember to shake hands firmly. I need to make eye contact.
>
> Wish me luck!

D **Read the story again. Circle *Yes* or *No*.**

1.	Monika has a job interview on Tuesday.	Yes	(No)
2.	She feels nervous about the interview.	Yes	No
3.	She needs to arrive at the interview on time.	Yes	No
4.	Monika should shake hands firmly.	Yes	No

E **GROUPS. Read the questions.**
Talk about job interviews in your country.

1. What happens at a job interview?

2. Should you shake hands? Should you make eye contact?

F **Write about job interviews.**

In my country, people _____.

They _____.

In the United States, people _____.

They _____.

G **GROUPS. Take turns. Read your sentences.**

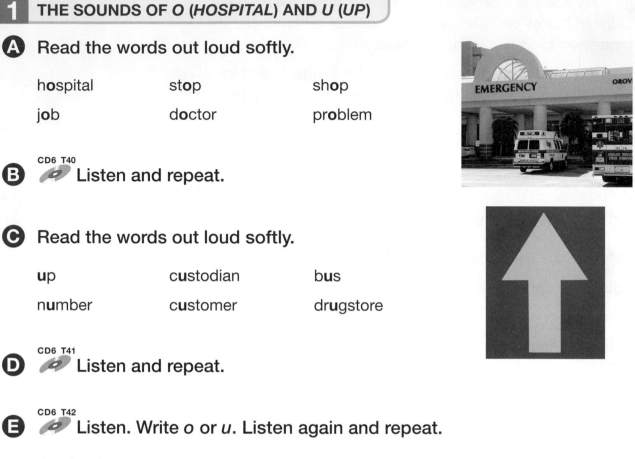

1   THE SOUNDS OF *O* (*HOSPITAL*) AND *U* (*UP*)

A   Read the words out loud softly.

h**o**spital	st**o**p	sh**o**p
j**o**b	d**o**ctor	pr**o**blem

CD6 T40

B   Listen and repeat.

C   Read the words out loud softly.

up	c**u**stodian	b**u**s
n**u**mber	c**u**stomer	dr**u**gstore

CD6 T41

D   Listen and repeat.

CD6 T42

E   Listen. Write *o* or *u*. Listen again and repeat.

1. j__b
2. d__ctor
3. st__p

4. __p
5. c__stodian
6. pr__blem

7. b__s
8. n__mber
9. sh__p

F   DICTATION. PAIRS. Student A, say three words from Exercise A. Student B, listen and write.

_____   _____   _____

G   DICTATION. SAME PAIRS. Student B, say three words from Exercise C. Student A, listen and write.

_____   _____   _____

2 VOCABULARY

A CD6 T43 Listen. Listen and repeat.

cashiers	mechanics	sales assistants	waiters
doctors	nurses	teachers	waitresses
housekeepers	office assistants	teacher's assistants	

B Write the answers. Use the words in Exercise A.

1. They use computers in offices. _____

2. They work in a garage and fix cars. _____

3. They clean houses and hotels. _____

4. They help sick people in hospitals. _____ _____

5. They wait on customers in restaurants. _____ _____

6. They help students in schools. _____ _____

7. They help customers in stores. _____ _____

C PAIRS. Compare answers.

3 SPEAKING

Your classmate asks: *What do you do?*
What do you say?

a. I'm doing homework.
b. I take the bus.
c. I'm a homemaker.

 Go to the CD-ROM for more practice.

1 APPLY FOR A JOB

A CD6 T44
Listen. Salma is applying for a job.

B PAIRS. Read the job ad.

Restaurant Jobs Available
Cook, Waiter/Waitress, Cashier
FT & PT wkdays & wknds
Apply in person
3073 Park Street

C Write a job interview. Use the information in the ad.

A: Hello. I'm interested in the _____ position.

B: OK. What job skills do you have?

A: _____

B: Do you have any other skills?

A: _____

B: When can you work?

A: _____

B: Please fill out this application.

A: OK. Thank you.

D CLASS. Take turns. Perform your conversation for the class.

2 FILL OUT A JOB APPLICATION

What kind of job are you interested in?
Fill out the form. Use true or made-up information.

POSITION INTERESTED IN: _____

PERSONAL INFORMATION

NAME _____
             First   Last

ADDRESS _____
                         Street

_____
City   State   Zip Code

_____
Telephone Number

Are you 18 years or older? Yes ☐   No ☐

AVAILABILITY

When can you begin work? _____
                       Month   Day   Year

Are you interested in a full-time job or a part-time job? ☐ FT   ☐ PT

3 WRITE ABOUT YOURSELF

Write about yourself. Use true or made-up information.

1. My name is _____.

2. I'd like to apply for the _____ _____ job.

3. I can begin work _____.

4. I can work _____ hours a week.

4 CONNECT   For your Team Project, go to page 218.

Team Projects

Unit 1   Meet Your Class   MAKE A CHART

TEAMS OF 4   Student A, Student B, Student C, Student D.

GET READY   Look at the chart. It is an example. You will make a new chart.

First Name	Last Name	Country
1. May	Chen	China
2. Pablo	Martinez	Mexico
3. Monika	Jasinska	Poland
4. Julia	Christian	Haiti

Materials
- A pen, pencil, or color marker
- Large paper
- A watch or clock

CREATE   **Student A:** Watch the time. Your team has 10 minutes.
Student B: Say where you are from. Then ask your teammates: *Where are you from?*
Student C: Write your team's answers.

REPORT   **Student D:** Show the class your team's chart. Say where your team is from:

_____ *is from* _____. *I'm from* _____.

Unit 2   Places in the School   MAKE A CHART

TEAMS OF 4   Student A, Student B, Student C, Student D.

GET READY   Look at the chart. It is an example. You will make a new chart.

Place	Location
1. bookstore	next to the office
2. Room 303	across from the library
3. cafeteria	across from the women's room
4. computer lab	next to the library

Materials
- A pen, pencil, or color marker
- Large paper
- A watch or clock

CREATE   **Student A:** Watch the time. Your team has 10 minutes.
Student B: Say four places in the school.
Student C: Write the places.
Student B: Say where the places are. Use *next to* and *across from*.
Student C: Write the locations.

REPORT   **Student D:** Show the class your team's chart. Say the places and the locations:

The _____ *is next to the* _____. *The* _____ *is across from the* _____.

Unit 3   Time to Get Up <u>MAKE A LINE</u>

Materials
• A watch or clock

TEAMS OF 4 Student A, Student B, Student C, Student D.

GET READY   Make a line in order of the times you get up.

CREATE   **Student A:** Watch the time. You have 5 minutes.

Student B: Ask your teammates: *What time do you get up?*

Student C: Listen to your teammates' answers. Put your teammates in order. Start with the person who gets up the earliest.

REPORT   **Student D:** Tell the class what time your team gets up. Start with the first person.

Say: _____ *gets up at* _____.

Unit 4   Birthdays <u>MAKE A LINE</u>

Materials
• A watch or clock

TEAMS OF 5 Student A, Student B, Student C, Student D, Student E.

GET READY   Make a line in order of your birthdays.

CREATE   **Student A:** Watch the time. You have 5 minutes.

Student B: Ask your teammates: *When is your birthday?*

Student C: Listen to your teammates' answers. Put your teammates in order. Start with January.

Student D: Check the order of the line. Is it correct?

REPORT   **Student E:** Tell the class your team's birthdays.

Start with the first person. Say: _____ *'s birthday is* _____.

Unit 5   Coins and Bills   MAKE PICTURES

TEAMS OF 4 Student A, Student B, Student C, Student D.

GET READY The coins and bills are examples. You will draw new pictures.

Materials
- A pen, pencil, or color marker
- Large paper
- A watch or clock

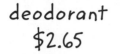
deodorant
$2.65

CREATE   **Student A:** Watch the time. You have 15 minutes.

Student B: Look at page 84. Say a drugstore item and give a price.

Student C: Listen to your teammate. Write the item and price. Draw the coins and bills that match the price.

Student B: Look at the price. Look at the pictures of the money. Is the total correct?

Students B and C: Do this activity two more times. Switch roles.

REPORT   **Student D:** Show the class your team's prices and pictures of bills and coins. Say the coins and bills needed for each price:
The deodorant is two dollars and sixty-five cents.
Two dollar bills, two quarters, one dime, and one nickel.

Unit 6 Plan a Party <u>WRITE A LIST</u>

TEAMS OF 4 Student A, Student B, Student C, Student D.

GET READY Look at the list. It is an example.
You will write a new list.

potato chips	soda
fruit salad	water
cake	coffee and tea

Materials
• A pen or pencil
• A piece of paper
• A watch or clock

CREATE   **Student A:** Watch the time. You have 10 minutes.

Student B: Tell your teammates: *We're having a class party.*
What food and drinks should we have?

Student C: Listen to your teammates' suggestions. Write the information.

REPORT   **Student D:** Read the class your team's list for the class party.

Unit 7 What's your home like? DRAW A FLOOR PLAN

TEAMS OF 5 Student A, Student B, Student C, Student D, Student E.

GET READY Look at the floor plan. It is an example.
Your team will plan a new home. You will draw a new floor plan.

Materials
• A pen or pencil
• Large paper
• A watch or clock

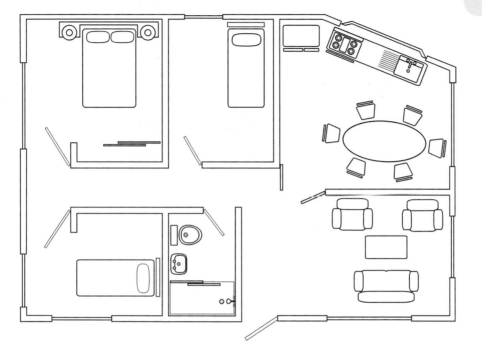

CREATE   **Student A:** Watch the time. You have 25 minutes.

            Student B: Ask your teammates what rooms to have in the new home.
Draw a floor plan.

            Student C: Ask your teammates to say the names of the rooms.
Write the words on the floor plan.

            Student D: Ask your teammates to say furniture and appliances for each room.
Draw the furniture and appliances on the floor plan.

            Student E: Ask your teammates to say the names of the furniture and
appliances. Write the words on the floor plan.

REPORT   **Student A:** Show the class your team's floor plan. Say the rooms,
the furniture, and the appliances: *There is a large kitchen.*
There is a dishwasher. There are four chairs . . .

Unit 8   A Clothing Sale <u>MAKE A SALE AD</u>

TEAMS OF 5 Student A, Student B, Student C, Student D, Student E.

GET READY Look at the clothing ad. It is an example.
You will make a sale ad for your team's store.

The Clothing Store
Sale!
Dresses $25
Men's pants $17.50
Shoes $15
Children's shoes $7.99

CREATE **Student A:** Watch the time. You have 20 minutes.

Student B: Ask your teammates: *What is our store's name?*
What clothing is on sale? What are the prices?

Students C and D: Listen to your team. Draw a store ad.
Write the store name, clothing, and sale prices.

REPORT **Student E:** Show the class your team's store ad. Say what is on sale.

Unit 9 Free-Time Activites <u>MAKE A BAR GRAPH</u>

Materials
- A pen, pencil, or color markers
- Large paper
- A watch or clock

TEAMS OF 5 Student A, Student B, Student C, Student D, Student E.

GET READY Look at the bar graph. It is an example.
You will make a new bar graph.

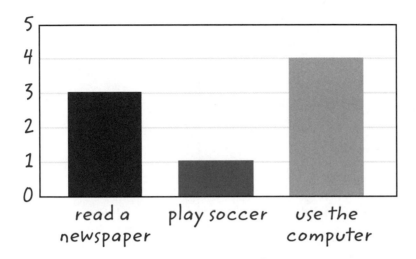

CREATE **Student A:** Watch the time. You have 20 minutes.

Student B: Choose three free-time activities.
Draw lines for the graph and write a number for each line.
Then write the activities at the bottom.

Student C: Ask your teammates about the activities:

Do you _____ in your free time?

Student D: Listen to your teammates' answers.
Count how many teammates do each activity.
Draw a bar for each activity that shows how many teammates
do that activity.

REPORT **Student E:** Show the class your team's bar graph.
Say your team's free-time activities:
Three teammates read a newspaper.
One teammate plays soccer.
Four teammates use the computer.

Unit 10 Places in the Neighborhood <u>MAKE A MAP</u>

Materials
- Color markers
- Large paper
- A watch or clock

TEAMS OF 4 Student A, Student B, Student C, Student D.

GET READY Look at the map. It is an example.
You will make a new map.

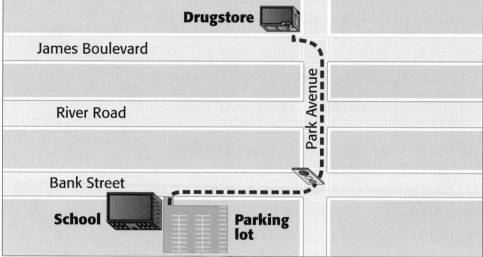

Turn right out of the parking lot.
Turn left at the light.
Go two blocks.
The drugstore is on the left.

CREATE **Student A:** Watch the time. You have 20 minutes.

Student B: Choose a restaurant or drugstore near the school.

Student C: Say the directions from the school to the place.

Student D: Draw the map. Write the directions.
Ask your teammates to check the information.

REPORT **Student B:** Show the class your team's map. Say the directions.

Unit 11   Give Health Tips   MAKE A LIST

Materials
- Color markers
- Large paper
- A watch or clock

TEAMS OF 4 Student A, Student B, Student C, Student D.

GET READY Look at the chart. It is an example. You will make a new chart.

Health Problem	Name	Country	What do you do in your country?
Headache	Anna	Poland	Lie down and cover your eyes.
	Hong	China	Rub a point on your hand near the thumb.
	Marco	Ecuador	Drink a special herb tea.
	Aysha	Somalia	Drink a special herb tea.

CREATE   **Student A:** Watch the time. You have 10 minutes.
Student B: Choose a health problem.
Ask your teammates: *What do you do in your country for this health problem?*
Student C: Write your team's information.

REPORT   **Student D:** Read your team's chart to the class.
Say each teammate's name, where he or she is from, and the suggestion.

Unit 12   Talk About Jobs   INTERVIEW SOMEONE

Materials
- A pen or pencil
- A piece of paper
- A watch or clock

TEAMS OF 4 Student A, Student B, Student C, Student D.

GET READY Read the interview questions. Find someone who works in the school. Ask for an appointment to interview the person. Use these questions.

CREATE   **Student A:** Watch the time. You have 10 minutes.
Students B and C: Ask the questions.
Student D: Write the answers.

Interview with: _____

Job: _____

1. What do you do? _____

2. What are your job skills? _____

3. What is your schedule? _____

REPORT   **Student A:** Tell the class about your team's interview.
Use the answers from the interview.

Word List

UNIT 1: NICE TO MEET YOU.

Page 8
Cambodia
Canada
China
El Salvador
Haiti
Korea
Mexico
Peru
Russia
Somalia
the United States
Vietnam

Page 9
country
name

Page 11
first name
last name

Page 12
zero
one
two
three
four
five
six
seven
eight
nine

ID number
student ID

Page 13
area code
phone number

Page 16
he
she

Page 20
a form
middle name
place of birth
student
    identification number

Page 23
bow
hug
kiss
shake hands
smile

UNIT 2: WELCOME TO CLASS!

Page 28
a backpack
a book
a cell phone
a dictionary
an eraser
a notebook
a pen
a pencil
a piece of paper

Page 30
Close your dictionary.
Open your book.
Put away your book.
Take out your pencil.
Turn off the light.
Turn on the light.

Page 32
bookstore
cafeteria
classroom
computer lab
library
men's room
office
testing room
women's room

Page 34
next to

Page 35
across from
teacher's room

Page 36
female
male
married
Miss
Mr.
Mrs.
Ms.
single

Page 38
ask the teacher questions
go to class
practice with my classmates
read signs
use a dictionary
write in my notebook

UNIT 3: ON TIME

Page 46
ten
eleven
twelve
thirteen
fourteen
fifteen
sixteen
seventeen
eighteen
nineteen
twenty
twenty-one
twenty-two
twenty-three
twenty-four
twenty-five

twenty-six
twenty-seven
twenty-eight
twenty-nine
thirty
thirty-one
thirty-two
thirty-three
thirty-four
thirty-five
thirty-six
thirty-seven
thirty-eight
thirty-nine
forty
forty-one
forty-two

forty-three
forty-four
forty-five
forty-six
forty-seven
forty-eight
forty-nine
fifty
fifty-one
fifty-two
fifty-three
fifty-four
fifty-five
fifty-six
fifty-seven
fifty-eight
fifty-nine

Page 49
at night
in the afternoon
in the evening
in the morning

Page 50
eat breakfast
eat lunch
get dressed
get home
get up
go to school
go to sleep
go to work
take a shower

Page 52
Monday
Tuesday
Wednesday
Thursday
Friday
Saturday
Sunday

Page 57
go to class
go to work
on time
on weekends

UNIT 4: FAMILY AND FRIENDS

Page 62
brother
children
daughter
father
grandfather
grandmother
husband
mother
parents
sister
son
wife

Page 65
child
grandparents

Page 66
clean the house
do the laundry
make dinner
take out the
    garbage
vacuum
wash the dishes

Page 68
January
February
March
April
May
June
July
August
September
October
November
December

Page 69
first
second
third
fourth
fifth
sixth
seventh
eighth
ninth
tenth
eleventh
twelfth
thirteenth
fourteenth
fifteenth

sixteenth
seventeenth
eighteenth
nineteenth
twentieth
twenty-first
twenty-second
twenty-third
twenty-fourth
twenty-fifth
twenty-sixth
twenty-seventh
twenty-eighth
twenty-ninth
thirtieth
thirty-first

UNIT 5: HOW MUCH IS IT?

Page 80
coins

a dime
a dollar coin
a half-dollar
a nickel
a penny
a quarter

Page 82
bill

fifty dollars
five dollars
one dollar
one hundred dollars
a single
ten dollars
twenty dollars

Page 84
aspirin
batteries
deodorant
lightbulbs
paper towels
razor blades
shampoo
shaving cream
soap
tissues
toilet paper
toothpaste

Page 85
aisle

Page 86
cents

Page 88
change
receipt

Page 89
check

UNIT 6: LET'S EAT!

Page 96
carrots
cucumbers
lettuce
mushrooms
onions
peas
peppers
potatoes
tomatoes

Page 100
apples
bananas
cherries
grapes
mangoes
oranges
peaches
pears
strawberries

Page 102
avocados
chicken
fish
ground beef

Page 103
a bag of rice
a box of cereal
a can of soup
a dozen eggs
a gallon of milk
a loaf of bread

bags
boxes
cans
gallons
loaves

Page 105
shopping list

Page 106
breakfast
coffee
juice
menu
pancakes
tea
toast

Page 107
dinner
lunch

chicken sandwich
fish sandwich
hamburger
taco

baked potato
french fries
green salad
rice

coffee
iced tea
juice
milk

cake
fruit salad
ice cream

Page 110
favorite
vegetables

UNIT 7: APARTMENT FOR RENT

Page 114
basement
bathroom
bedroom
closet
dining room
garage
kitchen
laundry room
living room

Page 116
large
modern
small
sunny

Page 118
bed
chair
dishwasher
dresser
dryer
lamp
refrigerator
sink
sofa
stove
table
washing machine

Page 122
apartment
avenue
boulevard
drive
lane
road
street

Page 126
rent

UNIT 8: LET'S GO SHOPPING.

Page 130
a blouse
a dress
a jacket
jeans
pants
a shirt
shoes
a skirt
sneakers
socks
a sweater
a T-shirt

Page 132
extra large
large
medium
size
small

Page 134
beige
black
blue
brown
gray
green
orange
pink
purple
red
white
yellow

Page 136
too big
too long
too short
too small

Page 138
sale
save
suit

UNIT 9: OUR BUSY LIVES

Page 146

free-time activities

exercise
go to the movies
listen to music
play soccer
play the guitar
read the newspaper
use e-mail
visit friends
watch TV

Page 147

once a week
twice a week
three times a week

Page 150

household chores

clean the house
do homework
do the laundry
make dinner
pay bills
talk on the phone
take out the
    garbage
walk the dog
wash the car

Page 152

workplace activities

answer the phone
count money
drive a truck
fix cars
help a customer
look for something
take a break
take orders
work on the
    computer

Page 154

caller
message

UNIT 10: WHERE'S THE BUS STOP?

Page 162

an ATM
a bank
a computer store
a drugstore
a gas station
a hospital
a parking lot
a restaurant
a supermarket

Page 164

City Hall
court house
Department of
    Motor Vehicles
    (DMV)
fire station
library
park
police station
post office
school

Page 166

transportation

carpool
drive
ride a bike
take a ferry
take a taxi
take the bus
take the subway
take the train
walk

Page 168

go straight
turn left
turn right

Page 170

traffic signs

no left turn
no parking
no U-turn
one-way street
speed limit/miles
    per hour
stop sign
train crossing
walk/don't walk
yield

UNIT 11: GET WELL SOON!

Page 178
body

arm
chest
ear
eye
foot / feet
hand
knee
leg
neck
nose
shoulder
stomach

Page 180
medical instructions

Breathe in.
Breathe out.
Lie down.
Look straight ahead.
Open your mouth.
Roll up your sleeves.
Sit on the table.
Step on the scale.
Take off your jacket.

Page 182
health

a backache
a cold
a cough
a fever
the flu
a headache
a sore throat
a stomachache
a toothache

Page 183
suggestion

drink a lot of liquids
get a lot of rest
stay home from work
take an aspirin

Page 184
emergencies

car accident
fire
heart attack
robbed

Page 186
capsules
cough syrup
prescription medicine
tablets
teaspoon

UNIT 12: WHAT DO YOU DO?

Page 194
a bus driver
a construction worker
a dentist
a homemaker
a housekeeper
a mechanic
a painter
a sales assistant
a teacher's assistant

Page 196
a cashier
a cook
a custodian
a doctor
a factory worker
a nurse
an office assistant
a security guard
a waiter/a waitress

Page 198
build houses
drive a truck
fix cars
help customers
help sick people
speak two languages
use a cash register
use a computer
use office machines

Page 202
experience
full-time
help wanted
in person
part-time
required
weekends

Page 209
application
availability

Audio Script

PRE-UNIT

Page 5, Exercise D

1. S   2. F   3. M   4. D   5. R
6. Q   7. V   8. I   9. U   10. A

Page 5, Exercise F

1. c   2. t   3. k   4. l   5. h
6. g   7. n   8. e   9. w   10. o

Page 6, Exercise C

a. 3   b. 7   c. 8   d. 10   e. 5
f. 1   g. 6   h. 9   i. 4

Page 6, Exercise D

a. 6   b. 3   c. 5   d. 7   e. 10
f. 2   g. 8   h. 1   i. 4

UNIT 1

Page 10, Exercise B

1. C   2. F   3. H   4. J   5. M   6. P
7. R   8. U   9. X   10. Z   11. L   12. Q

Page 10, Exercise D

1. hello
2. my
3. name
4. where
5. are
6. from

Page 12, Exercise B

a. 0   b. 2   c. 5   d. 6   e. 8   f. 9

Page 12, Exercise E

1. The student ID number is 02468.
2. The student ID number is 65378.
3. The student ID number is 05376.

Page 13, Exercise H

1. 231-555-7283
2. 434-555-0516

Page 13, Exercise I

1. 813-555-6291
2. 325-555-0478
3. 714-555-3924

Page 15, Exercise I

1. I'm a new student.
2. You're my English teacher.
3. You're a good teacher.
4. I'm in the classroom.
5. I'm from Russia.
6. You're my classmate.

Page 24, Exercise E

1. nice
2. from
3. map
4. number
5. phone
6. meet
7. answer
8. listen
9. welcome

Page 26, Exercise 1A

A: Hello. I'm Rosa.
B: Hi. I'm Rick. Nice to meet you.
A: Nice to meet you, too. I'm a new student here.
B: Welcome!

Page 26, Exercise 2A

A: What's your name, please?
B: Ana Sol.
A: Spell your first name.
B: A-N-A.
A: Spell your last name.
B: S-O-L.

UNIT 2

Page 31, Exercise H

1. Don't open your book.
2. Don't use a dictionary.
3. Don't put away your notebook.
4. Don't turn off your cell phone.
5. Don't take out your dictionary.
6. Don't close the door.

Page 33, Exercise H

1.
A: Where is your teacher?
B: He's in the computer lab.
2.
A: Where is your classmate?
B: She's in the office.
3.
A: Where is your book?
B: It's in the cafeteria.
4.
A: Where is your backpack?
B: It's in the classroom.

Page 42, Exercise E

1. number
2. practice
3. book
4. backpack
5. open
6. library
7. paper
8. pen
9. birth

Page 44, Exercise 1A

A: OK, everyone. Get ready for a test.
B: OK.
A: Use a pencil. Don't use a pen.

Page 44, Exercise 2A

A: Excuse me, where is the bookstore?
B: It's next to the testing room.
A: Thanks.

UNIT 3

Page 46, Exercise C

1. 20	2. 19	3. 24	4. 13
5. 15	6. 14	7. 26	8. 27

Page 49, Exercise H

The office is open from 8 A.M. to 6 P.M.
The computer lab is open from 7 P.M. to 9 P.M.
The cafeteria is open from 11 A.M. to 6:30 P.M.

Page 53, Exercise H

1. I get up at seven from Monday to Thursday.
2. I go to school from six to nine in the evening.

3. I play soccer on Tuesday.
4. I get home late on Friday.
5. I eat lunch at home on Sunday.

Page 55, Exercise F

1. Five forty-five
2. Three thirty
3. Ten fifteen
4. Six forty
5. Eight-oh-five
6. One fifty
7. Two o'clock
8. Four forty-five

Page 58, Exercise E

1. eat
2. day
3. dinner
4. time
5. Monday
6. get up
7. two
8. read
9. breakfast

Page 60, Exercise 2A

I'm busy on Saturday! I get up at 9 o'clock.
I eat breakfast at 9:30. I don't go to work.
I go to English class. Class starts at 11 o'clock.
We have a break from one to 1:30.
The class is over at 3 o'clock. Then I go to the library.
I study from 4 to 5. Then I go home.

UNIT 4

Page 68, Exercise B

1. December
2. June
3. October
4. January
5. May
6. April

Page 70, Exercise C

1. January 1, 2006
2. April 12, 1989
3. May 15, 1983
4. August 27, 2006
5. December 8, 2010

Page 76, Exercise E

1. father
2. daughter
3. that
4. date
5. mother
6. they
7. husband
8. there
9. laundry

Page 77, Exercise B

1. January
2. February
3. March
4. April
5. May
6. June
7. July
8. August
9. September
10. October
11. November
12. December

Page 78, Exercise 1B

My name is Marta. These are my parents Roberto and Linda. That's my husband, Pedro.
These are my children. These are my sons, Ernesto and Tino. That's my daughter, Ana.

Page 78, Exercise 2A

My name is Kato. In my house, my mother cleans and does the laundry. My sister makes dinner. My father takes out the garbage. I wash the dishes.

UNIT 5

Page 81, Exercise F

1.
A: Do you have change for a dollar?
B: Yes. I have three quarters, two dimes, and a nickel.

2.
A: Do you have change for a dollar?
B: Yes. I have two quarters, four dimes, and two nickels.

3.
A: Do you have change for a quarter?
B: Yes. I have one dime and three nickels.

4.
A: Do you have change for a quarter?
B: Yes. I have two dimes and five pennies.

Page 83, Exercise F

1.
A: Do you have change for a five?
B: Yes. I have five singles.

2.
A: Do you have change for a twenty?
B: Yes. I have two tens.

3.
A: Do you have change for a fifty?
B: Yes. I have two twenties and two fives.

4.
A: Do you have change for a hundred?
B: Yes. I have one fifty, two twenties, and a ten.

Page 85, Exercise E

1. Where is the shampoo?
2. Where are the paper towels?
3. Where is the shaving cream?
4. Where are the lightbulbs?
5. Where are the batteries?

Page 86, Exercise B

1. It's seventeen cents.
2. It's thirty-six cents.
3. It's forty-four cents.
4. It's sixty cents.
5. It's seventy-nine cents.
6. It's ninety-five cents.

Page 86, Exercise D

1. It's one twenty-five.
2. It's three-oh-seven.
3. It's four seventy-nine.
4. It's seven fifty.
5. It's eight ninety-nine.
6. It's ten forty two.
7. It's twelve fifty-five.
8. It's fifteen thirty-five.
9. It's seventeen ninety-five.

Page 92, Exercise E

1. go
2. drugstore
3. cash
4. computer
5. big
6. shaving cream
7. count
8. get
9. country

Page 94, Exercise 1A

A: Excuse me. Where is the shaving cream?
B: Aisle 4.
A: And where are the batteries?
B: Aisle 3.
A: Thank you.

Page 94, Exercise 2A

A: Excuse me. Do you have change for a ten?
B: Yes. I have a five and five singles. Here you go.
A: Great.

UNIT 6

Page 110, Exercise E

1. food
2. vegetables
3. fish
4. five
5. very
6. beef
7. have
8. fruit
9. favorite

Page 112, Exercise 1A

A: May I help you?
B: Yes. I'd like a fish sandwich and rice.
A: Anything else?
B: Yes. I'd like coffee.
A: Anything else?
B: No. Thanks.

Page 113, Exercise 2A

A: What do we need from the store?
B: We need a bag of rice and two dozen eggs.
A: Anything else?
B: Yes. A pound of grapes and two pounds of chicken.
A: OK.

UNIT 7

Page 119, Exercise H

1.
A: Is there a stove?
B: Yes, there is.

2.
A: Are there any chairs?
B: Yes, there are.

3.
A: Are there any lamps?
B: No, there aren't.

4.
A: Is there a washing machine?
B: No, there isn't.

Page 120, Exercise B

1. 270 John Lane
2. 15 City Street
3. 1460 Third Avenue
4. 60 Park Drive
5. 319 Sun Boulevard

Page 120, Exercise C

1. 75 Sandy Boulevard
2. 1325 West Avenue
3. 5 Main Street
4. 836 Jones Road
5. 1514 North Drive
6. 26 Town Lane

Page 126, Exercise E

1. large
2. rent
3. lamp
4. closet
5. chair
6. refrigerator
7. table
8. address
9. living room

Page 128, Exercise 1A

A: Guess what? I have a new apartment.
B: Really? What's it like?
A: It has a kitchen, a living room, and one bedroom.
B: It sounds great!

Page 128, Exercise 2A

A: I have some questions about the apartment. Is there a sofa?
B: Yes, there is.
A: Are there any lamps?
B: No, there aren't.

UNIT 8

Page 136, Exercise B

1. This shirt is too big.
2. Those pants are too short
3. This jacket is too long.
4. That dress is too small.
5. These pants are too short.
6. This skirt is too big.

Page 139, Exercise C

Dan's Clothing Store
Sale! February sixteenth to eighteenth
Dresses regular price $25.99, on sale for $15.99
Pants regular price $19, on sale for $14.99
T-shirts regular price $12.50, on sale for $8
Shoes regular price $32.99, on sale for $25
Sneakers, regular price $30.99, on sale for $25
Jackets, regular price $75, on sale for $50

Page 142, Exercise E

1. size
2. small
3. she
4. shirt
5. shopping
6. short
7. pants
8. dress
9. sale

Page 144, Exercise 1A

A: Can I help you?
B: Do you have this shirt in a large?
A: Yes. Here you go.
B: Do you have these pants in a size 12?
A: No, I'm sorry, we don't.

Page 145, Exercise 2A

A: Excuse me. Do you have this shirt in yellow?
B: No, we don't. But we have it in green.
A: OK. Do you have it in a medium?
B: Yes, we do.
A: And do you have those pants in blue?
B: I'm sorry, we don't.

UNIT 9

Page 149, Exercise H

1.
A: What are you doing?
B: I'm listening to music.

2.
A: What is Mrs. White doing?
B: She's going to the library.

3.
A: What are you doing?
B: We're visiting my sister.

4.
A: What's Rob doing?
B: He's watching a movie on TV.

5.
A: What are Sheena and David doing?
B: They're reading the newspaper.

Page 153, Exercise G

1. He's not fixing a car. He's counting money.
2. I'm not working on the computer. I'm on the phone.
3. They're not taking a break. They're helping customers.
4. She's not taking orders. She's looking for something.
5. We're not driving trucks today. We're taking orders.

Page 154, Exercise A

A: Hello?
B: Hi. This is Victor Mata.
   Can I speak to Mr. Green?
A: Mr. Green is not here. Can I take a message?
B: Yes. I can't come to work today.
   My wife is having a baby.
A: Congratulations! What's your phone number?
B: It's 917-555-9876.

Page 154, Exercise C

A: Hello?
B: Hi. This is Jane Black.
   Can I speak to Ms. Lark?
A: Ms. Lark is out of the office. Can I take a message?
B: Yes. I can't come to my appointment today.
   My son is sick.
A: What's your phone number?
B: It's 212-555-4366.

Page 155, Exercise E

A: Hello.?
B: Hi. This is Carlos. Can I speak to Dave?
B: I'm sorry. He's not here right now.
A: Please tell him I'm not playing soccer today.
B: OK. What's your phone number?
A: 212-555-0123.
B: 212-555-0123?
A: That's right.

Page 155, Exercise G

A: Hello?

B: Hi. This is Mira Lopez. Can I speak to Mr. Cohen?

B: He's taking a break right now. Can I take a message?

A: Please tell him I'm not coming to class today.

B: OK. Please spell your name.

A: My first name is Mira. M-I-R-A. My last name is Lopez. L-O-P-E-Z.

B: So that's M-I-R-A L-O-P-E-Z?

A: Correct. Thanks.

Page 158, Exercise E

1. every
2. later
3. name
4. message
5. date
6. newspaper
7. help
8. Wednesday
9. take

Page 161, Exercise 2A

I'm busy every week!
I work Monday to Friday.
I have English class on Monday and Wednesday night.
I go to the movies on Friday night.
I play soccer on Saturday.
And I have lunch with my family on Sunday afternoon.

UNIT 10

Page 168, Exercise B

1.

A: Where's the bank?

B: It's on Park Street. Go straight for one block.

2.

A: Where's the post office?

B: It's between the DMV and City Hall. Turn left on Third Street.

3.

A: Where's the school?

B: It's on Lake Street. Turn right at the corner.

4.

A: Where's the hospital?

B: It's on First Street. Turn right at the corner.

5.

A: Where's the computer store?

B: Turn left at the bank. It's next to the drugstore.

6.

A: Where's the police station?

B: Go straight for three blocks. It's across from the park.

Page 168, Exercise C

A: Is there a gas station near here?

B: Yes. Go straight. It's on the corner of Third Avenue and Church Street.

A: Where's the hospital?

B: Go straight for three blocks and turn right. It's on First Avenue and Bank Street.

A: Where's the drugstore?

B: Go to Third Avenue and take a right at the corner. Go straight for one block.

A: Is there a post office near here?

B: Yes. Go straight for two blocks and turn right at the corner. It's on the corner of Second Avenue and Bank Street.

A: Where is the school?

B: Go straight for two blocks and turn left at the corner. It's on Second Avenue and White Street.

Page 171, Exercise C

1. no parking
2. no U-turn
3. yield
4. stop
5. train crossing
6. speed limit 25 miles per hour

Page 171, Exercise E

1. only go in one direction on this street
2. don't walk across the street
3. stop first and then go
4. drive 25 miles per hour or slower
5. watch for a train crossing this street

Page 174, Exercise E

1. gas
2. ride
3. taxi
4. answer
5. library
6. write
7. sign
8. family
9. bank

Page 176, Exercise 1A

A: Where's the post office?

B: It's between the DMV and City Hall. Turn left on Third Street.

UNIT 11

Page 186, Exercise B

Conversation 1

A: Are you OK? You have a bad cough.

B: I know. I'm taking cough syrup.

A: How much are you taking?

B: I'm taking 2 teaspoons every 4 hours.

A: I hope you feel better soon!

Conversation 2

A: Hi, Mike. How are you?

B: I don't feel well. I have a fever and an ear infection.

A: Oh, that's too bad. Are you taking medicine?

B: Yes. I'm taking some prescription medicine.

A: That's good. How often do you take it?

B: I have to take 1 capsule twice a day with food.

A: I hope you feel better soon!

Page 190, Exercise E

1. give
2. knee
3. street
4. sick
5. feel
6. listen
7. sit
8. teeth
9. drink

Page 192, Exercise 1A

A: Hello. I'm Dr. Medina. Why are you here today?

B: I'm here for a checkup.

A: OK. Sit on the table. Look straight ahead.

Page 192, Exercise 2A

A: What's the matter?

B: I have a cold.

A: You should drink a lot of liquids.

B: OK.

A: Get well soon!

UNIT 12

Page 201, Exercise G

1.

A: Can Miss Tang wait on tables?

B: Yes, she can.

2.

A: Can Mr. Black use a computer?

B: No, he can't.

3.

A: Can you build houses?

B: Yes, I can.

4.

A: Can Marina and Pedro help customers?

B: Yes, they can.

5.

A: Can Mrs. Daniels speak two languages?

B: No, she can't.

Page 206, Exercise E

1. job
2. doctor
3. stop
4. up
5. custodian
6. problem
7. bus
8. number
9. shop

Page 208, Exercise 1A

A: Hello. I'm interested in the waitress position.

B: OK. Can you use a cash register?

A: Yes, I can.

B: Do you have any other skills?

A: I can speak English and Spanish. And I can use a computer.

B: When can you work?

A: I can work weekends.

B: Please fill out this application.

A: OK. Thank you.

Map of the United States and Canada

U. S. Postal Abbreviations

Alabama	AL	Montana	MT
Alaska	AK	Nebraska	NE
Arizona	AZ	Nevada	NV
Arkansas	AR	New Hampshire	NH
California	CA	New Jersey	NJ
Colorado	CO	New Mexico	NM
Connecticut	CT	New York	NY
Delaware	DE	North Carolina	NC
District of Columbia	DC	North Dakota	ND
Florida	FL	Ohio	OH
Georgia	GA	Oklahoma	OK
Hawaii	HI	Oregon	OR
Idaho	ID	Pennsylvania	PA
Illinois	IL	Rhode Island	RI
Indiana	IN	South Carolina	SC
Iowa	IA	South Dakota	SD
Kansas	KS	Tennessee	TN
Kentucky	KY	Texas	TX
Louisiana	LA	Utah	UT
Maine	ME	Vermont	VT
Maryland	MD	Virginia	VA
Massachusetts	MA	Washington	WA
Michigan	MI	West Virginia	WV
Minnesota	MN	Wisconsin	WI
Mississippi	MS	Wyoming	WY
Missouri	MO		

Canadian Postal Abbreviations

Alberta	AB	Nova Scotia	NS
British Columbia	BC	Nunavut	NU
Manitoba	MB	Prince Edward Island	PE
New Brunswick	NB	Quebec	QC
Newfoundland and Labrador	NL	Saskatchewan	SK
Northwest Territories	NT	Yukon	YT

Map of the World

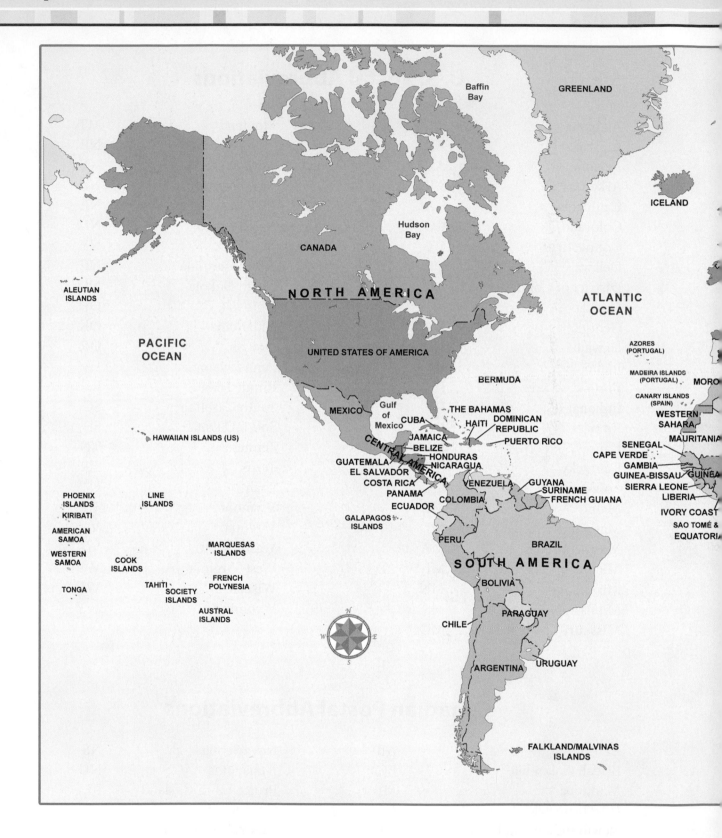

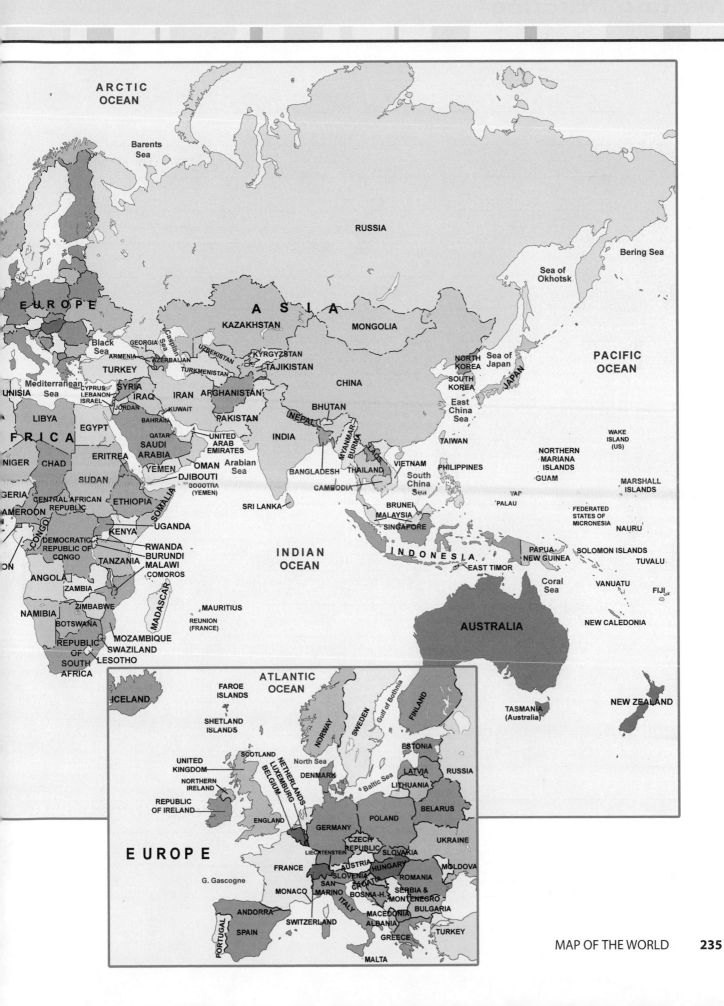

ARCTIC
OCEAN

Barents
Sea

RUSSIA

Bering Sea

Sea of
Okhotsk

EUROPE

ASIA

KAZAKHSTAN

MONGOLIA

PACIFIC
OCEAN

Black
Sea

GEORGIA

Caspian Sea

ARMENIA
AZERBAIJAN

UZBEKISTAN

KYRGYZSTAN

TAJIKISTAN

NORTH
KOREA

Sea of
Japan

TURKEY

TURKMENISTAN

CHINA

SOUTH
KOREA

JAPAN

Mediterranean
Sea

SYRIA

IRAQ

IRAN

AFGHANISTAN

East
China
Sea

UNISIA

CYPRUS
LEBANON
ISRAEL

JORDAN

KUWAIT

NEPAL

BHUTAN

LIBYA

EGYPT

BAHRAIN

PAKISTAN

MYANMAR
BURMA

TAIWAN

FRICA

QATAR

SAUDI
ARABIA

UNITED
ARAB
EMIRATES

INDIA

VIETNAM

PHILIPPINES

NORTHERN
MARIANA
ISLANDS

WAKE
ISLAND
(US)

NIGER

CHAD

ERITREA

YEMEN

OMAN

Arabian
Sea

BANGLADESH

THAILAND

South
China
Sea

GUAM

MARSHALL
ISLANDS

SUDAN

DJIBOUTI

GERIA

CENTRAL AFRICAN
REPUBLIC

DJDOOTIA
(YEMEN)

ETHIOPIA

SOMALIA

CAMBODIA

SRI LANKA

YAP
PALAU

FEDERATED
STATES OF
MICRONESIA

NAURU

AMEROON

CONGO

DEMOCRATIC
REPUBLIC OF
CONGO

UGANDA

KENYA

BRUNEI
MALAYSIA

SINGAPORE

ON

RWANDA
BURUNDI

TANZANIA

MALAWI

COMOROS

INDONESIA

PAPUA
NEW GUINEA

SOLOMON ISLANDS

TUVALU

ANGOLA

ZAMBIA

INDIAN
OCEAN

EAST TIMOR

Coral
Sea

VANUATU

FIJI

ZIMBABWE

MADAGASCAR

MAURITIUS

NEW CALEDONIA

NAMIBIA

BOTSWANA

REUNION
(FRANCE)

AUSTRALIA

REPUBLIC
OF
SOUTH
AFRICA

MOZAMBIQUE

SWAZILAND

LESOTHO

ATLANTIC
OCEAN

FAROE
ISLANDS

SWEDEN

Gulf of Bothnia

FINLAND

TASMANIA
(Australia)

NEW ZEALAND

ICELAND

NORWAY

SHETLAND
ISLANDS

SCOTLAND

North Sea

ESTONIA

UNITED
KINGDOM

NETHERLANDS
LUXEMBURG
BELGIUM

DENMARK

Baltic Sea

LATVIA

RUSSIA

NORTHERN
IRELAND

LITHUANIA

REPUBLIC
OF IRELAND

ENGLAND

GERMANY

POLAND

BELARUS

EUROPE

FRANCE

CZECH
REPUBLIC

LIECHTENSTEIN

SLOVAKIA

UKRAINE

AUSTRIA

HUNGARY

MOLDOVA

G. Gascogne

SLOVENIA

CROATIA

ROMANIA

SAN
MARINO

BOSNIA-H.

SERBIA &
MONTENEGRO

ANDORRA

MONACO

ITALY

MACEDONIA

BULGARIA

PORTUGAL

SPAIN

SWITZERLAND

ALBANIA

GREECE

TURKEY

MALTA

MAP OF THE WORLD   235

Writing Practice

A A

B B

C C

D D

E E

F F

G G

H H

I I

J J

K K

L L

M M

N N

O O

P P

Q Q

R R

S S

T T

U U

V V

W W

X X

Y Y

Z Z

a   a

b   b

c   c

d   d

e   e

f   f

g   g

h   h

i   i

j   j

k   k

l   l

m   m

n   n

o   o

p   p

q   q

r   r

s   s

t   t

u   u

v   v

w   w

x   x

y   y

z   z

A   A   A

B   B   B

C   C   C

D   D   D

E   E   E

F   F   F

G   G   G

H   H   H

I   I   I

J   J   J

K   K   K

L   L   L

M   M   M

N	n	n
O	o	o
P	p	p
Q	2	2
R	R	R
S	s	s
T	J	J
U	u	u
V	v	v
W	w	w
X	x	x
Y	y	y
Z	z	z

a	a	a
b	b	b
c	c	c
d	d	d
e	e	e
f	f	f
g	g	g
h	h	h
i	i	i
j	j	j
k	k	k
l	l	l
m	m	m

n	n	n
o	o	o
p	p	p
q	q	q
r	r	r
s	s	s
t	t	t
u	u	u
v	v	v
w	w	w
x	x	x
y	y	y
z	z	z

Index

ACADEMIC SKILLS

Grammar

Nouns
Singular and plural, 65

Prepositions
Prepositions of place, 34–35, 163, 165

Prepositions of time, 48–49, 52–53

Pronouns
Subject pronouns, 14–15, 16–17, 18–19

Verbs
Be, simple present full forms and contractions, 15, 17, 19

Be, *yes/no* questions and short answers, 87, 163

Can, affirmative and negative statements, 201

Can, *yes/no* questions and short answers, 179, 200–201

I'd like . . . for ordering food, 106–107

I'd like to + verb, 179

Imperatives, affirmative and negative, 3, 31, 180

Present continuous, affirmative and negative statements, 135, 148–149, 153

Present continuous, *yes/no* questions and short answers, 150–151

Questions with *How do you get to . . .*, 167

Questions with *How much is . . .*, 87, 121

Questions with *How often . . .*, 147

Questions with *What*, 68, 70, 102–103, 121, 136–137, 147, 179, 185, 195, 199

Questions with *When*, 52, 69

Questions with *Where . . .*, 9, 33–35, 85, 165, 167, 185, 197

Questions with *Who's that?*, 63, 197

Questions with *Who* and third person singular, 67

Simple present, affirmative statements, 15, 17, 19, 51, 53, 67, 99, 101

Simple present with *like*, affirmative and negative, 99, 101

Simple present with *need*, affirmative and negative, 102–103, 131

Simple present with *have*, 115

Simple present, questions with *Do* and short answers, 64, 81, 83, 97–98, 101, 132–133

Third person singular, 51

Other sentence elements
Adjective + noun, 116

Adjectives, 136

Contractions, 15, 17, 19, 31, 99, 101, 119, 149, 153

Expressions of frequency, 147

Suggestions with *should*, 183

There is/There are, statements and questions, 117, 119

This, that, these, those, 132–133

Sentence patterns
Affirmative and negative statements, 31, 99, 101, 117, 149, 153

Wh- questions, 9, 11–13, 18, 33–35, 66–67, 85, 197

Yes/No questions and short answers, 133, 151, 201

Critical Thinking Skills
Applying concepts to one's own life, 23, 41, 57, 75, 91, 109, 125, 141, 157, 173, 189, 205

Categorizing, 81

Comparing two pictures, 160

Connecting ideas, 25, 43, 59, 77, 111, 127, 143, 159, 175, 191, 207

Creating, 117, 214

Evaluating problems and recommending solutions, 183, 192, 218

Explaining, 23, 41, 57, 75, 91, 109, 125, 141, 157, 173, 189, 205

Planning, 213

Sequencing, 71, 77, 211

Summarizing information, 210, 216

Graphs, Charts, Maps
8, 34–35, 44, 52–53, 61, 163, 165, 168–169, 176–177

Listening
Addresses, 120–121

Apartments, 114–117, 124–125

Classmate introductions, 18, 22, 23

Classroom instructions, 30–31, 44

Classroom objects, 28, 29, 42–43

Clothing, 130–132, 136, 140, 141

Colors, 134–135

Common health problems, 182–183

Countries, 8–9

Doctor's appointments, 179

Drugstore items, 84–87

Emergencies (calling 911), 184–185

Families, 62–65, 78

Food quantities, 102–104

Forms (personal information), 20, 36, 72, 79

Free-time activities, 146–148, 156–157

Fruit, 100–102

Furniture and appliances, 118–119, 127

Household chores, 66–67, 74–75, 78, 150–151

Job interviews, 204–205

Job skills, 198–199

Jobs, 194–197, 207

Letters of alphabet, 4, 10

Meals, 108–109

Medical checkups, 180–181

Medical instructions, 180–181, 192

Medicine instructions, 186

Months and dates, 68–71

Numbers, 46

Ordering meals, 106–107

Personal introductions, 9, 11, 14, 26

Phone numbers, 13, 185

Places in community, 162–165

Places in school, 32–35

Schedules, 51–53, 56–57, 161

Credits

Photo credits

All original photography by David Mager. Page 3(L) Davis Barber/ PhotoEdit; 7(T) Shutterstock, (B) Redchopsticks Collect/age fotostock; 10 Shutterstock; 11 Jeff Greenberg/Omniphoto.com; 12(1A) Comstock Images/age fotostock, (1B) Corbis/Jupiterimages, (2A) Corbis/Jupiterimages, (2B) Oscar Malpica/age fotostock, (3A) Image Source/age fotostock, (3B) Pablo Delfos/age fotostock;16(TR) Image Source/age fotostock, (1) Blend Images/Jupiterimages, (2) Trevor Lush/Jupiterimages, (3) Redchopsticks Collect/age fotostock, (4) Image Source/age fotostock, (5) Image Source/Jupiterimages, (6) Corbis/Jupiterimages; 17(1) Comstock Images/Jupiterimages, (2) Myrleen Ferguson Cate/PhotoEdit, (3) Blend Images/Jupiterimages, (4) Corbis/Jupiterimages; 24(T) Shutterstock, (M) Shutterstock; 28(2) Shutterstock, (3) Tmeks/Dreamstime.com, (4) Shutterstock, (5) Michael Newman/PhotoEdit, (6) Shutterstock, (7) Stockbyte/ Getty Images, (8) Shutterstock, (9) Shutterstock; 33(TL) Thinkstock/ Corbis, (TR) Michael Newman/PhotoEdit; 36(T) Shutterstock, (B) Shutterstock; 38(T) Gary Conner/PhotoEdit; 42(T) Shutterstock, (M) Tmeks/Dreamstime.com; 58(T) Corbis/Jupiterimages, (M) Shutterstock; 62(TR) VStock LLC/age fotostock, (B) Myrleen Ferguson Cate/PhotoEdit; 76(T) Photos.com/Jupiterimages; 82(1) Bill Aron/ PhotoEdit, (2) Lushpix/age fotostock, (3) M Stock/Alamy, (4) David Young-Wolff/PhotoEdit, (5) Shutterstock, (6) Shutterstock; 88 Alex Serge/Alamy; 92(T) Glow Images/Getty Images; 96(1) Bluestocking/ iStockphoto.com, (2) Shutterstock, (3) Shutterstock, (4) Shutterstock, (5) Shutterstock, (6) Shutterstock, (7) Shutterstock, (8) Shutterstock, (9) Shutterstock; 97(T) Digital Vision Ltd./SuperStock, (B) David Young-Wolff/PhotoEdit; 100(1) Shutterstock, (2) Shutterstock, (3) Shutterstock, (4) Shutterstock, (5) Shutterstock, (6) Shutterstock, (7) Shutterstock, (8) Shutterstock, (9) Shutterstock; 106(column L) Bluestocking/ iStockphoto.com, Dana Hoff/Beateworks/Corbis, Shutterstock, (column R) Shutterstock, Shutterstock, Shutterstock, Shutterstock; 107(column L) Stockbyte/SuperStock, Burke/Triolo Productions/FoodPix/Jupiterimages, FoodCollection/SuperStock, Comstock Images/Jupiterimages, Shutterstock, Ciaran Griffin/age fotostock, Shutterstock, Shutterstock, (column R) Shutterstock, Shutterstock, Shutterstock, Shutterstock, Shutterstock, Photodisc/SuperStock, Lew Robertson/Jupiterimages, Bluestocking/ iStockphoto.com; 110(T) Shutterstock, (M) Shutterstock; 116(1) Peter Durant/Arcaid/Corbis, (2) Shutterstock, (3) BigStockPhoto.com, (4) Huntley Hedworth/Getty Images; 118(TL) Look Photography/ Beateworks/Corbis, (TM) BigStockPhoto.com, (TR) Abode/ Beateworks/Corbis, (BL) Bob Daemmrich/PhotoEdit, (BR) Minpin/ Dreamstime.com; 126(T) BigStockPhoto.com, (M) C Squared Studios/Getty Images; 130(1) Clayton Hansen/iStockphoto.com, (4) Shutterstock, (5) Canstockphoto.com, (6) Shutterstock, (7) Robert Lerich/iStockphoto.com, (8) Shutterstock, (9) Photos.com Jupiterimages, (10) Dorling Kindersley, (11) David Young-Wolff/ PhotoEdit, (12) Shutterstock; 132 Photodisc/Alamy, 138(TL) Photos. com/Jupiterimages, (TM) Shutterstock, (BL) David Young-Wolff/ PhotoEdit, (BM) Shutterstock, (BR) Photos.com/Jupiterimages; 139(TM) David Young-Wolff/PhotoEdit, (TR) Clayton Hansen/ iStockphoto.com, (BL) Shutterstock, (BM) Shutterstock, (BR) Canstockphoto.com; 142(T) Shutterstock, (M) Shutterstock; 146(1) Michael Newman/PhotoEdit, (2) Shutterstock, (3) Ijansempoi/ Dreamstime.com, (4) Donald Miralle/Getty Images, (5) Malcolm Case-Green/Alamy, (6) Sami Sarkis Lifestyles/Alamy, (7) Diane Macdonald/Getty Images, (8) Shutterstock, (9) Sandy Jones/ iStockphoto.com; 147 Donald Miralle/Getty Images; 150(1) Jennifer London/iStockphoto.com, (2) Shutterstock, (3) Kayte M. Deioma/ PhotoEdit, (4) Jupiterimages/Comstock Images/Alamy, (5) David J. Green - Lifestyle/Alamy, (6) Index Stock Imagery, (7)

RubberBall/Alamy, (8) Colin Young-Wolff/PhotoEdit, (9) I love images/Jupiterimages; 158 Malcolm Case-Green/Alamy; 162(1) David R. Frazier/PhotoEdit, (2) Will & Deni McIntyre/Photo Researchers, Inc., (3) Rob Crandall/The Image Works, (4) MedioImages/age fotostock, (5) Shutterstock, (6) Jeff Greenberg/The Image Works, (7) Photodisc/Getty Images, (8) Tom Carter/PhotoEdit, (9) Jeff Greenberg/PhotoEdit; 164(1) David R. Frazier/PhotoEdit, (2) David R. Frazier/PhotoEdit, (3) Tom Prettyman/PhotoEdit, (4) Pixtal/ SuperStock, (5) Cathy Datwani, (6) Andre Jenny/Alamy, (7) Jeff Greenberg/PhotoEdit, (8) Cathy Datwani, (9) Peter Bennett/Ambient; 169 Bill Aron/PhotoEdit; 170(1) Shutterstock, (2) Shutterstock, (3) Steve Hamblin/Alamy, (4) Shutterstock, (5) Shutterstock, (6) Shutterstock, (7) Shutterstock, (8) Shutterstock, (9) Shutterstock; 174(T) David R. Frazier/PhotoEdit, (M) Pixtal/SuperStock; 179(L) Custom Medical Stock Photo/Alamy, 181 Archivberlin Fotoagentur GmbH/Alamy; 190(T) Shutterstock, (M) Image Source/Corbis; 193 Alex Serge/Alamy; 194(1) Shutterstock, (2) Banana Stock/ age fotostock, (3) MedioImages/Getty Images, (4) Jeff Greenberg/ PhotoEdit, (5) Jeff Greenberg/PhotoEdit, (6) Kayte M. Deioma/ PhotoEdit, (7) Shutterstock, (8) David De Lossy/Getty Images, (9) Frank Herholdt/Getty Images, 195 David R. Frazier Photolibrary, Inc./Alamy; 196(1) Sean Locke/iStockphoto.com, (2) Shutterstock, (3) Shutterstock, (4) Dennis MacDonald/PhotoEdit, (5) Photoshow/ Dreamstime.com, (6) Index Stock Imagery, (7) Dynamic Graphics/ Jupiterimages, (8) Jeff Greenberg/PhotoEdit, (9) Michael Newman/ PhotoEdit; 203 Shutterstock; 206(T) Jeff Greenberg/The Image Works, (M) Shutterstock.

Illustration credits

Kenneth Batelman, p. 114; Luis Briseno, pp.13, 47, 63, 120; Laurie Conley, pp. 32-33, 66, 105, 135 (middle), 136 (top), 137 (bottom), 148, 180, 184, 198; Deborah Crowle, p. 8; Len Ebert represented by Ann Remen-Willis, pp. 2, 18, 29, 48, 63-64, 81, 98, 101, 115 (top), 119, 131 (top), 136 (middle), 153, 167 (top), 197 (top), 199 (top); Peter Grau, pp. 22, 40, 56, 74, 90, 108, 124, 140, 156, 172, 188, 204; Brian Hughes, pp. 4, 6, 84, 86, 94, 102, 103, 104, 132, 163, 165, 186, 217; Paul McCusker, p.78; Luis Montiel, pp. 64, 160, 191; Allan Moon, pp. 46, 61, 85 (bottom), 88, 95 (top); Chris Murphy, pp. 5, 11, 15, 31, 35, 51, 69, 71, 83, 99, 117 (bottom), 131 (bottom), 149, 167 (bottom), 179, 181, 197 (bottom), 199 (bottom); Roberto Sadi, pp. 34-35, 44, 55, 85 (top), 115 (bottom), 116, 117 (top), 127, 128, 143, 144, 145, 168, 169, 176, 177, 214; Meryl Treatner, pp. 31, 51, 67, 121, 135 (top), 151, 200; Anna Veltfort, pp. 3, 30, 36, 50, 133, 137 (middle), 152, 166, 175, 182, 183, 185; Neil Stewart/NSV Productions, pp. 7, 12, 48, 49, 53, 60, 68, 69, 70, 71, 89, 95, 106, 107, 112, 161, 187, 193

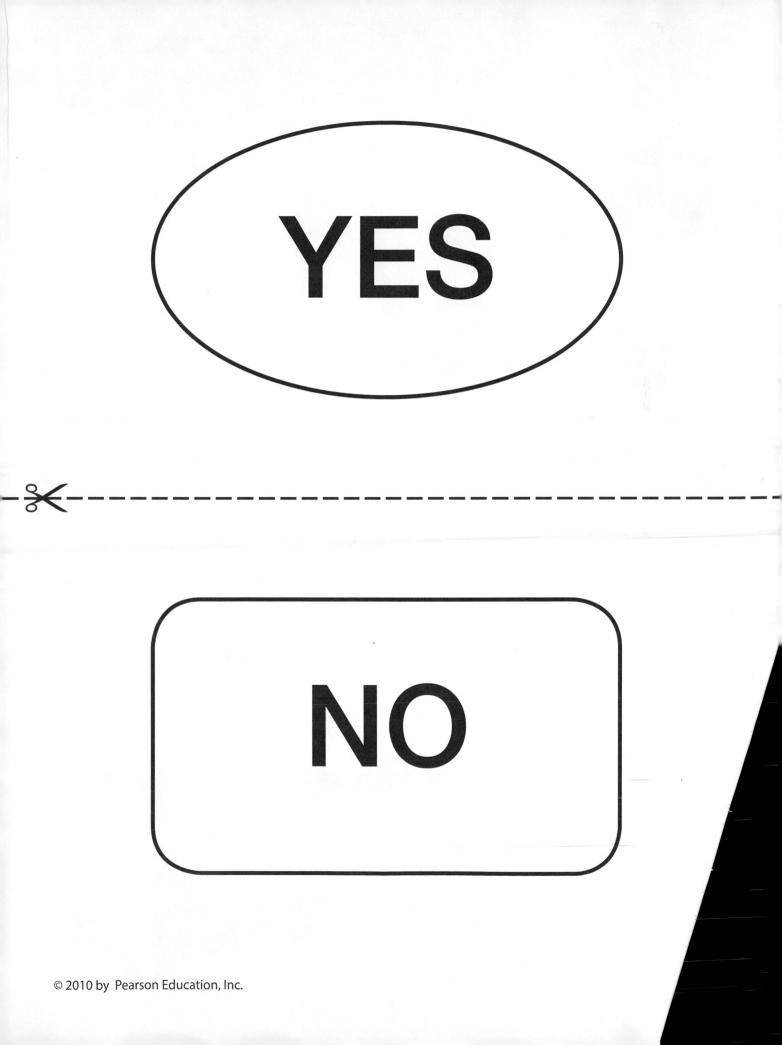

YES

NO